"Topgrading is not just desirable but essential for organizational success in this competitive world. Brad has helped me grow, and has helped DSC evolve from a warehousing company to a growth-oriented, leading-edge supply-chain management company."　　　　　　　　　　　　　　　　　　—Ann Drake, CEO, DSC Logistics

"Have you ever hired someone for whom you had high expectations only to suffer bitter disappointment in that individual's performance? Have you ever paid the heavy price of search, hire, and relocate, only to witness internal disruption as the person failed in his job? Have you ever chosen the wrong man or woman to advance to more responsibility? Dr. Brad Smart's groundbreaking research shows that 53 percent of such decisions are mis-hires. Winning companies have learned to topgrade—they succeed at getting and promoting the best. You can too. Dr. Smart tells how. Don't miss this one."
　　—Curt Clawson, President, CEO, and Chairman, Hayes Lemmerz International

"I have used Brad for over ten years in my ongoing efforts to build and enhance our own A team. Topgrading represents the kind of breakthrough I would expect from Dr. Smart. I will use it as standard practice here at DCM. American industry, I believe, will adopt topgrading as a necessary human resource optimization process in order to be competitive and survive on a global basis."
　　　　　　—David Gottstein, President, Dynamic Capital Management

"Brad narrows the target and then tells you how to hit it. For anyone who believes good people make a difference, this is excellent reading."
　　　　　　—Leslie G. Rudd, CEO, Standard Beverage Corporation

"Once again Doctors Brad and Geoff Smart have made the next quantum leap finding the keys to success in personnel selection . . . manpower planning; right person, right place, right tools for selection and placement. Use the knowledge in this book and you will succeed."
　　　　　　—John M. Eiden, President and CEO, Continental Woodworking Co.

"The author's lucid and crisp delineation of talent and its cultivation as the sine qua non of prosperous organizations and fulfilled individuals is cradled persuasively and absorbingly astride a savory introduction and an epilogue spiced with attainable, dazzling, and competitive futures for men, women, and the organizations and institutions they serve."
　　　　　　　　—Robert Perloff, Distinguished Service Professor Emeritus
　　　　　　　　　of Business Administration and Psychology, Katz Graduate
　　　　　　　　　　　School of Business, University of Pittsburgh

# TOPGRADING

How Leading Companies Win by

Hiring, Coaching, and

Keeping the Best People

**BRADFORD D. SMART, PH.D.**

**PORTFOLIO**

PORTFOLIO
Published by the Penguin Group
Penguin Group (USA) Inc., 375 Hudson Street, New York, New York 10014, U.S.A.
Penguin Group (Canada), 10 Alcorn Avenue, Toronto, Ontario, Canada M4V 3B2
(a division of Pearson Penguin Canada Inc.)
Penguin Books Ltd, 80 Strand, London WC2R 0RL, England
Penguin Ireland, 25 St Stephen's Green, Dublin 2, Ireland (a division of Penguin Books Ltd)
Penguin Books Australia Ltd, 250 Camberwell Road, Camberwell, Victoria 3124, Australia
(a division of Pearson Australia Group Pty Ltd)
Penguin Books India Pvt Ltd, 11 Community Centre, Panchsheel Park, New Delhi – 110 017, India
Penguin Group (NZ), Cnr Airborne and Rosedale Roads, Albany, Auckland 1310, New Zealand
(a division of Pearson New Zealand Ltd)
Penguin Books (South Africa) (Pty) Ltd, 24 Sturdee Avenue,
Rosebank, Johannesburg 2196, South Africa

Penguin Books Ltd, Registered Offices: 80 Strand, London WC2R 0RL, England

This revised edition published in 2005 by Portfolio, a member of Penguin Group (USA) Inc.

10   9

Copyright © Penguin Group (USA) Inc., 1999, 2005. All rights reserved

Publisher's Note
This publication is designed to provide accurate and authoritative information in regard to the subject matter covered. It is sold with the understanding that the publisher is not engaged in rendering legal, accounting, or other professional services. If you require legal advice or other expert assistance, you should seek the services of a competent professional.

LIBRARY OF CONGRESS CATALOGING-IN-PUBLICATION DATA
Smart, Bradford D., 1944–
  Topgrading: how leading companies win by hiring, coaching, and keeping the best people.
    p.  cm.
    Includes index.
    ISBN 1-59184-081-3
    1. Industrial management.  2. Leadership.  3. Employees—Recruiting.  4. Teams in the work-
      place—Training of.  5. Mentoring in business.  6. Employee retention.

HD31 .S5776  2005     658.4—dc 22           2004043178

Printed in the United States of America
Set in Minion
Designed by Joseph Rutt

To Mary,
My Super A Player

# PREFACE:
# WHAT'S NEW IN TOPGRADING

When originally published, *Topgrading* offered a radical vision. Topgrading is simply defined as achieving teams of almost all A players: those in the top 10 percent of talent available for the pay. Topgrading techniques in hiring, promoting, assessing, and coaching enable companies to hire 90 percent A players, promote 90 percent A players, and have 90 percent A players in management. When *Topgrading* was originally published, classic examples of companies that had successfully topgraded using Smart & Associates (see Appendix J for contact information) included General Electric, Allied-Signal, Travelers Express, and ACNielsen. But dozens of new topgrading success stories have emerged in the past six years — more large companies, small companies, not-for-profits, and individual managers. What does this mean?

## Every organization can topgrade.

Having personally assessed more than six thousand senior managers, scrutinizing all aspects of their careers, I've found that the most powerful skill for achieving career success is your ability to produce talented teams. By hiring people who make you shine, who embrace your principles and your vision for the company, you will earn promotions. Thousands of highly successful managers have used the powerful, efficient Topgrading[1] interviewing methods taught in this book to topgrade their teams and advance their careers. The inescapable conclusion:

---

[1] Topgrading Interview Guide (Topgrading). (See Appendix A.)

## Topgrading is a career turbo-booster.

The world has changed since the go-go 1990s, a decade in which premier companies topgraded, but lesser companies could sometimes perform spectacularly for a while without a lot of A players. With the tech collapse, stock market decline, and recession, companies with flawed business plans and not enough A players faltered. Companies that hung on to B or C players too long did what an increasingly competitive, Darwinian marketplace guaranteed: they went out of business. In the first half of the 2000–10 decade, companies that had sound strategies *and* topgraded through the decline flourished. This leads us to another inescapable conclusion:

## Topgrading is increasingly necessary for survival.

The primary reason companies and managers don't achieve A teams is that they fail to use accurate interviewing methods to assess talent. The Topgrading Interview has proven superior to all other methods of assessing both candidates for hire and internal talent. *Topgrading* reflects the broader experience of companies that have topgraded, and presents updated research to show that most companies mis-hire 75 percent of external candidates and mispromote 75 percent of internal candidates. Case studies show how conducting an internal tandem Topgrading Interview and/or a "second-opinion" Topgrading Interview by a topgrading professional achieves a success rate of 90 percent (or greater) A players hired and promoted.

Imagine trying to replace ten people, experiencing a 25 percent success rate and a typical cost of mis-hire of $1.5 million (documented in Chapter 2). You'd have to hire forty people, and suffer through thirty of your own mis-hires and $45 million in waste in those mis-hires, to end up with ten A players. It's such a costly and painful exercise, almost all managers give up and settle for a subpar staff—except topgraders, who use Topgrading Interviews, hire ten with one mis-hire, and get nine A players. The topgrader smoothly produces an A team, which outperforms teams with one-fourth As and the rest underperformers.

## WHAT'S NEW IN *TOPGRADING*?

In this revised and updated edition of *Topgrading*, you'll find many new case studies reflecting all types of organizations and success through various economic cycles. Eleven "obstacles to topgrading" have expanded to fourteen, with proven advice to overcome them. As before, you'll meet A players who used topgrading to improve their and their companies' performance, sharing their lessons and their best advice. With *Topgrading* entering Spanish and Korean markets, and with additional versions planned in other languages, *Topgrading* offers legal and practical advice for how to topgrade in countries that, frankly, protect underperformers.

I introduce a simple but revolutionary new talent model, the Topgrading Calculator. This model makes it easy to predict how many A players will result from your present hiring/promotion methods versus Topgrading-based topgrading methods. The Topgrading Calculator also enables you to accurately predict how much your present interviewing methods versus Topgrading-based methods will cost you.

The exciting promise for you, A player that you are, is this: abandon the shallow, incomplete interviews you use that have produced 75 percent mishires and mispromotions, substitute Topgrading Interviews, and you can have a team of 90 percent A players. It's about as simple as that, but topgrading is not simple. Since *Topgrading* was first published, we've learned more about how fragile topgrading can be. So, a new topgrading implementation model with case studies is presented, but read it carefully! C and B players hate topgrading and try to undermine it, so if even *one* of the essential topgrading steps is ignored, the A player standard you seek can evaporate.

A common reaction to *Topgrading* was "Topgrading is terrific, and I believe hiring/promoting success can be improved to 80 or 90 percent with it, but a four-hour interview is sooo long!" The revised *Topgrading* introduces the Self-Administered Topgrading Interview Guide, which, when completed before the Topgrading Interview, cuts a four-hour interview to two or three hours.

Something else is new. The universe of topgrading professionals has expanded. Appendix J offers you contact information to the largest and most effective companies of topgrading consultants. Finally, every page has been edited to reflect what we've learned from clients; their experiences are highlighted in new case studies, tools, advice, and a grand topgrading vision.

The revised, updated *Topgrading* retains the core foundation of *Topgrading*, and equips every reader to become an A player and create a topgraded organization of A players. Ultimately, the overall true benefit of topgrading your organization is one expressed by countless managers who have incorporated topgrading into their hiring practices:

---

**"Topgrading makes my life easier."**

---

# ACKNOWLEDGMENTS

My sincere thanks:

To Geoff Smart, a true intellectual partner in the evolution of topgrading, and the one topgrading professional to build a major consultancy, ghSMART & Company.

To the world-class topgraders who contributed new and updated case studies: Jon Boscia (Lincoln CEO), Bill McGill (MarineMax CEO), Geoff Smart (ghSMART CEO), Curt Clawson (Hayes Lemmerz CEO), Jack Harrington (Virtual Technology CEO), Greg Alexander (EMI VP Sales), Fred Rockwood (Hillenbrand CEO), Cass Wheeler (American Heart Association CEO), Roger Davis (Barclays CEO UK Banking), Bob Dineen (Lincoln Financial Advisors CEO & President), Jack Welch (General Electric retired CEO), Charles Butt (HEB CEO), and Phil Milne (Travelers Express).

To Chris Mursau, for performing the invaluable cost of mis-hire study; Margaret Brask, for her A player dedication in producing clean draft after draft after draft from my unintelligible scribblings; the two most conscientious peer reviewers of this manuscript, Brian Krueger and Geoff Smart; and finally to Seyfarth Shaw, the premier employment and labor law firm that wrote a terrific chapter on how to topgrade legally, both in the United States and outside the United States.

# CONTENTS

*Part Three*

## MASTERING THE TOPGRADING INTERVIEWING GUIDE AND LEGALITIES IN USING IT

## APPENDICES

# INTRODUCTION:
# TALENT WINS

*The ability to make good decisions regarding people represents one of the last reliable sources of competitive advantage, since very few organizations are very good at it.*
                                    Peter Drucker

In the face of increasing international and domestic competition, two senior managers vie to outperform the other. Both strive to improve their team's performance. Both have read about the latest management trends. Both have attempted some version of quality and process improvement. Both have discovered, rediscovered, and rerediscovered the customer. One senior manager has a team of a couple of A players, many B players, and a few C players. The other senior manager has almost all A players; she has been uncompromising in replacing C and B players with As. Hers is a *dream team.* Which manager would you bet on to win?

After studying literally thousands of successful and failed careers, and hundreds of successful and failed companies,[2] I've found that one overriding factor emerges: human capital. The single most important driver of organizational performance and individual managerial success is talent. The ability to actually do what every company and every manager professes to do—hire and promote the best—is what distinguishes premier ones from mediocre firms, successful careers from ordinary ones. The vast majority of organizations and managers simply can't figure out how to overcome the many obstacles to packing their team with A players. *Topgrading* shows how companies and individuals gain and hold that talent edge.

---

[2] In 34 years I have consulted with more than 200 companies. Roughly one-third have more than 20,000 employees, one-third have 1,000–20,000, and one-third have fewer than 1,000 employees. Half are manufacturing/construction, 43 percent are service (consulting, finance, government, not-for-profit, and so forth), and 7 percent are retail. Now with three separate topgrading companies and a few associated independent topgraders, we total 16 topgrading professionals, with combined experience well over 300 years, and we've consulted with over 1,000 companies.

Simply put, topgrading is the practice of packing your organization with A players. A players are the top 10 percent of talent available at all salary levels—best of class. With this radical definition, you are not a complete topgrader until your team consists of *all A players.* In practice, since people are not 100 percent predictable and the jobs they perform can dramatically change and require different competencies, we say successful topgraders are companies or individual managers with 90 percent A players or those with A potentials.

*Topgrading* shows you how premier organizations such as Lincoln Financial, General Electric, and American Heart Association gain a talent advantage, and how every manager can benefit from learning leading-edge techniques. *Topgrading* offers you:

- The enabler of all corporate initiatives to improve performance, because A teams make initiatives successful and lesser teams don't,

- A "silver-bullet" technique for near-perfect assessment of talent,

- A guide to effectively coaching your people,

- The ultimate personal career-development manual,

- Insight and advice acquired during my thirty-four-year career as well as the careers of fifteen other topgrading professionals and dozens of A player client managers in topgraded companies,

- An easy read.

### *Topgrading is* "the enabler of all corporate initiatives."

The Information Age has put a premium on talent, above any corporate resource. Topgrading will help you become very good at building this competitive advantage. Topgrading is the one catalyst that enables other initiatives to work, whether the economy is roaring as it was during the 1990s or sagging as it did during the subsequent recession. Process reengineering, Total Quality Management (TQM), globalization, and capital expenditures on technology all work best in topgraded organizations. Why? Because A players figure out how to make valuable management initiatives work, while C players kill good ideas.

Topgrading has turbo-boosted the talent advantage not only for mega-corporations, but also for fast-growth high-tech companies, not-for-profits, small family-owned businesses, and thousands of individual managers. From the executive suite to the shop floor, when your company has dream teams of A players and your competitors have fewer As and a lot more B and C players who suck energy out of everyone, you'll win. Companies with too many B and C players lose market share and lose profitability—lose, lose, lose! If the playing field is at all level except for talent, your superior talent will ensure that you win.

### *Topgrading* delivers a silver-bullet assessment technique.

When *Topgrading* was originally published, I guessed that about 5 percent of managers and companies were topgraders. It is maybe as high as 7 percent today, now that topgrading is catching on. That leaves 93 percent of managers and companies "making do" with only a few A players, the rest being chronic Bs and Cs who drag the organization down. Despite all the talk about the importance of human capital, *Topgrading* cites research showing that companies are poor assessors of talent, judging people to be A players when only one in four actually is.

---

### Our experience and research[3] show that 25 percent of managers hired or promoted turn out to be A players.

---

The primary assessment method is interviewing, and few managers are good at it. That's where the Topgrading Interview enters, for it is the closest thing to a silver bullet in assessing talent. With Topgrading Interviews, companies like Lincoln Financial and MarineMax hire and promote 90 percent As, not 25 percent. Because their interviewing techniques result in replacing B and C employees with almost all A players, they consistently watch their stock soar!

Few big companies survive fifty years, and one reason is talent deterioration. *The War for Talent* (Harvard University Press, 2001) notes that only about one-third of managers in high-performing companies (20 percent in low-performing companies) believe senior management can identify

---

[3] Research presented in Chapter 2.

the A, B, and C players. So much for "promote from within"! When B and C players assess talent, the A player standard erodes, because Cs and Bs are poor at judging As. That's why topgrading has to take place from the *top down*. When the performance management system, with one boss rating each subordinate, is not sorting out As, Bs, and Cs, topgrading can help. All the case studies in companies cited in Chapter 5 and elsewhere use a Topgrading Interview to supplement the boss rating, to assess internal management. Some companies prefer that topgrading professionals assess who are the As, Bs, and Cs initially, until internal managers prove capable at Topgrading Interviewing and have the time.

---

**Topgraded companies use Topgrading assessments, and 90 percent of the people they hire and promote turn out to be A players.**

---

The talent world today reminds me of a supermodern medical facility that, unfortunately, is lax on cleanliness. There are too many germs, so few patients get well. In the mid-1800s Dr. Joseph Lister invented and perfected antiseptic, surgical procedures. Lister (that's right, Listerine® is named after him) killed germs with antiseptic, and more than 90 percent of his patients survived. Surgeons not using antiseptics had patient survival rates of 25 to 50 percent. Similarly, topgraders assess talent with a 90 percent (plus) success rate, while the rest of the world stumbles along with a 25 percent success rate. Remarkably, the nontopgraders intuitively know they should assess talent better, but, stuck in their old ways, they don't overcome the obstacles to topgrading; they are like surgeons who fail to use antiseptics. Just as the doctors who used antiseptic procedures saved 90 percent of their patients, managers who rely on Topgrading Interviews hire and promote 90 percent A players.

This book thoroughly explains how to conduct the Topgrading Interview, so you can start using it tomorrow. Many managers rely on topgrading professionals for Topgrading Interviews, but thousands have learned the Topgrading Interviewing techniques, have conducted dozens of Topgrading Interviews, and have become very proficient. Topgrading is the *world-class standard* for achieving close to error-free hiring and valid assessment of internal talent.

### *Topgrading* is a guide to effectively coaching your people.

Smart & Associates' surveys[4] over the years have shown that only about half of employees at all levels consider their manager a good coach. That leaves about half of all managers deficient in coaching. The chapters on coaching can help all managers including those who neither like, nor are good at, coaching their people.

Armed with unprecedented insight provided by the Topgrading Interview, you can immediately tap your newly hired talent better and develop them with high-impact coaching techniques. Assessing your existing team with Topgrading Interviews will help you identify who are the As, Bs, and Cs; you will also be able to use those insights to better develop some B/Cs into As. Relying on Topgrading Interview insights, you can better spot "square pegs in round holes" and place them where even some C players become As.

*Topgrading* offers proven techniques for coaching A players to be even more effective, and for "fixing" weaker points to help B/C players become A players. And guess what! For reasons spelled out in Part Two, when you become a topgrader and surround yourself with A players, you *automatically* become a very good coach!

### Topgrading is the ultimate career-development manual.

My experience includes assessing and coaching more than six thousand executives. The Topgrading Interview approach scrutinizes *every* job a candidate has held. In my career, I found there were about ten jobs each for the six thousand managers I interviewed. Do the math—that's sixty thousand *job* case studies in which I asked the interviewee about their every accomplishment, every success, every failure, every disappointment, and every performance appraisal. The clearest insight from these sixty thousand case studies is:

---

[4] Involving hundreds of thousands of respondents to employee opinion surveys plus several more thousand participants in 360-degree surveys.

---

**Managers who don't construct high-performing teams experience career stagnation, while topgraders create A teams to achieve results, earn promotions, and enjoy very successful careers.**

---

**Topgrading provides insight and advice acquired during my thirty-four-year career, the careers of fifteen other topgrading professionals, and dozens of A player client managers in topgraded companies.** Since *Topgrading* was originally published, many other topgrading experts have evolved. Their wisdom is liberally shared throughout this edition.

**Topgrading is an easy read.** I don't know about you, but I skim books and articles for useful nuggets, and I appreciate authors who help me find the good stuff. But the good stuff for one reader wanting to learn specific details is different from the conceptual material of interest to another reader. I've tried to be generous with headings and summaries to help you spot the major conclusions found in this book.

**Part One** shows how premier companies topgrade, and presents compelling statistics to show why they have embraced topgrading. **Part Two** teaches how to become an A player and coach Non-As to become As. **Part Three** explains the basics of how to use the most important technique in topgrading—The Topgrading Interview, and concludes with advice on legal considerations, with extensive recommendations on how to topgrade outside the United States.

Almost all of the case studies identify the company or manager featured. Several clients prefer anonymity, however, because they are topgrading, their competitors aren't, and they don't want to give them a wake-up call. Rest assured that all the examples in this book are real-world. As in the previous edition of *Topgrading*, all new case studies have been approved by the company or individual.

*Topgrading* **is not for the fainthearted.** Those predisposed to protect "dead wood" will take issue with the basic underlying philosophy of this book. CEOs will fail if they ask their teams of As, Bs, and Cs if they want to topgrade, because C players will say, "Of course," but then undermine it. Managers who delegate topgrading to HR will fail because HR often lacks the clout to topgrade their peers. Those who, way down deep, would sooner see an organization die than nudge a hopelessly incompetent person out of a job are probably not A players, will not become A players, will not want to hire A players, cannot attract A players, cannot coach people to become A players, have difficulty retaining A players, and do not belong in a premier, topgraded organization. *Topgrading* is for A players and all those aspiring to be A players.

Everyone wants to know the key to individual and corporate success. I think I know. Sixty thousand job case studies devoted to scrutinizing fifty competencies provide some clues. Jack Welch, former General Electric Chairman and CEO, asked me which, of all those competencies, are *the most important ones* for helping someone become an A player. Mark Sutton, Chairman and CEO of UBS North America, asked the same question, as did most client CEOs. So did Bob Perloff, former President of the American Psychological Association. After the Topgrading Interview, managers frequently say, "Doc, since you've been studying careers in such detail for so many years, can you give me the secret to success?"

Yes. Topgrading. It will make your work life easier.

I hope *Topgrading* will be a pain reliever for your company and your career. It may not be Dr. Lister's cure-all, but it's the closest thing I've seen to one for corporate well-being and individual career success. *Topgrading* is chock-full of insights into how you can become, and remain, an A player, which is key to your success.

# TOPGRADING

*Part One*

# TOPGRADING FOR COMPANIES:

*Achieving the A Player Standard*

*One*

# TOPGRADING:
# EVERY MANAGER'S TOP PRIORITY

*Nothing our company does is more important than hiring and developing superior talent.*

> Larry Bossidy, Chairman and CEO
> Honeywell (retired)

How dramatically can topgrading improve talent? The average company today hires only 25 percent A players, promotes only 25 percent A players, and has 25–40 percent A players in management.[5] Topgraded companies, including those we'll study in Chapter 5, hire 90 percent A players, promote 90 percent A players, and eventually achieve 90 percent A players in management.

| The Topgrading Advantage: 90 Percent A Players | | |
|---|---|---|
| | Typical Company Results | Topgraded Company Results |
| Percentage hired who turn out to be A players | 25% | 90% |
| Percent promoted who turn out to be A players | 25% | 90% |
| Percent A players in management | 25–40% | 90% |

Most companies know they have too few A players, but they've given up and accepted their mediocrity. Managers with a 25 percent hiring and promoting success rate often conclude, "It's so costly and disruptive to hire four people, fire three, and get an A, I won't bother trying to get all A play-

---

[5] Research explained in Chapter 2.

ers." Topgrading companies hire 90 percent As, and expect all managers to be As. That's a real advantage in a competitive business world.

## WHAT IS TOPGRADING?

**Top·grade** (täp´grād) *v.* -graded, -grading, -grades, -tr. 1. To fill every position in the organization with an A player, at the appropriate compensation level.

This is an original definition[6] Dr. Geoff Smart and I came up with because we were unhappy with less potent terms like *upgrade.* Suppose a manager has a team of ten C players. One retires, and a B player replacement is hired. The team is still lame, but the manager is happy because she has "upgraded" her team. That's pretty weak. Upgraders lose to topgraders. Topgrading involves replacing underperformers until the entire team of ten consists of ten A players, or at least those who clearly exhibit A potential. When you are topgrading, you by definition are not accepting a mixture of A, B, and C players. You are proactively doing whatever it takes to pack your team with *all* A players.

Topgrading turns the typical hiring logic on its head. Typically, when there is a perceived talent shortfall, Human Resources will be asked to recruit "above the midpoint." That is, following a job analysis and preparation of a job description, a salary range is established, and rather than aim for the midpoint in the range, the company aims higher, to attract the higher level of talent needed. So, it might target candidates at the seventy-fifth percentile of the salary range. "You get what you pay for" is the rationale.

Trouble is, most companies *don't* get what they pay for. With a 75 percent mis-hire rate (see Chapter 2), companies are paying for A players and too often getting B/C players. *Topgrading* embraces a different perspective:

----

**Regardless of what you pay people, be sure to get top talent for the dollars you pay.**

----

Topgraders are not cheap; indeed, circumstances described in this chapter might justify paying above the *entire* accepted salary range. But the top-

----

[6] Bradford D. Smart and Geoffrey H. Smart, *Topgrading the Organization* (Directors & Boards, 1997), available free on www.Topgrading.com.

grader is more rigorous than the upgrader, more thorough in assessment, and more certain to "get what you pay for."

The United States has produced several (not all!) Olympic basketball dream teams who had no problem crushing competitors and winning the gold. What is the primary source of a dream team competitive advantage? Better strategic thinking? Better training? Better nutrition? Maybe, but dominant Olympic teams' fundamental competitive advantage seems to be talent. All other advantages flow from this primary driver of performance. When a team is comprised of high performers, or A players, they beat teams with B or C talent. If professional sports teams with talent superior to their competitors don't win, we blame managers and owners for being C players. Topgraded companies, like successful sports teams, truly value talent. There's no reason why your team shouldn't be a dream team.

There is an ever-growing body of research highlighting the impact of talent:[7]

- Paper plants managed by As have 94 percent higher profits than other paper plants.

- More talented investment banking associates are twice as productive as those average in talent.

- Return to shareholders for companies with top talent practices averages 22 percent above industry means.

- The top 3 percent of programmers produce 1,200 percent more lines of code than the average; the top 20 percent produce 320 percent more than the average.

- The top 3 percent of salespeople produce up to 250 percent more than average; the top 20 percent produce up to 120 percent more.

Proactively seeking out and employing the most talented people can have a multiplier effect on the creation of other competitive advantages. High performers—the A players—contribute more, innovate more, work smarter, earn more trust, display more resourcefulness, take more initia-

---

[7] McKinsey War for Talent Research, 2000, and Bob Eichinger, 2002, presented to Conference Board Integrated Talent Working Group.

tive, develop better business strategies, articulate their vision more passionately, implement change more effectively, deliver higher-quality work, demonstrate greater teamwork, and find ways to get the job done in less time with less cost. It's no coincidence that A player managers attract and retain A players, who want to be part of organizations that succeed.

## WHO IS TOPGRADING?

McKinsey & Co., a premier global consultancy, is known for its commitment to seeking out and employing the best people available at every level. Intel, Dell, Goldman Sachs, and 3M attract and retain A players and quickly redeploy C players. Clients Lincoln Financial, Hillenbrand Industries, General Electric, MarineMax, Hayes Lemmerz, American Heart Association, and UBS increase their percentage of A players yearly, and redeploy not just C players but B players too. Premier organizations topgrade as a way of life.

Under now-retired CEO Jack Welch, General Electric became the most respected company in the world, and at the time Welch was the most respected CEO. GE has been a premier topgrader. Fortunately, Welch continues to be a visible advocate of the A player standard. His bestseller, *Jack: Straight from the Gut,* makes it clear that every company's success derives from one primary source: talent. Welch's successor, Jeffrey Immelt, continues driving the GE A player standard.

There are, however, plenty of small companies that also topgrade. Dozens of leading private equity firms have embraced topgrading with the guidance of ghSMART & Company. You recognize topgraders every day, such as the grocery store with uncommonly friendly employees, the dry cleaner that goes out of its way to serve you, or the restaurant where every member of the staff seems competent, responsive, and enthusiastic. Topgrading can be more important in small companies, because there is no place a B/C can hide.

The most successful organizations in our experience have at least 90 percent of their people in the A player range (including those who clearly exhibit A potential). True topgrading companies strive for 100 percent A players but recognize there is always slippage. Achieving 80 percent who are As or demonstrate A potential is frequently good enough to beat competitors, though 90 percent is the typical corporate topgrading goal, and some companies achieve it. Hundreds of individual managers, A players who refuse to permit talent slippage, have achieved 100 percent A players. You'll read about many of the success stories in Chapter 5.

## WHAT IS AN A PLAYER?

A player (ā plā´ [ə]r) n. 1. One who qualifies among the top 10 percent of those available for a position.

An A player, then, is best of class. *Available* means willing to accept a job offer:

- at the given compensation level

- with whatever bonus and/or stock comes with it

- in that specific company, with a certain organization culture (family friendly? having dirty politics? fast paced? topgraded and growing?)

- in that particular industry

- in that location

- with specific accountabilities, and resources

- reporting to a specific person (positive A player or negative C?)

Goldman Sachs, the premier investment banking firm, may consider an A player the top one-tenth of 1 percent; with hundreds and hundreds of the best and brightest applying, it can afford such a selective definition. A few premier companies like Goldman earn a fabulous selection ratio of hiring the single best of five hundred applicants. Over the years most fine companies I have worked with have used these definitions:

*A player:* top 10 percent of talent available

*B player:* next 25 percent

*C player:* below the top 35 percent

# Figure 1.1

## Summary of Critical Competencies
### Position: President (base compensation level of $350,000)

| | A PLAYER | B PLAYER | C PLAYER |
|---|---|---|---|
| **Overall Talent Level** | Top 10 percent of those at this salary level | 65th–89th percentile at this salary level | Below the 65th percentile at this salary level |
| **Vision** | Facilitates the creation and communication of a compelling and strategically sound vision. | Vision lacks credibility; is somewhat unrealistic or strategically flawed. | Embraces tradition over forward thinking. |
| **Intelligence** | 130 or higher IQ; a "quick study" who can rapidly perform complex analyses. | 120–29 IQ; smart, but not as insightful as an A player. | 119 IQ or lower; has difficulty understanding and coping with new, complex situations. |
| **Leadership** | Initiates needed change; highly adaptive and able to inspire the organization to change. | Favors modest, incremental change, so there is lukewarm "followership." | Prefers the status quo; lacks credibility, so people are hesitant to follow; gives inconsistent direction. |
| **Passion** | Extremely high energy level; fast paced; 55(+)-hour workweeks (plus home email); driven to succeed. | Motivated; energetic at times; 50–54-hour workweeks. | Dedicated; inconsistent pace; 40–49-hour workweeks. |

| | | | |
|---|---|---|---|
| **Resourcefulness** | Impressive ability to find ways over, under, around, and through barriers; invents new paradigms. | Open-minded; occasionally finds a solution. | Defeated by obstacles. |
| **Customer Focus** | Extremely sensitive and adaptive to both stated and unstated customer needs. | Knows that "customer is king" but does not act on it as often as A players. | Too inwardly focused; misjudges the inelasticity of demand for the firm's products and services. |
| **Topgrading** | Selects A players and employees with A potential; has the "edge" to make the tough calls and redeploy chronic C and B players. | Selects mostly Bs and an occasional costly C player; accepts less than top performance. | Selects mostly C players; crises occur due to low talent level; tolerates mediocrity. |
| **Coaching** | Successfully counsels, mentors, and teaches each team member to turbo-boost performance and personal/career growth. | Performs annual performance reviews and gives some additional feedback; is "spotty," inconsistent in coaching. | Is inaccessible, hypercritical, stingy with praise, and late/shallow with feedback; avoids career discussions. |
| **Team Building** | Creates focused, collaborative, results-driven teams; energizes others. | May want teamwork but does not make it happen. | Drains energy from others; actions prevent synergy. |
| **Track Record** | Exceeds expectations of employees, customers, and shareholders. | Meets key constituency expectations. | Sporadically meets expectations. |
| **Integrity** | Ironclad. | Generally honest. | Bends the rules. |
| **Oral/Written Communication Skills** | Excellent. | Average. | Mediocre. |

Figure 1.1 provides an abbreviated set of competencies to give you a feel for how A players differ from Bs and Cs. This particular example includes competencies for division president; very different competencies would be appropriate for other jobs. Keep in mind that to qualify overall as an A player, one need not meet all of the A player competencies. (Appendix G provides a very complete list of fifty competencies.) Plenty of C players, for example, are very intelligent, honest, and customer-focused but short on drive, leadership, and resourcefulness.

People get confused about our definition of an A player. So, here is one more explanation, to make "top 10 percent" perfectly clear: Suppose that you had an opening for, say, systems manager paying $75,000. Suppose that you did a massive recruitment and had one hundred candidates representative of the total pool of talent, not just unemployed systems managers. Suppose further that you hired all one hundred, one at a time for one year—a hundred-year experiment. At the end of each year, the clock would be wound back and you would relive that same year, but with a different Systems Manager. At the end of the 100-year experiment, you would look back and rank all one hundred of the systems managers, from #1 to #100. The top ten in proven value of contribution, the top 10 percent talent, were by definition the A players. The next twenty-five (25 percent) were B players, and the rest were C players.

That explains a theoretical definition of A/B/C, but it will take some work to make it practical, for you to be "calibrated," to differentiate among them in a Topgrading Interview. It's relatively easy to judge salespeople in most industries, just as it is easy to determine who are top 10 percent athletes: performance is relatively objective. But for most jobs, you must immerse yourself, finding many ways to judge how much talent you can get for the compensation. To accurately differentiate among A, B, and C players, you might:

- Run ads, collect résumés, and interview candidates for Systems Manager.

- Collect information on your competitors' Systems Managers by asking vendors about them.

- In Topgrading Interviews of IT directors, follow the Topgrading Interviewing Guide and get appraisals of their subordinates, including systems managers.

- Participate in professional organizations to meet systems managers.

- Perform compensation surveys. (Online sites are presented in footnote 8 in this chapter.)

- Ask all your IT managers to offer opinions on how much pay attracts how much talent for systems manager.

- Ask recruiters to do a talent assessment of systems managers, utilizing their files and their skills at getting people in companies to give them information. One client asked a search firm to do a total analysis of competitors' executive teams.

As managers become calibrated, they inevitably make judgments about the talent reporting to them. *Topgrading* involves not just hiring As, but redeploying present employees who don't become As. As a practical matter, experienced topgrading managers develop a keen sense of which people internally are truly As . . . or not. They are generally confident their high performers are A players when:

- high performers they hire from competitors say they have superior talent,

- their performance management system is solid, with stretch goals, a culture of real accountability, and top bonuses only for truly outstanding performance,

- managers are given top performance ratings when rated by A players, and

- a manager has no fatal flaws—all critical competencies, such as integrity and topgrading are given high ratings.

Large companies, and all companies in a fast-growth mode, are naturally interested in screening talent not just for the present but for future jobs. They want enough promotable people to promote a lot from within (but not too many, or a lot of worthy people might not be promoted fast enough and quit). It's in your best interest to hire enough promotable people, but not everyone is equally promotable, so you can use the following scale of 1–2–3.

A1: promotable to Executive Committee level (EVP, COO, CEO)

A2: promotable one or two levels above present job

A3: not promotable

A topgraded organization expecting rapid growth has almost all A players, including a lot more A1s and A2s than A3s. Some companies don't have a need for A3s—A players who are not promotable. CPA firms, for example, typically fire them; the policy is "up or out," and if someone is judged to lack partner potential, he will be let go. However, most fast-growth companies need some A3s. A company's succession plan usually includes a chart indicating who the A1s, A2s, and A3 players will be for the next three to five years. Line managers must be able to look at the charts and say, "Damn, it will be impossible to achieve our strategic goals because we lack the bench strength!" Or, "OK, all of our managers are A players, only 20 percent are promotable. But that's fine, because we are not going to be adding management jobs for several years."

An added value in defining an A player as someone in the top 10 percent of talent available at all salary levels is not demeaning lower-level people just because they are not promotable. A players are not just the future superstars—future presidents or #1 salespeople. Everyone in the company should be an A player, and proud of it. A terrific store manager may not be promotable, but why demean her by saying, "She's only a C player." You don't see a Wal-Mart greeter awarded an "Employee of the Month" pin reading, "C Player Greeter." CEOs should treat all those A players the way Sam Walton treated all his A players, including A player greeters—with total respect.

Since 2003, articles have appeared extolling the virtues of B players. The common theme is "There are too many neglected B players, supercapable midmanagers, reliable workers who know how to get things done, who regularly go the extra mile for the company. They don't have the fancy MBA and will never be a top executive, but they are terrific, valuable employees." Hey, you just described not a B player, but an A player, an A3, who may not be promotable but who is among the top 10 percent of talent available within the pay scale for a midmanager!

Most companies must hire promotable people, do succession planning, and build talent "benches." But companies failing to topgrade this year waste their time talking about having all A players in five years. It starts

### Why B Players Are Not as Valuable as A3 Players

| B Player | A3 Player |
| --- | --- |
| Not promotable | Not promotable |
| Works medium hard | Works very hard |
| Delivers B results | Delivers A results for exactly the same compensation as the B player |

*now,* or it's not topgrading. The great topgraders say NOW is the best time to weed out underperformers, and almost all CEOs regret they did not topgrade faster. A global client that does "stealth" topgrading—hiring and promoting As but tolerating B/Cs until they retire or quit—qualifies as an upgrading company, not a topgrading one. They preserve their tolerant, forgiving organization culture at great risk: If two competitors have superior talent and financial/operational performance, who's got the advantage? Can you afford to incrementally, slowly upgrade?

## COMPENSATION AND TOPGRADING

We have defined A players as the "top 10 percent of talent available *for the bucks.*" To make that definition practical, you must do compensation surveys[8] or ask your Human Resources people to determine the "market" for various jobs. Assigning the right compensation can be complicated and extremely important; too often that judgment is screwed up by bureaucrats more concerned with organizational equity ("If a new hire gets close to Pat's salary, Pat'll quit.") than beating the competition. If you are a hiring manager, you must assert yourself to be sure compensation policy bolsters, not hinders, topgrading.

The amount of compensation necessary to attract a certain level of talent of course varies as talent supply and demand factors change. With the buildup to both Iraq wars, aircraft engineers were in demand, though previously they were a dime a dozen. During wartime, demand for engineers will be great, and entry-level engineers might be paid almost as much as the manager who hired them. You pay what you have to pay to get the human capital you need.

---

[8] Note: For readers whose employers are too small to have HR departments that acquire compensation surveys, the Internet has dozens of useful sites. See www.careerjournal.com and www.erieri.com.

During the year prior to Y2K there was a mad scramble to get IT systems fortified, and IT salaries shot up. When the supply of Y2K fixers in the United States and Europe was exhausted, anxious IT executives outsourced to India. Indian employees turned out to be so talented and inexpensive to hire that they kept a lot of IT jobs. It's all about supply and demand.

Paradoxically, organizations that topgrade do not necessarily pay more for talent than their competitors. Topgraders tend to look harder to find talent, screen harder to select the right people, and act more quickly to confront nonperformance. In relation to their competitors, these companies get disproportionately better talent for the compensation dollars they spend. A company that begins a serious topgrading effort finds it easier to recruit top talent because the company suddenly has a brighter future.

### A players are talent magnets.

A players are the most cost-effective employees, since their talent, the value of their contribution to the organization's performance, exceeds the value contributed by Bs and Cs for exactly the same pay. This is true at any given compensation level. For the foreseeable future, companies will be lean and people at all levels are now expected to do what two or three people did previously. C and B players simply can't cut it. Lean companies must have A players to perform well in increasingly demanding jobs.

A person can be enormously talented, but if those talents are not within the competencies for a job, they can be worthless. Your privately held company might not need a CFO with a CPA and extensive SEC experience. Too often companies fill jobs without determining exactly the competencies needed.

Remember, A players exist at all salary levels, and so do C players. Why would a board of directors pay a C player CEO $900,000? They didn't intend to hire a C player, but the mis-hired CEO turned out to be below the thirty-fifth percentile of executives available at $900,000. The board blew it. And why would an A player accept a $30,000 job? Perhaps that A player understands that her night manager job at a fast-food store is the highest-paying job where she qualifies among the top 10 percent of talent available. If she somehow were hired to manage a restaurant, a job paying $75,000, she would be a C player and likely fail. For now, she's smart to take a job where, as an A player, she can succeed and incrementally build her credentials for bigger, higher-paying management positions in the future.

If a supervisor can be an A player, and a CEO of a multibillion-dollar company can be a C player, how do we apply a common standard? You simply have to define the league and the salary range, and then determine how much talent can be attracted for that price. A conversation between two hiring managers might go like this:

> "Sally is an A player director of marketing, at an $85,000 base."
>
> "You think she's promotable to vice president of marketing, which has a $110,000 base?"
>
> "No, I'm sure she's among the top 10 percent of directors of marketing available at her pay, but she definitely is not in the vice president league yet, not an A player at $110,000."

Notice that these managers use job titles to define what job falls into what salary range. Another way to pin down how much talent can be attracted to a specific job, in a specific industry/location/company for a specific pay range, is to go online (see footnote 8). For $39 you can buy a quick and dirty compensation study. ERI also does a salary survey for executive positions by title, industry, and location for $189.

Correctly judging if someone is an A, B, or C player requires neverending research. Performing a compensation survey is not sufficient to make you "calibrated." If you are a manager who must consider investing in new equipment or software, it's your job to get calibrated, to accurately judge the value of the investments. Purchasing professionals and financial analysts devote a lot of time and energy to become calibrated in equipment expenditures. It's exactly the same with people.

Jack Welch is the most calibrated manager I've worked with. Welch insisted on a solid performance management system, so he could accurately gauge what managers actually did. I designed a tandem Topgrading Interview process supplemented with oral 360 interviews, for GE.[9] All interviewers were trained and coached to write comprehensive, hard-hitting

---

[9] The "360s" are surveys of opinions held by a manager's boss, peers, and subordinates. Also called "360-degree surveys," they can be administered orally ("oral 360"), on paper, or via email.

reports. Welch was always driving new initiatives ("Workout," "Six Sigma," etc.) to further test managers on resourcefulness, change management, and leadership. He oversaw hundreds of businesses, mastered dozens of industries, and constantly challenged every assessment, every offer of employment, every ranking . . . and every rating of every competency, for all 750 officers. He was a one-man topgrading hurricane, and he was calibrated so well that he could readily determine if an executive was describing an A, B, or C player subordinate. Welch and other super topgraders say:

---

**Managers must become calibrated as a topgrader
in order to qualify as an A player.**

---

To become calibrated, you must use the methods listed previously in this chapter (ask recruiters and other vendors to supply assessments, do compensation studies, use Topgrading Interviews to get assessment of bosses and subordinates, run ads, join organizations, etc.), but you should also:

- get Topgrading training,

- conduct Topgrading Interviews in tandem (more on that later), since two heads are better than one, and

- interview more candidates, from more companies than necessary, to broaden your perspective.

## CAN A PLAYERS BE INCOMPETENT?

Yes. One reason is that you've set the compensation too low. Suppose you advertise a salary at $25,000 rather than $75,000. What happens? You get wholly unqualified candidates. But you get 100 of them. Hypothetically, suppose you hire all one hundred, one at a time for one year, and one hundred years later you conclude not one was successful. Even the top 10 percent, the A players, weren't good enough. So, in this example, an A player in a C league (average compensation being in the $20,000–$30,000 range) is apt to be a C player in an A league (average compensation being in the $70,000–$100,000 range). If you underhire, if you hire at too low a salary for the job, you can hire a grossly incompetent A player.

---

### You must hire A players at the right salary level— in the right (compensation) league.

---

Another way you can wind up with a poorly performing A player is if the person is stifled by the boss. Or, if a product or project is canceled, rendering the job the A player is in unnecessary; or, if the performance bar is set so high no one, not even the #1 A player in the universe could succeed; or, the person might be a square peg in a round hole. We topgrading professionals find many more managers with A potentials than companies think they have, and they quickly perform at the A level when put in a job better matching their talents, or assigned to a boss who will unleash rather than stifle them.

A players can become B and C players in fast-growing companies. Let's say a company had $10 million in sales, so paying $50,000 for an operations manager was sufficient to attract and hold the necessary talent. The company grew to $100 million in three years. Naturally, midmanagers' salaries rose. The operations manager job became more complex and the operations manager is paid $80,000, not because he is worth it, but because the job is worth that much. But what if the company outgrew the talent? It happens all the time, so A players drop to B players, who drop to C players—not because their absolute level of talent has diminished, but because their talent has declined in relation to the salary they are paid. The operations manager could go back to a $50,000 job and be an A player. Perhaps he should, because his compensation skyrocketed 60 percent in three years and his talent (skills) increased at a lesser rate, making a former A player into an incompetent C player.

### WHEN TO "OVERPAY" A PLAYERS

Forward-looking, growing companies will *hire for the talent and compensation level needed three years from now.* We have a client (a biotech company) that grew from $2 million to $500 million in five years. Luckily they were prepared: they had sensibly hired senior managers for the $500 million level when the company was founded.

Another situation in which it may be wise to "overpay" for an A player at a high level of absolute talent is in a turnaround situation. Your pool of candidates may be too small and undertalented, due to the unattractiveness of the employment prospects of joining a troubled company. Therefore, you may decide to pay a higher level of compensation in order to be able to attract sufficiently talented A players. You also might have to overpay because of an unattractive location, a declining industry, or a reputation as a less-than-desirable boss. Ouch!

In these situations people are overpaid in relation to their skills and marketability in general, but are not overpaid in relation to what the troubled company requires. Granting a 50 percent signing bonus plus additional "battle pay" to work in difficult circumstances might be exactly what the company needs to attract and hold A players at the talent level necessary to succeed.

---

**Underpay and you might get too little talent, but overpay and you might give away the store.**

---

Overtalented people become bored and quit, or, even worse, retire on the job. It's all about supply and demand. Topgraded companies like GE plan for a few A players to be recruited elsewhere, opening up promotion opportunities for GE managers. If some A players are sliding toward B, the company will minimize bonuses and incentives to stay. But, As who are growing and becoming more promotable are rewarded with exciting opportunities and extra pay. You need to get the compensation right, and if that means paying bonuses to attract and retain turnaround specialists, you aren't overpaying at all.

## DEVELOPING Bs WITH A POTENTIAL

Companies that topgrade invest in their employees. Rather than passively watching the company outgrow its talent, they provide ongoing coaching, training, and development. Rather than battle courts in age-discrimination suits, they help aging employees maintain leading-edge skills. Topgrading is about hiring A players and developing them so that they remain A players. It's also about developing B/Cs to become As. Firing B/C players is essential to topgrading when the hiring and developing efforts have failed, when training hasn't produced A performance, and when efforts to redeploy B/C players in jobs where they could be As were futile.

When we're asked to help a company topgrade, we always start with a round of Topgrading Interviews and oral 360s. Generally we find that the management consists of approximately:

25 percent A players

50 percent B players

25 percent C players

The Topgrading Interviews also reveal who is that square peg in a round hole, and where some B/Cs can be placed in a job where they are A players. And they reveal which B players can develop into A players. Indeed, in every company there are even a few Cs who can develop into As. So, the picture is more favorable, with the typical client company having:

50 percent A players or A potentials (B/Cs who become As after developed and/or redeployed internally)

25 percent chronic B players (to be replaced)

25 percent chronic C players (to be replaced)

If 50 percent of managers are deemed chronic C or B players, how many are fired? Usually not many, even if the 50 percent are documented underperformers, failing to achieve the performance numbers they agreed to. Across decades of topgrading projects, here's how the 50 percent B/Cs break down:

15 percent retire/retire early.

15 percent resign, not wanting to hold the team back, fearing termination, and/or realizing that A player status will require changing employers.

10 percent are terminated ("mutually," with a severance package).

10 percent remain—the 10 percent who are new in jobs or fluctuate between A and B performance. They are the 10 percent preventing companies from achieving 100 percent A players.

Topgrading companies emphasize training and development a lot. With a positive attitude, tremendous effort, and a solid developmental plan, many B/C managers rise to the occasion and become solid As.

## WHEN TO PAY LESS FOR A PLAYERS

You pay less for talent when economic downturns, mergers and acquisitions, or outsourcing enable you to get the talent you need . . . cheaper. A top salesman in a client company earned $1.6 million just before the tech bubble burst, and was happy to earn one-fifth of that amount a year later because that was what he was worth. It's your challenge as a topgrader to stay on top of this issue—to pay more for the talent you need when jobs are scarce, and pay less when jobs are plentiful.

Retirees sometimes offer a lot of talent, cheap. In order to downsize and not be nailed with age-discrimination suits, some companies offer early retirement for managers. A players fifty-five years of age take the parachute along with C players. The A players typically do not want to fully retire and would be delighted to take an easier job for less pay.

Increasingly, talented people want part-time jobs, perhaps permanent part-time jobs. Ann Drake, CEO of DSC Logistics, has a part-time senior manager who could earn more money working full time for a much larger company, but has chosen a more balanced lifestyle instead. Hewitt Associates offers new mothers not only time off to have a baby, but part-time status after that.

---

**If a permanent full-time job isn't warranted, get a lot of talent for few bucks by hiring a part-timer.**

---

Entire industries—retailing, for example—favor part-timers to lessen healthcare costs. Outsourcing is on the rise, essentially institutionalizing what the techies predicted—that many would become "free agents," accepting "engagements" instead of "permanent" full-time jobs. As a management psychologist I frequently hear managers say, "There's no way I'll get approval to add that (marketing assistant, recruiter, strategy analyst)." I say to them, "How about using the Net or your personal network to find a freelancer or contractor to do that project?" After that you may determine that they are worth hiring.

## REDEPLOYING Bs AND Cs EXTERNALLY

Redeploying chronic B/C players externally is not downsizing. It does not necessarily mean having to fire anyone. It is acting on the recognition that someone places below the top 10 percent of talent available at a given salary level, and that's not good enough. By definition, A players are knocking at your door, available to you at not a dime more in compensation than your B/C players. B/C players suck the creative energy out of your organization. They fail to prevent problems and then can't fix them. A tremendous amount of your time is wasted undoing what B/C players did or doing what they should have done in the first place. Some screw up teamwork because A player teammates don't respect their perspectives. Instead of hiring A players, B/Cs hire more B/C players. These underperformers are your stealth "Dr. Kevorkians," assisting in your career suicide and your company's. As you'll see in Chapter 2, the costs of hiring B/C players—mis-hires—are huge.

Redeploying Bs and Cs initially involves progressive, documented steps to train or coach someone to become an A player. It involves careful assessment of individual talent, resulting in prying the square peg out of the round hole and inserting it in a square hole, maybe at a lower salary. And yes, it involves nudging misfits who can't be salvaged out of the organization. If it's done properly (see both Chapter 4 on style and Chapter 12 on legalities), B and C players feel they have been fairly treated but can't succeed, so they often quit before being fired.

## WHEN TO HIRE "UNDERQUALIFIED" A PLAYERS

Occasionally firms hire high-potential people who will be superior performers in future roles, but may seem underqualified initially. The person may be a B player in the near future with the potential to become an A player. For example, a CPA firm might hire a recent college graduate who has a limited technical background but exceptional intelligence, energy, and tenacity. The company might believe that the new recruit will be a B player auditor in the first year, but become an A player in the second year. At the time the entry-level auditor is hired, should she be referred to as a B player or an A player? Clients have all labeled such people "B player with A potential."

Here's another example: When companies are dissatisfied with prospects within their industry, they appropriately recruit outside their industry, seeking candidates who offer superior talent and potential, but who will have to experience a learning curve as they transition into a new industry. Usually they initially appear underqualified, but later when their results shine, they prove they were A player caliber all along.

My rule of thumb is this: If the person was a B player but became an A player within a year, he exhibited A player potential all along, merely growing into full A player performance.

## THE ONLY GOOD DESIGNATIONS ARE A PLAYER AND A POTENTIAL

Companies that topgrade designate A, B, and C players, but soon focus on the designations that are most practical and actionable:

A player

A potential

Non-A player

True topgraders regard a chronic B player (unable, despite training and coaching, to rise to A player status and not judged to be capable of being an A in a different job) to be as undesirable as a chronic C player. Neither is good enough. Both C players without A potential and B players without A potential must be replaced.

An "A potential" is someone who is predicted to achieve A player status within six to twelve months, typically. Figure 1.2 is a talent summary showing topgrading success for the top one hundred managers in a client organization. Initially the CEO said, "I think only 25 percent are A players." Our Topgrading Interviews and 360s resulted in his concluding that another 50 percent had A potentials, if they were placed better (square peg in square hole), and developed more (the previous CEO had neglected management development). This was a good company, with 75 percent A or A potential managers—and topgrading enabled it to become a great company, with 96 percent A/A potentials.

By year 3, the company's stock was at an all-time high. A topgrading score-

## Figure 1.2

### Talent Summary, Top 100 Managers

|                               | A and A Potential | Non-A |
| ----------------------------- | ----------------- | ----- |
| Year before topgrading started | 75%               | 25%   |
| Topgrading year 1             | 83%               | 17%   |
| Topgrading year 2             | 91%               | 9%    |
| Topgrading year 3             | 96%               | 4%    |

card like this can only occur when senior management consistently develops As, Bs, and Cs and redeploys chronic Bs, not just Cs, who aren't becoming As.

## WHEN IS A B PLAYER "GOOD ENOUGH"?

After redeploying C players, frequently replacing them with A players, companies wonder, "Do we have to go all the way and redeploy *all* the chronic B players?" Won't the disruption and cost of replacing Bs with As offset the advantages of having As in their place? Don't we need some blockers and tacklers, some good, solid B players who do the work but aren't necessarily promotable? The answer is, perhaps you need blockers and tacklers, but rarely is a B player "good enough." You need, and can get, A player blockers and tacklers.

Please remember that A, B, and C represent talent for the *current job*. Promotability is rated separately (1, 2, 3, or whatever) and if you don't need more promotable people to meet strategic goals, fine, keep your As who are not promotable. These are A player blockers and tacklers; they don't lose their A player designation just because they aren't promotable.

Now let's discuss your B players—your employees who are between the tenth and thirty-fifth percentiles of talent available, when A players (top 10 percent) are available right now, knocking on your door. Should you replace those Bs with As? "Give him a chance" is the battle cry, because:

"Half the time I replace someone, I end up with a C player."

"I can salvage my B player . . . I think."

"I can get the department's performance even with her B performance, because I work extra hard."

"Our competitors have less talent than we do."

"I don't have a network of As, so I'd have to pay a recruiter."

"Our organizational culture protects B players."

"He's a member of a protected group (minority)."

"In this (non-U.S.) country, Bs can't be fired."

If your recruiting processes are deficient, and three-fourths of the time you find yourself replacing loyal B players with mis-hired Cs or Bs, an edict to "replace the Bs" could be self-destructive. Your upgrading adventure could be a nightmare, with morale plummeting. Don't slow topgrading because of worry about the morale of chronic B and C players, who are understandably concerned about job security. Worry when A players' morale is low because you don't topgrade fast enough. A players reporting to chronic Bs are dispirited, and could be recruited by As in competitor companies. Firing B players and hiring C players as replacements will motivate your A players to quit.

Companies with performance management systems in which A players "Exceed Performance Expectations" and B players "Meet Performance Expectations" miss the point:

---

**In a topgrading company, A player performance
*is* the standard, so everyone who "Meets
Performance Expectations" is an A player. "Exceeds
Performance Expectations" corresponds to
A++ player performance.**

---

Whether to replace Bs with As, or not, depends in part on the competition. If you have upgraded and obliterated the competition, perhaps you can get by with some B players. But, if your less-than-topgraded company is number one in the industry, be careful—mediocre talent can invite in a new competitor. How high are the barriers to entry? What if a CEO with a topgrading mentality joined a competitor? Can you afford to bet that your B players will continue to be good enough?

Could McKinsey or Goldman Sachs be as successful if their percentage of B player professionals increased from, say, 5 percent to 25 percent? How about the New York Yankees? No way! In investment banking, entertainment, and general management consulting, premier firms soon die if their B players are not replaced with A players. We topgrading professionals work in every industry, and we sense that every industry is moving *toward* topgrading (though most quite slowly). Are you willing to bet your career and your company's future that your industry will not topgrade?

Are there exceptions, special circumstances in which retaining a B player is truly the smartest course of action? Perhaps, but ones I hear of are apparent, not real, exceptions. For example, suppose you plan to close the Houston plant in two years, and the plant management team there consists of all B players—people who have to be told what to do, but do it reasonably well. Other plant teams have A players who are much more creative and proactive. The Houston B players were going to be replaced until you decided to close the plant. To topgrade the plant would take six months, and it would take another six months for the team to gel and really make creative contributions. And then fire them all a year later? No. Actually, the moment you redefined their jobs as "holding the Houston fort" for two years, they became A players—the top 10 percent of talent available for a hold-the-fort job for two years. So, this situation is not an exception.

In a rare instance, the cost of disruption in replacing a B with an A might be excessive. Warren Buffett has been criticized for paying the division presidents of Berkshire Hathaway too much. He says they are doing a terrific job, so why not pay them above the normal rate? My guess is that this billionaire, whose time is worth so much, figures that the dozens of hours necessary to replace a president would not be as valuable as Buffett's using that time to manage his corporate portfolio. Saving $100,000 per year on a division president could have meant Buffett's missing that brilliant move to short the U.S. dollar in 2003, a decision worth hundreds of millions of dollars to his shareholders.

Just about the only reason to hang on to B players is if your recruitment approaches are so broken, you can't find A players to replace B players. You are certain As exist, but for various reasons (explored in Chapter 3) you just can't land one. That justification for accepting less than the A standard explains why most companies hire 25 percent As. Topgrading makes that justification a feeble excuse.

Your time is precious, so using some of it to replace a B with an A player is worth every minute. When you retain a B/C player in senior management, that bad apple spoils the barrel by hiring and promoting B/Cs, who hire and promote B/Cs, and you are inviting underperformers to cascade throughout the organization. If your recruitment machine is broken, don't throw up your hands in defeat—fix it! The smartest, sharpest A players I know in all industries never stop raising the bar on talent. That means they eventually achieve 90 percent A players, not 25 or 50 percent, and then they work hard to get as close to 100 percent As as they can. And their B players who have A potentials can be considered "special-circumstance A players."

## THE TOPGRADING CALCULATOR
## FOR PREDICTING ORGANIZATIONAL TALENT

STOP! This is a very important section. You're about to learn:

- why so few companies have topgraded

- why you as a manager have felt justified retaining some chronic underperformers

- a model that enables an entire company or you as manager to calculate how many total replacements will be necessary for you to have an A team

In Chapter 2, the Topgrading Calculator adds the costs of mis-hires, enabling you to project actual costs in replacing underperformers.

I am unaware of any company or manager, other than our clients, who predict talent levels such as the percentage of As that will exist in the future. Oh sure, talent meetings are held and projections of future managerial *needs* are related to anticipated attrition and strategic needs, but these methods overlook mass self-delusion regarding talent. Few managers ask:

"If we continue choosing people with our current methods and success rate, how good will our talent be?"

"Can we ever achieve 90 percent As?"

"If we emulate topgraders, how long will it take us to achieve a dream team of 90 percent As?"

The Topgrading Calculator helps to overcome talent self-delusion. Talent projections, until now, have been shams, assuming the people hired and promoted will be "good enough." Since the publication of *Topgrading*, we have helped clients calculate the percentage of As in management, percentage of As hired and promoted using old methods, and percentage of As hired and promoted using Topgrading-based methods. Now we connect the dots, *projecting* talent levels based on actual success in choosing talent.

If you are a perfect topgrader, you don't need a Topgrading Calculator to estimate the number of replacements necessary to achieve 100 percent As. If your success rate is 100 percent, you need only hire one person (who will be an A) as a replacement. If your likely success rate is 25 percent, you need to hire four people to get an A—three mis-hires and your good hire. Topgrading promises improving your success rate from 25 to 90 percent. In the meantime, to learn how many people you will have to hire, totally, to finally have 90 percent A players:

1. Estimate your current number of A players including those with A potentials.

2. Estimate Your Hiring Success Rate (your percentage of As and A potentials after hiring and promoting people).

3. Use the Topgrading Calculator (Figure 1.3). It will show the total number of people you must hire or promote in order to end up with at least 90 percent As, after replacing all those who turn out not to be As.

The implications of the Topgrading Calculator are profound. If you are a topgrader, picking people who turn out to perform at the A player level 90 percent of the time or more, you don't need to use the Topgrading Calculator! If you wish to replace ten underperformers, you hire or promote ten using Topgrading, and end up with nine or more A players. The right column of the Calculator is the topgrading goal, the achievable goal. That's your column for topgraders, who lead a charmed life. However, with a typical 25 percent success rate replacing underperformers, the disruption associated with replacing people is huge and you'd be smart to anticipate the problems. For example, replacing 40 people to achieve 90 percent As would

## Figure 1.3

### Topgrading Calculator
#### Total Number of Replacements to Achieve 90 Percent A Players
#### Your Current Success in Hiring/Promoting

| Number of Underperformers to Be Replaced[10] | 25% | 50% | 75% | 90% |
|---|---|---|---|---|
| 10 | 31 | 17 | 11 | 10 |
| 20 | 67 | 35 | 24 | 20 |
| 40 | 141 | 72 | 48 | 40 |
| 100 | 357[11] | 179 | 120 | 100 |

require hiring 141 replacements—and firing or otherwise redeploying 101 of them.[12] No board of directors would permit such a revolving door. And, by the way, what A player would want to join a massacre-prone company?

What would you do if you wanted to replace 10 underperformers and find that you have to fire the first, second, and third replacements before you end up with one A player? As the Calculator shows, you'd have to replace 31 people to end up with 9 As. You'd give up, right? You would only replace the worst C players, because it's just too painful to slash, slash, slash, to hire 31 and fire 22 to end up with 9 As. These simple statistics truly explain why so many companies give up, and perhaps why almost all of the largest companies no longer exist after 100 years.

Many managers inch into topgrading, replacing Cs but retaining Bs. The Topgrading Calculator shows this approach is doomed; it can *not* yield a team of 90 percent As. Suppose you had an organization of 100, including 60 A/A potentials, 20 Bs, and 20 Cs. And suppose your assessment methods

---

[10] For numbers less than ten, rounding errors are significant, but you can calculate averages from the 10 row. For example, replacing one person with a 25 percent success rate will necessitate 10 percent of 31, or 3.1 replacements on the average.

[11] You may wonder why, if your company replaced one hundred people with a 25 percent success rate, requiring three mis-hires to get one A, it doesn't mean hiring a total of 4 × 100 = 400. Hiring four to get one A achieves 100 percent As, and the Calculator is for 90 percent. The Calculator numbers come from spreadsheet calculations, rounding upward, since humans don't like to be dissected. Ninety percent As is the minimum acceptable; 88.5 percent was not rounded to 90 percent.

[12] Replace 40 leaving 30 (after Round 1), 22 (after Round 2), 16 (after Round 3), 12 (after Round 4), 9 (after Round 5), 7 (after Round 6), and 5 (after Round 7), for a total of 141.

produced a typical 25 percent As, 50 percent Bs, and 25 percent Cs hired or promoted. You can progress from 60 percent As to 66 percent in two rounds of replacing all Cs, but you can never exceed two-thirds As, since half of your replacements are Bs who are never replaced.[13] That's a lot of disruption to add six As and remove 19 Cs. Pity the upgrader if his competition topgrades, replacing underperformers efficiently with 90 percent As.

---

**An average company, using typical interviewing methods that select only 25 percent A/A potentials while replacing C players, can NEVER achieve more than two-thirds A players.**

---

Another important consideration is how long it would take you to replace people. Topgraders, using Topgrading, can replace 10 people in one year, and expect that nine will be As. But as was shown, the manager with a 25 percent success rate has to hire thirty-one people, removing twenty-two underperformers to end up with nine A players. That revolving door could easily take three years. It's so disruptive, painful, and (as will be shown in Chapter 2) costly that almost all managers will eventually live with a mixture of As, Bs, and Cs, only occasionally redeploying the weakest of Cs.

At organizations like MarineMax, Hayes Lemmerz, Lincoln Financial, American Heart Association, and Hillenbrand, 90–95 percent of those hired or promoted turn out to be As. You can achieve this rate too. Upcoming chapters will show you how.

## IS "ALL A PLAYERS" ACHIEVABLE?

Yes . . . and no. Yes, every manager should aspire to have all A players, and thousands have achieved that goal. We topgrading professionals are sure of

---

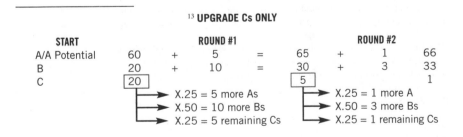

[13] **UPGRADE Cs ONLY**

|  | START |  | ROUND #1 |  |  |  | ROUND #2 |  |
|---|---|---|---|---|---|---|---|---|
| A/A Potential | 60 | + | 5 | = | 65 | + | 1 | 66 |
| B | 20 | + | 10 | = | 30 | + | 3 | 33 |
| C | 20 |  |  |  | 5 |  |  | 1 |

X.25 = 5 more As
X.50 = 10 more Bs
X.25 = 5 remaining Cs

X.25 = 1 more A
X.50 = 3 more Bs
X.25 = 1 remaining Cs

that because we have assessed all managers and replacements, and we sit in on talent meetings where performance *must* be at the A level or there is hell to pay. In topgraded companies CEOs and their A player managers insist on the A standard, and if performance is not to that standard:

- The underperformers are scrutinized, coached, and put on "performance improvement plans" to either improve or be redeployed, internally or externally.

- The hiring/promoting decision is analyzed to see who are the B/Cs and how they slipped through. Bonuses of hiring/promoting managers and their HR people are affected by their success in hiring.

We find that small companies, departments, and divisions with twenty or fewer managers, can have all As or Bs with A potentials, though typically there is slippage—10 percent mis-hires occur and goals change requiring new skills (and causing As to decline to B/Cs if they lack potentials to acquire new skills). Billion-dollar companies are doing very well to achieve 85–90 percent A/A potential standard, because they experience slippage for the same reasons, but with less agility. B/Cs with terrific images sometimes hide in big companies but are quickly found out in small companies. Business conditions change, strategies change, and the organization no longer requires existing skills and must have people with new skills. It takes a couple of years for large companies to adjust, whereas small companies are more adaptable.

Despite these big-company hurdles, I believe GE under Jack Welch achieved 90 percent As in management, as did ACNielsen (before Dun & Bradstreet spun it off) and American National Can (when Curt Clawson was COO and President). I hear the 90 percent standard is probably achieved by Goldman Sachs, Fifth Third Bank, 3M, The Limited, and other highly respected companies. Some of the case study companies in Chapter 5 have achieved 90 percent As, and others are "works in progress," topgrading but not yet fully topgraded, expecting to achieve that 90 percent As standard in the next year.

Some companies achieve 90 percent As without using topgrading's best practices. How do they do it? Executives we have interviewed from these companies explain that a critical mass of A players drive the A player standard in performance appraisals, succession planning sessions, and talent meetings. Those companies mis-hire a lot more than they should, because they use short competency-based interviews and not Topgrading, let alone tandem Topgrading Interviews. But they are quick to spot mis-hires and correct them with severance packages.

Bottom line:

---

**All managers should strive for *all* A players, and those with A potentials, and many achieve it. Billion-dollar companies can realistically achieve 85–90 percent A/A potentials.**

---

## WHEN IS TOPGRADING NOT SUCCESSFUL OR NECESSARY?

Topgrading does not guarantee success, but topgrading can give any company the best chance of success. Tens of thousands of mom-and-pops have been forced out of business by Wal-Mart; even tiny companies loaded with A players have found it impossible to compete against the colossus. Not many Davids slay Goliaths in real life. HEB is doing a fine job of competing with Wal-Mart, but it topgraded for decades *before* Wal-Mart entered their territory, and with sixty thousand employees, HEB is hardly a "David."

Gateway, however, is a David in relation to a Goliath, Dell. In the mid-1990s there were rumors that founder and CEO Ted Waitt would sell the company. Instead he topgraded. Based in North Sioux City, South Dakota, Gateway could not attract the talent necessary to compete. Waitt moved the headquarters to Southern California and changed much of the senior team. However, the changes were so dramatic, some of Gateway's magic was lost. With the simultaneous collapse of the PC industry and the stock market, and with clouds hanging over some of the newer managers, Waitt topgraded again. Waitt's advice: "Topgrade at a pace that the organization can handle and assimilate, be very sure new managers have the right values, and retain your long-term managers embodying the 'heart and soul' of the company in positions of power."

I've known fine companies strapped with such a heavy debt load that even a 100 percent A player team can't compete with B player competitors. The private equity world is getting smarter, assessing not just the financials but the talent in companies they are considering buying. ghSMART &

Company is the most prominent topgrading firm helping buyout specialists, many of whom will not purchase a company without a Topgrading-based assessment of the team.

As industries consolidate, smaller companies that topgrade can survive, and some flourish. I spent a week with Fifth Third Bank, a David in comparison to Goliath banks. The intelligence and energy of the top seventy managers impressed me. Like HEB, Fifth Third is hardly tiny—it has almost $100 billion in assets and twenty-thousand employees. It continues to grow rapidly through acquisitions, but it has not yet been acquired. Why? Fifth Third has a very high efficiency rating, which means there is no "fat" an acquirer could cut. Furthermore, the high stock price means an acquirer would have to pay dearly for it. Finally, all senior managers have substantial stock options and incentive pay, motivating all to continue to perform in a way that maintains a high stock price.

### Some companies at a competitive disadvantage can succeed by topgrading.

A well-known European company has a reputation for having mostly C players in management, but brilliant A players in R&D. The topgraded R&D department acquires patents that prevent competition. An executive told me, "The organization culture protects Cs, but what if a C player financial manager makes a huge error, or if a C player HR manager invites labor disputes?" *Not* topgrading is risky.

### Companies with a competitive advantage risk losing it to companies that topgrade.

The Soviet Union kept lame businesses alive. Europe, Japan, and even the United States sometimes rescue companies (like Chrysler and Harley-Davidson) or industries (steel and agriculture, for example). I felt a little foolish imploring the CEO of a huge, low-performing company to topgrade, when it became clear in a few weeks that his lobbyists had secured a huge competitive advantage in the form of protectionist legislation.

I reluctantly acknowledge the fact that state-supported monopolies reduce the need to topgrade.

---

**Topgrading makes markets efficient. State-protected companies don't topgrade, essentially imposing a "B/C player tax" on citizens.**

---

## A BRIEF SUMMARY OF TOPGRADING TECHNIQUES

Here's a brief summary of ways to topgrade, to achieve all A players:

1. Use Topgrading Interviews to identify who are your As, A potentials, and Non-As (Bs and Cs).

2. Use Topgrading Interviews to achieve 90 percent (or better) A players when hiring externally or promoting people.

3. Improve the existing human capital by providing employees coaching necessary to become and remain A players.

4. Redeploy chronic C players and B players into internal positions where they can be A players or outside the company.

## CHAPTER 1 CHECKLIST: ARE YOU A TOPGRADER?

**YES NO**

☐ ☐ My team consists of all A players or those with A potentials at the appropriate salary level.

☐ ☐ Instead of paying top dollar for talent, I get top talent for whatever dollars (salary) I pay.

☐ ☐ I know it's incorrect to say, "A $50,000 salary will only get me a B player, so we should pay $75,000 to attract an A player." The correct statement is "A players exist at all salary levels, but at $50,000 even the top 10 percent of talent is not good enough. We need an A player in a bigger league, someone in the top 10 percent of talent available in the $75,000 league."

☐ ☐ 90 percent or more of my external hires are A players.

☐ ☐  In relation to my competitors, I look harder to find talent, screen harder to select the right people, and act more quickly to confront nonperformance.

☐ ☐  I realize I can create a C player out of an A player by overpaying, stifling a person's talents, putting a square peg in a round hole, or failing to train someone.

☐ ☐  At least 90 percent of the people I promote turn out to be A players.

☐ ☐  My A, B, and C players all have Individual Development Plans to remain As or (for Bs and Cs) develop into A players, move into other jobs where they can be A players, or leave the company.

☐ ☐  I do not waste time "fixing" problems that B/C players should have prevented.

☐ ☐  I don't use short-term results as an excuse not to topgrade.

☐ ☐  I don't use "but the competition hasn't topgraded" as an excuse for me not to topgrade.

☐ ☐  I retain B players only in unusual circumstances, such as when replacing them with A players would be too disruptive or when the benefits would be too short-term (e.g., if a plant closing is coming soon), in which case they are truly "temporary A players."

☐ ☐  I run the numbers, using the Topgrading Calculator, to determine if and when my hiring and promoting success rate can lead to my having an A team.

☐ ☐  My minimum standard for subordinates (i.e., "Meets Performance Expectation") is one requiring A player performance.

☐ ☐  Even if my business enjoys government protection, I realize that protection could be withdrawn, so it is prudent to topgrade now.

If you answered "no" to more than two or three of the preceding questions, you are not a topgrader, and you are not alone. The practice of hiring and promoting the most talented people available at a given salary level is a powerful but unusual practice. Building a talent advantage over your competitors requires a high degree of focus and energy.

Every manager, from supervisor to CEO, is charged with the awesome responsibility of increasing shareholder value. Topgrading provides a powerful tool here. You can ask if you have the top 10 percent of the talent available and, if not, "Why am I paying for A players and not getting them?" You can measure if your hiring success rate is around 90 percent; if not, "Why am I not using the most effective selection methods available to screen people?" You can ask why so many B/C players are causing problems when, for the same salaries, A players can drive shareholder value upward.

All companies and individual managers can "do the math," using the Topgrading Calculator, to measure their hiring/promoting success rate to project what percentage of A/A potentials will exist after one or two more rounds of topgrading. Chapter 2, which explores the very real, very high costs of mis-hiring should further solidify your commitment to topgrade. By avoiding costly mis-hires and increasing the talent level, you can expect to see key performance indicators go up and your career prospects soar.

# Two

# THE FINANCIAL AND CAREER COSTS OF NOT TOPGRADING

*The toughest decisions in organizations are people decisions—hiring, firing, promotion, etc. These are the decisions that receive the least attention and are the hardest to "unmake."*
Peter Drucker

Chapter 1 laid the foundation for topgrading, promising that with better managerial hiring, promoting, and development, you can produce a true A team. Chapter 2 seeks to justify that promise by proving the following:

- Typical companies hire only 25 percent As, but topgrading companies hire at least 90 percent As.

- Typical companies find that only 25 percent of those promoted turn out to be A players, yet topgrading companies achieve at least 90 percent As.

- Typical companies have only 25–40 percent A players in management, yet topgraded companies achieve 85–90 percent or more As.

- Topgrading companies can improve from 25–40 percent As to 85–90 percent As with Topgrading interview-based managerial hiring, promoting, redeploying, and development.

- The financial and career costs in not topgrading are astronomical.

Mis-hires are costly to both companies and individual managers, and are demonstrably avoidable. The Topgrading Calculator introduced in Chapter 1 showed how Topgrading Interviews can eliminate a revolving door of mis-hires. This chapter adds the costs of mis-hires to the Topgrading Calculator, enabling you to *compute both how many replacements you* will require to achieve 90 percent As, and how much it will cost to get there. You can guess at the conclusion: Topgrading Interviews minimize the firings and measurable costs of mis-hires, making topgrading relatively quick, seamless, and inexpensive. This chapter ends with one of the most practical and beneficial exercises you will ever do—apply the Topgrading Calculator to your situation, including likely costs of mis-hiring, to have a much clearer understanding of the advantages of topgrading.

## HIRING 90 PERCENT A PLAYERS IS ACHIEVABLE

Topgrading case studies for years have shown how to achieve a 90 percent success rate in hiring. The CEOs of the following organizations estimated the percentage of upper management hires who turned out to be A players as follows:

| Organization | Percentage of As |
|---|---|
| Lincoln Financial | 90% |
| Hayes Lemmerz | 94% |
| ghSMART | 92% |
| MarineMax | 94% |
| TEKMORE (division)[14] | 92% |
| American Heart Association | 95% |
| Hillenbrand | 92% |

Prior to topgrading, most of these organizations experienced a hiring success rate of about 35 percent, and Topgrading Interviews took them to 90 percent and higher. Their typical topgrading discipline is for a group of managers to scrutinize each hire one year after the person was hired. B players without A potentials are deemed mis-hires. In some companies that evaluation of the hiree is so tough that if the hiree turns out to be a B or C without A potentials, the bonuses of the hiring manager and HR pro-

---

[14] Fictitious division name of well-known company.

fessional are reduced. So, there is great confidence that those deemed A
players truly are.

## TYPICAL COMPANIES HIRE ONLY 25 PERCENT
## WHO ARE LATER JUDGED TO BE A PLAYERS

Having Topgrading interviewed over six thousand senior managers, from
hundreds of companies, and having asked close to one thousand managers, "What percentage of external hires turn out to be A players in your
company?" the average response has been 25 percent. I sent out a questionnaire to fifteen topgrading professionals at ghSMART, The Mursau
Group, and other organizations, aggregating our combined experience of
over two hundred years and with over 1,500 companies.

The results:

### Topgrading Professionals' Estimates of
### Managerial Hiring (without Topgrading Interviews)
### in U.S. Companies

| | |
|---|---|
| A players/A potential | 25% |
| B players without A potential | 50% |
| C players without A potential | 25% |

In other words, based on our having professionally assessed talent in
1,500 companies, our collective opinion is that 75 percent of managers
hired externally (without Topgrading Interviews) are mistakes, underperformers, mis-hires.

When search firms are paid to recruit talent, do they deliver? A player
search professionals embrace the A player standard, but most don't. In
1998 and 2004, I surveyed one hundred senior managers, who reported:

### Executive Search Study
### (100 Senior Managers)

1. Percentage of retained searches in which the
   search firm failed to produce a candidate hired                          32%
2. Percentage of search engagements in which the
   search resulted in a manager hired who turned out to be an A player      26%

I decided to do another study in 2004, with one hundred more CEOs/ presidents and with topgrading professionals. The results:

## Estimates of the Quality of Managers Hired from Retained Searches

|  | 100 CEOs'/ Presidents' Estimates | 16 Topgrading Professionals' Estimates |
|---|---|---|
| A players/A potential | 21% | 23% |
| B players (without A potential) | 45% | 55% |
| C players (without A potential) | 34% | 22% |

All respondents were asked for search results when no Topgrading Interview was performed. Combining these various studies, it seems that a consensus among highly informed people is that no more than about 25 percent of managers hired externally turn out to meet the A player standard. The cold reality is that the average company suffers a 75 percent mis-hire rate, relying on interviews that are inferior to the Topgrading interview.

## PROMOTING FROM WITHIN IS A 25 PERCENT A PLAYER "SOLUTION"

Most large companies emphasize promoting from within. General Electric, for example, targets hiring 25 percent of managers externally, to enrich the mix of talent, but 75 percent of the time promotes managers internally. Human resource systems measure performance and provide annual assessments, and since most large companies have extensive 360-degree survey, feedback, coaching, training, and development processes, they should be terrific at selecting someone they know for promotion, right? Wrong! All those observations of managers do not ensure that those promoted will function as A players.

Relying on my two most trusted sources, the statistics are quite consistent, and quite negative.

## Estimates of the Quality of Managers in FORTUNE 500 Companies Promoted from Within

|  | 100 CEOs'/ Presidents' Estimates | 16 Topgrading Professionals' Estimates |
| --- | --- | --- |
| After promoted, are judged A player/ A potential | 25% | 20% |
| After promoted, are judged B player (without A potential) | 52% | 56% |
| After promoted, are judged C player (without A potential) | 23% | 24% |

Again, respondents were asked about promotion success when no Topgrading Interview was conducted. In our collective topgrading experience, B/C players contaminate managerial ranks, and B/Cs have difficulty attracting and retaining As, because As don't want to work for them. Underperformers are like termites eating away shareholders value—munch, munch, munch. Topgrading is a termite exterminator. The *War for Talent,* by Ed Michaels, Helen Handfield-Jones, and Beth Axelrod, showed that most managers, even in high-performing companies, believe top executives don't really know who are the As, Bs, or Cs. General Electric didn't want to trust the one annual appraisal of subordinates to determine who would get promoted, so it hired Smart & Associates to design and help implement a Topgrading-based program:

- Two managers in a tandem Topgrading Interview of a third manager in a different division.

- The tandem interviewers conduct extensive oral 360 interviews.

- A comprehensive report (typically with thirty strengths and a dozen areas for improvement) is considered along with boss appraisal, when promoting managers.

- The manager assessed receives the report and extensive coaching.

## NINETY PERCENT SUCCESS IN PROMOTING IS ACHIEVABLE

Topgrading companies not only hire based on Topgrading Interviews, but use Topgrading Interviews to promote managers. The GE Topgrading-based internal assessment tool is one embraced by Lincoln, Hillenbrand, MarineMax, Hayes Lemmerz, and many other companies. In excess of 95 percent of their managers promoted turn out to perform as A players.

One client, the CEO of a multibillion-dollar company and a very successful topgrader, offers a caution: it's important to reassess candidates, using Topgrading Interviews, for all promotions involving new competencies. At his company, the internal tandem Topgrading Interview approach was used to promote a manager who performed very well, and three years later was promoted to a job where he failed; in retrospect a new tandem Topgrading assessment at the time of promotion would have identified how poorly suited he was for the particular promotion.

## AVERAGE COMPANIES HAVE 25–40 PERCENT A PLAYERS, WHILE TOPGRADING COMPANIES ACHIEVE 85–90 PERCENT A PLAYERS

If typical companies (those not benefiting from Topgrading Interviews) experience only a 25 percent success rate in hiring and promoting managers, it stands to reason that they have a talent mix including only a minority of A players. Topgrading companies steadily approach a level in which 85–90 percent of all managers qualify as A players. Although some small companies have improved from 25 to 90 percent A players in one round of Topgrading-based topgrading, large companies experience some slippage along the way. It takes two to five years for topgrading to flow down, with the senior team topgraded and then their reports and so on. In the meantime, B/C players botch topgrading efforts; they don't do as well as As in conducting Topgrading Interviews, and some replacement As get frustrated reporting to Cs and quit. But topgrading companies ultimately prevail and achieve 90 percent As. These companies generally say that each year they deal with about 5 percent Bs and 5 percent Cs, underperformers who are on Performance Improvement Plans to either become As or be redeployed. When a C leaves and an A is hired or promoted, talent is ratcheted up. That's how topgrading works.

Why is the estimate of internal talent so broad—25–40 percent A players? Because we topgrading professionals identify a lot more As and A potentials than CEOs think they have. One hundred presidents and CEOs guessed the talent mix in U.S. companies:

*One Hundred CEOs' and Presidents' Estimates of Talent Mix in U.S. Companies*

23% A players

52% B players

25% C players

When asked to combine A players with A potentials, their statistics hardly budged. They are like Jack Welch before he discovered the developmental power of Topgrading-based coaching. He believed that A players could be trained in skills but that Bs or Cs rarely would become As. However, after seeing so many develop into the A category, he changed his mind and policies. Topgrading professionals say that across the United States, in average companies large and small and in most industries, a much more positive talent mix exists when those with A potentials are included.

*Topgrading Professionals' Estimates of U.S. Talent Mix Including A Potentials*

51% A/A potentials

49% Non-As (B and C players who can't become As)

Why the difference? Are topgrading professionals more lenient than CEOs in their talent assessments? No way! We're tougher, but also better at spotting talent potential.

Companies typically are shallow in their assessments of managers' talent and don't realize when square pegs are in round holes, or recognize when B/Cs can develop into As. Most companies rely on the appraisal of one manager to determine the future of that manager's subordinates. Most companies don't hold talent reviews, where half a dozen line and HR managers thoroughly discuss a manager's strengths, weak points, potentials, and career goals. But companies adding Topgrading Interviews and oral 360s to assess talent identify when a round peg will fit better in a round hole, so when the job change is made, voilà! A B/C becomes an A! The thoroughness of Topgrading-based assessment and coaching flushes out people's hidden talents, their developmental needs, and their true career goals. As noted in Chapter 1, in most companies that topgrade, most non-As retire, resign, or are redeployed internally, with only 10 percent fired.

Few companies have an annual Individual Development Plan (IDP)[15] with more than a perfunctory entry ("Attend a public speaking workshop."), whereas topgrading companies have imbedded a comprehensive IDP annually, addressing ways employees can maximize their strengths and minimize their weak points. Bs and some Cs kick-start their development and become A players. This coaching process is a major source of satisfaction for topgrading professionals and is a huge morale, talent, and performance builder for the individuals and their companies. So, topgrading professionals agree with CEOs that only about one-fourth of their managers are functioning as A players *now*, but we mine their talent and discover riches they overlooked—a lot of B/Cs with A potentials.

*How* to apply all the topgrading techniques for assessing and developing talent is covered in subsequent chapters. Please keep the basic topgrading

---

### Summary of Research on the Topgrading Standard[16]

### Percentage A Players

|  | Average Company | Topgrading Company |
|---|---|---|
| External Hires | 25% | 90% |
| Promotions from Within | 25% | 90% |
| Incumbent Managers | 25–40% | 90% |

---

[15] See Appendix H for a sample IDP.

[16] Respondents to various surveys in 1998 and 2004 are from dozens of companies including Boeing, Snap-on, T.J. Maxx, Amway, Rockwell, Idex, Stanley Works, Citibank, Chicago Title & Trust, Motorola, BICC General, ConAgra, Royal Bank of Canada, Office Depot, Comp USA, and FMC.

statistics (rounded off for clarity) in mind as we now look at the costs of mis-hires.

## THE COSTS OF MAKING HIRING AND PROMOTING MISTAKES

It may surprise readers of *Topgrading* that the estimated cost of mis-hires (including mispromotions) has been *reduced* since that book's earlier publication. Why? The higher the base compensation, the higher the cost of mis-hires. Including some mis-hires with over million-dollar salaries in the 1998 study seemed to weight the high salary/high cost-of-mis-hire examples excessively, skewing the results. The 2004 study did not include any cases with a base salary over $175,000. Here's the bottom line for the 2004 study:

---

**For midmanagers whose base salary is in the $100,000 range, the average cost of mis-hiring is fifteen times base salary, or $1.5 million.**

---

Let's delve into this topic, so you can judge the evidence for yourself. Intuitively you no doubt know that mis-hires are costly, but we won't even attempt to measure the costs of:

- Your career stalling because you failed to topgrade and your team's performance was mediocre.

- Unhappiness of mis-hired people.

- Your wasted time and energy redeploying B/C players.

- Your diminished fun and increased pressure because of your B/C players' deficiencies.

It doesn't make any difference if a person is "hired" from outside or inside the company. Mispromoting internally is about as costly as mis-hiring an external candidate.

At the "worker" level there are plenty of published statistics on turnover and even a few studies of the costs associated with mis-hires. A computer search of over two hundred studies and articles produced a hodgepodge of single-company results, with costs of mis-hiring factory workers to be

$1,500 in one company, salespeople $6,000 in another.[17] Governmental studies have placed the costs of mis-hiring programmers at two to three times their annual compensation.[18] At the managerial and professional levels, the data are even more sparse. In a world inundated with metrics from smallpox incidence to the population of snail darters, from soft-drink consumption to the numbers of nuclear warheads, the topic of managerial hiring success has been strangely ignored.

Having interviewed over six thousand managers in-depth, plus thousands more in shorter career discussions, I know that many managers in my sample have been a mis-hire in at least one job. I've heard thousands of accounts of what it's like to make a major career decision that goes awry. Being a mis-hire, a B/C player who eventually is fired, is painful. As topgrading consultants, we are sometimes asked to help correct an insidious corporate "death spiral" in which poor senior hires result in lower-level A players "bailing out," leaving B/C players who hire and promote more B/C players. The shareholders are left bleeding and wounded, and the company may become moribund. Mis-hires can kill companies, individual careers, and real people whose stress causes heart failure.

Dr. Geoff Smart's doctoral research[20] showed the economic costs of mis-hiring. He studied the talent assessment techniques of private equity firms, and those with the highest internal rate of return (financial success) scrutinized management of the firms they invested in (in a sense, hired). The private equity firms that used topgrading-like practices to evaluate management teams earned an average of 80 percent internal rate of return on their deals, compared to 25 percent or lower for firms that did not use topgrading practices. Many prominent private equity firms will only invest after the Topgrading Interviews are conducted by ghSMART & Company, in order to avoid misinvestments in weak management.

One hundred new (2004) client respondents supplied data on their

[17] (Anonymous) "Retaining Top Salespeople: How to Motivate Star Performers," *Small Business Report* 13(2) (February 1988), pp. 23–27.

[18] F. L. Schmidt, J. E. Hunter, and K. Pearlman, "Assessing the Economic Impact of Personnel Programs on Workforce Productivity." *Personnel Psychology* 35 (1982), pp. 333–347.

[19] "Human Resources Effectiveness Survey," *1987 Annual Report,* ASPA/Saratoga Institute (Saratoga, CA: Saratoga Institute, Inc.).

[20] Geoffrey H. Smart, "Management Assessment Methods in Venture Capital: Towards a Theory of Human Capital Valuation," Ph.D. dissertation, Claremont Graduate University, 1998.

costs of mis-hires, in interviews with Chris Mursau. The cost of mis-hires questionnaire is in Appendix I. Chris asked respondents to generate estimates on a *typical mis-hire*, not the most or least costly, and include mostly B player mis-hires, not more costly C player mis-hires. Fearing that respondents might have been inclined to hype costs estimates ("I'm a topgrader because I know mis-hires are *extremely* costly?"), Chris asked for *conservative* estimates. Of the fifty-two participants in this study who described mis-hires, about half are division presidents or above. The results are summarized in Figure 2.1.

Note that the $1.5 million mis-hire cost is the "bottom line," since costs were offset by contributions the person made.

Now, $1.5 million in costs for a single mis-hire is a lot of waste, but these numbers are probably a little conservative for several reasons. Several respondents assigned zero or very low costs to "maintaining," figuring the administrative assistant would have been employed anyway (to serve others), and the office would have been there anyway. The biggest *under-*

## Figure 2.1

### Cost of Mis-hire Study Results
### N = 52 cases

|  | Average (Mean) Statistics |
|---|---|
| Number of years in job: 1.6 | |
| Base Compensation: $102,692 | |
| 1. Cost in hiring | $31,643 |
| 2. Compensation (all years) | $255,452 |
| 3. Cost of maintaining person in job | $67,653 |
| 4. Severance | $33,962 |
| 5. Cost of mistakes, failures; wasted and missed business opportunities | $1,232,092 |
| 6. Cost of disruption | $242,356 |
| 7. Sum of costs (#1–#6) | $1,863,158 |
| Value of contribution | $360,721 |
| Net average cost of mis-hire | $1,502,436 (14.6 times base compensation) |

*stated* cost is the cost of disruption. More than half of the respondents registered the cost at $0. When asked why, they said that assigning a dollar value of costs was too difficult, too subjective. Almost all respondents, however, indicated that they believe costs associated with disrupting the workplace are huge. B/C players make mistakes affecting and disrupting many people. Instead of removing business land mines, they inadvertently plant them. Finally, the results of this study are probably conservative because many companies supplying the numbers are well-known companies. Some wrote best practices, including those pertinent to topgrading. These companies are quick to identify mis-hires and nip them in the bud. Lesser companies have more mis-hires and live with the consequences many more years.

The single biggest *estimated* cost in mis-hiring is the wasted or missed business opportunity. For decades I have witnessed multimillion-dollar fiascoes that clearly could have been avoided had an A player been hired instead of a B/C player. Gross neglect by a B/C player salesperson resulted in the loss of the #1 customer in one client company. In another, incompetent information technology consultants were hired. Why? Because they were friends of a B/C player CIO. The losses in information technology bankrupted the company.

One of the most insidious elements of "wasted or missed business opportunity" goes to the heart of topgrading. B/C players hire B/C players and drive away A players. Several of my clients carefully tracked the costs of B/C players mis-hiring people, and the cumulative costs through an organization where there are a lot of B/C player managers were astronomical. On the other hand, *not* hiring someone can cause business opportunities to be missed. A manufacturing client's customer said, "Designate a full-time customer service rep to us starting next week or we'll not sign the $10 million contract." This gun-to-your-head threat justified hiring a C player who, because of the unique situation, joined as what I would call a "temporary A player" and was replaced in six months—but the contract wasn't lost.

## RECURRING COSTS OF MIS-HIRES

Using the Cost of Mis-Hires Form (Appendix I), you can estimate what it costs you *not* to replace an underperformer. If the average cost of a mishire is $1.5 million, spread across 1.6 years, the recurring annual cost is $938,000 (or whatever). Total those recurring annual costs across your entire team, and the figure might convince you that there are huge financial gains to be made replacing B/C players.

## MIS-HIRES AT THE TOP

CEO mis-hires are the most serious. The media, if not behavioral scientists, cite at least some of the costs. Have you read enough about Ken Lay and Dennis Kozlowski? Their fine companies suffered because of their failures as CEOs. Gilbert Amelio was generally considered a disastrous CEO of Apple; although Apple's stock dropped 50 percent under Amelio, he left with a $9 million severance package. Michael Ovitz was hired and fired by his buddy Michael Eisner at Disney, and Ovitz walked away with $140 million in severance (challenged in later lawsuits). Not only the stockholders are hurt, but all business suffers a black eye when senior executives reap great financial rewards despite destroying companies and jobs.

CEO hiring is so seldom successful that the Sarbanes-Oxley Act (legislation holding boards more accountable) has been a wake-up call. Typically a committee of the board hires a search firm, and the search executive performs interviews and reference checks, with board members performing only perfunctory interviews. Many board members are CEOs, yet in this chapter we cited research showing CEOs and presidents believe that 79 percent of five executive searches result in mis-hires! Recently boards have been taking their CEO selection responsibilities more seriously, and relying on more thorough assessment approaches, including Topgrading Interviews.

## TOPGRADING CALCULATIONS

It is now possible to calculate, with reasonable accuracy, how much it costs you to:

- "live with" underperformers,
- replace B/Cs using your typical assessment techniques, and
- replace your B/Cs using topgrading techniques.

Suppose you have 20 B/Cs. Using the Mursau data,[21] the cost of mis-hiring them is 20 × $1.5 million, or $30 million, but the annual cost of leaving them in the job is 20 × $750,000, or $15 million.

To replace all 20 with As using a 25 percent successful assessment approach would involve three mis-hires for every good hire. You would have to hire 80 people, mis-hiring 60, to end up with 20 A players. The 60 mis-hires would each cost you $1.5 million, for a total of $90 million—a figure so high that it largely explains why otherwise talented managers live with Bs and even some Cs. It's simply too disruptive, painful, and costly to experience such a revolving door!

Using Topgrading-based assessment, 90 percent or eighteen of your replacements are As, and chances are the two mis-hires (costing a total of $3 million) would be replaced by As. Topgraders don't hesitate to replace all their underperformers, recognizing that $3 million is cheaper than $15 million or $90 million, and knowing disruption will be minor with the use of Topgrading-based assessments.

What about the "90 percent A player" standard embraced by many fine companies? The spreadsheet calculations have been done for you in Figure 2.2. Note that in replacing twenty underperformers with a 90 percent A player goal, the topgrading approach still involves $3 million in mis-hires, and the common assessment approach, with 25 percent As, "only" costs $74 million, not the $90 million to achieve all As. Some savings!

One more example: If you decide to replace forty Cs with ordinary 25 percent successful assessment, the cost of mis-hires is $158 million, but with the topgrading methodology of Topgrading Interviews, the costs of mis-hires would only be $6 million.

---

**Using Topgrading-based assessment, the cost of mis-hires is only 3–4 percent of costs using typical assessment approaches.**

---

Figure 2.2 expands this logic across a broad range of scenarios.

When you enter a new job and find underperformers, and if you want to estimate the costs of topgrading, DO NOT include the mis-hire costs for

---

[21] If the $100,000 average salary does not fit your situation, do your own cost of mis-hire study, using the template in Appendix I.

### Figure 2.2

### Topgrading Calculator Cost Matrix: Total Costs of Mis-Hires to Achieve 90 Percent As[22]

### (average cost of mis-hire: $1.5 million)

Your Current Hiring Success Rate

| Number of Underperformers to Be Replaced | 25% As Hired | 50% As Hired | 75% As Hired | 90% As Hired |
|---|---|---|---|---|
| 1 | $4 m | $1.4 m | $450 k | $150 k[23] |
| 2 | $8 m | $2.7 m | $900 k | $300 k |
| 4 | $16 m | $5.4 m | $1.8 m | $600 k |
| 10 | $33 m | $12 m | $3 m | $1.5 m |
| 20 | $74 m | $26 m | $9 m | $3 m |
| 40 | $158 m | $54 m | $18 m | $6 m |
| 100 | $401 m | $134 m | $45 m | $15 m |

those B/Cs you inherited. Blame your predecessor. Separately calculate the costs of not replacing them, if you wish, because you should be held accountable for their continuing costs to the organization. But when you quickly replace B/Cs, the estimated costs of mis-hires should begin with your hires, or more specifically, with the people you mis-hire.

Firing B/C players can be more costly than the averages our cost of mis-hire study shows. Two clients decided to "cut their losses" by paying severances to remove B/Cs rather than giving them a chance to become an A in the next year. One client spent $35 million severing about eighty B/Cs, another spent $55 million severing about one hundred B/Cs. All those B/C players failed to achieve their agreed-upon performance goals, the goals

---

[22] The matrix is equally applicable for mis-hires and mispromotions.

[23] $150 k is 10 percent of the $1.5 million cost of replacing ten underperformers with nine As, one mis-hire ($1.5 million). If you replaced one B/C, you'd have a 90 percent chance of hiring an A, with zero mis-hire costs, but a 10 percent chance your one hire would be a mis-hire, costing you $1.5 million. So $150,000 is an average cost.

expected of an A player. All had been given feedback, coaching, and training in the past, to no avail. Both companies topgraded and are certain those severance costs were worth it, because they got an A team and business success much quicker than if they had given all the B/Cs a year to reach the A category.

Other companies developed many and fired few. MarineMax has paid practically no severances, because many B/Cs were developed into A players, a few underperformers quit before being fired, and only a couple were let go.

We can debate the validity of various assumptions, and you can make whatever assumptions you choose regarding your success in hiring, costs of mis-hires, and how many people you need to replace. However:

---

**No matter how conservative your assumptions, failing to embrace a practice that picks 90 percent As is unnecessarily costly and disruptive.**

---

## CONDUCT YOUR OWN COST OF MIS-HIRE STUDIES

We should be as rigorous in hiring as we are in capital spending. For a piece of equipment costing $1.5 million we're disciplined in calculating ROIs, in comparative shopping, and in planning installation. Up front we have a meticulous process to justify and specify the type and amount of equipment we need and the expected outcomes, to be sure we are paying for precisely what we need to do the job. After the equipment is installed we debug it and then we systematically review the purchase to be sure it met our expectations. Did we get the capabilities we projected? The measured results? The Mursau study showed the average cost of a single mis-hire to be $1.5 million. But are we as rigorous in hiring as we are in capital spending? Nope. Most companies wing it on the front end without specifying the competencies, wing it in the hiring process with incomplete competency-based interviews, and let people sink or swim rather than debug any assimilation problems they experience. Unfortunately, most managers never go back to calculate benefits of good hires or costs of mis-hires, and never systematically study how we could do better next time.

To calculate the cost of mistakes at your own company:

### 1. Analyze every mis-hire.

Keep your Topgrading Interview Guide notes and your Candidate Assessment Scorecard (CAS). (CAS, which appears in Appendix E, is explained in Chapter 11. It's simply a form used after a Topgrading Interview to assess the candidate on all competencies.) Six months after you hire someone, pull out your CAS, and pat yourself on the back if your assessment proved accurate. When you have mis-hired someone, go back to your Topgrading Interview Guide notes to see where, specifically, you missed something. In this way you can remind yourself exactly how to improve your Topgrading Interviews in the future.

### 2. Calculate the cost of every mis-hire.

Use the template in Appendix I to understand what financial pain your organization suffered in a mis-hire. If you cut corners, perhaps reduced the Topgrading Interview time and didn't ask all the questions, or didn't conduct all the reference checks with all bosses in the past decade, a high cost of mis-hire experience will serve as a reminder to do it right next time. If the $100,000 salary level of the Mursau study doesn't fit your situation, or if the costs associated with your mis-hires are typically higher or lower than the averages in the Mursau study, conduct your own study. You must have realistic, credible assumptions.

### 3. Calculate the recurring costs of retaining underperformers.

In performing step 2, you simply divide line 2 (total compensation, for all years) by number of years in job. Thoroughly "digest" those recurring costs, and you will be more inclined to replace underperformers, those who were mis-hired or mispromoted.

### 4. Once per year use the Topgrading Calculator Cost Matrix (and ask your subordinate managers to do it too).

Using the Topgrading Calculator Cost Matrix (Figure 2.2), note your hiring success rate, calculate how many people you will have to hire to achieve your topgrading goal (presumably 90 percent As), and determine the total costs predicted from the inevitable mis-hires.

## THE CAREER COSTS OF NOT TOPGRADING

There is no clearer truth to a topgrading professional than this:

---

### The most powerful lever for career success in management is topgrading.

---

. . . and its corollary:

---

### There is no more certain career derailer in management than failing to topgrade.

---

More than six thousand senior managers have answered my exhaustive Topgrading questions about every job they held, an average of ten jobs. That's sixty thousand case studies. Successful careers all have a common pattern: creating more talented teams accounts for better results, earning managers more promotions. Sometimes the managers I spoke to admitted they were lucky—they inherited an A team because a boss assigned them the "best and brightest," or they went to work for a topgrading company that taught them how to do it. Most were motivated and resourceful, figuring out how to develop or replace Non-As.

The vast majority of managers I have interviewed experienced a stutter step—a failure to topgrade and a resulting failure to perform that led to career stagnation for a while or, in some cases, getting fired. The story of Ralph (not his real name) is typical. As Vice President Sales and Marketing, he inherited a mix of two A/A potentials, four Bs, and two Cs, as well as stretch goals for the year. The president of the company and I implored Ralph to topgrade, but all he did that year was develop one C into, maybe, a B-. A couple of underperformers convinced him they had "irreplaceable" relationships with customers. Ralph complained that HR wasn't recruiting A player replacements. This happened to be true, but he should have done his own recruitment. His feedback to his team was soft and ineffectual. When he failed to generate the sales results he committed to, he was fired.

I talked to Ralph after he was fired, and he was mad—at himself. "I was a C player because I didn't topgrade," he admitted. Ralph got a VP Sales and Marketing job at another company, topgraded at warp speed, and was promoted to President. He blossomed from a nontopgrading C player into a topgrading A player, and his career became much more successful.

Ralph's epiphany and subsequent topgrading are not unusual. Thousands of times we heard managers describe how failing to topgrade stalled their career:

"I limped along with a mix of As, Bs, and Cs, my results were mediocre, and I didn't receive a promotion."

"I upgraded, replacing the worst underperformers, and my results were OK, but it took five years for me to get an A team and three more years to earn a promotion."

The most successful leaders figure out the importance of topgrading, do it, get better results, and earn promotions. They say, "I topgraded, my results were terrific, and I was promoted in eighteen months." Every autobiography of a successful leader I've read emphasizes the importance of developing talented teams. It's no coincidence. Perhaps it could be equally revealing and instructive for unsuccessful careers to be analyzed, to dramatize how a failure to topgrade imperils careers.

## FINAL NOTE

Armed with accurate ROI information on hires, teams can make better human capital allocations, and all managers will embrace more rigorous selection. Why not raise the bonus of a manager who hires and retains A players and who becomes a provider of talent to other parts of the company? Why not lower the bonus of a manager who costs the company $2 million in mis-hires in a year and who drives away two A players? Topgrading companies use such incentives.

A 90 percent hiring success rate is achievable, both through external hires and when promoting from within. And, since management mis-hires cost $1.5 million (and more), mis-hires should be analyzed by individuals and companies, to improve interviewing skills and understand all of the true costs. The Topgrading Calculator Matrix is not a precise, scientific instrument, but I hope it will help you to better approximate scenarios in talent mix and relative financial advantages.

## CHAPTER 2 CHECKLIST: DO YOU KNOW YOUR COSTS OF MIS-HIRES?

**YES NO**

☐ ☐ I keep a Candidate Assessment Scorecard to record ratings on all competencies at the time a person is hired.

☐ ☐ I use a Candidate Assessment Scorecard to learn where I accurately, and inaccurately, assessed candidates.

☐ ☐ Upon reviewing a Candidate Assessment Scorecard six months after a person was hired, I revise my assessment techniques to improve, unless I was right on target.

☐ ☐ I calculate the costs of mis-hires/mispromotions.

☐ ☐ I connect my calculations of hiring/promoting success (Chapter 1) with my costs of mis-hires, to fully understand that the only way to achieve a dream team is to topgrade.

☐ ☐ I use the Topgrading Calculator annually to project my talent mix and associated costs.

☐ ☐ I require my team of managers to use the Topgrading Calculator Matrix annually.

# Three

# HIRING AND PROMOTING TALENT: THE TOPGRADING PLATINUM STANDARD

*It is a heck of a lot easier to hire the right people to begin with than to try to fix them later.*

Brad Smart

The hiring process is like dating. Overtures are extended, prospects play "hard to get," the relationship gets serious, a legally binding offer is made, and finally one is accepted. The spouses try to fix each others' foibles, but it doesn't work. Sometimes the marriage is made in heaven. Often it's not, and a major reason is the flawed way in which the two parties approach each other.

If you think a chapter that reviews hiring and promoting strategies is only for Human Resources professionals, think again. The main responsibility for hiring good people rests on your—the manager's or CEO's—shoulders.

## A TYPICAL HIRING STORY

Consider the following scenario: Suppose you are vice president marketing. Your marketing director just quit. She was superb at analyzing market data, developing product brochures, and coordinating advertising; she earned a $90,000 base salary.

Your company experiences only a 25 percent success rate in external hires, in part because your CEO has failed to set the recruitment bar high. There are no performance standards for hiring, no accountability, no policies that ensure that A players will be hired. There are no hiring scorecards for measuring percentage of hires who are A/A potential and no direct consequences for managers who mis-hire people. The costs of mis-hires are unknown.

You run to Human Resources, exclaiming, "Find me a new director, quick!" A job description is thrown together and a few competencies specified, but these are done superficially. You quickly consider a few internal candidates, but without conducting a thorough assessment of their talents. Your company made you attend a diversity workshop and you promised yourself that you would recruit more women, blacks, and Hispanics; however, in this crisis you forget to make it a priority. You ask around to see if someone can recommend a good external candidate. Nope. Unfortunately, neither you nor Human Resources has created a database of external talent. In addition, no one bothers to think about whether the job really needs filling; perhaps a sharp marketing analyst could perform the necessary functions, eliminating the need for a director; or, perhaps the three projects you need completed could be outsourced cheaper and better.

You call a headhunter, an executive search consultant who meets with you and the human resources director for two hours to learn the job specs. Snickering at your poorly constructed job description, the search executive promises to do better, but the result is a boilerplate job description thrown together with boilerplate competencies. The true essence of what it will take to do the job (coping politically with the cantankerous vice president sales, for example) isn't discussed. It's not that you want to deceive the search firm or candidates, but why turn off candidates with negatives? So, you put your best foot forward, concealing the dirty linen that could make a director of marketing's job hell.

Since the headhunter works for one of the country's largest search firms, 40 percent of Fortune 500 companies are its clients. This means that most of the largest firms are off limits to your search. You were not told the lockout list was so large, eliminating A player candidates from so many premier firms. You didn't think to ask.

The search executive delegates 90 percent of the work to a lower-level associate who hasn't even met the client—you. She screens résumés against the vague competencies. She lacks the horsepower to penetrate premier companies and tenaciously persuade A players to consider moving to a different company. You get occasional updates that are supposed to convince you that hundreds of people are being screened. You worry that since the search fee is 33 percent of the new hire's total compensation, the firm will say, "Gee, we're just not finding the level of talent you need at $90,000, so let's at least consider candidates in the $125,000 range."

The recruiter trots out three or four finalists for you to meet. The search firm partner has spent an hour with each, read his associate's reports, and scanned preliminary reference checks, which were all glowing (except for "sometimes too impatient with people who aren't doers"). The file on finalist candidates appears too good to be true.

You meet the candidates, perhaps for lunch, explain what the job needs are, ask a few questions about their experience and interests, sell the job a bit, and respond to their questions. If it looks like a mutual "go" for one or more finalists, your assistant organizes a day of interviews with some key members of your team. Current practice for "organizing" the interview sequence is like a fourth-grade fire drill. On the day of the interviews, two scheduled interviewers have crises to address, and so substitutes are thrown in at the last minute. The candidate is asked to be flexible, interviewing with a partial group. Most interviewers are ill-prepared, fumbling through candidate résumés for the first time ("Uh . . . tell me about yourself.") Interviewees go home feeling they've just been run through a hodgepodge of redundant, superficial, shallow interviews.

At the end of that disorganized day you talk with the other interviewers, but too often their thoughts are disjointed and contradictory. The scattergun interviews hardly provided deep, penetrating insights into any competency, except one—First Impression. The candidates don't match the search firm's glowing assessments. So the candidates are brought back for a second, equally disorganized visit.

Instead of hiring an A player marketing director, you're forced to choose the lesser of two evils, a candidate who now seems more apt to be a B player than an A player. Of course, three-fourths of the time your external hires turn out to be B/C players. The management psychologist's report hinted at some shortcomings, but his process, consisting of a half-day of tests and a one-hour interview, wasn't expected to be definitive.

The final compensation escalated to $110,000 base plus $40,000 bonus, so the search firm pockets $50,000 (not the $35,000 initially expected) plus all expenses. You get headaches and a career black eye for a mis-hire and HR ducks to avoid any complicity. No one—not you, not HR, not the search firm—is held accountable for the disaster, making it probable that the same thing will happen the next time someone at your company needs to make a hire.

## IMPROVING THE EXECUTIVE SEARCH PROCESS

How familiar was this story to you? Unfortunately, most companies' hiring process go something along these lines. Experienced topgraders minimize their hiring search by relying heavily on A players in their Rolodexes and excellent promote-from-within processes; but external searches are very common at most companies, so it's worth exploring the process more thoroughly.

A distinction should now be made. "Retained searches" are conducted by executive search firms, who are paid (usually one-third of first-year salary and bonus) regardless of whether their client hires someone they found. Executive-search professionals are at the top of their profession; they help to fill senior-management positions. "Contingent-fee recruiters" get paid (usually 15–25 percent) only if they produce a candidate who is hired. Contingent-fee recruiters usually work at lower levels—midmanagement, professional jobs, sales positions, administrative assistants. Both retained- and contingent-fee recruiters are headhunters, the former hunting for higher-salary "heads" than the contingent-fee recruiter. Since my practice involves assessing candidates for upper-management positions, the headhunters referred to in the remainder of this chapter are retained, not contingency.

When challenged with the dismal statistics on searches, A player search executives often fire back:

- "B/C player hiring managers say they want A players but won't hire one who threatens their status. This search firm shouldn't be blamed in this case."

- "Hiring managers initially say they will be flexible on budgets and other resources, but then restrict new hires who can't perform. When clients misrepresent the job, it's not the search firm's fault when there is a mis-hire."

- "We produce A player candidates who have other job offers and need to meet our client now, but the client is too disorganized to schedule a visit and loses good candidates."

- "Many times I have tried to put the client through the paces of job analysis and construction of meaningful competencies, but the client is lazy. It's clear they haven't really thought through the job requirements, and when I try to pin them down they become evasive and defensive."

- "We in the search industry have done a poor job of instructing clients on how they can get the best results."

I believe A player search executives accept assignments only where they are very confident they will succeed. It's the C player search people who incur the wrath of CEOs, who complain:

- "Large search firms are ethically prohibited from penetrating their client companies, but they don't tell you which ones are on their lockout list unless you ask."[24]

- "I asked for a lockout list and found that the search firm was ethically forbidden to search in two-thirds of all Fortune 500 companies in our industry—their current clients. So, their pool of potential A players is one-third of what we expected."

- "Some large companies hire every large search firm for one search every other year, just to keep them from pirating their A players. You have to pay to keep the vultures away."

- "They know darned well a C player manager won't hire an A, but they take the assignment anyway."

- "Instead of pushing clients to figure out if the job is really needed, they take the fee and don't care if the search is canceled."

- "Their lockout list contains only the divisions they worked in. If they found a manager for Division X, they feel entitled to steal a manager from Division Y. They say they need to ask about talent in other divisions to understand the total company and then go after our people in other divisions for their other clients."

---

[24] The Association of Executive Search Consultants' (AESC) published Code of Ethics states, "Disclose to present and prospective clients information known to the member about relationships, circumstances or interest that might create actual or potential conflicts of interest."

- "The search partner is the salesperson; he closes the search deal and then low-level associates do all the work. But those associates aren't sharp enough to get to the A players and entice them away from good jobs."[25]

- "The search industry is the only industry I can think of that hasn't undergone a major transformation in thirty years. It attracts C players from the business world—sales types who can make a quarter of a million bucks a year selling searches while mostly playing golf."

- "If they are hired by corporate HR, they don't view divisions as clients, so the division gets terrible service."

- "Reference calls by search firms are a joke. They never kill a candidate. They use reference calls to bolster, not screen, finalist candidates. They occasionally throw in an example of how reference calls eliminated a candidate, but the person was an obvious misfit to begin with."

- "The percentage of salary commission structure, 30–33 percent of first-year compensation, motivates search people to ignore superb talent that is cheaper in favor of acceptable talent that is much more expensive."

- "Search executives sometimes do long interviews, documenting accomplishments, but there is too much hype, no mention of failures, no mention of mistakes, and too much concealment of weaknesses that we see within weeks of hiring someone."[26]

## HOW TO MANAGE SEARCH FIRMS

There are many ways to achieve a high level of professionalism for retained-fee executive search firms:

---

[25] The AESC Code of Ethics requires members to define "the scope and character of services to be provided."
[26] AESC Code of Ethics requires members to "thoroughly evaluate potential candidates, including careful assessment of the candidate's strengths and weaknesses."

- Favor boutique firms of fewer than ten professionals. Large search firms have some A players, but if they can't invade their premier clients to attract A players for you, their value is diminished. Use large search firms to fill positions in which industry-specific competencies are not required: for example, functional positions such as director of human resources or vice president/controller. Be wary of firms specializing in an industry (computer software), because many top companies might be their clients and therefore locked out of your search.

- Require a written list of client companies they cannot penetrate—their lockout list—before you or HR signs a contract.

- Check references of the key search executive before signing a contract. This is very important—companies new to topgrading often buy slick pitches without checking that specific search consultant, and later they regret it. Accept nothing less than rave reviews on the consultant you hire, and be sure she does 75 percent (or more) of the work, and is not mostly a salesperson who delegates the work to low-paid "associates."

- Sign a fixed-fee contract that removes the incentive for the search firm to find expensive candidates, and requires the professionals you want to do the work (and not delegate it to underlings you haven't met or approved).

- Require original job descriptions plus several dozen competencies, written after a minimum of two full days of on-premise meetings with hiring managers and key team members.

- Expect the search executive to consider the CEO the major client, the eight-hundred-pound gorilla, but also to serve you (the hiring manager) and HR as clients.

- Require the firm to produce A player candidates who will help to achieve your diversity (inclusivity) goals. For example, if your company needs more women in management, require a minimum of 25 percent female candidates be presented.

- Require weekly updates—names and discussions of prospects, not just statistics. ("We screened 100 people.")

- Insist on Topgrading Interviews of all finalists, with written reports citing mistakes and failures, not just accomplishments. Tell the search executive, "If you cannot motivate candidates to disclose failures and shortcomings, you're not the right professional for us." Be reasonable—don't punish search firms when they present candidates with shortcomings. After all, there is no perfect candidate.

- Require candidate reports to disclose at least six real weak points—everyone has that many.

- Require reference check summaries that disclose negatives, not just positives. Repeat reference calls with all bosses in the past decade after you and the topgrading professional conduct Topgrading interviews.

- Sign a contract requiring the search firm to not steal your company's employees for three years. Make your entire company off limits, not just your division. So, if a search firm does a search for GE Capital, it cannot target managers at GE Medical Systems or any other GE entity for three years.

- Evaluate some résumés and career history forms and review some telephone screens early on to be sure you're "on the same page" as the search firm.

- Be very accessible to meet with candidates and to meet with search people to do job analyses and so on. Return their calls promptly.

- Be creative. Consider out-of-the-box relationships with recruiters, such as a reduced fee for these searches.

## THE BEST SEARCH FIRMS LOVE TOPGRADING

C player search people hate topgrading, because the clients require so much from them, but A players love it! Every couple of weeks I receive a box of *Topgrading* books FedExed from one search executive or another, asking me to autograph them so they can distribute them to their clients. An article in *Recruiter Magazine On-Line* said that nudging clients to topgrade is one of very few powerful actions recruiters can take to build business. One put it succinctly: "*Topgrading* makes the most compelling case to replace B/Cs with As, and when clients topgrade, they hire us to find those A players."

Although CEOs are critical of the executive search industry, premier companies manage to find A player search professionals and get good results. But there are many links in the recruitment chain, and one rusty or nonexistent link can result in a mis-hire. What additional approaches can help companies convert a 25 percent success rate in external hiring to 90 percent? The remainder of this chapter offers several.

## TOPGRADING MUST BE DRIVEN
## BY THE CEO, NOT HUMAN RESOURCES

The CEO job is to achieve results by getting the strategy, talent, and organization culture right. No CEO can survive poor results for long, blaming a low-performance culture on his managers, blaming the VP strategy for a failed strategic plan, blaming the CFO for the stock's tanking, or blaming the VP human resources for too many B/C players and not enough A players in the company. Only in a *Saturday Night Live* sketch could a CEO who has been in the job several years stand up before the shareholders, board of directors, and investors and say, "Have confidence in me! Our company is in a tailspin, we have to close ten plants, and there is mediocre talent at all levels, but I have a plan—I'll replace the vice president of human resources!"

Not so funny, is it? Topgrading must be thought of as a function permeating the entire company, supported by HR but driven by the CEO. When delegated to HR, topgrading fails, even when HR is a fully topgraded function.

HR cannot drive topgrading because it lacks the line authority and political clout, and because a lot of HR systems (compensation, performance management, hiring, succession planning) require CEO intervention to maintain the A player standard. HR managers can devise a world-class performance system, but cannot require their peers to use it properly to reinforce the A player standard. When performance appraisals are too generous, the HR manager can plead with peers to stop being so generous, but it's the CEO who ultimately must tell a division head, "Your division has fallen short of the goals you committed to achieve, so how can all ten of your direct reports be rated A players, and how can their performance appraisals be 'meets performance expectations' or 'exceeds performance expectations'? Spread out the distribution, tell your people the truth, hold them accountable, and don't think of nominating some B/C players for promotion . . . or I'll consider you a C player!"

I'm not criticizing HR, just acknowledging human nature. Politics can cause HR and line managers to join together to "game the system," a cancerous affliction only the CEO can cure. Short-term results can undermine topgrading when a division manager says, "I believe in topgrading, but if I make my numbers this quarter, I'll get a promotion. There isn't enough time for me to replace two B/C players so I'll hide them, keep them from screwing things up, and work my A players and myself extra hard. And I'll leave topgrading to my successor."

The HR manager reporting to that division manager can hardly fight the boss, and risks being a snitch, a tattletale, by telling the corporate VPHR or CEO, "The division manager is protecting two C players." Talent meetings conducted by the CEO and the corporate VPHR can flush out the division manager's narrow self-interest, to hold him accountable for topgrading NOW, but seldom can the division HR manager impose topgrading on an unwilling peer.

It was stated earlier in this book that anyone can topgrade—*any* department manager can topgrade a department, *any* division manager can topgrade a division. But from a corporate topgrading perspective, the CEO cannot assume that A player subordinates are doing it. That's why Jeffrey Immelt (CEO) and Bill Conaty (HR) literally spend months in the famous Session C talent meetings at GE. The same principle holds for you if you are a function head or operating division head. As a division president you can topgrade, but it is foolish to assume that all your A player plant managers will topgrade (even though they would not be considered A players without being topgraders). In your talent meetings as well as daily discussions you must be sure that no one is gaming the system or eroding your A player standard for political reasons.

In addition to politics eating away at topgrading integrity, limited experience undermines valid assessments. You have experience with hundreds of plant managers and their staffs, so you are better calibrated than they are. This means that you can judge them and their people with a more accurate understanding of who qualifies as an A, A potential, or chronic B/C.

Dave Robertson, the VPHR who initiated topgrading at Hillenbrand

Industries, says, "Even world-class compensation, performance management, and succession systems have flaws, and HR gets caught up in exceptions and fixes that cause topgrading to suffer. That's why the CEO, not us in HR, must lead topgrading."

## CEO ROLE IN TOPGRADING, HIRING, AND PROMOTING

When topgrading the hiring and promoting process, a CEO should:

- Take responsibility for topgrading success, including hiring/promoting results, policies, and processes. The CEO must approve a best-practices blueprint. Most topgrading CEOs require tandem Topgrading when people are hired externally and when they are promoted internally.

- Maintain the A player standard *daily* by prohibiting exceptions to creep in. Fight pressures to try to get by with a B who can be hired now; push managers to recruit better and to hold out for the A player.

- Set specific management hiring goals—numbers to be hired, diversity (I prefer the term *inclusivity*) goals, and the requirement that only A players or people with A potential will be hired. Typically all managers are required to have at least 90 percent subordinates deemed A players or A potential, zero C players, and no more than 10 percent in the "I'm not sure yet" B/C category. Although 100 percent As is the goal, there is always some slippage in topgrading, as described in Chapter 1.

- Hold all managers accountable for topgrading (including hiring and promoting success). Award bonuses for topgrading and withhold bonuses when managers fail to achieve topgrading goals.

- Monitor topgrading progress, including hiring success.

- Devote one-quarter of work time to topgrading (Jack Welch estimated one-half of his time); challenge every key hiring decision, asking questions to be sure an A is hired.

- Minimize the use of external recruiters by personally encouraging everyone in management to build their networks, keep their Rolodexes updated, and recruit like mad.

- Occasionally call the big plays (override subordinate ratings of candidates to be sure A players are hired).

- Be sure all vendors (recruiters, management psychologists) understand that the CEO is the key client, so that if there are attempts to undercut topgrading, they are required to notify the CEO.

- Manage search firms according to guidelines spelled out in this chapter.

- Conduct talent meetings (once or twice per year), including reports on hiring and promoting success.

Hiring is a daily opportunity for CEOs to drive topgrading policies and values. Curt Clawson, CEO of Hayes Lemmerz, reads all psychologists' Topgrading reports on internal assessments and selection candidates, complimenting hiring managers and HR for going the extra mile to hire a true A rather than get by with a B. Ann Drake, CEO of DSC Logistics, generates one or two management candidates from most industry meetings she attends. She has exactly the right perspective, one to be emulated by every manager: "I recruit all day long, every day, with everybody I meet." Bill Gates personally calls recent college graduates—"Hi, this is Bill Gates. I can sure use you at Microsoft." That makes Gates the highest-paid recruiter in the world—and if he makes time for this crucial topgrading activity, shouldn't you?

## TALENT MEETINGS

A CEO can reinforce topgrading in talent meetings, in large part by making decisions to replace B/C players who are not becoming As.

Let's back up. An organization's strategy is converted to organization charts with boxes—jobs to fill this year and maybe five years from now. A simple coding is A player, A potential, and Non-A in present job, with promotability indicated by numbers (1, 2, and 3) or by color (yellow for promotable one or two levels, green for promotable to executive committee level, and red for someone who has plateaued). Whirlpool Corporation has the "bunker," a 15 × 25-foot room in which the only topic of discussion permissible is talent. This locked room has the pictures of managers, with ratings of promotability. Typically the CEO, HR, and a business unit or function head will meet to discuss, thoroughly, the two levels of managers reporting to the head.

Performance appraisals, topgrading professionals' Topgrading assessments, and task-force accomplishments are presented in talent meetings in order for the group to compare people. In large companies, assessment reports on managers by trained tandem Topgrading interviewers (supplemented by oral 360 interviews) are included; this establishes a common standard across functions and divisions. "Intelligence" on competitors' teams is introduced to determine who has the talent edge. HR produces the latest compensation studies to enable valid conclusions about who are A players (top 10 percent of talent for the compensation). The CEO is the final arbiter of how strong a manager has to be to qualify as an A player, what happens to B/C players (termination, transfer, demotion, forced retirement), or exactly which A player will be promoted.

In talent meetings the CEO should ask in any number of different ways:

- Do we have the talent to meet our strategic goals? Will we have it? Let's review the last, updated Talent Scorecards to see how many As, A potentials, and Non-As we have in the company overall, broken down into every division, function, and department.

- How successful are we at recruiting people, internally and externally? What is our hiring batting average? Let's review the latest, updated Hiring Scorecard for the company, broken down into every division, department, and function.

- Where are we strong and weak in management?

- Which A players should be promoted, and to what jobs, in order to retain and develop them, but not put them in over their heads?

- How many external searches should we do, for what jobs?

- Have we made progress in redeploying the chronic B/C players? Why not? Who's responsible?

- Are we all in a full-court press by developing our Rolodexes, our networks, to generate candidates? How strong is our "virtual bench" of talented A players we can recruit, when needed, and bypass search firms?

- Are we managing the search firms for our benefit?

- How are we progressing on developing an internal "bench," so we can have an optimal blend of promoting people from within and enriching the mix with talent from outside?

- For specific jobs, do we need A players at higher ($150,000) or lower ($100,000) levels, in bigger or smaller leagues? How does our talent stack up against our competition's talent?

- Do our HR systems (compensation, performance management) reinforce topgrading?

- Which managers are topgrading and which are not?

- Are we all in agreement that there should be As in every job, and that there is nothing more important for the success of the company than driving, driving, driving toward that standard?

The chairman of a $6 billion company that topgrades (but wishes to remain anonymous so as to not alert competitors to the benefits of topgrading) offers these suggestions for talent meetings:

1. Be sure that it's the manager, not HR, conducting the talent discussions. That reinforces the fact that talent is the division president's job, and it's not delegated to HR.

2. At the end of each talent review, summarize the actions to be taken, and hold people accountable for follow-through.

3. Communicate with the board of directors about topgrading, before topgrading is launched (to get their buy-in and support), and periodically present the results—increase in percentage of A players, what happened to an A player who declined to a B, hiring success, and so on.

## THE HIRING MANAGER'S ROLE IN TOPGRADING, HIRING, AND PROMOTING

As the hiring manager, you must fully "own" your topgrading results, including hiring and promoting decisions. Even if the company does not topgrade, you can hire and promote As, develop managers to become As, and remove B/Cs. If you can't topgrade because of a C player culture, find another job or risk becoming a C player yourself. You are the boss, the manager who will conduct the performance appraisals of the people you hire and promote, and your overall performance will depend on your talent choices. Of course, any hiring manager can adopt the perspective of an A player CEO, but have authority over a smaller domain. Your talent meeting simply becomes a regular part of your staff meeting. Your role is to:

- Set a goal of having everyone reporting to you be an A player within one year, and everyone reporting to them be an A player within the next year, and so on.

- Hire A players at the right level. It's your job to overcome the obstacles. No excuses.

- Continually build your network of potential A player candidates, lessening dependence on search firms. Keep a talent Rolodex of dozens of names. "Recruit like mad" for life. If Bill Gates and Ann Drake can make the time to do it, so can you.

- Work with HR to analyze jobs and write behaviorally based job descriptions. Entire books have been written on how to analyze a job, but the basic steps are straightforward: talk to incumbents and former incumbents, ask informed coworkers for their insights, obtain best practices information, ask HR consultants and search firms to contribute. See Appendix G for an example of behaviorally anchored competencies. Produce a "first-year accountabilities" scorecard.

- Manage search firms effectively (advice appears in this chapter).

- Conduct a Topgrading Interview, preferably a tandem Topgrading Interview, of every finalist for hire.

- Conduct three to six reference calls, with a minimum of all bosses in the past ten years. Talk to some peers, subordinates, and customers, both present and past.

- Conduct candidate evaluation meetings at the end of visits by selection candidates.

- Evaluate yourself on your hiring success (bring out the Candidate Assessment Scorecard[27] six months later to learn where assessments were accurate, or not). Conduct your own cost-of-mis-hire study for any mistakes, to reinforce your commitment to improve.

- Work with Human Resources to be sure the Hiring Checklist (Figure 3.1) is completed, with every component done to an A player standard.

### FIGURE 3.1
### SAMPLE TOPGRADING HIRING CHECKLIST

Date_____

Candidate Name _____

Position Applied For _____

Hiring Manager _____

☐ Job Description Completed

    ☐ Job-Specific Competencies

    ☐ First-Year Accountabilities (for Bonus) Specified

☐ Career History Form Completed

☐ Tandem Topgrading Completed

Tandem Interviewers_____    Date_____

                _____    Length_____

---

[27] Appendix E, described in Chapters 2 and 11.

☐ Coworker Interviews

    ☐ (interviewer) _____ competency _____

    ☐ (interviewer) _____ competency _____

    ☐ (interviewer) _____ competency _____

    ☐ (interviewer) _____ competency _____

    ☐ (interviewer) _____ competency _____

☐ Topgrading professional Topgrading (n/a if not needed)

☐ Reference Checks by Topgrading Interviewers (minimum: all bosses in past ten years)

_____ interviewer      _____ reference's name and title

_____ interviewer      _____ reference's name and title

_____ interviewer      _____ reference's name and title

_____ interviewer      _____ reference's name and title

_____ interviewer      _____ reference's name and title

_____ interviewer      _____ reference's name and title

_____ interviewer      _____ reference's name and title

☐ Candidate Report

    Executive Summary

    Job-Specific Competencies Rated

Lists of Strengths, Weaker Points

Developmental Recommendations

Approval by _____     Date _____

A similar process is used by topgrading companies in order to promote A players who succeed. Remember, research shows only 25 percent of those promoted turn out to be As, proving that the usual performance appraisals are weak predictors of promotability success.

In topgrading companies it is typical for everyone in management to be Topgrading-assessed, to create an overall talent picture of As, A potentials, and Non-As. Managers are developed and become As or are redeployed, and eventually there are 90 percent As. Companies relying on a current performance review and a three-year-old Topgrading assessment fail to achieve 90 percent success in promotions.

---

**To achieve a 90 percent success in promotions, supplement performance appraisals with a fresh, current Topgrading-based assessment.**

---

The Topgrading-based assessment can be done several ways:

1. Manager conducts Topgrading Interview of subordinate candidates for promotion.
   Advantage: easy, quick.

2. Manager conducts tandem Topgrading, and both interviewers conduct oral 360s (like reference calls for hiring) with peers, subordinates, and other coworkers.
   Advantage: more reliable and objective than #1.

3. Interviewers from different part of the company conduct tandem Topgrading Interviews and 360s, or topgrading professional conducts Topgrading Interviews and 360s.
   Advantage: most likely to produce a promotion that turns out to be an A player.
   Disadvantage: more time consuming and/or costly than #1 or #2.

The hiring checklist can easily be modified for a promotion candidate, and should be. Bear with me for repeating myself by emphasizing the importance of a full and current Topgrading process when promoting people, because a few clients have slipped on this banana peel; they mispromoted managers and later realized they had cut corners, experiencing avoidable high costs in mispromotions.

## HUMAN RESOURCES' ROLE IN TOPGRADING, HIRING, AND PROMOTING

The HR role vis-à-vis the CEO has been stated, but let's review it with a particular focus on hiring and promoting. A player HR professionals are increasingly valuable, in part because although CEOs must drive topgrading, HR must be topgraded to support topgrading. I know of fifteen companies in which the HR person is the "right arm" of the president or CEO. In many premier companies the senior HR manager is finally on a par with peers in terms of overall influence and pay. A major reason for HR's ascendancy in respect is their effectiveness in motivating managers to topgrade, including hiring and promoting A players. They sell, cajole, challenge, coach, and browbeat their client managers to topgrade. The A player HR role is to:

- Topgrade HR, serving as a role model, recruiting all A players for HR, coaching people to become As, redeploying chronic B/C players, and using tandem Topgrading-based approaches for both hiring and promoting.

- Support the entire team in topgrading, including hiring and promoting; partner with managers, serving those managers to be sure that A players are hired and/or promoted.

- Drive best practices in recruitment through upholding A player standards, encouraging hiring managers to "recruit for life." HR should embody "recruit for life" as a role model.

- Coordinate job analyses and the creation of job descriptions that really describe the jobs, have up to fifty competencies, state major challenges, spell out first-year bonus accountabilities, and build Candidate Assessment Scorecards.

- Create strong recruitment sources (prescreen search firms, find A player recruitment professionals, build a powerful image in college-campus recruitment and Web sites); provide internal recruiters, when appropriate, for outside searches that might otherwise have been assigned to outside search firms; explore "bounty" systems ($1,000 to an employee who refers an A player who is hired).

- Lead design of topgrading systems, including hiring/promoting practices and policies.

- Adjust the level of pay for A players at the right level ("Is an A player at $100K or $150K necessary?"), tap personal network, and acquire pay surveys to get the money–talent ratio right.

- Coach the team (peers and boss) to help them write and follow through on their Individual Development Plans.

- Coach the team on legalities of hiring/firing and on achieving diversity (inclusivity) goals.

- Organize interviewing training, talent meetings, visits of candidates, assimilation of new hires, and Topgrading selection interviews and coaching by topgrading professionals.

- Calculate the numbers to measure topgrading success; track each hiring manager's "batting average" and summarize all company topgrading scorecards periodically (costs of mis-hires, percentage of A/A potentials at each level in the organization); follow through on Individual Development Plans and hiring success.

Topgrading scorecards are key measurements of success, and teams of A players see the present results and figure out ways to improve. For example, simply presenting the hiring scorecard can create intense peer pressure for a non-Topgrading interviewer to embrace Topgrading. The American Heart Association tracks hiring success and states that in the past two years, internal and external hiring at the executive level (corporate and field) has produced 100 percent success with Topgrading:

## American Heart Association
## Senior Executive Hiring Scorecard

|                              | A/A Potential Hired | A Not Hired |
|------------------------------|:-------------------:|:-----------:|
| Topgrading Interview Used     | 10 | 0 |
| Topgrading Interview Not Used | 0  | 0 |

At the American Heart Association there initially was widespread concern that Topgrading Interviews took too much time, but success stories ("I avoided two mis-hires last week because of Topgrading.") helped build what now is deep acceptance of Topgrading.

HR's volunteering to be a tandem partner can help build commitment to the discipline. In one large service company, a division had stretch sales and profit goals and six months remained to achieve them, but the division was in jeopardy of missing its numbers because Charlie, the vice president sales, continued to mis-hire sales representatives. He used a short competency interview and mis-hired three out of four account representatives. His peers were concerned that they were going to lose their bonuses because he kept mis-hiring. The HR manager offered to be a tandem Topgrading interviewer with Charlie, who had a couple of finalists coming in the next couple of weeks. Charlie acquiesced, hired nothing but A player sales representatives, and became a vocal advocate of tandem interviews. And yes, Charlie met his sales goals and the division team achieved maximum bonus!

HR can further support topgrading and hiring by ensuring that HR systems impacting recruitment are world-class. Those HR systems are:

- *Applicant tracking systems* to be sure that recruitment activities are consistently reaching A/A potential candidates through the entire selection cycle. This candidate database should be developed to become a valuable source of talent managers have gleaned from their personal networks. An ATS can be a high-tech corporate Rolodex.

- *Performance management* to be sure that the system is fair and hardhitting in identifying A, A potential, and non-A players, and has the minimum acceptable performance rating ("Meets Performance Expectations") corresponding to what A players achieve.

- *Management development* to be sure that managers are powerfully developed, in order to qualify as A players now and when the bar is higher—when the company is bigger, when the jobs are more complex.

- *Succession planning* to be sure that promotions achieve what is intended: that A players succeed in bigger jobs, that the system is fair, that A players are retained because they grow, that B/C players are put in jobs where they can be As, and that the company has the right bench strength.

- *Compensation* to ensure that packages (including benefits, stock, and perks) reward desired behavior leading to the company's success (including pursuing the right strategy, achieving sufficient talent, and maintaining a high-performance organization culture).

- *Midyear career review* to adjust conclusions about each manager's career goals, strengths, and weak points and to adjust the comprehensive Individual Development Plan for the next six months. (The reason it is midyear is to have career discussions separated from the tension of annual performance reviews, bonus awards, pay increases, and promotions.)

HR must be a topgraded function, because the top HR executive will be in the limelight, driving integrity into each system that affects recruitment. Inequities in performance appraisals come to light in topgrading meetings. If a B player should be replaced through external recruitment or given another chance depends on the CEO's decision, which will be a better decision with a solid management development system. If someone is considered a C player because of being a poor team player, yet the compensation system rewards not cooperating with other departments, the CEO will decide to change the compensation system, and HR must implement this change.

## A PLAYER HR PROFESSIONALS
## LOVE TOPGRADING

In topgrading organizations HR is held accountable for *quality* of hires, not just speed to hire and cost per hire. They don't drive topgrading, but HR A players are essential in supporting it. Their bonuses depend on it. If they slack off and let a B/C slip through, the CEO will be all over them, demanding to know why a B/C player was promoted or hired. HR has historically dodged real accountability, but A players welcome it.

Instead of a résumé stating that they "upgraded the HR organization," A player HR managers can cite, "Topgraded HR, and then helped the CEO topgrade the company, contributing substantially to a 50 percent increase in the stock price in three years." A players are resourceful, and A player HR managers get up every morning looking forward to a day full of challenges and opportunities to make a real difference.

But even A player HR executives who topgrade all of HR cannot topgrade a company if the CEO doesn't drive topgrading. HR can train people in Topgrading interviewing (even B/C players want to learn it) and offer coaching by topgrading professionals (B/Cs like that too); HR can create topgrading scorecards to track the company's percentage of As in the company and percentage of As hired (even Cs can be politically savvy and if they are required to have more As, they'll game the system and explain why their coaching has converted Bs to As). But, as soon as the HR executive mentions *assessment* with the real possibility of replacing B/Cs with As, B/C players don't want to be assessed, so they run to the CEO with one thousand reasons why topgrading should not be done ("The timing isn't right," "It will be so disruptive we'll miss our quarterly numbers," etc.).

A player HR managers are extremely marketable, and can readily join a company led by an A player who will topgrade. They can only love topgrading when and where they can do it, and that means reporting to an A player CEO who will personally drive topgrading.

## HOW TO MANAGE TOPGRADING PROFESSIONALS

Are the management psychologists and other topgrading professionals the good guys, riding to the rescue—sorting the As, Bs, and Cs whom search firms produced so hiring managers can be sure that only A players are hired? Sometimes. We psychologists are a mixed bag, however, with our A, B, and C players. As in the search industry, C player psychologists work in a sea of mediocrity. The CEO should be the main client, always, to guard against C player managers manipulating HR, search firms, and psychologists in ways that result in mis-hires.

My personal bias is in favor of Topgrading Interviews and against reliance on psychological tests for upper-management hires or promotions. Tests, properly validated, are moderately useful predictors of job performance at the lowest levels—factory worker, salesperson, typist. For management jobs, tests such as Myers Briggs Type Indicator are fine in workshops—"thinkers" go to that corner and "feelers" go over there, and you all talk to each other to learn how people with different thinking styles can communicate better. But for management selection, all tests are dull instruments. The psychologist should know the company strategy, the culture, the hiring manager, the job, and the competencies, and then use the Topgrading Interview to reveal fit and no-fit factors. I wish tests worked—I could earn 50 percent more, assessing three managers in a day rather than two. But I have never heard of a psychologist relying on test profiles and a one-hour interview and achieving an excellent batting average in assessment. Require your psychologist to use a Topgrading Interview. Then track the accuracy of the psychologist's report—pull it out six months after a person has been hired and require 90 percent (or better) accuracy.

How valid are topgrading professionals' Topgrading assessments? It would be a tad self-promoting to discuss myself, but two other firms that guarantee their results are ghSMART & Company, Inc., and The Mursau Group, Inc. Both are included in case studies in Chapter 5.

This book offers the tantalizing prospect of improving from 25 to 90 percent A players hired or promoted, but there are in-between levels of success. So that you have realistic expectations, the following success rates are noted, based on decades of topgrading professionals' experience:

25 percent success (A/A potentials hired or promoted): typical, average results across all industries and levels in management, with no Topgrading Interview.

50 percent success: typical result with solo Topgrading by interviewer with experience conducting ten to twenty Topgrading Interviews.

75 percent success: achievable result with tandem Topgrading Interview conducted by trained interviewers with experience in ten to twenty Topgrading Interviews.

90 percent (plus) success: best result attained by trained tandem Topgrading Interviewers with experience conducting fifty to seventy-five Topgrading Interviews, Topgrading Interview by topgrading professional, or both

In large companies we professionals are used until internal managers are trained, get experience, and prove 90 percent successful.

## RESOURCEFULNESS, THE MEGACOMPETENCY

Before we get into the hiring blueprint, let's pause to review the competencies we hire against. Now would be a good time to read the fifty management competencies in Appendix G.

If you've already read the original *Topgrading,* you'll notice that a new competency, Resourcefulness, replaces Initiative. *Resourcefulness* refers to your ability to passionately figure things out, like how to surmount barriers. It wasn't listed previously in *Topgrading* as a separate competency because it is a composite of many: Intelligence, Analysis Skills, Creativity, Pragmatism, Risk Taking, Initiative, Organization/Planning, Independence, Adaptability, Change Leadership, Energy, Passion, and Tenacity.

Earlier in this book I said that A players are almost all topgraders and all are resourceful. Since resourcefulness contains so many competencies, it's easy to understand why it's a megacompetency. The *American Heritage* dictionary defines *resourcefulness* as, "able to act effectively or imaginatively especially in difficult situations." Not bad, but I prefer action, not readiness, so *doing* something with passion seems more apt. *Initiative* is defined as "ability or instinct to begin or follow through with a plan or task." Close, but no cigar. Maybe dictionary writers are short on resourcefulness, because "ability or instinct" could reside in passive people, devoid of initiative. A dictionary definition of *enterprising* falls short of the mark with "readiness to venture."

I asked two hundred A player managers how important resourcefulness is, and all two hundred said it was not just desirable, but essential to their success and their identity. A typical statement was "If I were ordinary in resourcefulness, I wouldn't be me. I live to figure things out, to meet challenges."

Dr. Kate Smart Mursau, in her doctoral dissertation, confirmed the importance of resourcefulness in accounting for success in management.

## A HIRING BEST-PRACTICES BLUEPRINT

Let's connect some dots. Now that we've discussed the roles of CEO, hiring manager, and HR, provided advice on how to get the best results from search firms and topgrading professionals, and highlighted the importance of resourcefulness as a competency, a blueprint for structuring the entire hiring process can now be laid out. This blueprint:

- Further breaks down your responsibilities as hiring manager and those of your key partner, Human Resources.

- Outlines a practical visit schedule, assuming two visits to the company by a finalist.

- Proposes an interviewer-focus matrix, in which each interviewer delves into a competency rather than "wing it."

- Presents a sample structured interview guide for one of those short structured focused interviews.

Exactly how to conduct good interviews (the Topgrading Interview or the shorter structured interviews) is covered in Chapter 11. Chapter 12 spells out important legal considerations.

Let's begin with how responsibilities are typically divvied up between Human Resources and the hiring manager. See Figure 3.2.

## Figure 3.2

## Responsibilities of Hiring Manager and Human Resources

|  | Hiring Manager | Human Resources |
|---|---|---|
| 1. Requisition forms . . . completed by | X | |
| submitted to | | X |
| 2. Job analysis, job description, competencies created by | X | X |
| 3. Posting | | X |
| 4. Internal recruitment | Network | Various |
| 5. Search firms hired and managed | X | X |
| 6. Résumés screened by | X | X |
| 7. Career history forms or SATI guides | X | X |
| 8. Telephone interview (in-person interview, if local) | Technical | Routine |
| 9. Visits coordinated by | | X |
| 10. Visit #1: Structured short competency interviews | | |
| coordinated by | | X |
| Written evaluations collected by | | X |
| Decision to continue or reject candidate | X | |
| 11. Visit #2: Exchange of perspectives interviews | | |
| coordinated by | | X |
| Topgrading Interview (preferably tandem) | X | tandem? |
| Written Evaluations collected by | | X |
| Decision to Continue or Reject Candidate | X | |
| 12. Factual record checks | | X |
| 13. In-depth reference checks by Topgrading interviewers | X | If tandem |
| 14. Topgrading by topgrading professional coordinated by | | X |
| 15. Meeting to decide hire/not hire coordinated by | | X |
| Decision to Hire/Not Hire | X | |
| 16. Negotiate salary | X | |
| 17. Send rejection letters/offers | | X |
| 18. Retain records | | X |
| 19. Research hiring success | X | X |

1. You, the hiring manager, determine that a job needs to be filled, so you complete the necessary requisition forms and submit them to HR.

2. Job analysis is performed, with HR working closely with you. For a new management job, three or four hours of analysis can produce a "real" job description, rather than boilerplate. The two of you modify my generic list of fifty competencies in Appendix G, writing behavioral definitions of what it will take to do the job. If HR is to do preliminary screening, this step 2 can ensure that you are both "singing out of the same hymnal."

3. HR posts the job, both internally and externally, to produce internal candidates, candidates generated through employee referrals, and external candidates.

4. Recruitment of outside candidates is apt to initially be done by you and HR. You will tap your personal network, which often is the only way to quickly hire an external A player. Keep your Rolodex full and updated. If this approach fails, HR might ask an internal recruiter to help you.

5. If recruitment of internal candidates (step 3) and use of your network and other internal recruiters of outside candidates fail, a search firm might be hired. The search firm should view the CEO or non-HR hiring executive as the main client, but on a day-to-day basis you and HR are the key contacts and operational clients. You and HR both manage the search firm (using guidelines presented in this chapter).

6. Don't delegate all of the résumé screening to HR or to a search firm. Share the responsibility initially to be sure that HR is screening internal and internally generated candidates the way you want. Do the same for search firms with external candidates.

7. Do the same as in step 6 with Career History Forms (application forms) and Self-Administered Topgrading Interview (SATI) Guides. How to use the Career History Form (Appendix C) and SATI Guide is discussed in Chapter 11. Briefly, the Career History Form is typically modified to be the application form of the company, and it provides

a lot more information (total compensation history, for example) than most application forms. Examining both the résumé and Career History Form (or SATI Guide) screens out B/C players and screens in A players more effectively than is possible with just the resumes.

8. Search firms screen, but for internal searches (conducted by you and HR), initial telephone screens can be done by HR. However, if you are a lot better equipped to determine technical expertise (engineering, finance, and the like), you could screen quickly on this essential competency and HR could screen on other competencies. Short "verbal surgery" telephone interviews are appropriate here. If you are apt to be "selling" the interviewee, try to arrange a face-to-face interview. This is more time consuming for an initial screen, but is worth it if you are strapped for viable candidates. All interviewers should write a brief report, and HR should collect them. You decide if you want to proceed with each prospect.

9. HR coordinates visits to the company. The two one-day visits are typically a month apart. If there is a decision to proceed with visit #2, it usually takes a month for calendars to align all of the interviews. In a time crunch, however, for an apparently outstanding candidate, visit #1 and visit #2 could be combined into a single two-day visit. The risk, of course, is that after the first day you may reject the candidate. Sending the candidate home in the middle of a two-day visit is more awkward than not inviting a person back after a one-day visit. And, the extraordinary effort to coordinate two days of interviews is wasted.

10. For the initial day of interviews, both HR and you are apt to be on the schedule. You will have already talked with the candidate, so the two of you are on a first-name basis. By now you know how to balance your question asking versus question answering as well as your screening versus selling the candidate on you and the job. You are apt to take the candidate to breakfast, and at the end of the day talk with all interviewers and review their written reports. HR will be one of the interviews during the day; it will also coordinate the schedule and collect reports. You decide whether to drop the candidate or continue.

11. In the second visit, a couple more short structured interviews are conducted, along with the tandem Topgrading Interview conducted by you (preferably with a peer such as your HR person). Some companies place the Topgrading Interview the morning of visit #1, so the hiring manager can cancel all subsequent interviews if the candidate "washes out." The visit #2 Topgrading Interview is for well-oiled topgrading machines, where very few visit #2 candidates are eliminated. The advantage is more available data, so the visit #2 Topgrading Interview is a little more revealing. Additional "sharing-perspectives" interviews are appropriate—no more grilling the candidate, but instead several prospective coworkers talking with the candidate as colleagues. Then HR collects the reports and, again, you decide to continue the selection process or reject the candidate.

12. Factual record checks should be done by HR (or the search firm). *Factual* means obtaining confirmation of education records, dates of employment, and so forth. Background checks for criminal records might also be done. Chapter 12 spells out the legal considerations.

13. You or the other internal Topgrading Interviewer, or (typically) both, should conduct in-depth reference checks. You can bond with the candidate's previous bosses and only you can ask the really penetrating questions. The interviewee actually coordinates those interviews (see Chapter 11 on reference checking). Any reference checks conducted by internal recruiters or search firms are considered preliminary.

14. If a Topgrading Interview by a topgrading professional is conducted, it is at this "final check" time.

15. A final meeting to hire/not hire and compare various candidates is coordinated by HR, but you make the decision.

16. And you, not HR, should negotiate the job offer (salary, etc.).

17–18. HR retains all records (EEOC and the like), and sends out offer and rejection letters. Topgrading HR departments also track hiring success with a Hiring Scorecard so you, they, and the company can continually refine the selection systems and achieve that 90 percent success rate. Even if HR does not, you should track your own success.

## Figure 3.3

### Candidate Visit Schedule

#### VISIT #1

2 weeks before *Hiring committee meets.* Hiring manager reviews status of search (how many prospects, how good they are), revisits importance of job to strategy, organizes Visit #1 (who is available to interview, who should focus on what competencies), distributes paperwork (résumé, job description, Candidate Assessment Scorecard). HR is partner and "quality control coach," but also keeps the calendar, reminds interviewers of schedule, scrambles to replace interviewer if one becomes ill, and so on.

7:30–9:00 A.M. *Hiring Manager* picks up candidate, goes to breakfast, drives candidate to offices, reviews schedule for day with candidate.

9:00–10:00 *Interview #1: Intellectual Competencies*

10:00–10:15 Interviewer completes written summary; candidate gets short break.

10:15–11:00 *Interview #2: Personal Competencies*

11:00–11:15 Summary/break

11:15–12:15 P.M. *Interview #3: Interpersonal Competencies*

12:15–12:30 Summary/break

12:30–2:00 *Interview #4: Management and Additional Leadership Competencies* (during lunch)

2:00–2:15 Summary/break

2:15–3:15 *Interview #5: Motivational Competencies*

3:15–3:30 Summary/break

3:30–4:15 *Meeting.* Hiring executive and candidate (Wrap-up— "let's touch base tomorrow to talk about next steps"). Candidate takes tour of facility.

4:15–5:00 Hiring committee meets. Hiring manager reviews all interviewer summaries with committee to get all opinions on person's strengths, weak points, fit, and consensus on whether to proceed with Visit #2. Discussion of how best to "sell" attractive candidates and how family needs of candidate can be addressed (help spouse get job, introduce kids to coaches, make real estate agent available).

## VISIT #2

| | |
|---|---|
| 2 weeks before | (same as for Visit #1) |
| 7:30–11:30 A.M. | *Interview #6:* Hiring manager conducts tandem Topgrading interview followed by answering questions by interviewee. |
| 11:30–12:00 | Interviewer completes Summary. |
| 11:30–11:45 | Candidate break |
| 11:45–1:30 P.M. | *Interview #7: Exchange of Perspectives* (over lunch) |
| 1:30–1:45 | Summary/break |
| 1:45–2:45 | *Interview #8: Exchange of Perspectives* |
| 2:45–3:00 | Summary/break |
| 3:00–4:00 | *Interview #9: Exchange of Perspectives* |
| 4:00–4:15 | Summary |
| | Hiring executive and candidate meet for brief wrap-up. |
| 4:15–5:15 | *Hiring committee.* Hiring manager runs meeting to summarize all data from both visits, to refine consensus on candidate strengths, weak points, and fit, to decide whether to proceed with in-depth reference checks and psychological appraisal, and to discuss how to best sell candidate on joining company. |

An Interviewer Focus Matrix (Figure 3.4) may help to clarify what the one-hour short structured interviews cover in relation to the Topgrading Interviews. Both you (in tandem with a peer) and the topgrading professional (if one is used) conduct the full Topgrading Interview, which—as you see in Appendix A—covers all competencies: intellectual, personal, interpersonal, and so forth. The short structured interviews focus on one group of competencies, although Figure 3.3 shows that all interviewers are apt to get some insights into interpersonal competencies.

What specific questions do the shorter structured interviews cover? These interview guides really should be created for each job—by you and HR. Figure 3.5 is an example—all of the focused questions on intellectual competencies are taken from the focused questions section of the Topgrading Interview Guide (Appendix A). And, let me repeat, Chapter 12 highlights simple but important legal guidelines.

## Figure 3.4
### Sample Competency Interview Guide

Applicant _____

Interviewer _____

Date _____

### Interview Focus: Intellectual Characteristics
Scale: 6 = Excellent; 5 = Very good; 4 = Good; 3 = Only Fair;
2 = Poor; 1 = Very Poor

*Rating*

_____  1. **Intelligence**

a. Please describe your **learning ability.** _____

_____

b. Describe a **complex situation** in which you had to learn a lot, quickly. How did you go about learning, and how successful were the outcomes? _____

_____

_____

_____

_____  2. **Analysis skills**

a. Please describe your **problem analysis** skills. _____

_____

b. Do people generally regard you as one who diligently pursues every **detail** or do you tend to be more **broad brush?** Why? _____

_____

c. What will references indicate are your style and overall effectiveness in "**sorting**" the wheat from the chaff? _____

_____

    d. What **analytic approaches** and tools do you use? _____

_____

    e. Please give me an example of digging more deeply for facts than what was asked of you. _____

_____

_____ 3. **Judgment/Decision Making**

    a. Please describe your **decision-making** approach when you are faced with difficult situations in comparison with others at about your level in the organization. Are you decisive and quick, but sometimes too quick, or are you more thorough but sometimes too slow? Are you intuitive or do you go purely with the facts? Do you involve many or few people in decisions? _____

_____

_____

    b. What are a couple of the **most difficult** or **challenging** decisions you have made recently? _____

_____

    c. What are a couple of the **best** and **worst** decisions you have made in the past year? _____

_____

_____

    d. What **maxims** do you live by? _____

_____

_____

_____ 4. Conceptual Ability

Are you more comfortable dealing with concrete, tangible, short-term issues or more abstract, **conceptual,** long-term issues? Please explain. _____

_____

_____ 5. Creativity

a. How **creative** are you? What are the best examples of your creativity in processes, systems, methods, products, structure, and services? _____

_____

b. Do you consider yourself a better **visionary** or implementer? Why? _____

_____

_____ 6. Strategic Skills

a. In the past year, what specifically have you done in order to remain **knowledgeable** about the competitive environment, market and trade dynamics, products (services) and technology trends, innovations, and patterns of consumer behavior?

_____

_____

b. Please describe your **experience** in strategic thinking, including successful and unsuccessful approaches. (Determine the individual's contribution to team strategic efforts.) _____

_____

c. Where do you predict that your (**industry/competitors/function**) **is going** in the next three years? What is the **conventional wisdom,** and what are your own thoughts? _____

_____

_____ 7. **Pragmatism**

Do you consider yourself a more **visionary** or more **pragmatic** thinker? Why? _____

_____

_____ 8. **Risk Taking**

What are the **biggest risks** you have taken in recent years? Include ones that have worked out well and not so well.

_____

_____

_____ 9. **Leading Edge**

a. How have you copied, created, or applied **best practices**?

_____

_____

_____

b. Describe projects in which your **best-practice solutions** did and did not fully address customer/client needs. _____

_____

_____

_____

c. How will references rate your **technical expertise** . . . are you truly leading edge, or do you fall a bit short in some areas?

_____

_____

_____

d. How **computer literate** are you? _____

_____

e. Please describe your professional **network**. _____

_____

_____

_____

_____ 10. **Education**

a. What **seminars** or formal **education** have you participated in (and when)? _____

_____

_____

b. Describe your **reading habits** (books and articles—global factors, general business, functional specialty, industry).

_____

_____

_____

_____ 11. **Experience**

a. (Compose a series of **open-ended questions:** "How would you rate yourself in _____, and what specifics can you cite?" For Finance, "How did you gain expertise in, for example, treasury, controller, and risk management areas?" For Human Resources, "How did you gain expertise in selection, training, compensation, and so on?"

• Question: _____

_____

• Question: _____

_____

• Question: _____

_____

b. What are the most important **lessons** you have learned in your career? (Gives specifics with respect to when, where, what, etc.) _____

_____

____12. **Track Record**

Looking back in your career, what were your **most and least successful** jobs? _____

_____

## Other Competencies Observed

Rating _____

Competency _____

Comments _____

Rating _____

Competency _____

Comments _____

Rating _____

Competency _____

Comments _____

Rating _____

Competency _____

Comments _____

Rating _____

Competency _____

Comments _____

Rating _____

Competency _____

Comments _____

Rating _____

Competency _____

Comments _____

## Figure 3.5

### Interviewer Focus Matrix

| | Intellectual Competencies | Personal Competencies | Interpersonal Competencies | Management and Additional Leadership Competencies | Motivational Competencies | Exchange of Perspectives | Visit |
|---|---|---|---|---|---|---|---|
| #1 George | X | | X | | | | #1 |
| #2 Leslie | | X | X | | | | #1 |
| #3 Geoff | | | X (major focus) | | | | #1 |
| #4 Bill | | | X | X | | | #1 |
| #5 Chris | | | X | | X | | #1 |
| #6 You (Topgrading) | X | X | X | X | X | X | #2 |
| Tandem Interview | X | X | X | X | X | X | |
| #7 Mary | | | X | | | X | #2 |
| #8 Will | | | X | | | X | #2 |
| #9 Kate | | | X | | | X | #2 |
| #10 Psychologist | X | X | X | X | X | X | After Visit #2 |

## HOW AND WHEN TO "SELL" CANDIDATES

When do you "sell" a candidate? Always, from the very first contact, throughout every interview, and even after an offer has been accepted. It's preferable to not interrupt the Topgrading Interview much to "sell," but instead ask all your questions and then invite the candidate to ask you questions. There are no hard and fast rules, however, except one: you can best sell candidates by having keen insight into their needs, and that comes from Topgrading Interviews. The recruitment mating game fluctuates between selling and probing, selling and probing. You can do both. A players want you to assess them. All topgrading professionals hear, constantly, that A player candidates welcome a tandem Topgrading with the hiring manager and another Topgrading by the psychologist because they embrace topgrading, want to join an A team, and frankly don't want to be a mis-hire.

Your professionalism and thoroughness help sell candidates. You don't stop selling when the new hire arrives on the job. Employers the candidate rejected in favor of your company haven't necessarily given up. Maybe their full-court press is still on! So keep selling the candidate.

Your A team sells candidates. Taking over a company soon to be in Chapter 11, CEO Curt Clawson had to be very persuasive to attract A players. A year later a critical mass of As made the job a lot easier, so the fact that the company had not yet emerged from Chapter 11 did not discourage most candidates. They were impressed with the high-performing, nonpolitical culture, and down-to-earth A players throughout management, and contagious A player enthusiasm sold candidates.

One final selling point that is becoming more popular is location flexibility. Ten years ago relocation was a standard requirement, but not so much anymore. With both spouses working it's a lot easier to recruit talent, saying, "Relocation is not required, but attending key meetings at Corporate an average of three days per week is, and it's up to you to figure out how to make working out of a remote location successful." Topgrading provides the opportunity for candidates to prove they have made it work.

## TOPGRADING AND DIVERSITY ("INCLUSIVITY")

The soul of topgrading embraces discrimination on the basis of talent and potential, not religion, gender, race, or the absence of handicaps. That soul cringes at the thought that white male C players would bypass female A players because "We are uncomfortable with female managers." Topgrading can shake up the management ranks. If a company is underperforming, topgrading can result in changing one-third of all managers. Therein lies opportunity to bring in A players and achieve diversity goals. (I prefer to use the term *inclusify*.) As companies globalize, they seek not to emphasize differences but to include more, to enrich the mix of human capital. They hire and promote more Hispanics/Latinos, because they start doing business in those neighborhoods, and they include more women in management because more women are customers. By inclusifying, they incorporate a broader spectrum of background, experiences, and perspectives upon which to build a world-class organization.

Companies guilty of discrimination sometimes toss bodies into jobs to avoid or resolve class-action suits, to make the problem go away. In their eagerness to prevent or resolve a "disparate impact"[28] charge, they might lower the performance bar. The soul of topgrading cringes at tokenism.

Forward-looking topgraders inclusify without lowering standards. If a retail company is going to move into Asian geographic areas, they want more A player store managers who are Asian. There aren't enough qualified Asian store managers? Then they recruit like mad, broadening the target area from ten square miles to twenty or two hundred miles. They hire early and train Asians so that when the stores open, A player Asians are prepared. They work the previously all non-Asian organization culture to make it more attractive to Asians. *Talent* is the key word. They don't solely staff with Asians, but it would be foolish to attempt to build a retail division to serve Asians without plenty of Asian marketing, operations, and human resources involvement.

I conducted a team-building meeting for a U.S.-based international company. Not one executive was a white American male. Why? Because of an EEO lawsuit? No. Because of pressure by minority politicians? No. This executive melting pot was designed by market forces and topgrading values. Sure, there are white American male marketplace constituencies to be included, but in the choice of these ten managers, whiteness, maleness, and American birth were not so important as talent.

---

[28] See Chapter 12 for explanations of legal terms such as *disparate impact*.

My wife, Mary, when president of the Junior League of Chicago, advanced ongoing efforts to inclusify the basically white, upper-income organization of two thousand women. By identifying A player blacks, Hispanics, and Asians and inviting them to visit headquarters, the League "salted the mines" with talent. The minority women were more interested in joining after finding that other minority A players were doing the same, and any lingering doubts among the long-term members regarding whether such a rapid change would work, were nonexistent.

Some companies need a legal threat to inclusify. Most, in my experience, are motivated far more by market forces. A multibillion-dollar international (not yet global) company, a government supplier, passed its affirmative action audit with flying colors. The CEO said, "That is a hollow victory. The government says we have enough females, but we don't. Our marketing studies show our ads appeal to males; our management is 95 percent male, but our customers are 60 percent female, and our competitors are killing us advertising and building products to meet female customers' needs." A year later the company had a lot more female managers. Because those female managers are A players, the company is coming back in the marketplace. It's hard to topgrade without diversity, or inclusivity, today.

## LINCOLN FINANCIAL GROUP—HIRING A PLAYERS TO DRIVE A DIVERSITY STRATEGY

Lincoln is a $5 billion financial services company whose strategy includes offering clients all full-suite financial planning services. Since the majority of high–net-worth individuals are women, it is smart business to have women embedded in all parts of the business.

Lincoln's topgrading commitment has long included diversity. Officers include 34 percent women and 7 percent minorities. The board of directors includes three women, and women are well represented in management ranks. Topgrading interviewing has been embraced, with hundreds of managers trained, and with Topgrading Interviews (usually tandem) used for external hires and internal promotions. The results are very good.

---

**Of forty-three managers hired since 2000, 91 percent are evaluated to be A or A potential.[29]**

---

The same A player standard, and the same thorough Topgrading Interview, have been used when hiring recent college graduates. Sixty percent of college recruits are women. A special two-and-a-half-day training program helps train six high-potential women each year; it includes executive coaching. Seven of twelve women participating in this program have earned promotions.

With its emphasis on excellence in hiring and its commitment to developing women for top management, Lincoln has been featured in *Working Women* as one of America's best companies for women to work for, and has been recognized by the National Association of Female Executives and *Working Mother.*


## RETAINING A PLAYERS

Un-topgraded companies and those in the process of topgrading struggle to retain A players. Topgraded companies usually experience little difficulty holding on to their superior talent. Topgraded companies like those featured in case studies in Chapter 5 report that they lose only 5 percent of their managers in most years to external searches.

The same incentives used to attract top talent to begin with also provide "golden handcuffs":

- a winning, high-performance organization culture

- the fun and excitement of working with dream teams of A players

- the opportunity to grow, to meet challenges, and to rise in stature and title

- competitive pay and stock options

---

[29] A few in the past year have not been formally rated, because that evaluation takes place one year after they are hired; until that formal evaluation they are considered "A potential."

But what if simply being part of a topgraded company is insufficient to lock in loyalty? In the very late 1990s A player managers were in such demand that weekly calls from search executives were the rule, not the exception. Equally attractive companies were offering 50 percent increases in total compensation, so "Why should I stay here?" Topgraded companies have A players at the helm, executives who don't wait to hear their top talent complain that they are undercompensated, underutilized, or underappreciated. Topgraded companies are seldom so desperate as to offer a secret "retention bonus" to keep an A player on board. Instead, they anticipate external offers and proactively increase pay to compensate A players with what they are worth. I've known dozens of senior managers who, in fact, rejected a retention bonus, saying, essentially, "Boss, now you'll increase my pay 25 percent to match my outside offer, but forget it. If I was worth it, why didn't you pay me that amount before I'm about to leave? I'll resign and join a company that doesn't need a threat of quitting to pay people appropriately."

Topgraded companies communicate with their talent and get the major, tangible reward mechanisms—pay, stock, benefits—right. A player managers also tend to be experts in creating the psychic gratification people want, through any means conceivable, such as:

- Job movement/enrichment. (A players would sooner find a job elsewhere than stagnate in a job that is no longer enriching and challenging.)

- Special projects, task forces, and seminars.

- Personal coaching; lots and lots of honest feedback.

- Social activities and team building events.

- Business travel with spouses (who otherwise feel left out).

- Status (for example, being featured in a company magazine).

- Permission to commute (if, for example, a relocation by a spouse would otherwise mean your manager would quit).

Methods for retaining lower-level employees go beyond the scope of this book, and have been written about extensively. Our premier clients are becoming increasingly family-friendly, offering daycare centers, sabbaticals, casual attire, and superb communications. They improve morale and earn greater loyalty through these initiatives.

Topgraded companies found it relatively easy to retain A player managers during the incredible bull market of the 1990s, because stock options were too valuable to walk away from. However, during the subsequent economic downturn, stock options obviously diminished in value, and those "golden handcuffs" were less golden. Premier companies directed task forces to create retention programs—career paths requiring less frequent relocation, special projects to enhance people's skills, presentations to the CEO for visibility, whatever it took.

Watch out! Though topgraded companies keep their A players, lesser companies frequently experience high turnover among the A players they hire. They can retain a few A players—the chosen few "fair-haired boys or girls" who actually like being in a mediocre company because there are so few A players with whom to compete. Even sluggish, bureaucratic companies try to hire an occasional A player with the promise "Things will get better around here." But if things don't get better, the A players quit, leaving B/C player managers saying, "I guess we just can't hold on to supertalented people." (Translation: "We're meekly going through the motions of topgrading.") A players are talent magnets and that fact is a two-edged sword. Hire one A and other As follow—a "two-fer" or "three-fer." But when that A leaves, other As follow, so failing to retain As can be doubly or triply costly.

When department managers topgrade, but the rest of the company is lame, retaining A players is challenging. The excitement of being part of a dream team is offset by the frustrations associated with working with B/C players in other departments. Therefore, the more pervasive the topgrading commitment in a company, the easier it is to retain the As.

When an un-topgraded company launches a major topgrading initiative, retaining A players is also challenging. Pockets of B/C players not yet topgraded drive A players crazy. Saying, "Hang in there as B/Cs are replaced by As," satisfies the As who have worked there for years and are thrilled that the company is finally getting its act together. However, A players recruited from terrific topgraded companies become impatient. These A players need care and feeding—encouragement, support, pep talks. The perceptive boss must pull the right levers—a vision of how the stock will skyrocket for one person, a commitment to accelerate top-grading for another, or simply saying, "Pat, you've been killing yourself for us and we appreciate it, but dammit, it's the Fourth of July weekend, so get the heck out of here for three days and turn off your cell phone!" Take heart. Though retaining A players requires finesse, sensitivity, and bold action during the early stages of topgrading, it's not very difficult when you have arrived, when your organization qualifies as topgraded.

In general, the best results in management retention come from bosses regularly "taking the pulse" of their A players ("Are you happy?" "Is there anything we need to do to lock you in for several more years?") and re-sponding before an external job offer is seriously considered. If you sense a key member of your team may be looking, then talk, listen, and cut through the bureaucracy to find golden handcuffs. And, above all, top-grade your entire organization and encourage your CEO to do so compa-nywide, so your A players are preoccupied with maximizing the success of a powerful team, not frustrated and looking elsewhere.

## TOPGRADING HOURLY EMPLOYEES

Topgrading is for all jobs, including hourly jobs. With companies wanting workers who generate ideas to improve productivity, work in teams, share jobs, vote on each other's pay, know the economic drivers of the company, own stock, and help to screen candidates for hour team jobs, Topgrading Interviews are appropriate. Some companies hire employees on a trial ba-sis, as trainees for a couple of months, to thoroughly assess them. Many companies find that a Topgrading at the hourly level requires only a couple of hours. As Cliff Waits of Dayton Power & Light commented, "Topgrad-ing works perfectly in the plants; we're definitely improving our hiring suc-cess rate."

This chapter has covered a lot, so let us conclude with Figure 3.6's ab-breviated contrasting of the typical and topgrading approaches to hiring.

### Figure 3.6
### Typical versus Topgrading Hiring

*Typical Hiring*                    *Topgrading Hiring*

| | |
|---|---|
| Expensive search | Network ("virtul bench") |
| Emphasis on speed | Emphasis on quality |
| Vague job description | Job description with competencies and accountabilities (scorecard) |
| | Network provides A candidates |
| Résumés for screening | Résumé plus Career History Form or SATI Guide |
| Hodgepodge interviews | Tandem Topgrading Interview plus competency-based Interview by boss/peers |
| Reference calls by search firm | Reference calls by Topgrading interviewers |
| No feedback to hiree until one-year review | Thorough feedback session, with creation of Individual Development Plan, within first month |
| Hiring success not measured | Hiring scorecard reviewed regularly |
| Success not measured (but is 25 percent) | Success measured at 90 percent or higher |

## CHAPTER 3 CHECKLIST: ARE YOU A BEST-PRACTICES HIRING MANAGER?

**YES NO**

☐ ☐  CEO drives topgrading, including hiring and promoting processes, that achieves 90 percent As in management.

☐ ☐  CEO holds managers accountable for hiring A players.

☐ ☐  CEO conducts periodic talent meetings, retaining final authority over who is hired, promoted, and fired.

☐ ☐  CEO drives "recruitment as way of life."

☐ ☐ Everyone in management continuously updates his Rolodex with possible recruits; HR retains cumulative Rolodexes to be searched when jobs are to be filled.

☐ ☐ HR is topgraded, with strong recruitment staff/systems to produce an ample pool of A player candidates.

☐ ☐ HR creates world-class processes for succession planning, performance management, compensation, and midyear career reviews.

☐ ☐ The entire senior team considers topgrading, including hiring and promoting, crucial to achieving strategic goals.

☐ ☐ Job descriptions are written by the hiring manager (with HR input), including first-year job accountabilities. Competencies, written into Candidate Assessment Scorecards, reflect reality (politics, budget constraints, etc.).

☐ ☐ Search firms are managed properly (an acceptable list of target companies that cannot be penetrated is required, partner does the work, Topgrading Interviews ask for failures and mistakes, reference calls produce significant negatives, reports include significant negatives, and weekly updates are provided).

☐ ☐ Every manager "owns" responsibility to hire and promote A players.

☐ ☐ All interviewers are trained in how to conduct tandem Topgrading Interviews and stay within complex legal requirements.

☐ ☐ Visits to the company are well organized (producing valid insights into candidates, "selling" them, and portraying high level of professionalism).

☐ ☐ Hiring manager conducts tandem Topgrading Interview.

☐ ☐ Topgrading professional conducts "second-opinion" Topgrading until internal tandem Topgrading produces 90 percent As hired, or if job is crucial and candidate is a little controversial.

☐ ☐ Internal candidates are assessed with the same high level of rigor as external candidates, using Topgrading Interviews.

☐ ☐   Spouse/significant other/family are incorporated into the hiring process (dinners make person feel welcome, help in job search is provided, kids meet coaches, real estate agent available).

☐ ☐   I conduct final reference calls (after talking with all other interviewers and reading the Topgrading report by topgrading professional), with my tandem interviewer conducting some as well.

☐ ☐   Assimilation activities are ongoing, with specific activities before first day and during weeks #1, 12, and 14.

☐ ☐   Hiring and promoting success are measured by HR and me (hiring manager), so I can improve.

☐ ☐   To retain my A players, I "take their pulse" regularly and proactively meet their needs.

☐ ☐   I inclusify without lowering performance standards.

☐ ☐   I drive topgrading, including Topgrading interviewing, throughout my organization including hourly jobs.

*Four*

# REDEPLOYING CHRONIC B AND C PLAYERS: A MORAL APPROACH

*It is not good to be better than the very worst.*
Seneca, c. 4 B.C.–A.D. 65

If topgrading means packing teams, even the entire company, with A players, then it usually involves removing chronic C and B players. *Chronic* means they don't even try to become A players or else they have embraced an Individual Development Plan (IDP), but simply aren't improving sufficiently to qualify as A players in a reasonable amount of time (usually six to twelve months). Some B/C players can be redeployed internally into jobs where they can be A players. If this isn't feasible, they are redeployed externally. They're let go, "changed out," though typically with an appropriate severance and outplacement counseling; and, having worked on their IDP, they have good insights into themselves and a clear understanding of what sort of job would enable them to be happy and . . . A players! Unfortunately, topgrading requires some firing, or asking people to resign. It's painful, but it's not immoral if companies:

- use the best selection techniques, which leads to hiring 90 percent As,

- use the best assessment techniques, which identify as many people with A potential as possible,

- use the best coaching techniques, which give A potentials the best chance of becoming As,

- look for other internal jobs where the person would be an A, and

- fire people only if they fail to achieve agreed upon standards for performance.

This book is all about using the assessment and coaching practices that are so thorough and fair that even those who are chronic underperformers, who cannot be placed in a job where they can be an A, feel fairly treated. They are! Chapters 9 and 10 spell out these coaching techniques and Chapter 12 articulates the legal nuances. This chapter expands on the gut issues, the pain in firing, to help fortify your commitment to making the tough people decisions.

As companies embrace topgrading, someone with a little too much creativity inevitably "invents" the word *bottomscraping*, meaning "firing the dregs, to make room for A players." Ugh! Bottomscraping has a particularly disdainful connotation. It evokes images of the 1800s, with general stores full of barrels that held crackers, pickles, you name it. Periodically the bottoms of the barrels would have to be scraped to remove the grunge. I like to remind people that the fine Muscadets and Cognacs come from the scrapings at the bottom of the barrel. Deployed properly, the scrapings enable the fermentation of "nectar of the Gods." Anyone can be an A player. Anyone. So, please discourage the use of team "bottomscraping" in your organization.

While we are discussing language, let me clarify what I mean by "firing." In management, people are technically "fired" only under extreme circumstances—for theft, for example. Ordinarily, if a B/C player can't be redeployed internally, he is asked to resign in exchange for signing a severance agreement. A typical severance agreement might provide pay and benefits for half a year or longer, depending on length of employment and level in the company, along with the requirement that the person not steal secrets, pirate employees, or sue. This is a forced resignation, which has almost the same psychological effect as a termination, since the person has no choice but to go. But at least the person forced to resign gets to say, "I resigned," or "The decision was mutual"—a face-saving approach that helps the person retain as much dignity as possible. During the remainder of this chapter, please consider "firing" to include forcing resignations.

## BUSINESS REALITY AND THE PAIN OF FIRING

Key questions are "Does business necessity require removing chronic B and C players?" "If I retain B/C players, am I putting my company in jeopardy?" and "Is it moral to fire underperformers?"

Decades of experience, serving over two hundred companies as clients and interviewing managers from over seven hundred companies, have convinced me that the world is a much more painful place when companies fail to redeploy B/C players. In an increasingly globalized economy, there is no place where companies with many B/C players can hide. Companies packed with A players mercilessly annihilate companies burdened by B/C players—it's inevitable, and it's happening at an accelerated pace. Successful business models can be replicated across an industry, but it's people that truly make the difference between corporate winners and losers. Therefore, protecting incompetent people is corporate suicide.

Corporate Darwinism is all-powerful today. Companies sprout and flourish, but many die in a few years. Even some A players become C players, not because they changed, but because the world changed around them and they failed to adapt and grow. People and companies need to adapt quickly, or they suffer. Is this bad? Is it immoral? No, this is reality. If you agree, then:

---

### It is immoral NOT to remove B/C players and imperil the jobs of everyone else.

---

Is it being nice to people to tolerate their underperformance? As Debra Dunn, Vice President Strategy and Corporate Operations at Hewlett-Packard, said, "I feel there is no greater disrespect you can do to a person than to let them hang out in a job where they are not respected by their peers, not viewed as successful, and probably losing their self-esteem. To do that under the guise of respect for people is, to me, ridiculous." Or, to give people higher performance ratings than they deserve and not give them honest feedback about their weak points can leave them in the dark. That dishonesty can continue for years, particularly if a company is doing well. Then a company falters, the performance management system is tightened to weed out C players, and fired people are understandably indignant: "Why didn't you level with me ten years ago? I could have been working to overcome the shortcomings you now say are so serious you're firing me. Thanks a lot!"

---

### It is immoral treatment of B/C players to leave them in the dark regarding their weaknesses and leave them in the job in which they fail.

---

*The War for Talent* (Harvard Business School Press) provides some shocking statistics:

- Only 19 percent of managers surveyed believe their company removes low performers quickly and effectively.

- Only 16 percent say their company knows who the high and low performers are in the senior ranks.

We in the topgrading world may seem a bit cold and dispassionate when managers excuse their retaining B/C players. We've heard all the excuses a thousand times. But hanging on to chronic underperformers hurts the company, division, managers of the B/C, and the B/C players themselves. And surely a nation of topgraded companies is apt to be more productive than a nation of companies with 75 percent Non-As.

Firing B/C players need not be a major obstacle to topgrading, if a CEO or other senior manager says, "Do it!" and lower managers comply. Most managers are sensitive to the pain firing brings, however, and they hate it. The vast majority of managers I've interviewed told me that the hardest, most agonizing actions they take involve letting people go. They avoid it. They rationalize: "It's only fair to give B/Cs more of a chance." "It will be too disruptive." "Our organizational culture is against firing." "What if I replace a B with a C?" "How can I fire a subordinate who is friendly?" "She's over forty and we could get sued for age discrimination."

Many managers I've assessed have been fired at least once. They might have been relieved to finally be extricated from an unbearable boss, an untenable strategy, an unreasonable profit goal, or a job requiring more talent or energy than they possess. However, the ego usually takes a significant hit. They know what it's like to announce to the family, "I'm no longer needed." The family pretends not to believe, "You're a loser," but that thought enters everyone's mind. The kids say, "We understand," but if a relocation results, it means losing friends. A relocation could force an unwanted job change on the spouse. Depending on the severance agreement, the family's lifestyle may decline. Marital and family discord are more likely.

Failing to fire B/Cs punishes their subordinates. The dozen topgrading professionals I'm associated with conduct a lot of oral 360 interviews, following a Topgrading Interview, when we assess and coach managers. I've probably conducted twenty thousand oral 360 interviews. We all talk about an overlooked source of pain—the pain experienced by A players when their B/C player boss is *not* fired. McKinsey asked thousands of employees if they would be "delighted" if their company got rid of underperformers, and 59 percent strongly agreed, though very few believed their companies actually did it. While managers talk a lot about the pain in firing B/Cs, they should communicate more with teams reporting to B/Cs. Eventually, the As quit, which is disruptive to their families, but in the meantime, they suffer every day. The B/C player boss stifles their creativity, keeps them hidden (for fear of being upstaged), provides deficient direction, and hardly serves as a good role model.

Firing people makes a powerful statement regarding who you are and what you stand for—your character. Firing is also a macro issue, a reflection of the architecture of a society, even human nature. If you have traveled on business, you know how European and other nations consider the United States "uncivilized" because we have "employment at will," with too little concern for the pain, the anguish inflicted on workers and their families. My prediction is that the United States will gradually increase job protection of workers, and the importance of topgrading will increase. It will then seem even more important to hire and promote only As, because demoting or firing mistakes will be legally prohibited or more costly. And coaching and training B/Cs to give them the best chance of becoming an A will not just be more fair, but perhaps be legally mandated. In the meantime, embrace topgrading practices now and you can hold your head high, knowing you are doing what is right for the individual (fairness), your career (success), your company (more ability to survive and flourish), and your nation (economic strength).

The firing component of topgrading should not be confused with downsizing. Even premier companies cut jobs when there is an economic downturn. Sometimes companies must alter strategy to survive, and as a result entire divisions are sold or disbanded; even A players are no longer needed. Downsizing is necessary and moral when it will permit a basically good company to recover or grow. But, downsizing has a bad name because sometimes it's a last-ditch effort of a failed CEO to pump up profits. Often, slashing jobs doesn't improve performance enough, and the CEO is fired. A successor is then hired to pick up the pieces. Please, don't call that topgrading! Al Dunlap ("Chainsaw Al") was fired by the board of Sunbeam, not because he ruthlessly fired people (though he did), but because he was destroying shareholder value. Geoffrey Colvin of *Fortune* lamented that the executives of General Motors can lay off 15,000 workers, Whirlpool 6,300, and Aetna 2,400, but those same executives agonize over and delay firing individual underperforming managers. He observes that high-performing companies remove B/C player managers every day. Topgrading is not laying off thousands of hourly workers while retaining C player managers whose decisions put those thousands on the street.

## A FIRING MODEL

Firing some can be the right, ethical, and legal action, but how it is done can make a huge difference in how the action is perceived. How do you stack up in:

• **Ease of deciding to fire someone.** Do you conscientiously assess all your people and take your B/C player through the appropriate steps of coaching, training, and looking for alternative jobs internally? And if all those steps have failed to produce an A player, do you then easily conclude, "He has to go"? Or, do you waver, procrastinate, avoid confronting the issues with the B/C player, or perhaps even ignore the fact that you have an underperformer?

• **Ease of implementing the decision.** When the decision to fire the B/C player is made and will be implemented shortly, how easy or hard is it for you to fire the person? Are you a cold ("Hey, this is business. Nothing personal.") sort, pulling the trigger on the B/C player without empathy? Or, do you sympathize and show human concern as you say, "Sorry, Charlie, but you have to go"?

### What Type of Leader Are You?

Ease of Deciding to Fire Someone

| Ease of Implementing the Firing Decision | | Easy | Hard |
|---|---|---|---|
| | Easy | Hatchet Person | Ostrich |
| | Hard | Topgrader | Wimp |

The **hatchet person** is thorough and fair in the decision to remove the B/C player, and the firing is conducted with surgical coolness and precision. No tears, no sympathy. Team members respect the hatchet person's decision, but are frightened by her callous, uncaring style and seeming lack of humanity. Some A players might even find another job rather than work for that heartless robot. Instead of firing being perceived as necessary, people suspect vindictiveness by the hatchet person, who loses credibility and respect.

The **wimp** frets and avoids dealing with the B/C player. He knows he has a chronic underperformer, but he is so soft that he procrastinates in making the decision to fire, and is extremely apologetic when the deed is finally done. Team members might like the wimp as a neighbor but don't respect him in business because he's too soft. The whole team has suffered because the wimp gave fifth and sixth chances to a chronic underperformer. They know the wimp is a weak leader, not a winner. A players on the team get frustrated and look for jobs where they can be on winning teams.

The **ostrich** ignores evidence that he has a B/C player, so he can't determine if the person can be salvaged. Softness is not his problem, it's naiveté and lack of judgment. When a C player fails dramatically, the ostrich has no difficulty implementing a firing decision. Ditto if the boss makes the decision. An A player boss might say, "Ostrich, you just don't get it. Your B/C player is killing us! Either you fire the B/C or I'll fire you!" Firing a B/C becomes easy for the ostrich, because it wasn't his decision. And, the ostrich is so oblivious to business reality and so wrapped up in himself, he tends to ignore the pain the B/C will experience in being fired. Even if the ostrich has otherwise been a topgrader, hanging on to one C player might make team members consider the ostrich a C player. A players he inherited are more apt to look for better opportunities elsewhere if the ostrich continues to carry that C player, who, to the rest of the team, is an obvious underperformer.

The **topgrader** is professional and caring. The B/C player has been thoroughly assessed and coached, has worked hard on a developmental plan, but continues to be an underperformer. The B/C player's hopeless situation is recognized and dealt with properly. The topgrader does not delay firing the B/C, but she is humane. She conveys a moral sense, questioning what went wrong and wondering if she should have coached better or hired better. She is genuinely sympathetic to the B/C player's pain. Team members respect the topgrader for her quick but fair decision, and they are happy she cared.

This model has a simple but clear message: retain your moral sense and human caring while quickly and professionally ratcheting up talent by replacing B/C players with A players.

## HOW PREMIER COMPANIES FIRE PEOPLE

Managers are of course fired for failing to achieve agreed-upon performance goals established with the boss. During the past two decades more companies have also fired people who "made their numbers" but failed to exhibit the company's stated values or the essential competencies for the job. So, a manager achieving sales and profit targets will be fired for committing an ethical violation, harming teamwork by failing to share resources with others, showing lack of respect by publicly berating people, or . . . failing to redeploy B/C players. But in most companies a subordinate is judged by one boss. Is this fair?

The topgrading practices used to fire people have already been introduced. They are exactly the same practices used to develop As to remain As, to develop B/Cs to become As, and to supplement the performance management system that holds people accountable for achieving goals. The development approach I designed for GE, emulated now by dozens of fine companies, consists of:

- Tandem Topgrading Interviews by higher-level managers from a different part of the company,

- Oral 360s by the tandem interviewers,

- Extensive feedback and coaching of the manager assessed, and

- A comprehensive Individual Development Plan, with a timeline and regular measurements of progress, so that improvements will be clear to all, and a failure to improve will help the manager decide to look for a job (internally or externally) where A player status is realistic.

Since only the biggest companies have the talent depth to ask two managers to devote forty hours each (eighty hours total) to assessing and coaching one manager, alternatives are:

- Ask another Topgrading-trained manager to pair up with you for tandem Topgrading of your people.

- Hire topgrading professionals (sorry, it's self-serving, but some clients want outside professionals to do it until internal managers are trained and have enough experience to be very good). For B/Cs who have disregarded their boss's criticisms, the impartial Topgrading and plenty of oral 360 comments and ratings are highly credible, convincing B/Cs they are failing. The "second opinion" of Topgrading-based assessment and coaching provides feedback and advice to develop managers.

## PREMIER COMPANIES DON'T NEED TO FIRE MANY PEOPLE

When 85–90 percent are A players, firing is uncommon. When the boards of premier companies pick A player CEOs and senior managers who get the strategy right and topgrade the whole company, there aren't many awful business decisions that have to be corrected by removing people. There are few B/C player managers who immorally fire A players who might upstage them. Rigorous hiring prevents many mis-hires. Topgraded companies quietly redeploy B/C players to become A players internally and seldom nudge a person out of the company. Firings and forced resignations don't occur much, and when they do, they are done with integrity and class, and for credible, solid strategic reasons.

Premier companies protect a few B/C players, just a little, to maintain a positive, humane organization culture. When some people have to be removed, normal attrition and early-retirement options are fully explored. If former A players near retirement become C players, they are given token jobs with prestige for a year or two. They no longer function in a key decision-making role, but do special projects and remain available to mentor up-and-coming managers. People who have an unusual personal crisis that hurts their performance are afforded slack. For example, letting someone decline from A player to C player during a period of mourning can produce an even more motivated A player when things are back to normal. At a minimum, such tolerance of temporarily lower performance gives a positive tone to the organization culture and usually inspires coworkers to pitch in and take up the slack. "After all," they say, "a crisis like that could happen to me." Is this tolerating mediocrity? No, it's accepting normal, temporary slippage, which occurs to almost all A players. It's like Michael Jordan or Tiger Woods experiencing a slump.

Premier companies minimize the Peter Principle (getting promoted to one's level of incompetence). Topgrading is an antidote to the Peter Principle. In a premier, topgraded organization there are frequent career discussions. B players talk to their boss or HR about the need to be redeployed in a different position, where they can qualify as an A player. They want to get up each morning, confident that they will have fun, contribute, and grow.

Ross Perot once told me that he liked to fire failed trainees in one of his businesses by removing them from the training center in the middle of the night. He thought that the remaining trainees would be more motivated if they awakened to the realization that a couple more trainees were axed. I doubt that this version of "business necessity" worked. In my experience, successful organizations do not bludgeon the reputation of trainees who fail or A players who decline to C players because the company outgrew them. Smart CEOs and senior managers apply their creativity to find ways to retrain people, restructure jobs, and flex in order to permit loyal C and B players to become loyal, highly productive A players in other roles. They look for ways to protect honest people's dignity, not humiliate them to make an example.

## HOW NOT TO FIRE PEOPLE—THE FORD DEBACLE

Ford announced a forced ranking system suddenly, with little explanation and too little flexibility.[30] Managers ranked in the bottom 10 percent were told that they would not receive what had been an automatic annual increase in pay for years, and that they had to improve enough to get out of the bottom 10 percent within two years or they'd be fired. Some of the

---

[30] I take this case study information from published articles, former Ford executives, and Detroit-area attorneys. This case study was sent to the top HR executive at Ford to get confirmation of accuracy of statements and to provide an opportunity to describe the improvements in their system, but in his reply, he declined to comment.

thirty managers who initiated the class-action suit felt that efforts to help them improve and get out of the bottom 10 percent were minimal, or simply ways of documenting their underperformance to justify termination. Some of the firing managers doing the rankings lacked credibility, in part because they felt in a bind—the ranking criteria were vague, and even if they had all high-performing subordinates, they still were required to do the rankings and deny salary increases to the bottom 10 percent. This seemed grossly unfair to managers and their subordinates. It wasn't clear to the bottom-ranked managers that their bosses, the ones doing the rankings, were A players. This added to their concern about validity and fairness. One former Ford executive told me, "That top-down, rigid imposition of change, with hardly enough input from the managers who had to implement it, caused morale problems and support to be halfhearted."

If the goal was to fire C players, it failed, because those bottom-ranked managers, over forty years of age and members of a protected class, found a lawyer in Detroit (no surprise) to file the class-action suit. The low-ranked managers won, perhaps because Ford had problems in their practices and systems: *compensation* (automatic increases for years, which were not merit based), *communications* (limited), *assessment* (one boss did the ranking for each subordinate, and the bosses were not all considered A players by those doing the ranking), *development* (minimal), and *change management* (lack of support by managers required to implement the forced ranking system).

Ford Motor Company got a lot of negative press for their forced ranking system that would have, eventually, led to terminations of bottom-ranked managers. The Ford process generated a class-action lawsuit, which it lost, with a modest monetary settlement and promises to fix their system.

## FIRING C PLAYERS THE RIGHT WAY: A SCRIPT

If you believe retaining B/C players is self-defeating, you must be able to lead them to leave the job or look them in the eye and say, literally, "It's time to go." Let me paint a picture from your entering a new job as a senior manager right up to saying, "C, it's time to move on." You are vice president operations and C, a plant manager, is very likable but failing. C was a very good financial analyst; he asked to transfer into Operations and has been struggling for two years as manager of a small plant. The problems in his plant are not being solved, yet C is eager to be named your successor as VP operations.

In the dialogue that follows, a discussion lasting many hours, over a period of two months, is compacted into paragraphs. Please assume there would be a lot more meaningful communication and fewer blunt statements by you, the manager.

*January 5:*

*Manager:*  Hi, C, I'm Pat, your new manager. I'd like to spend several hours with you next week in a Topgrading Interview, to get to know you—to review your background, accomplishments, and developmental needs and to hear what your goals are and what you'd like to see from me. I believe two heads are better than one, and our human resources manager has also been trained on Topgrading and will help interview you. OK?

*C:*  Great, a boss who wants to know all about what I can do!

The tandem Topgrading Interview was conducted January 12, and you and the HR manager agreed C was a C player. You assessed dozens of competencies in your diagnosis. C's level of commitment to doing well is high, his basic values (ethics, respect for people, high standards) are fine, and his confidence is normal—a bit low, but understandably so, because he's failing. The problem is skill, and you sense that there is no easy fix with C, that C cannot acquire the many competencies, the skills to succeed in this job in a reasonable amount of time. But you decide to observe C a month to be sure. If C cannot be salvaged, you want to nudge him out the right way. Here's the conclusion of your January 12 Topgrading Interview . . .

*January 12:*

*Manager:*  C, you say that you hope to grow from plant manager to vice president operations. I don't want to wait for a year for a performance review to discuss how realistic your goals are. Do you?

*C:*  No way! What do you have in mind?

*Manager:*  Let's meet in a week. Here is the job description and competencies for vice president operations and for your job, plant manager. I've also included your bonus accountabilities for this year. I consider these stretch goals, but fully achievable, and I want to know your opinion. Are these the right goals and can you achieve them? Please rate yourself on all the competencies for both jobs: plant manager and VP operations. When we meet in a week, let's discuss all of this—your performance goals for this year, how realistic you feel they are, how you intend to achieve them—in relation to how strong you feel you are in the essential competencies. And, let's discuss your career goal of vice president and how you stack up on those competencies.

Consistent with legalities discussed in Chapter 12, you consulted with Human Resources and Counsel. They reminded you that the company policy manual requires you to give a written warning to a person, stating that termination can occur in ninety days if performance accountabilities, stated in writing, are not met. They asked you to document everything—accountabilities, every discussion about nonperformance.

*January 19:*

*Manager:*  C, you've put a lot of time into preparing for this meeting by rating yourself on essential competencies and stating that you believe the goals are the right ones, and you can achieve them. We've been talking two hours and I think we've clarified a lot of things. Your and my ratings of you on the competencies for both plant manager and vice president operations are about the same on several competencies. However, based mostly on the tandem Topgrading interview, discussing your entire career in depth, the HR manager and I rate you lower than you do on Assertiveness, Performance Management, Selecting A Players, and Resourcefulness. Because you know you have slipped in your goal attainment, maybe we should stop talking about your becoming vice president operations and focus on this year and how you can improve and succeed in your present job as plant manager.

*C:*  You're right. I haven't been on track to meet my performance goals. I need to learn some things to do a better job as plant manager. Only a couple of years ago I was a financial analyst, so I'm still learning. I agree I should hire better, and as for Performance Management, I just don't want to be an autocrat. I'm still learning lean manufacturing and Six Sigma, but I know I have to improve productivity, quality, and safety to earn my bonus.

*Manager:* OK, but let's clarify something right away. I thought I was clear when we met previously that your performance goals for this year must be met for you to keep your job. Those are for a "Meets Performance Expectations" rating.

*C:* Oh, I know. It used to be that the performance level you require would result in an "Exceeds Performance Expectations" rating, but that's fine. You want all A players, and that means A player performance. I've got to show I'm in the top 10 percent of talent you can get for the pay I'm getting. Fair enough!

*Manager:* Let's see if we can make a plan. You agree you should hire better. I'll personally teach you Topgrading interviewing so maybe we can eliminate those costly mis-hires. And if you want, I'll do tandem interviews with you.

*C:* I'd like that, and with two supervisory openings, I can use help now. I think I talk too much in interviews.

*Manager:* People like you a lot, and maybe I can help you use your winning personality to learn more about candidates' competencies.

*C:* Sounds good.

*Manager:* Let's talk about Assertiveness. My hunch is that you would come closer to meeting your production goals if you could schedule the shop better. To do that, you need to engage the salespeople so they get you the projections sooner.

*C:* But I ask, and they're just late and make excuses.

*Manager:* I could talk to the vice president sales, because you really need the projections delivered on time. But my preference would be for you to show a little more Resourcefulness and Assertiveness rather than relying on me.

*C:* I don't know. The VP sales is pretty stubborn.

*Manager:* OK, I'll handle it, for now. Let's move on to Performance Management. I've observed your asking your people to do things.

*C:* I'm not an autocrat. I ask, not tell.

*Manager:* That's fine, but what I wonder about is if people feel really accountable. I heard a lot of excuses.

*C:* Yeah, they say I ask two people to do the same thing, so I guess I should communicate better. Some crises have arisen, so we're not able to do as much. I don't know if those are excuses, but it's hard to keep everyone focused.

*Manager:*     You don't conduct weekly staff meetings, I've noticed.

*C:*     No. I have had staff meetings, but there doesn't seem to be time to have them weekly. Not even monthly.

*Manager:*     But if people are confused, crises are occurring, and your team isn't focused, I wonder if you might not save time by getting everyone coordinated in a weekly staff meeting.

*C:*     OK, I guess.

*Manager:*     You're hesitating.

*C:*     Yeah, my meetings wander. We don't seem to get a lot done. Your staff meetings are really productive, but I just don't have the knack.

*Manager:*     Would you like it if I were to colead one or two of your staff meetings to get you started? I'm big on agendas, fast-moving discussions, participation, action plans. Consensus is desirable, but I call the shots if we stall out. For every decision someone is accountable to do something, and I follow up to be sure results are achieved. No excuses. If someone this week says he'll do an analysis by next week, he has to do it.

*C:*     Phew! Yes, I'd like you as a partner, coleading. Maybe you can set a better tone and then pass the baton to me. I have trouble pushing these guys, because, well, when I was in Finance a couple were my drinking buddies. I'm Mr. Nice Guy, I guess.

*Manager:*     I see. You're Mr. Nice Guy, not just because you need to be liked but because you have some social friends reporting to you.

This "data dump" in real life could have taken several hours and multiple meetings, and there would have been a lot of give-and-take and better coaching in order to give C the very best chance to improve his skills. You want to also boost C's confidence, but not in a shallow, artificial way. My point here is that you, as a manager, need to be both positive and hard hitting. Take as long as necessary to be sure your subordinate gets the message. Summarize this conversation in writing (not email), to be clear C understood, and to protect against a wrongful termination suit. Let's return to your January 19 meeting with C.

| | |
|---|---|
| *C:* | I know, I know. I'm not leading so well. |
| *Manager:* | Do you want to move to a different plant to get away from your buddies? |
| *C:* | No, if I can't become a good leader with this bunch, I'm not cut out for leadership. Your standards are awfully high, though. |
| *Manager:* | I guess so. I'm asking for you to achieve the targets you agreed to. Can you do it? |
| *C:* | I don't know. You're trying to help me, and I appreciate it. |
| *Manager:* | I'll continue to help any way I can. I haven't raised the bar, just held all ten plant managers to what I consider necessary and achievable by A players. We have a plan to help you improve both skills and results. In addition to tandem interviewing your finalists for those two open jobs, I'll colead a couple staff meetings to show you how to incorporate Performance Management. And I'll set up a weekly update with the vice president sales, so you can get sales projections sooner and adjust your production schedule more quickly. I'd like you to show more Resourcefulness and Assertiveness in getting results. Is that a pretty complete summary? |
| *C:* | Yes, and I do think the goals are correct. I feel I'm letting you down, but I appreciate your help. I'll write all this up in my Individual Development Plan. |
| *Manager:* | Let's follow up in one month to see how we're doing. |
| *C:* | See you February 19. |

By February 19 you are fully convinced C is a chronic C player who has to leave the job. Perhaps he can return to his former job as a financial analyst, which would be a demotion. If not, he'll have to leave the company. You have followed through on the plan to help C, but C is still Mr. Nice Guy, letting his team avoid accountability. The manager coaches C through several progress assessment meetings in which C acknowledges too little progress. C agrees to quietly look for a financial analyst position inside the company and explore opportunities outside the company.

By March 5, C will have another job. This wasn't the prettiest, easiest scenario. C was a C player plant manager, and his short-term goal of becoming vice president operations was totally unrealistic. The manager was honest, helpful, and direct—a topgrader in the firing model presented earlier in this chapter. If C quits for a job with a different company, there will be a nice going-away party, a cake at lunch, and best wishes. Maybe C will suck it up—remain with the company as a senior analyst, live on a lower salary, and tell everyone he benefited from the cross training. If there is no job available for him in Finance, and no other position where C will be an A player, you as manager have to fire him (or ask him to resign). An appropriate severance package would be offered, including perhaps six months' pay and outplacement counseling.

If C really works on improving, perhaps he will overcome fatal flaws in Assertiveness, Resourcefulness, Selecting A Players, Removing C Players, and Performance Management. This could take years. If so, he could become a division controller. His career will be a lot more successful than if he had been "carried"—permitted to get by with nonperformance, poor accountability, frequent mis-hires, and Mr. Nice Guy softness.

This redeployment scenario contained all the necessary moral elements:

- Thorough and accurate assessment

- Reasonable performance goals with the A player standard for "Meets Performance Expectations"

- Tandem Topgrading assessment, including oral 360s

- Help in the creation of an Individual Development Plan

- Ongoing honest, comprehensive feedback

- Role modeling (Topgrading Interview, conduct of staff meetings) by manager

- Comprehensive coaching

- No hard feelings

- C's increasing self-awareness and taking responsibility for his career

- Increasing skills by C, who will be more marketable when he is fired, and more successful in the next job

- Opportunities for ego protection and financial protection during redeployment

- Outplacement counseling

Everyone wins. C is better equipped to become an A player and to take responsibility for his self-development for future positions. You documented each discussion in memos, partly for legal protection and partly to be sure communications were clear. This is only fair. You, the manager, serve the shareholders and yourself by removing a C player (and presumably by replacing C with an A player). The company is stronger, being better able to preserve jobs, increase employment, and pay taxes.

The manager, in this scenario, is competent, professional, and humane. In real life, managers all have flaws, and our firing C players is more moral if we are less flawed. Chapter 8 is devoted to minimizing our weak points. In an ideal world, a manager would be so inspiring, so perceptive, so fantastic in all respects that B/C players would be magically converted to A players. In my experience, such superleaders account for less than 1 percent. Coach Gene Keady, Purdue's successful basketball coach (who retired in 1998) had a reputation for converting a B team of talent to an A team, the Big Ten Champions. Good for him! Aspire to be like Coach Keady. But don't limp along with B/C players, if you are not such a talented coach and developer.

Would you like to read another script with a manager dealing with an underperformer? Chapter 10 has one that shows more of the coaching techniques.

Chapter 12 includes common "do's" and "don't's" in order to function within the law when firing B/C players or forcing their resignation. Please read it carefully and use your HR people and expert attorneys to be certain you are operating within the law. Bottom line, when companies consider firing members of protected groups in the United States, CEOs of topgrading companies have a common perspective: "Diversity (or inclusivity) is a business necessity so embrace it, and if a chronic C player is in a legally protected group (age, race, and the like), don't retain the person just because a lawsuit is more likely." Those CEOs say, "Hire A players to begin with, but don't 'carry' chronic B/C players because you fear a lawsuit. Do your homework, work with Human Resources and Counsel to document nonperformance and its consequences, coach like crazy to help the person succeed, and if worse comes to worst, fire the person." Permitting C player members of protected groups to keep their jobs while C players who are not members of protected groups are redeployed is divisive. It smacks of tokenism and is deeply offensive to A players in that protected group, because it diminishes their value.

## CHAPTER 4 CHECKLIST: ARE YOU A MORAL REDEPLOYER?

**YES NO**

☐ ☐ I believe, deep in my soul, that redeploying chronic B/C players is moral for companies and for B/Cs fired.

☐ ☐ My company has a world-class performance management system.

☐ ☐ Regardless of the quality of our performance management system, I personally provide thorough, regular performance feedback to every one of my direct reports.

☐ ☐ My B/C players are given a fair chance to become A players, because I use tandem Topgrading assessments to help my people prepare Individual Development Plans, and I support those plans.

☐ ☐ I give B/C players months, not years, to prove they can be A players.

☐ ☐ In redeploying chronic B/C players, I look hard for an internal role where they can be A players, but only if they will be happy and successful in their new role.

☐ ☐ In redeploying B/C players internally, I look for creative ways to protect people's dignity.

☐ ☐ I retain B/C players a year or two from retirement, usually maintaining performance by transferring some responsibilities to others.

☐ ☐ I consult with Human Resources and Legal Counsel to be sure I am functioning within the law in redeploying B/C players.

This entire chapter on firing C players would not be necessary in a book on screening people for the entertainment industry. Here it is obvious that talent counts. No one buys the CDs of C player musicians. A C player news anchor in Chicago is quickly dispatched to be a weather reporter in Peoria. Fans boo C player athletes, and the owners and fans keep the heat on any manager who accepts poor performance. In the rest of the business world (and not-for-profit world) it is sometimes considered immoral to fire a salesperson who can't sell, though her continued employment is not good for the company, not good for the shareholders, not good for any of the other team members, and not good for her, either.

I hope this chapter has acknowledged how painful, unfair, and immoral firing people can be, and how ostriches, hatchet people, and wimps unnecessarily contribute to pain. In the next chapter a variety of case studies will show there are pain relievers available between the covers of this book. Because topgraders mis-hire 10 percent (not 90 percent), mispromote 10 percent (not 90 percent), and coach and develop people with topgrading best practices, there are few people to fire. But when firing is necessary, topgraders do it in a professional, fair-minded, moral way that minimizes disruption and pain. Perhaps after reading the explanations of this chapter and the case studies in Chapter 5, you will understand why many topgraders receive Christmas cards, not lawsuits, from people they have fired.

# Five

# TOPGRADING CASE STUDIES: A PLAYERS, NO EXCUSES

This chapter showcases a broad range of new topgrading case studies and revisits case studies from the first edition of *Topgrading*. Many readers have asked, "What are the specific steps we should take to implement the topgrading best practices?" Before presenting the various case studies, let's integrate a lot of material covered in the first four chapters and organize it for practical application. All of the case studies exemplify the Simple Topgrading Model, and companies like Lincoln, Hayes Lemmerz, Hillenbrand, and MarineMax embraced the Successful Topgrading Rollout Plan. It's a reasonably detailed and complicated plan, because billion-dollar companies don't dramatically improve talent without carefully thought out, communicated, and implemented plans. If you are an individual manager wanting to topgrade in a company that won't topgrade, or if you are part of a small company that will, modify the "big-company" topgrading templates as several case studies show. With the general guidelines for how to topgrade spelled out, please assume they took place in the case studies, so the model and plan are not repeated in each case study.

A delicious smorgasbord of new case studies is laid out. Feast your eyes on:

- Lincoln Financial, a $5 billion financial services company that changed strategy, topgraded, and experienced dramatic performance improvement.

- MarineMax, an IPO of boat dealers that went public as the stock market tanked and used topgrading to succeed anyway.

- ghSMART & Company, Inc., a firm of topgrading professionals that has succeeded as a result of following the topgrading advice it gives clients.

- Hayes Lemmerz, a remarkable company that topgraded its way out of Chapter 11.

- Virtual Technology, a high-tech startup that has leveraged its success through topgrading.

- Greg Alexander, who read *Topgrading* and got a little coaching from Geoff Smart and took his EMC sales region from twelfth (of fourteen) to #1 in one year.

- Hillenbrand Industries, a $2 billion company that used topgrading to unclog its bureaucratic arteries and turbo-boost its stock price.

- American Heart Association, a not-for-profit that uses topgrading to, literally, save lives.

- Claude Hanson, who as president of a division of TEKMORE, launched his own topgrading initiative without corporate direction and succeeded. (All names in this case study are fictitious because Claude left the parent company, whose CEO might not appreciate being asked, "Why did a great topgrader leave?")

- Barclays, a three-hundred-year-old British company that reinvented itself with topgrading.

- Bob Dineen, who, while with Merrill Lynch, invented his own version of voluntary topgrading.

At the end of this chapter we revisit case studies from the original *Topgrading:* GE, Travelers Express, Nielsen International, Dominick's, and HEB.

|  | *New Case Studies* | *Revisited Case Studies* |
|---|---|---|
| **Large companies** | Lincoln Financial | General Electric |
|  | Hillenbrand | HEB |
|  | Hayes Lemmerz | Nielsen |
|  | Barclays |  |
| **Midsized companies** | MarineMax | Dominick's |

| | | |
|---|---|---|
| **Small companies** | Virtual Technology | |
| | ghSMART | |
| **Division** | TEKMORE | Travelers Express |
| | (fictitious name) | |
| **Plant** | Hayes Lemmerz | |
| **Not-for-profit** | American Heart Association | |
| **Individual manager** | Greg Alexander | |
| | Bob Dineen | |

## TOPGRADING MODEL

As you know, to qualify as a company that topgrades, the A player standard has to be embraced, but that alone is insufficient. The A player standard is not achieved without superb methods to assess and develop internal talent, and assess candidates for selection, and that's why Topgrading is so crucial. The simplest model for topgrading includes four essential components:

---

### Simple Topgrading Model

1. Topgrade from the top down.
2. Assess internal talent using Topgrading Interviews.
3. Coach people using Topgrading-based Individual Development Plans.
4. Hire and promote people using Topgrading Interviews.
5. Redeploy (fire, demote, transfer) people who fail to achieve the A player standard.

---

Topgrading has to start at the top. The CEO topgrades the executive team, and when it consists of almost all A players (or those deemed to have A potential), it topgrades the next level down, cascading topgrading down to the lowest level. Any A player manager, at any level, can successfully topgrade, but in general "top down" is best. The reason is simple—until a level is topgraded, B/C players undermine the process, mostly out of fear that they'll lose their jobs. A players love topgrading, enthusiastically embracing it. B/C players fake it; they game the system, defending their teams' B/C players, because they have trouble managing A players. They are lousy coaches of As, who don't respect them, and they have difficulty recruiting As for the same reason.

Topgrading-based assessment is simply using the Topgrading Interview to gain additional insights into internal talent, to validly peg As and non-As, and choose who will be promoted. The program I built for General Electric has been emulated by dozens of premier organizations, and consists of:

- Topgrading assessors, line and human resources professionals, are thoroughly trained.

- Tandem (two) interviewers travel to a division they don't work in, conduct Topgrading Interviews followed by oral 360 interviews (with bosses, peers, and subordinates), write a thorough assessment report, give feedback to and coach the manager, and help the manager compose a comprehensive Individual Development Plan. A tandem approach is used because Topgrading is difficult, and two interviewers help each other ask questions, analyze interview responses, write reports, and provide coaching and feedback to their assessee. Tandems also help offset each interviewer's biases and gaps in knowledge; tandem Topgrading provides a rich supplement to the typical "one manager rates one subordinate" performance management system in determining who are the As, Bs, and Cs. Because even trained Topgrading assessors are short on experience, topgrading professionals are typically used the the first time in assessing internal managers.

The Topgrading Interview is of course also used to assess external candidates for selection. I say "of course," but frankly I'm amazed and pleased that so many companies have embraced such a long, complex interview. Topgrading is difficult, and it takes time to master. Some companies simply hire us professionals to do the Topgrading, noting that we have all done a lot of them (six thousand in my case). The CEO of a $6 billion company said, "Brad, I've known four CFOs in twenty-five years; how many have you assessed with Topgrading?" "I don't know, probably 250 or so," I replied. We're "calibrated," able to peg managers as A, B, or C players, but we encourage and train client managers to master Topgrading skills. In many companies no one is hired without a tandem Topgrading Interview—tandem for the same reasons in Topgrading assessment of internal people: two heads are better (more valid and legally defensible) than one. When trained Topgrading interviewers "bat 900," hire 90 percent A players, the topgrading professional is seldom used for that outside "second opinion." Until then, however, candidates might participate in multiple Topgrading—one by the search executive (if a search firm is used), one in tandem by the hiring manager and another manager, and a third by the topgrading professional.

References are performed by the hiring manager (or Topgrading partner, or both) after all the Topgrading Interviews, so that laserlike questions can confirm or disconfirm whether the candidate truly is an A player. Is it worth it? All of the case study topgraders mentioned in this book are certain of it. Don't A players get impatient with multiple Topgrading? Naahh. The Topgrading Interviews are spread out across several weeks, each interview is different because the personalities and perspectives of the interviewers differ, and, most importantly, A players don't mind devoting half a day to discussing one of their favorite subjects—themself! A players report that they love Topgrading Interviews: "You have A players here and I want to join an A team, so I welcome your thoroughness and professionalism in determining that I will be an A player that fits with this team!" Topgrading is an A player magnet, not an obstacle.

Finally, those who fail to achieve the A player standard, even after coaching them to conscientiously implement their Individual Development Plan, are redeployed. This means they are demoted or transferred to a job where they can perform at the A level, or they are fired.

## SUCCESSFUL TOPGRADING ROLLOUT PLAN

Large and small companies alike, embracing the four essential components of the Simple Topgrading Model, tend to follow a similar, logical sequence in rolling out topgrading, to make it a "way of life," not a one-time program. Common steps are:

1. All managers read *Topgrading*.

2. Senior managers participate in a two-day Topgrading Workshop, which explains the topgrading vision and rollout plans, and trains

participants in how to conduct tandem Topgrading Interviews and provide useful feedback and coaching.

3. Human Resources participates in a two-day Topgrading Workshop to be able to serve as tandem Topgrading partners and to support managers in all aspects of topgrading.

4. For the time being, all managers who have participated in a two-day Topgrading Workshop use tandem Topgrading Interviews to assess external candidates for hire. The Career History Form (Appendix C) or Self-Administered Topgrading Interview Guide (Appendix B) supplements the résumé in prescreening candidates, offering a lot more detail such as complete compensation history. The Topgrading Interview Guide (Appendix A) is used for the Topgrading Interview. References from a minimum of all bosses in the past ten years are set up by the interviewee and conducted by a Topgrading Interviewer using the In-Depth Reference Check Guide (Appendix D).

5. Topgrading professionals conduct a "second-opinion" selection Topgrading Interview until managers are (a) confirmed to be A players and (b) so good that 90 percent A players would have been hired without the psychologists' Topgrading Interview.

6. Topgrading professionals assess upper managers using Topgrading Interiews and 360s. The CEO receives an assessment report. The assessed manager receives coaching, feedback, and help preparing a comprehensive Individual Development Plan (Appendix H) to:

   • Help A players remain A players.

   • Help Bs and even Cs with A potential eventually qualify as A players.

   • Help B and C players who will not become A players realize the futility of their developmental efforts so that they either find a job internally where they qualify as an A player, or leave.

7. The CEO makes topgrading decisions, resulting in a senior team of all A players. We are outside consultants, and although we make recommendations (hire, fire, develop), it is not appropriate for us to decide who should go or stay. Our clients are the topgrading decision makers.

8. IDPs are updated annually, as part of the performance appraisal process.

9. Topgrading cascades down, throughout the organization, with steps 1–8 repeated sequentially.

10. Topgrading-based assessments (with 360s) are used before every major promotion.

## TOPGRADING ONGOING PRACTICES

Throughout the introduction of topgrading, from initial rollout and indefinitely, there are seven key ongoing practices:

1. Topgrading is driven by the CEO and A player line managers, not Human Resources. The quickest way to kill topgrading is for a CEO to delegate it to HR. A player HR executives who topgrade HR rapidly become powerful partners to CEOs, however.

2. Topgrading Interviews are used for all hiring and promoting decisions.

3. Talent meetings are held every six months initially and, eventually, annually. For example, a president/CEO with a team of six vice presidents will meet to achieve consensus on the fifty managers at the next level and reach consensus on who are the As, Bs, and Cs, and on who has (and hasn't) followed through conscientiously on their Individual Development Plan, and with what improvement. The team assessment considers performance appraisals, assessments by topgrading professionals, or tandem Topgrading assessments by internal managers. Team discussions help calibrate the team to provide valid conclusions about each person discussed.

4. Scorecards are kept to track topgrading success, year by year:

## A Player/A Potentials in Management Scorecard

|  | Year 1 | Year 2 | Year 3 | Year 4 |
|---|---|---|---|---|
| Number (%) A and A potentials in senior management (*N*=10) | 5 (50%) | 8 (80%) | 10 (100%) | 10 (100%) |
| Number (%) A and A potentials in midmanagement (*N*=60) | 15 (25%) | 30 (50%) | 40 (67%) | 55 (92%) |
| Number (%) A and A potentials in lower management (*N*=200) | 50 (25%) | 80 (40%) | 120 (60%) | 170 (85%) |

Note topgrading is top down, with senior management topgraded before midmanagement, which is topgraded before lower management.

## Hiring Success Scorecard

|  | Topgrading Interview Process Used | Not Used |
|---|---|---|
| Number (%) A or A potentials hired | 20 (91%) | 2 (18%) |
| Less than A or A potentials hired | 2 (9%) | 9 (82%) |
| Total | 22 | 11 |

The Topgrading process in hiring consists of a tandem Topgrading Interview by trained interviewers, and reference checks by Topgrading interviewers with a minimum of all bosses in the past ten years.

The Hiring Success Chart is reproduced for each level (senior, mid-, and lower management), each year. With 91 percent As hired using Topgrading Interviews and 25 percent As hired without using Topgrading Interviews, a typical result, managers soon embrace Topgrading Interviews.

Every manager follows the cost-of-mis-hire template (Chapter 2) to identify the costs, and these costs of mis-hires are aggregated across the company, and disclosed to all managers annually. The result is increased peer pressure to follow Topgrading Interview hiring practices.

5. The A player standard is reinforced. Up to 50 percent of bonus potential is tied to topgrading results. Managers are eventually required to have at least 90 percent A or A potential managers. The goal is 100 percent, but the *requirement* is 90 percent; otherwise managers (fear-

ing loss of bonus or promotability) may "game the system," portraying underperformers as A potentials.

6. Coaching is used to help drive the A player standard. Instead of an A player representing "Exceeds Performance Expectations" in a performance management system, the A player standard is "Meets Performance Expectations." Coaching is so comprehensive, and annual Individual Development Plans so detailed, that every individual is given a terrific opportunity to improve.

7. Topgrading professionals occasionally monitor the system, a quality-control check.

Let's now review a broad array of case studies, all with a common pattern: topgrading best practices were embraced, and contributed clearly to the improved talent[31] that boosted organizational performance.

## LINCOLN FINANCIAL TOPGRADES TO DRIVE A BOLD NEW STRATEGY

Founded over a hundred years ago, Lincoln was a traditional insurance company based in Indiana. The executive team in the mid-1990s began a strategic reorientation. In 1998 Jon Boscia was named chairman and CEO, and he continued to execute the new business strategy, transforming Lincoln from a traditional life insurance company to a diversified financial services powerhouse. *Topgrading* ("the most important business book I've read," says Boscia) was key to the success of that transformation.

Today Lincoln, with $5.3 billion in revenues and $131 billion in assets, is a different company, one of the nation's leading providers of wealth accumulation and protection, financial planning, and investment advisory services for the fast-growing segment of affluent and retirement markets. Topgrading required dramatic changes in management, not because the company had weak talent, but because some of the managers in the traditional insurance

---

[31]With a January 2005 release date, 2004 case study numbers for talent (management's percentage of As) and organization performance (stock performance) are estimates, inserted in the manuscript as late as feasible, and are expected to be very close to actual 2004 records.

company lacked necessary competencies to drive the new strategy. The corporate office and two divisions were relocated to a financial hub.

Says Boscia, "About half of the top one hundred managers were A players in the old Lincoln and became As in the new Lincoln, but others simply did not have the necessary skills for the new strategy."

The topgrading rollout followed the template at the beginning of this chapter. Smart & Associates, Inc., psychologists assessed and coached approximately two hundred managers from 1999 to 2003, trained managers in Topgrading interviewing, and screened candidates for selection and promotion. By 2004 Lincoln was almost fully self-topgrading, with hundreds of managers conducting Topgrading Interviews. Outside consultants are occasionally used, where a professional second opinion seems appropriate.

The performance numbers for Lincoln track perfectly with topgrading results. Despite the severe bruising financial services companies took at the turn of the century, Lincoln steadily gained on its competitors. After years of stagnant results, two key success indicators—net cash flow and total gross deposits—have increased every year since 2000. Stock performance versus peers (Figure 5.1) and versus the S&P 500 (Standard & Poor's index of 500 leading companies, Figure 5.2) are impressive.

### Figure 5.1
### Lincoln National Groups' Stock Performance (Average Return) Compared to Its Peers'

|  | 1 Year | 3 Years | 5 Years | 10 Years |
|---|---|---|---|---|
| Life insurance industry group | -9.4% | -3.7% | 6.1% | 12.8% |
| Lincoln National Group | 5.4% | 8.8% | 16.3% | 17.5% |

Topgrading has permeated all levels, all jobs at Lincoln. It started at the top, where half the top one hundred managers have changed jobs or been replaced. Designations of A player versus non-A have come from the best practices spelled out at the beginning of this chapter—internal tandem Topgrading Interviews, Topgrading Interviews by outside professionals, and final ratings made in talent meetings overseen by the CEO and top HR managers.

## Percentage of A Players Among Officers[32]

|  | 2000 | 2003 | 2004 (est.) |
|---|---|---|---|
| A and A Potential | 50% | 92% | 97% |
| Non-A | 50% | 8% | 3% |

Lincoln's hiring success at upper levels has improved similarly:

## Figure 5.2
## Lincoln Stock Chart

### Price History—Lincoln National Corporation (7/3/2000–4/27/2004)

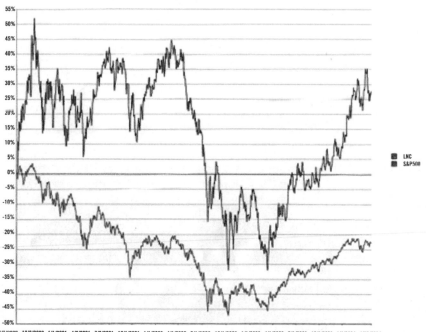

---

[32]Due to reorganizations, the populations of the "top one hundred" have changed. The 2004 estimates are considered accurate, though they include a couple of new hires.

### Percentage of Senior Managers Who Proved to Be As after Hired Using Topgrading[33]

|                  | 2000 | 2003 | 2004 (est.) |
|------------------|------|------|-------------|
| A and A Potential | 30%  | 94%  | 99%         |
| Non-A            | 70%  | 6%   | 1%          |

"We want 100 percent As in management," says Boscia, "but we hold managers accountable for 85 percent, so that they won't be incented to game the sytem." Superior hiring (100 percent As—nineteen of nineteen managers hired) was achieved very quickly in 2000, using topgrading professionals, and has continued as Lincoln managers and human resources professionals have mastered Topgrading.

Topgrading processes are well ingrained. All managers receive training in Topgrading, emphasizing the importance of tandem interviews to assess candidates for promotion and external candidates for selection. Rigorous talent meetings ensure that A players truly are As, not just B/Cs the boss thinks are As. Scorecards on percentages of As and As hired are kept, but until 2004 the software did not exist to aggregate the numbers across all the business units. The new software will permit accurate feedback to management on whether topgrading is progressing or slipping.

Yes, there have been some slips. A few A players were unable to lead the next transformation, became B/C players, and had to be replaced. A few people were hired or promoted on the basis of internal tandem Topgrading plus an outside tandem professional Topgrading, then performed at the A level and were promoted to a very different job, and failed. Says Boscia, "We should have re-topgraded them in relation to a different job with different competencies." And, far down in the organization some corners were cut (abbreviated Topgrading training, solo Topgrading, partial reference checking), and some mistakes were made. Concludes Boscia, "No talent management process is perfect, and when mistakes are made, it hurts the shareholders, the communities we serve, and very good people. Topgrading is no panacea, but it has been key in packing Lincoln with the talent that has turned the company around, which of course is in everyone's best interest."

---

[33]As in the previous chart, as of late 2004 when we went to press, it was too early to tell about performance of the most recent hires.

Lincoln's executives advise would-be topgraders:

1. "Topgrade from the top down. That's what we did, and in retrospect any other approach would have severely slowed our progress."

2. "Go internal. Companies with thousands of employees are big enough that managers can be trained, so there is progressively less reliance on outside consultants."

3. "Re-Topgraded candidates for promotion. Even two-year-old Topgrading conclusions are almost irrelevant if the promotion is to a job with some different competencies."

4. "Don't let up. The CEO, HR, and every manager must measure topgrading results and trace adherence to the discipline. Business pressures can lure people into cutting corners. Topgrading must be reinforced and kept fresh and alive."

## MARINEMAX

How would you like to launch a new company, selling yachts, just before a recession hit? MarineMax did exactly that, and despite some early success in the waning months of the go-go '90s, the arrival of a significant economic downturn, coupled with a relatively unseasoned management team from a corporate perspective, made their chances of weathering the turbulent financial climate difficult, to say the least. "We had a great vision for our company and the opportunity to provide our customers with something not seen before in our industry—hassle-free boating. We all talked enthusiastically about *'delivering the boating dream'* to customers. Unfortunately, our initial stock performance was mixed, partially because we lacked all of the talent we needed. With topgrading, we have been much more successful," says Bill McGill, CEO.

MarineMax began in 1998 with six independent boat dealers merging their businesses, and an IPO took place that year. The company in 2004 approached $750 million in sales, with almost seventy dealerships throughout the United States. The stock chart (Figure 5.3) suggests something remarkable was done to grow profitably, selling a discretionary luxury item, despite several recessionary years. That "something" was topgrading.

Says McGill, "In retrospect we had only 25 precent A players. We visited Brad at the end of 2001 after reading *Topgrading,* and he got us started right by assessing and coaching the top team, so we got A players in all the senior jobs, and then training us to take over."

---

**"Topgrading had to be done at the top first."**
**Bill McGill, CEO**

---

The top managers include seventy store managers, five regional presidents, and twenty-five managers in the corporate office called Team Support. Figure 5.4 shows topgrading results:

### Figure 5.3
### MarineMax Stock Chart

### Figure 5.4
### MarineMax Talent Distribution

|  | Before Topgrading | 2002 | 2003 | 2004 (projection based on pre-2004 results) | 2005 Goal |
|---|---|---|---|---|---|
| A/A potential | 25% | 41% | 76% | 90% | 92% |
| Non-A | 75% | 59% | 24% | 10% | 8% |

Topgrading took hold quickly at MarineMax. The initial senior team consisted mostly of B/C players, but many of them had A potential. Having run individually successful boat dealerships but not being familiar with the more sophisticated and complex corporate structure, some very sharp, high-potential managers simply had a huge amount to learn about information sciences, human resources, marketing, mergers and acquisitions, and the best practices and processes necessary to run a nationwide company. In addition to bringing his senior management team up to speed on these efforts, McGill made the staunch commitment that topgrading would become an integral and lasting part of the company's culture. All managers now receive training in topgrading, by (1) reading *Topgrading*, (2) participating in Topgrading Interview training workshops, (3) learning online through the company's E-learning system, in innovative training sessions featuring lessons from successful topgrading managers and topgrading professionals, and (4) for managers who have not yet performed a Topgrading interview, doing one in tandem with those who have as soon as the opportunity arises.

Hiring A players has become a MarineMax towering competency. Several acquisitions were walked away from, after internal Topgrading interviews conducted by Jay Avelino (VP Team Support) and senior operating executives found that the company to be acquired lacked management talent. In the pre-topgrading era about one-fourth of new hires and promotions turned out to be As or A potentials. McGill says, "In talent meetings we're tough graders, but we're proud that now 94 percent of our external hires have been A/A potentials."

Few B/Cs have actually had to be fired. "We're a people-oriented company, equally passionate about helping our customers live their boating dreams and sincere in helping our own people progress from B/C to A," McGill relates. In a coaching atmosphere, every senior manager updates a comprehensive Individual Development Plan annually and helps his direct managerial reports to do the same. The results can be quite dramatic. On the other hand, if they don't comply or aren't able to achieve their goals, they generally quit, because the company has done all it can to help them grow. "Everyone knows the expectations and there aren't any surprises," explains McGill, "and we are fully committed to having over 90 percent As and A potentials by 2005, because only A players can *deliver the boating dream* to our customers."

MarineMax executives advise:

1. "Topgrade from the top down."

2. "Use topgrading professionals to initially assess management and screen replacements to be sure of an all–A-player senior team."

3. "Make topgrading integral to the company culture, not a 'program.'"

4. "Emphasize why topgrading is necessary—to *deliver the boating dream* and to provide great careers for our people."

5. "Use Topgrading assessment on management of possible acquisitions *before* the acquistion."

## ghSMART & Company, Inc.

Can topgrading professionals topgrade? In our case, the cobbler's son did not go without shoes. In fact, Geoff Smart, my son and collaborator on the concept of topgrading back in 1997, has gone to the extreme in his use of topgrading principles in building the firm ghSMART (see Appendix J for contact information).

ghSMART today is the #1 management assessment and coaching firm serving the private equity investor market. These are the savvy investors who buy, topgrade, and sell companies for a living. To serve this high-brow clientele, Geoff had to field an exceptional team. Geoff has been extremely selective, hiring fewer than 1 percent of the applicants for ghSMART who make it to the interview process, rendering it one of the most selective professional services firms anywhere. From 1995 to 2004, Geoff and his team interviewed over 1,400 professionals to choose the ten "best of the best" consultants who currently comprise his team. ghSMART has had a 100 percent acceptance rate of people who are given an offer—A players are indeed drawn to work with other A players. And no consultant has left the firm voluntarily in nine years. It really is considered a great place to work. There has been minimal involuntary turnover. Two early professionals proved to be less of a good match as the firm's strategy and product mix evolved. And ghSMART has had one hiring mistake, which was almost immediately recognized and the person was released.

The selection process at ghSMART is very thorough and by-the-book Topgrading. One advanced tactic that ghSMART has used since 2003 is working with "recruiting researchers." These folks are not recruiters per se, but researchers who gather data. They penetrate top consultancies and research markets that provide leads, but do not do extensive interviews. They provide a great bang for Geoff's buck, since he wants candidate names, and does not wish to pay for somebody else to do extensive screening interviews. Using a recruiting researcher, Geoff and his team have been able to generate a very rich flow of candidates. The full recruiting process has a multistep process that is sudden death—failure at any step means a candidate is out of the running:

## ghSMART's Recruiting Process

1. Researcher identifies a candidate based on two or three referrals in a market.

2. Researcher piques candidate's interest with a job description and asks her to fill out a Key Data Sheet (summary of accomplishments, etc.).

3. A ghSMART partner conducts one or two thirty-minute screening interviews.

4. A ghSMART partner conducts a full four-hour SmartAssessment® interview, Geoff's version of Topgrading. At this point, a successful candidate goes on the "Virtual Bench." This means that she is "on deck" to be activated in the firm when the timing is right for both parties. People have occupied the bench for as many as two years prior to being hired. To move from the virtual bench to the team, the candidate chooses to "run the gauntlet." The running of the gauntlet

is a series of interviews with every member of the ghSMART team, as well as extensive reference and background checks. So the process continues:

5. Every partner and principal conducts a ninety-minute interview.

6. A *second* ghSMART partner conducts a full four-hour SmartAssessment® interview.

7. Between ten and fourteen reference interviews are conducted by a partner. Finally,

8. Kroll® is hired to perform background checks to verify education and employment information, and check criminal history.

ghSMART is driven mostly by client satisfaction, not sales or profits. For example, the ghSMART performance management system emphasizes evaluations by clients. Client satisfaction surveys and interviews are conducted every six months. Client satisfaction is guaranteed. If the client is unsatisfied, the fee is returned. Feedback from clients is aggressively sought, analyzed, and used to coach not only the consultant who provided the service, but all consultants on the team in biannual ghSMART "Summits." Staff members on the team receive incentive-based performance reviews on a *monthly* basis. There is no waiting for the annual review. Feedback and incentive dollars flow to team members in bursts on a monthly basis. Performing at the A or A+ level means more money to pay the mortgage, put kids through college, and order nice wine at dinner. A dip into the A-level means less money. A dip into the B level for more than a couple of months would mean a parting of the ways. It is this real-time feedback linked to compensation that helps to keep ghSMART on its toes and focused on maintaining A performance.

Topgrading ghSMART has led to the building of a client-satisfying, high-end consulting boutique that has enjoyed profitable growth and provides a fun atmosphere of talented colleagues. Geoff and the ghSMART team recognize that the firm could have grown faster in the short term if it lowered its standards to accept Non-A players. But the team feels proud that they are building something that is sustainable and meaningful and could have only been accomplished through strict adherence to Topgrading principles.

Geoff's advice may be a bit biased:

- "Read *Topgrading*!"
- "Follow *all* its principles!"

## HAYES LEMMERZ

Hayes Lemmerz today is a premier automotive supplier, with #1 market share worldwide in wheels. Just a couple of years ago, however, it was stumbling, mired in Chapter 11 bankruptcy protection. When Curt Clawson joined as CEO, he was one of the youngest CEOs of a multibillion-dollar company, and he expected to make a good company great, utilizing his lean manufacturing and topgrading skills learned at AlliedSignal and American National Can. Surprise! The week he entered the company, he discovered accounting irregularities that meant Chapter 11 was inevitable. That was late in 2001, and Hayes Lemmerz began topgrading immediately, emerging from bankruptcy protection in 2003. Only a couple of years into topgrading, Hayes Lemmerz has improved managerial talent to 89 percent As, and the 90 percent goal will be achieved by the time this book is released.

Topgrading is not a cake walk in a declining industry (automotive), based in a city not usually listed among the most desirable to live (Detroit), with a very uncertain future (Chapter 11). If there were a Black Belt in topgrading, Clawson would have it, and he needed it. He tapped his personal network, attracting As to key division president and corporate positions, hardly using search firms. Over a three-year period managers participated in Topgrading-based assessment and coaching conducted by outside topgrading professionals. Two-day Topgrading Bootcamps were conducted for all managers. External candidates participated, and continue to do so, in internal tandem Topgrading Interviews plus Topgrading Interviews by outside professionals. As hiring managers and Human Resources (a topgraded function, of course) have become proficient at Topgrading, outside professionals are used less, and as HR professionals have become capable trainers, they have taken over the conduct of Topgrading workshops.

Talent meetings have documented a major improvement in talent (see Figure 5.5). Nine out of the top ten executives are new, and it's an A team: 100 percent A players. Among the top seventy-seven managers, from plant manager to CEO, the percentage of As has skyrocketed from 38 to 90 percent and is improving rapidly.

### Figure 5.5
### Hayes Lemmerz Talent Distribution
### (Top 77 Managers)

|                | Pre-topgrading (2001) | 2003 | 2004 | 2005 Goal |
|----------------|:---------------------:|:----:|:----:|:---------:|
| A/A Potential  | 38%                   | 78%  | 90%  | 93%       |
| Non-A          | 62%                   | 22%  | 10%  | 7%        |

Typical hiring and promotion-from-within policies had left the company talent poor, with 65 percent in the Non-A category. Since the rollout of topgrading, however, careful talent assessment by teams, not just the hiring manager, has produced different statistics (see Figure 5.6).

### Figure 5.6
### Topgrading-Based Hiring

|                | Pre-topgrading (2001) | 2003 | 2004 (est.) |
|----------------|:---------------------:|:----:|:-----------:|
| A/A Potential  | 35%                   | 94%  | 100%        |
| Non-A          | 65%                   | 6%   | 0%          |

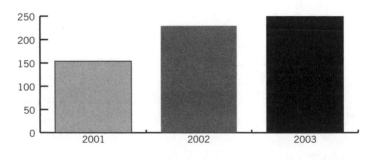

**Hayes Lemmerz International Financial Results**

Adjusted EBITDA

Of thirty-seven management hires in 2003, one was not Topgrading interviewed, and that person failed. Thirty-four of the thirty-six hired have been deemed A players. As of late 2004, thirteen managers have been hired, and all are considered As. However, a couple of managers joined a month or two before this book went to press, so it is too early to tell (hence Figure 5.6's 2004 statistics are estimated).

As Hayes Lemmerz has emerged from Chapter 11, the A players have created a better company. Losses of $211 million in 2001 have been replaced by breakeven (2002) and earnings from operations of $62 million (2003). Adjusted EBITDA has shown the same trend.

Talent selection has improved from 35 percent to 94 percent A players; B/Cs have been removed or redeployed; replacements have come one-third from promotions, one-third from search/recruitment, and one-third from personal networks and ads. A full 100 percent of the promoted managers are considered A/A potential. Clawson says, "Promote-from-within can work, if topgrading assures that *only* A players are making the decisions, if Topgrading-based assessments are used, and if A players in talent meetings reach agreement."

## Topgrading at the Plant Level

Hayes Lemmerz, like all serious topgraders, drives topgrading throughout the organization, ultimately including all jobs. At the plant level, topgrading was launched in 2003 in the largest division, North American Wheels.

In four plants, Topgrading-based assessments, combining internal tandem Topgrading and external topgrading professional (Chris Mursau) Topgrading, dramatically improved talent. Of twelve new managers screened by two Topgrading Interviews, all have been rated A players. Four additional managers passed the internal tandem Topgrading, but Chris Mursau's Topgrading reports were convincing that all four would have been C players. If that conclusion is correct, the external Topgrading increased the success rate from 71 to 100 percent. Overall, after eighteen months since topgrading began, the results in this work in progress in the four plants is improvement from 20 percent A/A potential to 88 percent.

As of late 2004 their open positions are still being filled, yet barely a year into topgrading:

Scrap is down          36%

Production is up        22%

Internal quality is up  39%

Headcount is down       13%

Senior Hayes Lemmerz managers advise:

- "Even if you face major business obstacles, topgrade!"
- "Launch topgrading from the top. Otherwise, B/C players will undermine it."
- "Pay signing bonuses to attract a critical mass of A players during Chapter 11. After that, As want to join As and have fun turning a company around, so signing bonuses decline and finally, are nonexistent."
- "Treat Bs and Cs who leave well, to show the company has a heart and to avoid lawsuits (there have been none)."
- "Hold talent meetings twice per year, to keep all managers focused and accountable for topgrading."
- "Train Human Resources early in the process."
- "Use quality of hire (A/A potential metrics) to gauge success."
- "Because managers in remote locations with negligible turnover aren't necessarily 'calibrated,' pair them with experienced interviewers for tandem Topgrading interviews."
- "Topgrade all jobs—100 percent—not just upper management."

## VIRTUAL TECHNOLOGY CORPORATION

Do you have any high school kids who waste endless hours playing computer games? Maybe one day they will work for Virtual Technology Corporation (VTC). "We build video games for generals," says CEO Jack

Harrington. Like flight simulation environments that train pilots, VTC's simulator environments train military officers in amazingly realistic battles. These are deadly serious games, ones that ultimately save money and lives. Founded in 1994, VTC grew to a hundred employees in 2004, but topgrading is accelerating its growth. Harrington says, "All we have is our reputation; one C player can destroy that reputation."

Harrington has received some excellent business guidance through Gazelles, the premier outsourced corporate university for companies with thirty to two thousand employees. Tom Peters called Gazelles founder Verne Harnish "*the* guru of fast-growth companies." Through Gazelles, Harrington, cofounder Rich Briggs, and several executives attended a one-day topgrading workshop conducted by Geoff Smart (ghSMART & Company) and were struck by the topgrading bolt of lightning.

States Harrington, "As a company whose business model is to provide the best and brightest people to our customers, we were not satisfied with our employee selection. In the past, hiring other than A players led to turnover and other problems that hurt our growth. Following topgrading guidelines Rich hired twenty people last year—one (who failed) without using Topgrading, and nineteen with Topgrading, eighteen of whom were As, and one was a B we moved into a job where he became an A. I don't know if that's 95 or 100 percent success, but our business has taken off." This year twenty-five more have been hired, and five are considered "superstars," and . . . so far all seem to be As. With more As, bigger contracts are sought, won, and delivered with top quality. Turnover is down, and sales and profits have skyrocketed.

Harrington returned to a topgrading workshop for a "tune-up," getting reinforcement on the basics. He recalls, "We were always good at recruiting bright talent because we sell a positive vision—a culture that is entrepreneurial (so people can make a difference), fun (including a game room), nonpolitical, and, best of all, important (because what we do saves lives). But the discipline of Topgrading interviewing is the silver bullet, enabling us to pick As from the crowd of applicants. I'm continually amazed at how *patterns* tell the whole story. Last week I interviewed someone who hated all twelve of the bosses he'd had. Duh! Do I want to be lucky 13?"

Advice from VTC founders for how small and midsized companies can topgrade:

1. "Start with aggressive recruitment, and for a small company, *sell* candidates an exciting entrepreneurial vision."

2. "Craft a job Scorecard—a job description but with all the competencies and first-year accountabilities. It sounds like big-company bureaucracy, but it isn't. This exercise helps us determine exactly what we want."

3. "Exercise Topgrading discipline, discipline, discipline! Just DO IT and you will be amazed to see how easy it is to see trends of success, failure, or mediocrity. You will be surprised by what interviewees will tell you about themselves and by the results that come from avoiding problem people and hiring A players."

## GREG ALEXANDER TOPGRADES A SALES REGION

Greg Alexander was one scared, brand-new EMC regional vice resident. "I was totally unprepared for the promotion," he lamented. His region was thirteenth of fifteen in sales. He floundered until he discovered topgrading and embraced its principles. His performance then shot to the top—#1 of fifteen—and has remained there ever since. When the tech bubble burst Greg was the only VP to achieve his quota, and core account sales have increased dramatically in the several years since.

According to Alexander, "The competition was doing well, and the only thing they really had that beat me was talent. But I didn't know how to topgrade, yet. With seventeen regional and district managers and eighty-four sales reps, I knew I needed better people, so I started firing the worst performers, but I mis-hired 75 percent of the replacements. I was a bull in a china shop, working a hundred hours a week, ignoring my B and C players, and spending all my time with the few As. Having gained thirty pounds, I was on the verge of burnout."

Greg read *Topgrading* and called, asking for my help. I suggested he contact Geoff Smart, who coached him through topgrading steps. "Greg really did it all himself," says Geoff, "and he did it well. He Topgrading interviewed all of his managers to conclude that fifteen of seventeen should be replaced (most returned to being sales reps, where they were A players). He achieved the goal of *all* As or A potentials."

Alexander continues, "There have been reorganizations and natural attrition, but I'm always topgrading. I've had to relearn a lesson: Don't cut corners. Initially to hire all A players I required two Topgrading Interviews of sales reps—one by the regional, one by the area manager—and it worked. When I reduced it to one Topgrading, my mis-hires increased, and it's dumb. It's so much more costly and harmful than doing two Topgrading or a tandem Topgrading!"

Recently Greg was named Sales Manager of the Year by *Sales and Marketing Management* (March 2004). His direct reports nominated him without his knowing. He was selected over two thousand other entries, "I was totally surprised," he said, "and in the interview I said you and Geoff, and topgrading, were key to my success." Like other case study managers, Greg learned that B/C managers were incapable of topgrading their sales reps. "There's a temptation to get all managers topgrading, NOW, but the only way it can work is to topgrade management first."

Greg's advice is:

- "Stick with all the topgrading basics; don't cut corners."

- "Topgrade from the top down."

## HILLENBRAND INDUSTRIES

Hillenbrand Industries is a $3.5 billion market capital publicly traded holding company headquartered in Batesville, Indiana, a rural community located approximately forty miles from Cincinnati. Although the company increased its earnings and shareholder value during the 1990s, the stock languished—performing below the S&P 500. This lackluster performance forced the question, "What will it take for Hillenbrand Industries to succeed in the future and move to the next level?"

Dave Robertson, former Vice President of Administration, led the initiative to build greater leadership talent. Robertson remarks, "We had too many people, and not enough talent . . . and that had to contribute to our dismal stock performance."

In 1999 Dave asked Gus Hillenbrand, CEO, to meet with me. Topgrading was launched in 2000. In addition, Steve McMillen, Vice President of Executive Leadership Development and Performance, was hired to help

## Figure 5.7

### Price History—Hillenbrand Industries (7/3/2000–4/27/2004)

lead the topgrading effort. After three years of building a performance culture based on talent, the new CEO, Fred Rockwood, says, "Hillenbrand has been transformed through topgrading. Our new A-level executive management team has created an exciting strategy, and our organizational culture is much more positive and performance oriented."

The Hillenbrand stock remained in the high 20s from 1990 through 1999. Figure 5.7 shows the stock's rapid improvement with the infusion of A players who replaced underperformers.

How did Hillenbrand do it? Among other things, they followed the guidelines just presented—the Topgrading Model, Successful Topgrading Rollout Plan, and Topgrading Ongoing Practices, all modified and supplemented by Hillenbrand's A team. Two associates and I assessed the top 150 managers. As one senior executive puts it, "You confirmed what a small group of As believed were the As, Bs, and Cs, but external validation was necessary for us to act." Feedback and coaching sessions were held with all 150 managers, who were helped to write Individual Development Plans (IDPs). Since topgrading started at the top and cascaded down through the managerial ranks, each manager who had received feedback and coaching helped the direct reports or teams at the next level develop and implement their IDPs. To further institutionalize the topgrading practice in the organization, I conducted two-day Topgrading Workshops for HR professionals, who have since trained hundreds of managers.

Fred Rockwood says, "Topgrading is never a finished program, it's an ongoing part of our culture, and our present percentage of As will continue to grow and develop. We can achieve even greater results." But the improvement in talent is impressive. Among the top 109 managers, by the end of 2003 40 percent had been hired, and 60 percent had been promoted or redeployed. Topgrading decisions began being made in 2001 and by the end of 2003 all 109 managers were in different positions, with 81 percent functioning as A players. A potentials are not included in that 81 percent (which would raise it closer to 90 percent). Hillenbrand has dramatically

**Figure 5.8
Hillenbrand Curve**

**Managing the Performance Distribution Curve**

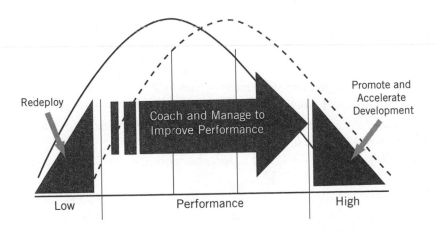

improved its managerial talent, and, according to a senior executive, "Clearly, the shareholders were best served by topgrading faster, not slower—that's always the case."

Since the beginning of the topgrading initiative, Hillenbrand Industries has greatly improved its human resources systems—compensation, performance management, succession planning, and leadership development. According to McMillen, "It was imperative to build a talent culture. To consummate a large acquisition, we would need a bench strength of A players to place in an acquired company."

In addition to assessing talent, the company makes the development of A players a top priority. Parts of the organization use a forced ranking system (Figure 5.8) as a way to identify the top 10 percent for accelerated development.

The bottom 10 percent have been thoroughly evaluated and coached by a variety of sources—internal (boss) and in some instances an external consultant. They are told they are in the bottom 10 percent, and an Individual Performance Improvement Plan is implemented.

Since the topgrading journey began, there have been very significant changes in management at the top. At the most senior level, Fred Rockwood was promoted to CEO of Hillenbrand Industries, the first non–family member to hold this position. Ken Camp was promoted to CEO of Batesville Casket Company (BCC), a division whose business mission is to protect market share and generate stable earnings and cash flow for Hillenbrand to invest in its growth strategy. But Camp has also developed and contributed managers for healthcare division Hill-Rom, and his topgraded team has grown shareholder value at a compound annual growth rate of 18 percent, in a declining market. A players Ernest Waaser (CEO of Hill-Rom) and Scott Sorensen (corporate CFO) proved the truth that A players are talent magnets, having topgraded their organizations with spectacular results. Their new teams have enabled the company to strengthen its foundation and then make three acquisitions in a matter of a few months to jump-start the growth strategy.

As is always best, Hillenbrand topgraded from the top down. Change at the executive-committee level has resulted in all seven members being A players. Naturally, they insist on all As reporting to them, and that's why the A standard has permeated the entire company.

John Dickey, VP Human Resources of the BCC division, has conducted dozens of Topgrading workshops, and has received a special sales award for his contribution. When BCC customers heard about topgrading, they asked to be trained in the skills. When prospective customers heard they would be trained in topgrading, one customer began placing big orders. "They probably would have become customers anyway," Dickey relates, "but learning about topgrading solidified the order."

Topgrading is not simple; it is complex and fraught with emotional and political barriers. For organizations undertaking a topgrading initiative, Hillenbrand executives advise the following practices:

- "Topgrade at the top first. B/C players are threatened by A players and will avoid hiring or not recognize A talent. Having B/C players at the top makes attracting A talent difficult. A players don't generally go to work for B/C players."

- "Don't ignore your A players. Sustaining the talent edge requires the organization to invest in the development, recognition, and appreciation of A players. When As leave the organization they are talent magnets, and other As in the company will follow them."

- "Listen to your As—they want challenges, growth, honest feedback, and fair pay. Meet their needs or you'll lose them."

- "Use topgrading professionals initially to assess managers, and to learn how to topgrade. They provide additional confirmation of the organization's talent assessment, which helps the organization move with the decisiveness to replace Non-As. Use internal managers to assess people when they have proven they are A players and have mastered Topgrading skills."

- "The CEO must drive the topgrading initiative or it will be compromised and fail."

- "Overcommunicate. Develop an effective communication plan that describes the purpose and process of topgrading. It's the best practice, and it's fair, so tell that story again and again."

## AMERICAN HEART ASSOCIATION

Of the two hundred disease-specific charities, the American Heart Association is second only to American Cancer Society in the amount of money raised annually: one-half billion dollars. Those dollars are used to reduce the incidence of heart disease and stroke through medical research, education (programs in schools, businesses, and the community), public information ("Heart disease is the #1 killer of women and men."), and advocacy (working for heart disease and stroke legislative and policy issues). In 1999 the CEO initiated topgrading, with this belief:

---

### "Topgrading AHA will help save lives."
### Cass Wheeler, CEO

---

AHA launched topgrading in 1999, just before a recession hit and charitable giving declined. Nonetheless, with a higher percentage of A players at the senior levels, better strategy was formulated, and A players in the field improved execution.

When topgrading began, the four main voluntary health organizations had all beaten the AHA in the percent increase in revenue over the prior year. But this soon began to change. By 2002, the AHA's rate of increase was higher than all but one; 2004 produced exceptional results, with fund-raising up 18.5 percent, the AHA's best yearly percentage increase in forty-seven years, far higher than any other leading nonprofit voluntary health organization. In fact, the AHA's five-year campaign has exceeded the growth in any previous five-year period for the past nineteen years.

But the benefits of topgrading extend far beyond revenue generation. In 2004, the AHA had a tremendous year, launching its highly successful "Go Red for Women" campaign, funding advertising initiatives, forming new strategic alliances, and seizing opportunities to aggressively expand existing programs. Such successes increased organizational momentum and effectiveness, setting a course for continued future achievements. Ultimately, the AHA's success will be measured in lives saved, as it advances toward its strategic goal of reducing coronary heart disease, strokes, and the risk of those diseases by 25 percent by 2010. Since 1999, through the leadership of the American Heart Association and others, the death rates from coronary heart disease and stroke have already dropped 9.1 and 6.3 percent, respectively.

The twelve regional organizations (Affiliates), with staffs totaling 2,600, have executives who are hired and managed by volunteer leaders in consultation with Wheeler and the COO of field operations. The National Center of the organization has the power of moral suasion, and Wheeler used it. He distributed copies of *Topgrading* to all the field executives, who discussed it in several meetings. The group, along with National Center department executives, voted to be "topgraded by Brad Smart," and Wheeler decided to go first. He and his corporate team went through the Topgrading, oral 360s, and feedback process with me. Then I Topgrading-assessed and coached the top field and National Center executives. An associate did the same with some midlevel field managers. After discussing my A, B, and C conclusions with Wheeler and agreeing on the appropriate designations, I shared my conclusions and recommendations with each executive. All embraced Individual Development Plans.

A Train-the-Trainer model of spreading topgrading was launched, so that HR conducted Topgrading workshops throughout the United States. Annual talent meetings involve Wheeler, Human Resource VP Bill Achenbach, and COO Field Operations Gordon McCullough, who meet leaders from each region (Affiliate) and the National Center to ensure progress toward all A players. AHA licensed all the topgrading forms, and standard practice is to hire and promote people only with the Topgrading guides.

Of the top 250 managers, in 1998 20 percent were A or A potentials, compared to 60 percent in 2004. The results are impressive, but as Wheeler says, "The topgrading job is a work in progress. We will achieve higher percentages of As and A potentials every year."

Topgrading advice of American Heart Association senior executives is:

- "Use Topgrading results to aggressively sell Topgrading internally. Initially managers felt Topgrading Interviews were too long, but hiring managers and internal recruiters broadcast success stories and published the hiring scorecard, and that convinced the slower adapters to get on board."

- "Hold jobs open longer to hire top talent. The pressure to accept a B now, rather than continue recruiting for an A, was intense. A common mantra was 'I know candidate X isn't the best we can find for that salary, but a B player now can at least get some programs going!'

Others had to work harder for a while, doing two jobs, but it was worth it. When an A would finally start, the hiring managers knew the wait was justified."

- "Topgrade with emphasis on a mission. At the AHA, that mission is saving lives. In another company a mission might be to provide terrific service, or make the highest-quality food product. Sure, managers know their career is going to be more successful when they topgrade, but making tough people decisions is better justified with a bigger purpose."

## CLAUDE HANSON TOPGRADES TEKMORE

Can you topgrade even if your company is not supportive? Division President Claude Hanson did it, with Corporate lukewarm on his topgrading initiatives.[34] Many readers of *Topgrading* have launched topgrading in their department and report plenty of interference; their insights and suggestions to minimize corporate interference are presented at the end of this case study.

Late in 2001, after successfully leading a $200 million high-tech manufacturing business and achieving record earnings growth at that company, Claude was given the most challenging assignment of his career. A $550 million revenue company was acquired, and he was promoted to president of the combined global entity, TEKMORE. With $750 million in total revenue, TEKMORE was the largest division in the company. Unfortunately, the company acquired was devastated when the high-tech bubble burst at the turn of the century. Morale was low, efforts to rebound were halfhearted, and management exhibited a "deer in the headlights" complacency. The industry was in turmoil: the high-tech world was in severe decline in the short term, major customers had consolidated and were squeezing their suppliers, and the competitors were cutting prices and losing money, hoping to stay alive. Further complicating the situation, the company acquired was really made up of seven different companies and cultures all over the world, and several had

---

[34]Hanson left TEKMORE and TEKMORE's CEO interfered with Hanson's disclosing his name and company names, so identifying information (but not anything substantive) has been changed.

never integrated into the global company. Thus, while owning the best-known brands in the industry, TEKMORE was positioned poorly both strategically and operationally.

This was the largest acquisition in the parent company's history, and expectations for TEKMORE were high. Plans were to improve operating profit significantly, globalize the company, and focus on global customers, all while leading simultaneous integration, cost reduction, business rationalization, and strategic growth initiatives, anticipating a tech rebound. In short, Claude had to redefine the strategy and deliver superior returns. Speed was of the essence.

Claude decided that his first priority was building his leadership team. With very high expectations for the current year, it was generally assumed that Claude would "make do" with his management team; although several were not A players, any changes could be disruptive, harming short-term results. Having used topgrading as the focal point to drive great operating performance and success in his previous leadership positions, Claude thought differently. He was determined to topgrade all levels of management fast! But this was a huge challenge—a new, large team, scattered around the globe, eight new direct reports, and an acquisition that had a disjointed culture of its own. Changing managers would be disruptive, but hanging on to B or C players in key positions too long would make achieving the stretch goals impossible.

First, Claude communicated the vision of his people strategy: "We can only win by having the best people in the business, A players. We have to make talent our highest priority." He started very quickly with this communication, even before the acquisition closed. He ordered twenty copies of *Topgrading* and made it required reading by all his reports and the other key leaders in the business. He constantly communicated that having the best people was key to success. Next, he launched topgrading, instituting all the essential practices. Claude led it and asked his VP of HR to drive the day-to-day execution, focusing initially on the top team but cascading it rapidly throughout the company.

Time was critical and he had to assess the top team quickly, but do it in a way that gained their respect and earned him credibility. He announced that he would be spending time with each manager to get to know them better, and it would take the form of several steps over the course of a month:

1. Lunch or dinner.

2. A three-hour meeting to review their current objectives and top priorities of their job, performance targets, and any issues that they may have. Usually this took the first hour. Then he used the next two hours for a short version of the Topgrading Interview, concentrating on the most recent two jobs and reviewing the manager's HR file.

3. A full four-hour Topgrading Interview by a topgrading professional.

4. Interaction in the meetings and reviews.

5. Follow-up on their key objectives and priorities that they were supposedly already working on.

6. Daily, ongoing coaching to help them succeed and build teamwork.


Claude scheduled the psychologist's Topgrading assessments over a three-week period for all the twenty managers, even though he was certain that a couple were A or A potentials and some were hopeless B/C players. The consultant's reports confirmed the As and B/Cs. Feedback helped focus the As and ignite their energy, while it helped "soften up" the B/Cs, preparing them to exit.

Overall Claude's top team was very weak, with only a few A players, some in wrong positions, and an organization structure that didn't fit the business needs or strategy. Specifically, before topgrading his senior team Claude had one A player and three with A potentials, and after replacing the four Non-As and adding three As, the team of eleven managers was 100 percent A or A potentials. The A potentials all became full-blown A players within one year.

Claude smoothly removed a C player who, in the Topgrading Interview, made it clear he would not embrace the changes needed. Another B was a square peg in a round hole, and happily moved laterally and became an A. Two others in the organization lacked some business skills or the high-performance leadership style needed; they embraced developmental plans, were coached by their boss, and improved enough to qualify as A players.

The hiring success by managers before topgrading is estimated to have been no better than 25 percent good hires—that is, A or A potentials. The acquired company was not disciplined at all in their hiring process, but new A players enthusiastically embraced improvements. As topgrading rolled out in the company, Topgrading Interviews caught on because they ensured that almost all As were hired. Topgrading Interviews were also used to make decisions to promote managers or move them laterally. Even some C players became A players when moved into the right job.

| Hiring and Promoting Success, Using Topgrading | | |
|---|---|---|
| | Number | Percentage A/A Potentials |
| External Hires | 70 | 97% |
| Internal Promotions or Transfers | 25 | 95% |

Claude's A team turned the business around quicker than anyone thought possible. Operating profit tripled over the two years as TEKMORE gained the confidence of major customers around the world. Claude's hands-on involvement declined, as he delegated more to A players. The team became recognized as the best in the industry.

Essential parts of the hiring process are:

- Hiring managers personally do a three- or four-hour Topgrading Interview on the first or second visit. Subordinates of the hiring manager focus on the most important competencies.

- If the first visit goes well, the second visit simultaneously zeros in on areas of concern in the candidate while "selling" the job by addressing the candidate's questions. Usually, dinner is arranged with key staff to get to know the candidate in a more personal and informal setting.

- If the candidate appears to be an excellent fit and A player, a full four-hour Topgrading Interview with an outside topgrading professional is scheduled.

- Finally, Claude and every other hiring manager personally call references, including bosses, but also others whose names emerge from Topgrading Interviews—perhaps a key subordinate, a peer or two, or even a key customer.

## How to Minimize Corporate Interference

Although Claude's corporate officers did not interfere with his division-level topgrading, he was lucky. Dozens of readers of *Topgrading* have shared their frustrations, insights, and advice. After all, if only 7 percent of companies topgrade, most readers are faced with some sort of interference, from a nonsupportive boss to a corporate office that forbids topgrading.

Nonsupportive corporate officers rarely give good reasons why they discourage topgrading. "The timing isn't just right," and "It would be too disruptive to our culture," are typical. You might respond, "Then is it OK if I use Topgrading Interviews? After all, it's a proven best practice and all I want is four hours to be more thorough." Unbelievably, many senior HR executives have said, "We have a selection process that works just fine, and if we let people start changing things, it will fall apart."

A lot of bosses and corporate functions will interfere with topgrading. Claude Hanson notes:

- "Too many C players fear that topgrading could cause them to lose their job."

- "Topgrading is complex. The hiring processes are like a chain with many links, and a corporate HR manager assigned to me didn't want to use the Career History Form, learn Topgrading, serve as a tandem partner conducting Topgrading, do thorough reference checks, or maintain the A standard. The HR manager assigned to my division was a C player, lazy and incompetent."

- "People accuse you of showing off or grandstanding by laying out a process that is far more thorough, systematic, professional, and valid."

- "As soon as a functional manager begins topgrading, B and C players are exposed, and secretly use their political connections to sabotage topgrading."

Fortunately, Claude and other managers not supported in topgrading found a solution:

## Topgrade quietly, under the radar screen, to minimize interference. Use "stealth topgrading."

If someone asks why you want four hours for an interview, don't mention Topgrading. "I've made too many hiring mistakes, so I'm trying to be more thorough."

"Why are you using that Career History Form?" "Uh, I just can't read a résumé and get a sense that I'm seeing the whole truth, and this form is more thorough and helps me prescreen people better."

"What's this about your conducting a tandem interview?" "No big thing—I'm just not very good at asking questions, taking notes, anticipating questions, and maintaining rapport, all at the same time. I guess I'm a slow learner, but in my case, two heads are better than one."

When you are as successful as Claude in your stealth topgrading, don't expect corporate to beg for your secrets of success. Or, if they do and other divisions want to emulate your topgrading program, coach them. But don't expect more than lukewarm support at best from corporate. You'll know when an A player CEO is serious about talent, when you can openly share your topgrading success story, but until then be stealthy, lurk below the radar, and topgrade ever so quietly.

Here's Claude Hanson's topgrading advice:

- "Quickly make the tough people decisions, because procrastinating is worse for everyone."

- "Be thorough and professional in the assessment process by using all available information on a manager, multiple meetings, and a complete Topgrading Interview."

- "If you haven't mastered Topgrading, use a professional to assess both internal talent and candidates for selection."

### BARCLAYS

Barclays has been in banking more than three hundred years, and is one of the largest and most revered financial institutions in the UK. A bold new strategic plan led to benchmarking best practices in talent management of high-performing organizations, which led to topgrading.

Four components of Barclays' human resources strategy are:

1. A distinctive and compelling employer brand.

2. Value-driven leadership at all levels.

3. A rigorous performance management ethic.

4. Attracting, retaining, and deploying exceptional talent at all levels.

---

**"The topgrading philosophy and best practices have enabled us to make progress in each of our People (HR) Strategy priorities."**

---

The application of topgrading principles has been tailored to the needs of various divisions. For example, Barclays Capital's recruitment needs made Topgrading-based selection interviewing the topgrading tool most applied, and Retail Bank has used Topgrading-based coaching[35] to satisfy the need to develop managers. Topgrading-based coaching is being rolled out at levels reporting to Retail Bank CEO Roger Davis and below, and topgrading is spreading across various divisions. Davis did not simply ask managers to go through Topgrading-based assessment and coaching. He built support by participating himself and telling his team, "The personal feedback and coaching was immensely valuable."

The Bank is favoring the use of topgrading professionals so far for selection and coaching. As the internal skills are built, there will be less and less need for outside consultants.

The Barclays topgrading experience has emphasized training managers in Topgrading-based hiring and coaching. Hundreds of managers have been trained in two-day workshops in which two managers, a tandem pair, Topgrading Interview a lower-level manager. The topgrading approach and workshop have received such good reviews that line managers' demand for training has become the main driver of its talent building program.

---

[35] Topgrading Interview and oral 360 interviews followed by feedback and coaching, with a topgrading professional.

Conclusions and advice from Barclays management are:

- "Topgrading is a critical enabler in ensuring that a candidate's perception of the brand becomes as attractive as leading organizations such as Microsoft or Virgin."

- "The Topgrading Interview is as valuable in development (with 360s and feedback) as it is in selecting A players."

- "Topgrading works equally well across operating and staff areas. In topgrading workshops, delegates practice full Topgrading Interviews on real selection candidates. It considerably enhances the learning experience."

- "Commit four hours to the Topgrading Interview in order to achieve a quality result. It cannot be completed adequately in less time."

- "Build a powerful recruitment process that enables managers to fill their vacancies with A players; that way they are more apt to replace underperformers. Topgrade a team from the top down, with the philosophy cascading from the most senior team member of the team."

- "Don't just rely on reading *Topgrading* to teach Topgrading interviewing. Practice sessions are essential."

## BOB DINEEN'S VOLUNTARY TOPGRADING

Today Bob Dineen is CEO and president of Lincoln Financial Advisors, Lincoln Financial Group's two thousand financial planners. Earlier in his career, when he was a regional manager for Merrill Lynch, his assignment was a tough one—bring ML's high-performance New York standards to Arkansas, Oklahoma, and Louisiana, a region in which performance was subpar.

Bob entered the Little Rock office, finding twenty-five out of twenty-eight trainees failing to achieve five performance goals (number of new accounts, amount of fees for financial planning, etc.). He felt certain that the national standards set by New York–based Merrill Lynch were achievable throughout the United States, yet many in his offices felt those standards were inappropriate. Bob said, "When I arrived in Little Rock, they expected me to be a hard-driving New Yorker who would immediately impose unrealistic goals and then fire everybody." Firing twenty-five new brokers in a town like Little Rock would have given Merrill Lynch a bad name, only confirming the insensitive New York stereotype; furthermore, it would have made it difficult to recruit. Besides, it's simply not the Bob Dineen style, for he is an A player who achieves high-performance goals by inspiring A players to join and by positively coaching them to be their best.

Early on, Bob convened a meeting of those twenty-five underperformers, and as they looked around the room, they figured Bob was about to drop the ax. Instead he said, "Although you have all fallen short of the national standards and could be let go, I'm not going to fire anyone. Instead, I'm going to add two new goals: attitude and effort. I'll meet with you one-on-one monthly, and you rate yourself on the previous month, on a ten-point scale with ten high, on attitude and effort. As long as you rate yourself a seven or better on both, you have a job here. If you rate yourself below a seven on either dimension, please resign, and I'll do my best to help you get another job."

One broker asked, "What if you think someone's effort has been poor, only a two on the ten-point scale?" Bob replied, "I don't get a vote. You are the only one who will judge whether your attitude or effort met the seven goal." Within six months twenty-three of the twenty-five resigned, all amicably. Bob had offered comprehensive coaching and developmental planning to all twenty-five, and nine took him up on the offer. The only two who hadn't resigned within six months were still completing their developmental plans, but eventually they resigned, as well.

Bob suggested the same methodology in the other Arkansas, Oklahoma, and Louisiana offices, but did not mandate it. He made it clear to his branch managers, however, that they all had six months in order to have 100 percent of the broker trainees meeting all five numeric goals. Some simply continued to measure numeric performance and fired brokers who failed to achieve the five numeric goals, though some emulated Bob's voluntary topgrading technique.

Sounds easy, doesn't it? "Hey, you all just tell me if you're trying hard and your attitude is positive, and if so on both, you keep your job!" That could be an approach that a C player manager would use, and it would flop. Lazy and negative brokers would put on their golf pants at noon and wave to the manager as they went off to play golf. Instead, Bob showed the office he could put an A team in place. He interviewed every registered representative (broker) in all three states, articulating a compelling vision—to be part of the most successful, highest-performing, most respected brokerage company in the region. And, he assured them, the financial rewards would follow as a result of first doing what was right for the clients and aligning their practices with a firm like Merrill Lynch, which has the exact same philosophy as an overall organization.

He hired A player brokers, all of whom met the five national performance goals, and these high performers formed a "critical mass" of exceptional performers, making it increasingly awkward for the underperfomers to come to work each day. The notion that only hard-driving workaholic New Yorkers could possibly achieve at a very high level was proven untrue, day after day after day. The new A player brokers were hardworking as a positive, exciting team, infusing the office with energy and optimism. Bob continued to coach the underperformers, but it became increasingly obvious that they were mis-hires, truly incapable of exceptional performance. And that's why they quit. Bob's "ace in the hole" was the fact that Merrill Lynch had such a fabulous training program, that even brokers who could not meet the Merrill Lynch performance standards could easily find a job with another brokerage firm.

Bob's "voluntary topgrading" approach comes with a warning label, "Do not try this unless you are an A player, and you are confident it will work in your circumstances." In Bob's organization, C players quit because they visibly dragged down the office. Financial planners (no longer called "brokers") in Bob's organization, then at Merrill Lynch and now at Lincoln Financial Group, are committed to a noble mission—helping people realize their financial goals. They want to come to work every day and feel that they are highly ethical and competent, and always maintain the highest professional standards. They want to have fun, share ideas with other A players, and creatively solve problems. And they want to be respected in the community. As the A players Bob hired showed that this vision was not idealistic but very practical and achievable, C players found it increasingly difficult to march into his office once per month, look him in the eye, and tell him that their effort and attitude were very high, if they weren't. And, even if attitude and effort were high, but performance continued to be low, C players resigned because they knew they were failing, and they knew everyone in the office knew too. The new brokers Bob hired were absolutely required to meet the five financial goals, and the twenty-five people given "special treatment" eventually became too embarrassed to have a job that everyone knew they didn't deserve.

In an unusual way, Bob Dineen topgraded, simultaneously hiring all A players, coaching As to remain As and B/Cs to become As, and redeploying (voluntarily) B/C players who couldn't become As. Bob's main advice is:

- "How you treat people as you topgrade is as important as the topgrading process itself."

## REVISITED CASE STUDIES

The first edition of *Topgrading* featured topgrading case studies, several of which are updated:

### General Electric

GE continues to be a talent generation machine under CEO Jeffrey Immelt. It was retired CEO Jack Welch, however, who convinced the business world that the A player standard was not only achievable, but necessary for any company to flourish. In retirement Welch continues to be a highly visible and effective proponent of topgrading principles.

Welch was great to work with. Every idea I had, he multiplied by ten. He initially didn't think face-to-face coaching after Topgrading-based assessment was necessary; "Give the guy the report and if he's an A player he'll figure out how to improve," he said. But he let me try it, and he saw A players embracing far more comprehensive Individual Development Plans than they would otherwise and improving more than he expected, so he approved it. I introduced 360s to GE, where I was told, "The 360s are counterculture, because at GE you don't rat on your boss." When assessing and coaching executives, I just did 360s, and Welch was surprised that subordinates opened up to me. I told him, "Managers will learn more and the shareholders will benefit," and Welch approved selected use of 360s.

He asked me what GE could do that other topgrading companies did, and I replied, "Forced rankings, but be careful. They have to be done right or they'll backfire." Welch instituted forced rankings. He had always considered executive coaching a waste, saying "Leopards don't change their spots," but when managers like Tom Brock (a case study in Chapter 10) increased their emotional intelligence and achieved better results, he required all managers to be positive and empowering. Welch fired four executives who made their numbers but even after coaching continued to be autocratic, showing he was dead serious about every leader discarding old autocratic ways.

Though Welch sometimes mandated change, he did so in a way that inspired his many A players. But as he said in *Jack: Straight from the Gut*, political dynamics and personal favoritism can result in managers "gaming the system." Under Welch those games were smoked out every day. His strongest message to topgraders might be just that: Fortify the A player standard in *every* meeting, *every* day, and don't let any manager get away with overrating someone.

## ACNielsen

Nielsen International's CEO topgraded the non-U.S. business of the world's largest marketing firm. I assessed presidents of country organizations, finding mostly C players who were comfortable with slow growth, and who couldn't bring themselves to do what their customers demanded: combine regional reports throughout the world. All but two of the top fifty managers changed jobs; some were promoted or reassigned, but many left voluntarily or were terminated. The topgraded organization achieved record results; CEO Christos Cotsakas was promoted to CEO of Nielsen Worldwide (including the United States) and achieved a superb record. The parent company (Dun & Bradstreet) was subsequently broken into parts, and many A player Nielsen executives departed.

## Dominick's

Dominick DiMatteo had sold his grocery chain, bought it back, and topgraded. His son Jim DiMatteo became CEO and led profitable growth of the company, eventually selling Dominick's with a fifteen-fold gain in its value.

My role was to convince Dominick to promote his son Jim to CEO, add a new president and several senior vice presidents, and roll out topgrading throughout the entire company—all of which he did. Topgrading-based assessments and coaching took place every two years for the senior team. One-fourth of the store managers were deemed chronic B/C players and replaced. Unfortunately, since the company was sold, the topgrading processes have been abandoned, and performance of the company has declined.

## Travelers Express

In the 1990s Travelers Express was a small division of Dial. I saw several C player candidates for president and advised the chairman/CEO of Dial to require the search firm to produce A player candidates. Bob Bohannon was hired, topgraded Travelers Express, and was subsequently promoted to chairman and CEO of the newly formed parent company, VIAD. I Topgrading assessed/coached the top team at Travelers Express, helping to nudge B/Cs out, and did Topgrading Interviews to be sure only As were promoted and hired. Today Travelers Express topgrades on its own, without my involvement. It's a large and very profitable division of VIAD. Topgrading processes continue in full force under Travelers Express CEO Phil Milne, who requires:

- Topgrading Interviews of finalist candidates for selection or promotion.

- Forced rankings in talent meetings, where consensus on As, Bs, and Cs is achieved. The bottom 10 percent are redeployed when they fail to move up to A player status.

- Hard-hitting performance rankings and 360s that fortify the A player standard.

VIAD Chairman Bob Bohannon says, "Topgrading was essential to our success at Travelers Express." During the first few years of topgrading, 40 percent of the managers were deemed B/C players and were replaced, almost always with an A player. In recent years, Milne's focus has been on maintaining the A standard because, as he puts it, "Topgrading can never stop."

## HEB

HEB is a big company you've probably never heard of, but it has $11 billion in revenues and sixty thousand employees. It's been listed as the eleventh largest privately held company in the United States. I began working with CEO Charles Butt in the early 1970s, when this South Texas grocer had $200 million in sales. HEB was soon to be challenged by major grocers, but because it topgraded, it has enjoyed consistent growth in a saturated field.

For two decades I assessed, coached, and screened candidates for all management positions from store manager to COO. I still occasionally

Topgrading Interview a finalist for a very senior position. Dozens of Topgrading training sessions were held over the years.

A lot of topgrading notions were formed at HEB, like the definition of an A player. In the early 1970s I asked, "Why should this store manager, who's weak on most managerial competencies, earn the same salary as a Texas Instruments manager who is strong on most managerial competencies?" Charles Butt agreed he should get the talent he was paying for, and has maintained that A player standard ever since. Morale is measured, and typically it is extremely positive. Unions have tried unsuccessfully to invade the company, but employees have consistently chosen to trust HEB's A player management instead.

---

**"Topgrading has enabled us to remain competitive through hiring and developing A players; identification of A players has been essential to our progress. Brad Smart's guidance over the years has been highly valuable."**
**Charles Butt**

---

Charles Butt's main advice regarding how to maintain the A player standard is:

1. "Hiring and promotion decisions are the hardest work I do. When we rush the decision process, costly mistakes begin to occur."

2. "Attracting and choosing great leaders requires balancing intuitive interviewing and careful reference work."

3. "Internal promotion decisions are just as challenging, and how well they are done adds up to what a company becomes."

## CONCLUSION

Joseph Lister saw the medical establishment slowly accept antiseptics; I've been gratified that topgrading principles have become increasingly accepted. And maybe one day the full utilization of talent through topgrading will be part of the business establishment and even commonplace.

# Six

# OBSTACLES TO TOPGRADING, AND HOW A PLAYERS OVERCOME THEM: A REVIEW OF MAJOR TOPGRADING PRINCIPLES IN PART ONE

*Man is not the creature of circumstances. Circumstances are the creature of man.*

Benjamin Disraeli, 1805–81

Many managers are committed to the idea of employing only highly talented people, but find topgrading challenging. I have asked thousands of senior managers to describe why, and their responses, gleaned from over three decades, show most prevalent psychological and organizational obstacles that managers face in ratcheting up their organization's talent. This chapter briefly presents the major obstacles to topgrading and the best practices to overcome them—approaches that have succeeded in dozens of topgrading engagements in which I have been involved.

Here in the final chapter in Part One, we review the obstacles and solutions to the key topgrading principles covered in Chapters 1 through 5. If you like tests, read the 14 obstacles in quotation marks and see if you can state their answers, the topgrading solutions.

## 1. "I CAN'T GET MY B/C PLAYERS TO HIRE A PLAYERS."

### Solution 1: Topgrade from the top down.

The single biggest deterrent to topgrading is the understandable reality that B/C players rarely hire As and As rarely want to work for B/Cs. If I'm a

C player, why in the world would I hire or promote someone who could get my job? Besides, A players ask too many embarrassing questions, are disruptive, and, in frustration, quit. A players are usually perceptive enough to avoid going to work for Cs, and because they are the most employable, they can afford to be choosey. CEOs make a big mistake attempting to simultaneously topgrade multiple levels in an organization that has B/C players. B/Cs are like reverse magnets to As—they avoid each other.

As you topgrade from the top down, expect your As to get enthusiastic and want to topgrade their organization NOW. They have discovered the magic of Topgrading, and are confident they can assess their organization accurately and then use tandem Topgrading Interviews to screen replacements for underperformers. They don't want to wait until you've topgraded all managers at their level. But if you let them topgrade, B/Cs will want to and they'll botch the job. It's a quandary with a solution.

### Solution 2: Require Your A Players to Make the Topgrading Judgments for Their B/Cs.

Perhaps a B player will retire in two years, so A players can be attracted with a chance for a promotion. Say to B, "I'll make the topgrading judgments because you won't be around to live with the results." Conduct a tandem Topgrading on selection candidates to both assess candidates accurately and let A players see you are an A, committed to choosing As now and promoting an A in eighteen months. And steadily remove the most important responsibilities from the B player, assigning them to the promotable A player.

Suppose you have a couple of B players who seem to have A potentials, but you aren't certain. They are implementing comprehensive Individual Development Plans and have six months to move into the A category or be redeployed. In the meantime, require them to hire As. Talk to recruiters yourself to be sure they don't cull A player candidates (because of "signals" from your B players). Interview finalists yourself. If your B/C players grow and become A players, terrific. If you are sure a B or C player should be replaced, sensibly impose an A player successor.

Here's how to combine solutions 1 and 2: empower A players to topgrade, and you and the A players make all topgrading decisions for B/C players, as they either develop into As or are replaced.

## 2. "WE THINK WE ARE HIRING A PLAYERS, BUT THEY TURN OUT TO BE B/C PLAYERS IN DISGUISE."

**Solution: Perform More Accurate Assessments Using the Topgrading Interview, Preferably in Tandem.**

As Chapters 1 through 5 made clear, frequent mis-hiring is a powerful deterrent to replacing B players, not just C players. It isn't worth the costs and hassles to remove a B player with only a 25 percent chance that the replacement will be an A, and the average cost of a mis-hire is fifteen times base salary. At that rate, the typical hiring manager of $100,000 managers would mis-hire three and waste $4.5 million to hire one A player. With 90 percent As hired using tandem Topgrading Interviews, however, A player managers cull B/Cs, smoothly and quickly building a team of all As.

## 3. "OUR HUMAN RESOURCES PEOPLE ARE OVERWORKED AND UNDERSTAFFED, SO WE DON'T EXACTLY HAVE A PIPELINE OF A PLAYERS GOING THROUGH THE OFFICE."

**Solution: Constantly Recruit Your "Virtual Bench," Your Network of A Players in Your Rolodex, Who Are Ever Available to Join You. And, Require All Your Managers to Constantly Build Their Virtual Bench.**

Don't blame HR if you can't find talent. I've interviewed hundreds of managers who were fired for failing to achieve their numbers, when their excuse was "I wanted to topgrade, but HR didn't find me A player candidates." Curt Clawson could not have pulled Hayes Lemmerz out of Chapter 11 if he hadn't filled most of the top jobs with A players in his Rolodex. Jason Chandler, Regional Director at UBS, turbo-boosted his career by personally recruiting top financial planners on a daily—that's right, *daily*—basis.

## 4. "SEARCH FIRMS JUST DON'T PRODUCE ENOUGH A PLAYER CANDIDATES."

**Solution: Manage the Search Process, Including Search Firms, Much More Thoroughly.**

There is widespread dissatisfaction with search firms these days. Chapter 2 cites original research on searches and Chapter 3 spells out how search firms can be managed effectively and produce A player candidates.

## 5. "I WANT TO RAISE THE PERFORMANCE BAR, BUT ALMOST EVERY TALENTED PERSON I BRING IN FROM THE OUTSIDE IS REJECTED BY THE CURRENT ORGANIZATION CULTURE AND ENDS UP QUITTING."

### Solution: Provide New A Players Air Cover, Protection from Undermining By Existing Personnel.

This is a common problem. A manager realizes her company, unit, or department is far from world class. The low-performance culture is often characterized by lack of accountability, fear of change, minimal innovation, and lots of excuse making. It reinforces itself with an incestuous promote-from-within policy. B/C players chew up and spit out A players, saying, "Gee, too bad, she just didn't fit in here."

It is critical to seek out and employ A players who will help drive the culture-change process with finesse, not a sledgehammer. Those A players must have the competencies, skills, and attitudes to simultaneously earn the respect of the present culture while creating the new, *desired* culture. That's a tall order; A players can be rejected by the old culture unless you provide them protection. Make it clear to the others that these new hires have your full support, monitor that support, reward active supporters, and quickly correct those who plant landmines to destroy the "outsiders."

## 6. "WE CAN'T AFFORD TO HIRE A PLAYERS."

### Solution: Yes, You Can—You Already Pay for *All* A Players.

This was a trick question. Did you get the correct answer? If not, please reread Chapters 1 and 2. A players are available at *all* compensation levels: They are people above the ninetieth percentile of overall talent of all potential candidates at every compensation level. You already are paying for A players, whether or not you get them. That means that a company that is paying its C player marketing director a $90,000 base salary could hire an A player for the same salary. The definition of A player is closed, airtight; you cannot *not* pay for an A player. Is this a semantic game? No! But, what if A players at $90,000 aren't good enough to beat the sophisticated competition with $150,000 marketing directors? You can afford to hire only an A player in your B league or a B player in your competition's A league, but realize that you need an A player to compete in an A league. Figure out a way to afford it, or expect to suffer—hundred-hour workweeks for yourself, burnout in the person you underhire, or failure by the person you hire. At best you'll hire a B with A potentials, perhaps someone short on experience but highly resourceful and on a rapid learning path—and your long hours carrying and developing that manager will eventually pay off.

Given our definition of A player, can you afford to not hire A players? Perhaps, if your competition will guarantee they will *not* topgrade. Don't count on that!

If you still think it might be too costly to topgrade, please use the Topgrading Calculator Matrix. Compare the costs of retaining underperformers versus topgrading. A players all conclude, "We can't afford *not* to topgrade."

## 7. "I DO NOT WANT TO FIRE LOYAL B/C PLAYERS."

### Solution: Redeploy Chronic B/C Players Because, Painful As It Is to Fire Someone, Failing to Do So Is Almost Always More Painful— to the Company, Your Career, and the Underperformer.

B/C players should be given a fair chance (though sometimes brief) to become an A player, with extra training and coaching. If this does not work, it may be wise to narrow the person's job to include only those responsibilities that the person is competent performing, and pay accordingly. A B/C player can be considered one who is overpaid and/or underperforming. By reducing pay and/or improving performance, B/C players can become A players. Obviously a caricature can be made of this; cutting pay across the board is more apt to cause massive departures of A players than conversion of B/Cs to As. People are B/C players when they are mis-hired, mispromoted, or misdeployed within their companies. Not facing *your* mistakes or *your* inherited problems is *your* responsibility. Face it, or maybe someone will conclude that you aren't an A player.

Theoretically, everyone can be an A player. The best organizations ask the question, "In what sort of role (and for what level of pay) can this person be an A player?" Such organizations creatively align individuals' responsibilities to be consistent with their strengths, weaknesses, and interests. Every year since 1980 about fifty thousand companies have failed; they go out of business for many reasons, but deficient talent is almost always a key factor. CEOs tell me all the time that their biggest failure is not moving fast enough to remove long-term, underperforming managers. Just as A players provide an uplifting force to an organization, B/C players can sink the ship. The best way to avoid firing loyal, beloved B/C players is to not hire or promote them over their head and to redeploy them into a position where they can become an A player.

## 8. "OUR PROBLEMS WILL SOON CLEAR UP BECAUSE WE ENGAGED A MANAGEMENT CONSULTING FIRM, AND THEIR REPORT LOOKS GREAT, SO TOPGRADING ISN'T NECESSARY."

### Solution: Topgrade First.

In *Good to Great,* author Jim Collins noted that all eleven newly appointed CEOs of companies they took from good to great first assembled their A teams, *then* launched new strategic initiatives. Great management initiatives combined with a cast of A players can reasonably be expected to increase a company's performance. However, expensive consulting engagements typically fall flat when the company managers lack the talent to drive successful implementation. In chess, great strategy will not prevail if one player has all pawns while the opponent enjoys a board full of royalty. Talent is a necessary ingredient to making management initiatives convert to shareholder value. Indeed, talent is the grand enabler of all management initiatives. I cringe every time I hear about an undertalented company trying to implement process reengineering or some other initiative and push decision-making responsibility down in the organization. Underskilled or undertalented employees are given decision-making authority and end up making bad decisions. Performance inevitably suffers.

In contrast, organizations that topgrade are able to drive improvements in strategy, productivity, innovation, quality, customer service, and speed-to-market. They experience greater success in these areas because they have the most competent employees on whom to rely. Having consistently strong operational performance can be a powerful force in building shareholder value. Of course, other factors such as macroeconomic trends, currency fluctuations, industry changes, and customer preferences can all affect shareholder value as well.

---

**"At the end of the day, you bet on people, not on strategies."**
**Larry Bossidy**

---

I am not saying that talent is the only driver of shareholder value, but that it is a key one—and one of the few that managers can directly control. Ratcheting up the talent level of a company is a lot easier than trying to affect the strength of the U.S. dollar.

The idea behind topgrading is so simple that I am continually shocked that so few companies do it. Far too often, managers at all levels make the costly mistake of trying to "manage their way" to excellence with underperformers on their team. That is truly a losing strategy.

### 9. "WE COULD NEVER ATTRACT A PLAYERS BECAUSE OF OUR LOCATION, INDUSTRY, CURRENT FINANCIAL PROBLEMS, AND SO ON."

**Solution: Pay More in Compensation to Attract the Level of Talent Necessary to Beat the Competition.**

Or if location is a terrible recruitment obstacle, consider moving. Hire A players who are such terrific leaders (like Curt Clawson, in Chapter 5) that they attract As despite undesirable aspects to the job.

The president of a division of Honeywell found that he had to pay senior managers a 25 percent premium to attract them to a small rural town. You pay what you need to pay in order to attract the talent necessary to achieve your goals. Compensation is closely connected to the definitions of the A, B, and C players. No NBA franchise will pay $100 million per year for the next Michael Jordan, because at that salary level, no one is worth it. It is extremely important to determine the right level of pay, but it is equally important to understand the relationship between pay and talent, supply and demand. If you own a football franchise and decide to advertise a job as place kicker for a salary of $15,000, the top 10 percent of talent available (the A players) might include no one, absolutely no one who can consistently kick a forty-yard field goal. All NFL franchise owners have concluded that they need A players available and willing to sign on at a pay level considerably above $15,000 in order to achieve the team goals.

Some managers overcome hiring obstacles by performing the equivalent of a full-court press. They seek to understand and address every individual need of the candidate and convey unrelentingly how enthusiastic the firm is about him, how much "we need you and like you," and so on. Passive hiring managers say, "Let's touch base next week," while the most successful managers never end the recruitment pressure until the person is physically on the job. Even then, they assume that another job offer may be lingering, so they lock in the new hire with continued attention, involvement, and respect.

The Topgrading Interview is especially helpful for identifying the candidate's needs as they relate to the job. What does the candidate really want in her boss? What types of responsibilities does the candidate love to have? What does she dislike? What are her long-term goals? What does she want to learn? Conducting a Topgrading Interview provides the answers to these questions. It helps companies craft "dream jobs" for A players by modifying the job description a bit and increases the likelihood of both attracting and retaining A players, even for unattractive jobs. I Topgrading interviewed a prime candidate for a job with a science-based company. The candidate told me he was about to accept a job elsewhere because my client had tried to sell him on pay, location, and prestige advantages—all of which were almost inconsequential to him. The Topgrading Interview disclosed his strong desire for *variety* of assignments, which another company offered. Fortunately, my client recrafted a job offer to include enough variety to attract the candidate, but it was the Topgrading Interview that disclosed a pattern across courses taken and aspects of jobs he liked or disliked that produced the effective sales pitch.

---

### To "sell" a candidate, use the Topgrading Interview to find out what the person really wants in a job.

---

In the 1990s a lot of companies reluctantly accepted "commuter managers." There was a dearth of talent, and finalist candidates said things like "My spouse has a career, too, and I promised not to move for the next three years," or "I've relocated my family so much I just won't move." But they also said, "I'd be willing to commute." A players usually make commuting work. They fly in Monday, stay through Thursday, and if necessary are on premises Friday or Saturday, or arrange teleconferencing or videoconferencing. Bottom line: Most companies can attract better talent if they are flexible on locations of at least some managers.

### 10. "MY SUBORDINATES TEND TO GIVE 'THUMBS-DOWN' ON A PLAYERS."

**Solution: Don't Let Them Have a Vote. Make the Hiring Decision Yourself.**

Having your subordinates interview a prospective peer of theirs is desirable, almost necessary. A player candidates might insist on it. But don't forget obstacle #1 ("I can't get my B/C players to hire A players."), because a corollary is "A players might not want the competition of other A players." So, get their opinions, but don't give them a vote.

Your job is not to preserve the status quo. Get the A players in, help Bs to rise to the occasion, and remove the untrainable B/C players who drain the energy from your group. If your A players don't want competition, that's tough. Maybe if you changed the compensation system so all are paid bonuses on team performance, A player peers would be more welcome. Always make it clear that hiring A players for your team is not a democracy— it's your responsibility and you will meet it.

### 11. "WE ARE DOWNSIZING AND MY JOB IS ON THE LINE; I NEED SHORT-TERM RESULTS AND DO NOT HAVE TIME TO TOPGRADE."

**Solution: Improve Short-Term Results *by* Topgrading.**

For years I have noticed a dangerous death spiral that can occur when organizations become leaner. Survivors of massive downsizings have more work to do; stress levels increase; the more marketable people, the A players, quit. Managers may not feel that there is time to find A players. A futile mistake is to try to squeeze A player results out of the remaining B and C players. Stress increases even more and drives the best of the remaining talent to quit, causing the death spiral to continue. *Death spiral* may be more than a metaphor; more people seem to have heart attacks and strokes in high-pressure client companies than ones with a less stressful culture, and I wonder if topgrading might have alleviated some pressure and the resulting health problems.

OK, if you are talking about keeping a C player for three more months until your new software is installed, fine. Perhaps that C player is lazy and disruptive, but is an expert in this particular software package. A replacement in midstream could be terribly disruptive. Consider that C player a "temporary A player." Coasting along with B/C players for more than six months, however, is almost never justifiable.

## 12. "I KNOW I SHOULD REDEPLOY A B/C PLAYER, AND I HAVE CONFIDENCE THAT BY USING TANDEM TOPGRADING INTERVIEWS AN A PLAYER WILL BE A REPLACEMENT, BUT I JUST CAN'T PULL THE TRIGGER."

### Solution: Recruit the A Player Replacement Now and Then You'll Find It a Lot Easier to Remove the B/C.

It's amazing how easy it becomes to make a change when an eager, sharp A player is ready and willing to take the job. It's "the devil I know is better than the devil I don't know" syndrome that causes managers to limp along with marginal talent. So get to know an A devil and you'll no longer tolerate the B/C devil.

If you have As in your network, it's easy to talk informally, then talk some more, eventually do a tandem Topgrading, and *know* the replacement will outperform the person replaced. But if the alternative is to sign a contract for a search fee, it's understandable that you might want to give the B/C six months more to move into the A category. It's understandable, but usually regrettable to delay the inevitable.

## 13. "EVEN MY A PLAYERS AREN'T CALIBRATED. THEY DON'T ACCURATELY JUDGE WHO ARE THE As, Bs, AND Cs."

### Solution: Build Corporate Expertise and/or Rely on Topgrading Professionals While Improving Your A Players' Calibration Skills.

Inbred organizations or those in remote locations can have A players who are simply out of touch with the talent marketplace. They don't know how much talent might be available, for how much money, because they haven't experienced much turnover and, when they do, they recruit within the community or stay narrowly within their industry.

In some multilocation organizations like GE, Hillenbrand, MarineMax, and American Heart Association, the CEO and corporate HR people travel to conduct talent meetings. They become calibrated and help those in the field become calibrated. Initially, however, all those organizations relied on topgrading professionals to help them become calibrated.

Individual managers can become better calibrated by casting the recruitment net further, beyond the industry and nearby area, getting information on talent from vendors including recruiters, and volunteering to do tandem Topgrading Interviews in other locations.

## 14. "THE BOARD OF DIRECTORS IS MORE INQUISITIVE ABOUT TALENT, FOLLOWING THE SCANDALS OF THE EARLY 2000s, AND I FEAR THEY WILL RESTRICT MY TOPGRADING EFFORTS."

### Solution: CEO Topgrade and Keep the Board Fully Apprised.

Directors are increasingly held accountable for misdeeds of CEOs, CFOs, and other executives, as they should be. The CEO should welcome board pressure to topgrade, do it, and communicate both processes and conclusions. When boards understand the thoroughness of topgrading processes and the accuracy of assessments, they have more, not less, confidence in the CEO and his team. When a change is required, the CEO should review the Topgrading-based assessment and performance reviews of an executive, progress (or lack of it) implementing an IDP, 360 survey results, and the Topgrading-based assessments of A player replacements. The board can and should ask a lot of questions to be sure topgrading is working. With thorough topgrading processes in place, when more A players produce improved operating results, boards will praise, not restrict, CEO topgrading.

## WILLIAM BRADFORD, AMERICA'S FIRST LEADER, OVERCOMES OBSTACLES TO TOPGRADING

The final case study is almost four hundred years old. America's first great leader, William Bradford, was a topgrader.[36] Before telling his topgrading

---

[36]Bradford D. Smart, "America's First Great Leader: William Bradford, Governor of Plymouth Colony," *The Mayflower Quarterly* 62(1) (1996), pp. 6–19.

story, let me intrigue you with a brief assessment of a man you might not have heard of. William Bradford is one of a handful of leaders in history who was both pure of heart and very successful at changing the world. Ghandi and Lincoln were two others. It is an exclusive club.

Here's his background: Within a year after the *Mayflower* landed at Cape Cod in 1620, William Bradford was elected governor of Plymouth Colony; he was reelected thirty more times. Under his leadership America was truly founded, 150 years before the Revolutionary War. Bradford led his team of A players (Winslow, Brewster, Standish, and others) as he:

- **Established what John Quincy Adams called the world's first true democracy.** The Greeks had slaves. Puritans flooded the New World after the Pilgrims (who weren't technically Puritans) showed families could survive, but the Puritans had a theocracy. Bradford's creation of democracy led the way to our Revolution and the spread of democracy throughout the world.

- **Abandoned socialism for free enterprise.** In 1621 the Pilgrims were near starvation. Their contract with European venture capitalists called for socialism—all Pilgrims would farm and send back almost all the money to Europe to pay off the debt. People weren't motivated. Bradford, in America's first privatization, let each family sell a portion of its goods on the open market after contributing its fair share to the common store. The GNP of Plymouth shot up.

- **Began the first community Thanksgiving.** Bradford's free-enterprise effort permitted the Pilgrims to survive in the New World (otherwise we'd all be speaking Spanish or French), and our holiday of Thanksgiving began with him.

- **Ensured separation of church and state.** Devout but no religious fanatic, Bradford insisted that rule by law, civil law, be separate from religious edict.

One leader, William Bradford, led the Pilgrims to these foundations of our society 150 years before the signing of the Declaration of Independence! For fun let's see how Bradford's topgrading withstood some common obstacles to topgrading listed in this chapter.

- **Misassessment.** Instead of Topgrading assessments, the Pilgrims self-assessed. How's this for a selection test: risk your life fleeing a monarchy, face a horrible Atlantic crossing, survive disease that will wipe out 50 percent of your team in the first year, face a mutiny by some hired hands, risk war with the natives . . . and in your spare time build a town, a government, an entire society. Any takers? The Pilgrims who jumped aboard the *Mayflower* were all Michael Jordans or Lance Armstrongs. Bradford was the best and brightest—the A player most respected to lead this miracle. How rigorous are your assessment methods compared to this?

- **Inadequate recruitment.** Only one hundred Pilgrims and hired hands volunteered and boarded the *Mayflower*. Quality, not quantity, permitted our nation to be founded. The Pilgrims recruited *Mayflower* passengers from among their ranks for more than a year. B and C players were asked to remain in Europe. Do you cop out and accept B players because you don't want to wait a couple more months for an A player?

- **New A players can be chewed up by C players.** To have enough people to launch a colony, the Pilgrims permitted societal rejects to be hired hands onboard the *Mayflower,* and upon arriving in the New World, they threatened mutiny. The hired hands were a mixed lot, including A players, but also some B/C players. The A player Pilgrims were such a strong and capable team that they were sure their reason and pureness of spirit would win over the misfits. They did. Almost all the hired hands embraced democracy, became A player citizens, and helped elect Bradford their leader thirty-one times! How good are you at creating policies that show such contagious belief in the reason and goodness of people?

- **We don't want to fire loyal C players.** Bradford was magistrate, and he banished repeated lawbreakers. Even this generous Christian removed C players who threatened the viability of Plymouth colony. He hung one man (in forty years), a man who killed an Indian. He banished several crooks. Do you banish C players who wound your organization? (Don't try hanging C players.)

- **Topgrading isn't necessary with key initiatives determined by others.** The economic model the Pilgrims began with was trade, but the trading vessel leaked and never made it to the New World. So Bradford and his team altered strategy, introducing farming. Changes in strategy work best with teams of A players. Do you use internal A players to alter strategy?

- **But location makes finding A players difficult.** Finding A players is always possible, but you may have to pay more to get the level of talent you need. The Pilgrims had a burning vision of economic and religious freedom. The recruitment pitfall was "Do you have what it takes to succeed in the most difficult circumstances?" The Pilgrim pay was psychic, spiritual, and practical. It was inspiring going to work each day and building a close-to-perfect society. It's hard to beat a team willing to risk all for a vision. How compelling is your vision?

OK, launching a new society is not exactly like running a business. But the principles are applicable. It is utterly amazing that America succeeded, because it required the first government to be original (democracy) and flexible (handling a changed economic system) and despite all odds (50 percent mortality in the first year) serve as a beacon for the future of the world. The massive and constant problems required Bradford and his A players to make a lot of decisions on the fly, and they had to be right.

In some of the most prophetic words in American history, William Bradford wrote,

> *Thus, out of small beginnings greater things have been produced by His hand and as one small candle may light a thousand, so the light here kindled has shone to many, in some sort to our whole nation.*

Bradford wrote these words to suggest that Plymouth Colony's democracy paved the way for democracy across the New World. Perhaps the quotation can also mean that a small topgraded organization grew to the most powerful in the world. This strange, truly unique topgrading case study of William Bradford sets a very high standard. As William Bradford did, Curt

Clawson, Bill McGill, Fred Rockwood, Cass Wheeler, Jack Welch, and Larry Bossidy know what it is to topgrade with a passion, with a vision that will prevail. Like all these leaders, you can overcome obstacles to topgrading.

## CHAPTER 6 CHECKLIST: DO YOU OVERCOME MAJOR OBSTACLES TO TOPGRADING?

**YES  NO**

☐ ☐ I understand that I should not have any B/C player managers, but until I redeploy them I force them to hire only A players.

☐ ☐ If I'm a B player, I hire As who will help me function as an A player.

☐ ☐ I know the tandem Topgrading Interview is the most powerful tool I can master to achieve a 90 percent or better success rate in hiring.

☐ ☐ I don't blame HR if I can't find A players to hire. I must be in the recruitment business all day, every day, with everyone I meet.

☐ ☐ If external recruiters fail to produce A player candidates, I realize I must manage recruiters better.

☐ ☐ To avoid A players being chewed up and spit out by existing personnel, I provide them political protection or "air cover."

☐ ☐ I realize that if I say, "I can't afford to hire A players," I'm confused. A players exist at all compensation levels. Perhaps I mean that A players at a low salary are not good enough, and in order to attract the level of talent necessary, a higher salary will be required.

☐ ☐ I know that everyone can be an A player in *some* job.

☐ ☐ Although I may hate firing chronic B/C players, it is best for them that they move on to be A players elsewhere, best for the shareholders that As replace B/Cs, and best for my career to have a dream team, not a flawed team.

☐  ☐  I know that all management initiatives are ill fated when carried out by B/C players and have the best chance for success when implemented by a team of A players.

☐  ☐  To attract the level of talent I need to an unattractive location, industry, or company, I'm willing to offer a "battle pay" premium in compensation.

☐  ☐  I minimize "battle pay" in recruitment with a superpositive, superaggressive "full-court press."

☐  ☐  To topgrade, I let my people interview a new member of the team, but I'm the one who decides whether the person will be offered a job.

☐  ☐  When I'm sure a B/C won't become an A, I recruit the A, making it easier to *then* remove the B/C.

☐  ☐  I keep myself calibrated by recruiting broadly, talking to vendors (including recruiters) about talent, and volunteering to conduct tandem Topgrading interviews in other locations.

☐  ☐  As CEO, I keep my board of directors fully apprised of my topgrading processes, and how topgrading changes produce improved business performance.

*Part Two*

# TOPGRADING FOR INDIVIDUALS:

*Developing Yourself and Your Team*

# Seven

# BECOMING AN A PLAYER: HAVING YOUR CAKE AND EATING IT TOO

*The stepladder is gone, and there is not even an implied structure of an industry's rope ladder. It's more like vines, and you bring your own machete. You don't know what you'll be doing next or whether you'll work in a private office or one big amphitheater or out of your house.*
Peter Drucker, *Managing in Times of Great Change*

Everyone can be an A player today in the right job, in the right industry, in the right league. My job in this chapter is to help you figure out how to become an A player in the biggest league you can . . . and want. This chapter begins Part Two, which also will help you master a major leg of the topgrading platform—coaching and developing A players to remain As and B/Cs to become As.

As an A player, you will qualify as the "cream of the crop" or "best of class." Your career options will be magnified. You will be sufficiently on top of your job to develop competencies needed in bigger jobs. Maybe, if you play your cards as I suggest in this chapter, you'll be happy too. And I'll guarantee you, as an A player you will be better equipped than Non-As to judge talent, which will help you topgrade your organization. As a topgrader, you will perform at your peak and earn promotions faster than managers who don't topgrade. Remain an A player and a topgrader, and you will have the best chance of becoming an A player senior manager.

Even if you are not in the career major leagues yet, this chapter will alert you as to how A players in that league look at talent, careers, and developmental planning. After citing commonplace bad advice in career planning, I present you with nine keys to becoming an A player at the highest level. It includes some unconventional wisdom. By enriching and deepening your insights into the entire spectrum of career success principles and patterns, you will simultaneously learn how to be a better topgrader and how to have your cake and eat it too in your career, meaning that you will be successful *and* happy. You will also learn some principles to help you coach and develop your team members.

## HAVE YOUR CAKE AND EAT IT TOO

When managers learn about the thirty-four file cabinets with more than six thousand career dossiers in my basement, a predictable dialogue ensues. They ask what is the fastest route to career success and I respond, "You may sacrifice a lot of happiness to get there." Most senior managers I work with are ambitious and eager to learn secrets of career success. The more discerning executives ask what are the major mistakes high-potential managers make, and there are many to learn from. Thirty-four years ago I paid particular attention to what interviewees said they regretted in life, and I've diligently followed the main principles. The best question is "How can I be both happy[37] and successful?" Bingo!

Since the mid-1980s, my coaching has sought to help high-achieving managers answer what impresses me as the most important question: How can I maximize both my success and happiness? In topgrading terminology:

### How can I become an A player in the biggest league, while maximizing my overall happiness in life?

Some of the happiest people I know are low achievers. They enjoy serenity, rock-solid character, wonderful friends and family, spiritual grounding, respect in the community, a job they like, good health, a few bucks in the bank, and love. You aren't a low achiever. You *need* career success. You are ambitious, or you wouldn't be reading this book. This chapter will help you achieve your maximum potential *and* balance—yes, you can have your cake and eat it too. Perhaps you have been focusing *much* more on how to succeed in business than in life. If so, you have probably bought into a career mythology that won't work.

---

[37]*Happy* means enjoying deep fulfillment in life, not shallow pleasure, and certainly not being happy-go-lucky.

## BAD CAREER-PLANNING ADVICE

"New paradigms" for career success are popping up all over, but in most respects they are not new. The same old post–World War II career-development principles are dressed up in words such as *virtual, global,* and *temporary.* The baby boomers bought into the same career myths as their Depression era parents, merely "tweaking" the paradigm. Generation Xers and Yers are different in some respects. Many don't trust marriage (their parents split up) or big companies (Dad was downsized out of one company and right-sized out of another), and they want to be high tech entrepreneurs (yes, high tech has continuing appeal, even after the tech bubble burst and left many jobless). Some are career "free agents" in careers they control; many are still like their predecessors—career slaves.

The "new paradigms" for career success are based on compelling statistics. You have heard it all. For example:

- Only sixteen of the one hundred U.S. companies with the most revenue in the year 1900 survived until the end of that century.

- Manufacturing jobs have dropped from 73 percent in 1970 to 9 percent today.

- A Christmas card that sings "Jingle Bells" today contains a chip with more computer power than existed in the entire world in 1960.

With globalization, national boundaries disintegrate, with profound career implications. Lean manufacturing is here for the foreseeable future, outsourcing overseas is growing steadily, and contract employees/managers appear to be the wave of the future. There will be more career free agents in the future, experiencing a series of short-term employment relationships, without career-long job security. Intel's Andy Grove writes *Only the Paranoid Survive,* and he's right. No business, no manager, can rest comfortably for a second because the velocity of change is increasing. In certain industries, some companies pump out an average of two new product innovations per day. How can old career-success principles be applied today? Simple—the old, and fundamentally *flawed* principles have simply been repackaged and continue to mislead people the way they misled our parents' generation!

## THE BAD CAREER-PLANNING ADVICE

Here's the bad career-planning advice:

1. *Work harder.* It's fine to talk about "balance," but in this increasingly competitive, globalized marketplace, bad advice #1 encourages you to focus almost totally on your career. After all, while you're attending a concert or participating in community service, your peer might be running a spreadsheet that will earn her a promotion you want. Downsizing and outsourcing are here to stay, so do the work of two people and be happy you have a job. If you aren't willing to work seventy hours per week, someone else will. Delay gratification. Sacrifice balance in life now so that you and your family will later reap the rewards of your rising as high as you can. If you don't, you might be rightsized out of your job. Enjoy your vacation!

2. *Live a little beyond your means.* Spend money, because that's the American way! Social Security will dry up, but retirement will be paid for through your 401(k), profit sharing, IRA, and stock options. You work hard, so spend some dough. All Americans have big debts! Besides, a nicer abode, cars, and clothes will enhance your business image, and your career marketability. Living in a classy neighborhood can open doors. If working so hard has caused some problems at home, purchase some domestic harmony. ("Honey, I'll be traveling more, so I want you to travel in luxury—look at your new Beemer in the driveway!")

3. *Don't pass up a job opportunity people say you can't refuse.* A really big jump in income and responsibility can put you in that bigger league. So what if your skills aren't fully there or the job is fraught with major risks? So what if the relocation will disrupt your family? You're resourceful, you'll learn. Do it! Go for it! When people say you can't refuse the offer, they mean, "Don't make excuses. Don't be a wimp."

4. *In job interviews, hide negatives.* With job security a thing of the past, job mobility is in. You will be interviewed more, because you'll change jobs more often. Don't blow it with a naive "come clean" attitude. Get the job offer and worry about doing the job later. You're

more talented than some people who are concealing their shortcomings, so why shoot yourself in the foot?

5. *Develop your strengths to the max, and don't waste time trying to fix your shortcomings.* Bad advice #5 might seem to defy logic, but it assumes your success thus far has come from those strengths, so put all your developmental time and energy into maximizing them. What could be illogical about that? And, face it, you're not going to change your weaknesses. Leopards don't change their spots. People don't really change. Old dogs don't learn many new tricks.

6. *Let your spouse or hired surrogate (teacher, babysitter, coworker, etc.) raise your kids.* Seriously! Sure, bond with your kids and by all means take them to McDonald's Saturday morning and occasionally attend one of their activities. But totally devoted dads and moms are the B and C players at work. They put family first, career second, which makes it easy to blow right on by them. You love your kids, right? Of course, so give them some quality time now and then and devote 90 percent of your energy to career success. That will give the kids the financial resources for expensive activities, and, most important, they'll see you as a great role model—hardworking, honest, persevering, resourceful, and skillful at persuading and impressing people.

Many high achievers continue embracing the paradigm underlying these myths. So, they work harder, grasp at higher brass rings, sacrifice more for the future, and think "some day the pain will be gone, the fear will seep away, and my insecurities and inner demons will no longer run my life." Good luck. Most senior managers lie awake at night, listening to their heartbeat: *thump-thump, thump-thump.* Worrying. Worrying about their performance, about company politics. About that goddamn bar being raised. About balance. Don't tell yourself, "Screw balance. I'm in a survival mode."

A players have a much better chance than B and C players of achieving balance and happiness. After all, A players are the top 10 percent available for their job—the best and the brightest, the cream of the crop. They can *afford* to get their life in balance. But plenty of A players have screwed up their lives; they suffer sleepless nights worrying about how to perform the best now, so that they can get an even better job. Trouble is, they fritter away their golden opportunity to have their cake and eat it too. A players at least have more power to get control of their lives *and* be successful. Here's how:

## NINE KEYS TO BECOMING A HAPPY A PLAYER AT THE HIGHEST LEVEL

### 1. Perform a Periodic Life Balance Review, and Focus on Becoming "Good Enough" in All Eight Critical Life Dimensions

How are you doing on all the dimensions of life you consider essential? Score yourself on the Life Balance Scorecard in Figure 7.1. Hundreds of managers have said this short exercise changed their life. So, I'll explain it in detail.

To introduce the Life Balance Scorecard, let's return to one of the new ideas in this edition of *Topgrading,* as defined in Chapter 3:

---

**Resourcefulness is the most important competency.**

---

Resourcefulness was described as a megacompetency, a composite that is demonstrated in passionately figuring out how to get around, through, under, and over barriers to success. It's what A players live for, the thrill of figuring things out.

What? Aren't the topgrading competencies (Hiring A Players, Coaching, Redeploying B/C Players) the most important? Yes and no.

Resourceful A players learn topgrading and quickly figure out how to make the tools effective. C players lack resourcefulness and generally can't figure out how to topgrade, how to overcome obstacles like the fact that A players rarely will work for C players. There are exceptions. A few C players over the years have acknowledged their C player status and managed to topgrade, promising their A player recruits a fun, nonpolitical team experience . . . and it has worked, even though the hiring executive otherwise lacked resourcefulness. But generally A players stand out as extremely resourceful and persistent topgraders.

My daughter (Dr. Kate Mursau) and I wrote *CAN-DO KIDS: How to Raise Resourceful, Happy Children* (AMACOM, 2005), a book that has involved our studying who are the happiest, most fulfilled people. We concluded,

**The happiest people are those who apply resourcefulness across all the life dimensions they consider important.**

We found extremely happy people in all walks of life—teachers, small business owners, professors, and, yes, some CEOs too. These truly fulfilled, happy people recognize when some dimension of their life is out of kilter, which happens in all lives. It's that simple, but it's not simple, because so many people are resourceful in only *some* life dimensions and incredibly lacking in resourcefulness in others. The two thousand unhappy and two thousand "sort of, sporadically happy" businesspeople I've studied have been incredibly resourceful in pursuing Career Success and . . . well, that's about it. Oh, many gave something back to the community, but too often running a fundraiser is just another part of the career success plan. Ditto for recreation—golf is for business relationship building.

How good are you at utilizing your resourcefulness across all important parts of your life? Please complete the Life Balance Scorecard in Figure 7.1. The particular set of dimensions in Figure 7.1 is pretty common, but may not be the perfect set for you. You might have a burning need for physical adventure, power, or daily freedom to do what you want. Add or delete

## Figure 7.1
## LIFE BALANCE SCORECARD

| | *Good Enough* | *Not Good Enough* | *Critical Life Dimensions* |
|---|---|---|---|
| 1. | ☐ | ☐ | Career Success |
| 2. | ☐ | ☐ | Wellness |
| 3. | ☐ | ☐ | Family (and Other Relationships) |
| 4. | ☐ | ☐ | Pleasure (Recreation, Hobbies) |
| 5. | ☐ | ☐ | Spiritual Grounding |
| 6. | ☐ | ☐ | Financial Independence |
| 7. | ☐ | ☐ | Giving Something Back |
| 8. | ☐ | ☐ | Being Creative |

dimensions and then simply check "Good Enough" or "Not Good Enough." Most executives decide they want to keep Career Success first, but improve in two dimensions: Family and Pleasure. They want to have more discretionary time for pleasure (fishing, attending sports events, or whatever) because emphasizing Career Success is exhausting, and devoting more time to Family is a difficult responsibility. Putting Pleasure higher in priority makes it worth it (they say) to be so conscientious in Career Success and Family.

You may not feel the need for Giving Something Back. Then eliminate it from the list. But where there is a deep, soul-wrenching ache that says your Family (and Other Relationships) (#3) are Not Good Enough, you know you'd better adjust your life, or you won't truly be happy. Estimate what it will take—converting a few minutes per week one-on-one with each child to an hour? Perhaps four (rather than two) hours of quality time per week with your spouse/significant other?

Score yourself, right now, and be honest. Then formulate a plan to adjust your life to achieve Good Enough in all eight Critical Life Dimensions. Do that and you will embody the one most important "truth" lurking in the thirty-four file cabinets of client reports in my basement. Hundreds of senior managers, successful in their careers, have told me in various ways that they would give anything, anything, to be able to wind the clock back and have another chance to achieve better balance.

Completing the Life Balance Scorecard is just a first step. Self-awareness usually is. You can rate yourself Good Enough on five dimensions but Not Good Enough on #2 (Wellness) and #3 (Family) and be destined for a not very happy life. If you think the Bad Career-Planning Advice earlier in this chapter is good advice, not myth, you might simply follow the same path, put career success *way* above the other seven, and end up unfulfilled, with an impressive title and half of an impressive bank account (after a divorce).

The Life Balance Scorecard is an amazingly quick exercise. It takes only ten minutes. Score yourself, and if two dimensions are weak, give a rough estimate of the adjusted time allocation necessary to achieve *all* Good Enoughs in a year. If someone put a gun to your head and said you absolutely must figure out how to achieve all eight Good Enoughs within a year, you could do it, because you're resourceful, right? In a very real way destiny *has* put a gun to your head. The result of this exercise could be a major reallocation of time and energy. It could incur risk, such as crafting a major career change, throttling back your lifestyle, spending more quality time with your spouse, exercising half an hour per day—any one change could be major. Don't bite off more than you can chew.

Will eight Good Enoughs make you happy? For most high-achieving, ambitious managers, yes. That is the clearest, simplest operational path to happiness I know. Eliminating the Not Good Enoughs enabled thousands of executives I've interviewed to improve their overall happiness level.

Having been fascinated with resourcefulness for years, I love saying, toward the end of a Topgrading Interview, "You have been highly resourceful in your career. Are there any ways *other* than in your career you have been very resourceful?" The happiest managers have, on their own, figured out their Life Balance Scorecard and in their own way figured out how to achieve all Good Enoughs. One man, early in his career, chose running a small business over big business, because he figured that would enable him to take a lot of time with his kids, and avoid disrupting the family with relocations; he has taken three months of vacation time for years, and allocates enough time for a wide variety of community and recreational interests. "I think I could have been a pretty good CEO," he noted, "but I wouldn't have been as happy." All these smart Life Balancers recognize that

### Maximizing happiness necessitates compromises in life dimensions.

So, they use resourcefulness to constantly make adjustments, tweaking their plans, figuring out how to achieve more Good Enoughs.

After the terrorist acts of 9/11 a lot of people have reassessed their lives, pursuing their own version of the Life Balance Scorecard and readjusting their priorities. Many business executives have left Career Success at the top of their list of Critical Life Dimensions, but they have used a lot more resourcefulness to elevate involvement in Family (and Other Relationships), and they are determined to live a fuller, more meaningful life—to have their cake and eat it too.

### My best career advice is to set overall happiness as the goal and use your resourcefulness to achieve it. Measure all

**your Life Dimensions and work to make all Good Enough
every year. It's OK to list Career Success first, as long as you
achieve balance that maximizes your happiness.**

---

## 2. PERFORM A PERIODIC PERSONAL CAREER REVIEW

There are major talent dislocations in which mediocre talent skyrockets in hot industries and superb talent languishes in stagnant industries. There are midmanagers I know who are A players at $100,000 per year in manufacturing industries on the decline, though they could become financial planners and soon earn 50 percent more money. They would still qualify as A players in that higher-paying league. Only about one-third of the thousands of managers I have interviewed in-depth had a good handle on how to manage their career—knowing their strengths and weak points and how they might proactively take advantage of career marketplace trends. Two-thirds focused on the job at hand and maybe the next promotion, but were in the dark about what to do to maximize attractive job options over time, what industries to join, and what companies to pursue.

It's all about supply and demand, and your career review should ask, "Where can my competencies achieve the biggest bucks in the foreseeable future?" You shouldn't necessarily go after the biggest bucks, but you should constantly inform yourself about how the marketplace trends are valuing what you have to offer.

People finish school, take the best job offer, and stay in that function, that company, that industry, too long. By the time they realize it, the demand for their skills has declined. "Downsizing can't happen to me" or "Outsourcing overseas won't happen in this industry" . . . until it happens. Some industries (automotive, financial services, and defense, for example) are highly cyclical. I saw Gulf War generals thanking General Electric engineers for having designed twelve of thirteen jet engines used in the war. Despite concerns about dust and sand, the engines worked superbly. After watching a general's appreciative speech, I returned to a conference room where plans were being made to lay off seven thousand talented engineers. The defense industry tanked until the 9/11 attacks began a new war, one on terrorism. You owe it to yourself to keep your antennae tuned to those forces that will impact your career options, your marketability. Not many defense engineers could foresee 9/11, but all could have understood the cyclical nature of their industry.

Suppose you are division controller and want to become general manager in five years. It's time for a quick Personal Career Review. Create your own, using this model:

## PERSONAL CAREER REVIEW

- What must I do to become marketable as an A player candidate for general manager?

- Is this the industry for me to stay in? Is it growing? Does it generally reward technical skills (software engineering) I lack?

- If this industry is the right one, is this the right company for me? Can I rise in it? Will it grow profitably?

- What is the competition like for general manager? What will it be like in five years? What skills (like international experience) do I lack that will be essential as the industry globalizes? Is my company developing general managers, or is it apt to recruit general managers from premier companies?

- What are future A player candidates for general manager doing developmentally?

- How do I stack up now, and how will I stack up five years from now, on all competencies necessary to be an A player candidate for general manager?

How do you get career supply-and-demand information? Use your resourcefulness.

- Develop a network of at least ten people who are in the know, people on top of industry and job trends. Some should also be people who can kick open doors to help you get the ideal job.

- Read, read, read. Read your trade publications and general business magazines such as *Forbes, Fortune, Business Week, The Econ-*

*omist,* and *The Wall Street Journal.* Use the Internet for tons of career information.

- Attend at least two seminars per year for one to three days each, plus a trade show or two. While learning technical or management skills, or industry trends, you can expand your professional network. At the same time you can be recruiting (remember Chapter 3).

- Stay in touch with at least five of the highest-powered headhunters who will talk to you. There is a clear pecking order— senior partners at top executive search firms don't have time for $60,000-per-year salespeople. Pump your headhunter associates not just for job possibilities, but for feedback: how strong is your résumé, what are your career strengths and shortcomings, what do you need to do so they can market you best?

A Personal Career Review conducted annually is a reality check. It nudges you to keep abreast of career-relevant trends, including supply and demand, through reading and by checking with your network. The Personal Career Review can and should lead to action plans, so that you continue feeling on track when you conduct your next review, next year.

## 3. Live Below Your Means

What? Is #3 like "Brush your teeth regularly"? I'm serious, dead serious. Financial freedom is central to becoming an A player at the highest level and being happy.

In our consumer-driven society, we spend like mad. Other nations save in the double digits, but our savings rate is low single-digit. Rising managers spend like mad to show off, and to buy off the neglected spouse or significant other. Most rising managers are strapped for dough, and a career setback would be catastrophic, causing a significant decline in lifestyle. This is exactly what happened to thousands of dot com millionaires when the tech bubble burst in the late 1990s. That sort of personal financial mismanagement leads to regrettable career choices.

At least 10 percent of high-achieving managers I have worked with have caused themselves big problems because of financial desperation. They take jobs in which they are unlikely to succeed, because they "have to have the income." They get caught up in a lifestyle that is hard to break out of. What would the neighbors think if they took a slightly lesser job in order to move into a higher-growth industry, or spent more time with the family, or got healthy, or . . . got a life? They hardly know the neighbors, yet a frenetic compulsion to be successful is driven by a need for public show. A lot of WorldCom, Enron, and Wall Street crooks lived *way* beyond their means, no doubt magnifying their greed and dishonesty.

A Fortune 500 executive, Bruce, lived below his means, and it enabled him to have a more successful career than peers who didn't. When his company was bought out, Bruce and others received lump-sum severances. Most of Bruce's peers jumped at the first decent job offer, but Bruce took nine months to make a job choice. He performed due diligence on a lot of job possibilities. He was slower than his peers to get the next job, but years later he is the most successful and happy. He had his cake and ate it too. His peers were stretched financially and grasped for the highest-paying jobs fast, and most have changed jobs three times since. They never screened jobs well, because they bought Bad Advice #2 (live a little beyond your means) and #3 (don't pass up a job opportunity people say you can't refuse). They are chronic B players if not worse, whereas Bruce can "afford" to be an A player.

Bruce's example is somewhat unusual but not rare. Many A players live below their means but don't advertise it. They quietly build their nest egg and relish their growing financial freedom. Bruce became financially independent by forty years of age. His peers' stories are commonplace: "I guess I didn't perform due diligence on the next job" is a tune I hear every week. How can a smart manager get into such a hopeless job? "I had to—my expenses were high and that was the only job offer I could live with." That is saying, "I'm not smart enough to get my finances in order, so I destine myself to be a B or C player." You can "afford" to be an A player. Anyone can.

A measure of financial independence permits quitting jobs on principle. A division VP told me he "had to go along with cooking the books" for a couple of years because "I had no other job choice." If the conflicted manager had two years' savings, he could have easily quit rather than risk going to jail! Can you "afford" to be a person of high integrity?

How much should you save? Several hundred happy A players gave me a common rule of thumb:

---

**Save 25 percent of pretax income for the first twenty years
of full-time work. Then live more luxuriously without saving,
and watch your nest egg continue to grow.**

---

For example, picture a husband and wife, both managers at fast-food stores. The median income in the United States is about $45,000 and they each earn $50,000, for a total of $100,000. For simplicity, let's say their incomes remain constant enough to offset inflation. Suppose they each save $12,500 (for a total of $25,000), invest conservatively in their 401(k)s, and put the rest in exchange traded funds (ETFs, which have rock bottom expenses, boast terrific tax efficiency, and are traded like stocks). Suppose they both started saving at twenty years of age. Let's run the numbers for an 8 percent return.

### Saving $25,000 per Year

| Age | Savings at 8% ROI |
|---|---|
| 20 (start saving) | $0 |
| 30 | $362,000 |
| 40 | $1.1 million* |

At age 40 they have over $1 million saved and can let it grow without additional savings from their salaries. Their nest egg will double every 9 years, totaling $2.2 million when they are 49 years of age, $4.4 million at 58, and $8.8 million if they don't touch it until they are 67. Suppose they stopped saving the 25 percent when they were 40, so suddenly their disposable income shot up. By living lean for the first 20 years of saving, they now can spend a lot while their nest egg grows and grows. Most of their friends who try to start saving at 40 will never catch up.

---

**"The most powerful force in the universe is the
power of compounding."
Albert Einstein**

---

* Thanks to Susan Schildt, Lincoln Financial Advisors, for providing this scenario.

Most executives don't save early, and by age 45 discover the magic of compounding and realize it's too late to let the money earn money for 40 years or even 30 years. So they ratchet up their ambition, figuring financial independence will only be possible with a much higher income in their last decade of working. They forget balance and become certifiable, card-carrying members of the rat race . . . for the rest of their lives. As bad as that common scenario sounds, the worst part is the frustration, marital conflict, and fear that result from living on the financial edge. Our savers managing the fast-food stores had money for a rainy day, even after a year. After five years they had the savings to quit working and go to college, relocate to Santa Fe, or pay for an expensive medical procedure not covered by company benefits. If fire destroys their house, insurance won't cover everything, but they can tap savings and bounce back just fine.

The career benefits of living below one's means, and saving for financial independence, are:

- Ease in maintaining high integrity in your career. (There's less temptation to cut ethical corners and rationalization.)

- Flexibility in making job changes. (It's easier to walk away from highly stressful jobs.)

- Confidence in seeking and accepting jobs where you can be an A player and grow more. (You can afford to look longer and scrutinize jobs more thoroughly.)

- Quiet satisfaction in knowing you are doing something important to win the game of life, to have your cake and eat it too.

There is only one disadvantage: you can't show off as much, materially, for a few years. You can show off after that and be financially independent, however. This is the deal: you get more integrity, flexibility, confidence, quiet satisfaction, and growth opportunities in exchange for less show for a few years. That's a terrific deal, for all except those who are deeply insecure.

## 4. Only Accept Jobs Where You Will be an A Player

Turn down (almost all) those opportunities people say you simply can't refuse. I hear the excuse for failure all the time—"It was an opportunity I couldn't refuse." Finish the sentence with "so I took the job, failed because I was a C player in it, and I later regretted my decision."

The "can't refuse" rationale typically means there was a big jump in money and title. As long as the Life Balance Scorecard registers Good Enough in all dimensions, as long as your Personal Career Review questions are satisfactorily answered, and as long as you have the competencies to be an A player in the opportunity, fine, consider the job move. Perform exhaustive due diligence on the job—what challenges you'll encounter, your resources to fix things, and exactly what are the accountabilities you must achieve to earn your first year's bonus. Talk to prospective peers about the organization culture, the boss, and the finances in the company. Talk to people who have left the company too.

A bad job choice is an indication of bad judgment. You shouldn't blame the hiring company if you accept a job and you turn out to be a B or even a C player. It's your life, your responsibility. Trouble is, poorly-thought-out job moves tend to feed on themselves. Your compensation jumps, you buy a bigger house, and you quickly get accustomed to that country club. It's hard to admit failure and go back, and it's very hard if your spouse went along with a major relocation largely because of the income "bribe." So, as the bullet nears your head, you talk to your search network: "You gotta get me a job with $150K base, minimum!" Struggling to *not* get fired becomes a way of life. In that state of desperation, the Life Balance Scorecard becomes a joke. Forget family, forget working out, forget getting a life!

There is comfort and personal security in accepting bigger jobs only when you are sure that you will be an A player, among the top 10 percent of people available for the bucks you'll earn. Having personal security does not mean avoiding career risks. Becoming an entrepreneur, starting a company, is a career home run for a lot of folks. In my experience, successful entrepreneurs are very confident, but they are insecure overachievers with something to prove: they are highly motivated and very resourceful. They may stumble once or twice, but they figure out what to learn, they adapt, and then they succeed. They know they are or will be A players in the league they seek to play in. Their problem frequently is recognizing when their company has outgrown their skills, when they need professional management. But that's a different story. Here's my point: Accept jobs where you will be an A player, and that does not mean being highly conservative. Seizing opportunities on the fly can be damned foolish—take calculated risks, ones well within the scope of your A player talents.

## 5. Work on Overcoming Your Weak Points More Than on Maximizing Your Strengths

That's heresy. In the career section of every bookstore the "ten guaranteed success secrets" books say to forget working on your shortcomings. It's a waste of time and effort. Recognize the competencies that got you to your present level, and build on them. If you're a discus thrower, work on discus throwing and forget trying to be a sprinter. Square peg, avoid the round holes. Sound logical? It is, for individual contributors, who early in their careers have no hire or fire authority. It is *not,* for anyone in management.

Career individual contributors such as tax attorneys, compensation analysts, and medical researchers have technical expertise to develop throughout their careers. Leadership is not a high priority. They need to work on being organized, showing initiative, and broadening their experience in their specialty. For those who will remain individual contributors, learning how to hire A players would be a waste of time, so they should continue maximizing their strengths. For them, this career myth isn't a myth at all.

For those pursuing management, however, the story is different. From first-level supervisor to CEO, the game is totally changed. You still need your strongest assets—brilliant creativity, fabulous sales ability, or whatever—but the limiting factors in your career will be your serious shortcomings.

Please glance through Appendix G, a list of fifty generic management competencies. You tell me on which of these fifty competencies you can, as a manager at any level, afford to be Very Poor. None? How about Poor? None again? How about Only Fair? OK, you might be promoted and succeed, despite being Only Fair in Education (take some classes), First Impression (your bosses can buff you up), Communications—Oral (get a coach), Communications—Written (get a good assistant), or Selecting A Players (read this book). But, if you are Very Poor, even in these competencies that can be "easily" compensated for, you may have an Achilles' heel, a fatal flaw, a potential career derailer.

At General Electric, Chairman Jack Welch shocked and impressed the world when he rolled out a simple model showing why superperformers might be fired for being Poor or Very Poor on a few competencies.

## GE Model

### Make Your Numbers

|  |  | No | Yes |
|---|---|---|---|
| Exhibit GE Values | Yes | Yes/No | Yes/Yes |
|  | No | No/No | No/Yes |

Welch said if you both achieve your annual performance numbers *and* you exhibit the positive, empowering GE values, you stay. Miss on both, you go. Miss the numbers but show the values, or make the numbers and not show GE values, and you get a second chance. My coaching work with GE executives helped show Welch that if autocratic number achievers learned to positively lead teams, the operating results would be even better, in some cases dramatically better. Some executives getting second chances succeeded. After some second chances failed, however, Welch rolled out this simple model and fired chronic values violators. Arrogant, condescending managers destroy teamwork, stifle good ideas, and drive away A players. They fail to optimize shareholder value. So, the bullet catches them. Please note that one of the most valuable corporations in the world got that way in part by firing managers who were Very Good or Excellent on dozens of "hard, objective" competencies, but were Only Fair or Poor on a handful of "soft" competencies, the emotional intelligence competencies.

No A player in management can be awful on *any* of the fifty competencies. So, no matter how strong your strengths, working on developing your Very Poor, Poor, and Only Fair competencies so they are at least Good is time well spent.

---

**High-potential managers can better advance their careers by devoting personal development time to fixing their weak points than making strengths even stronger.**

---

Chapter 8 is devoted to exactly how you can improve in various competencies to fix your weaknesses. Chapters 9 and 10 (on Coaching) address when people can change, and when not, and how coaching can help. For now, I hope you can understand why all of those publications saying, "Ignore your shortcomings," are wrong, except for niche players, individual contributors, or fringe specialists. For managers, my advice is:

---

## Fix your Very Poor and Poor competencies, or get out of management.

---

## 6. Develop A Player Competencies Before You Need Them

If you have fatal flaws, key #5 says fix them, and forget key #6 until you do. But if you have no career derailers, key #6 becomes a high priority. Just because you recently accepted a promotion and you're sure you're an A player, don't be self-satisfied for a second. If your company is growing and you stop growing, C player status is fast approaching. Here's why: If your company doubles in revenues, your salary will automatically grow from, say, $100K to $150K. It's inevitable, whether or not you've earned the increases. As the company grows, pretty soon you'll need to hire managers at $100K, so obviously your salary can't stay at $100,000. We all like Human Resources departments that perform salary surveys, because they keep us "current." A bigger company requires that you get paid more. Heh, heh. But, if you were an A player at $100K and haven't grown enough, you could easily be a B or C player at $150K. Oops. Companies outgrow some people's talents. So:

---

## Stay in the personal development business forever.

---

If financial acumen is an essential competency to move to the next level, don't count on getting the job and then learning it. Take the courses and then offer yourself as a better candidate because you already meet the job specs. If understanding Asian/Pacific cultures is an increasingly important competency in a global company, read about those cultures. Volunteer for a special project that will take you to Singapore. Take your vacation in

Thailand and meet businesspeople there. Talk to managers who have relocated to that region, to learn what they consider important to know. Attend lectures on the Asia/Pacific region. Then let your bosses know you have prepared yourself to succeed in that first international job.

Such resourcefulness is one mark of an A player. A players at $50,000 base salary just express that career development initiative differently from someone at $500,000. If you don't have any fatal flaws, use developmental time to acquire competencies early, not late.

## 7. In Job Interviews, Reveal Negatives

More and more companies are topgrading, and they thoroughly reference check prospective hirees. You may not be able to hide negatives, even if you want to.

You're an A player now, have your life in balance, and need only consider offers for jobs where you can be pretty sure you will be an A player—in a bigger league. So, why would you deceive a prospective employer? The commonplace answer is that books, search firms, outplacement firms, and former employers all make it "convenient" to conceal your negatives. Your own greed and unbridled ambition could be contributors too.

Publishers for years have tried to persuade me to write a book on how to pass the Topgrading Interview: *How to BS Your Way into a Much Bigger Job: The Brad Smart* (BS, get it?) *Method.* Go to the career section of any bookstore and 95 percent of the books imply the advantages in hyping positives, while concealing negatives. There are dozens of such books, but not one I've seen until *Topgrading* advises getting a job in which you will qualify among the top 10 percent. They're all about getting more, moving higher, regardless of the consequences.

People are changing jobs more often, so they go through more selection interviews, which are the defining moments of job choice, the vehicles for communicating truth or fiction about one's self. More interviews, more deception, more lies. It becomes easier to omit that failed three-month job, and as long as no Topgrading Interview uncovers it, why disclose that little blip in career judgment?

Some headhunters believe that if you reveal your weaknesses, they might be criticized for not producing flawless candidates. Only the most ethical search executives (and there are many) would press you to reveal your full job history, warts and all. There are also many ethical outplacement firms but, frankly, some less ethical firms reward "moving inventory," not "helping people become A players." Ordinarily honest candidates become "packaged" with résumés that hide negatives and hype accomplishments, with references persuaded to be kind, with role plays that teach how to avoid disclosing failures.

So, there you have it, a massive societal imperative that creates too many miserable C players. A greedy, materialistic society induces people to live beyond their means, to accept jobs where they fail. Books and outplacement counselors reinforce deception, former employers help conceal negatives (for fear of lawsuits), and job failures occur—half the time or more. Note that search and outplacement firms benefit from that revolving door, that 75 percent failure rate for outside hires. It's a nasty, painful death spiral.

You can break the cycle by "just saying no" to deception. Put your best foot forward, but reveal your shortcomings. Be positive, but 100 percent honest in job interviews. Accept job offers only when you anticipate being an A player—and a happy one. Don't let search or outplacement firms twist your arm into accepting the wrong job or hiding negatives. Your refreshing honesty will help you get job offers, and your integrity will become a towering competency, magnifying your career success. We topgrading professionals, when conducting Topgrading Interviews on selection candidates, have a high level of confidence in A players who readily reveal their mistakes, failures, and weaker points. They are eager for thorough reference checking to be done because they want the hiring company to know them, warts and all. Their perspective is "I won't accept an offer unless I'm confident I'll be an A player, and I want you to offer me a job only if you know me well and are sure I'll succeed."

"Hmmm," you say, "but if 97 percent of companies don't topgrade, don't use Topgrading, and put candidates through short, shallow, 'tell me about yourself' interviews, how can an A player candidate get the facts of his strengths into interviews?" Good question. When asked something irrelevant like "What are your hobbies?" say, "Actually, I don't have much time for them, because in exceeding all three key goals last year, I was working pretty hard. Would you like to hear how I did it?" Here's another idea: complete the Self-Administered Topgrading Interview Guide and hand it to interviewers, in advance of interviews, when possible. Email interviewers saying, "Attached is a complete summary of my career, and it's unusual for it shows details of not only successes, accomplishments, and strengths, but my failures, mistakes, and weak points as well." A players report that interviewers are very impressed, and say that this approach is honest and confident and shows a willingness to put faith in the interviewers.

## 8. Question Whether Big-Company Life Is for You

A life spent working in big companies these days is too often no life at all. Despite the media attention to "family-friendly" companies, it is difficult for managers in them to achieve balance, to have their cake and eat it too. Managers work sixty to seventy hours per week, not including time for commuting, business traveling (getting there and back), general business reading, or casually pecking away at the computer. The pace is rapid, and it continues to accelerate. Change is on the fly, and that's good; companies are adapting and flexing, but stress is high. Reorganizations are nonstop. A client executive told me, "The only reason we don't reorganize more often is we're too disorganized." New structures. New people. Team dynamics change. Organizational Darwinism is at work; less effort or less dedication won't cut it, unless the competitors suddenly go lax, which is not very likely.

Are there jobs where people have it "made"—moderate stretch jobs where success is almost a given, where spurts of frenetic activity are occasional, not a way of life? Sure. If you are CEO of a niche company with very high barriers to entry, you might be able to build a team of A players and perhaps spend your life as you want. An alternative for some might be to get out of management and go back to being an individual performer, be a consultant rather than office head, a key account sales representative rather than VP sales. These are versions of #4 (Only Accept Jobs Where You Will Be an A Player). That's smart, because it will free you to address the other six legs on your life platform. Cutting back may be best for balance and happiness, but most high achievers want more.

The single biggest decision affecting the success–happiness ratio, for many managers, is whether to work in large companies or smaller firms. As I edited these paragraphs I got a call from a man (I'll call him Ron) who I believe could become chairman of his Fortune 500 company someday, if he could just put up with the company politics. He couldn't force himself to get along with two consecutive bosses he didn't respect. The second boss fired Ron, who four months later called to tell me he is thrilled to be joining a smaller ($350 million) firm, with a 5 percent equity stake. This is not a lose/lose outcome, but win/win. The big company got outstanding results from Ron for ten years, but no longer could tolerate this "loaded cannon." Ron didn't need the further agony of playing the game. Ron is not suited for big-company life, not now anyway.

Large and complex organizations can consume people's lives. Some A players thrive on the complexity, the grand scale, the internal competition. Some A players don't. CEOs implore managers to figure out how to achieve balance, and they are remarkably tolerant of an afternoon off for a child's soccer game or concert. Some A players in large companies are successful and happy, cutting deals with coworkers to free up time to take the kids to school or enjoy an uninterrupted three-day weekend. But, some managers can't achieve balance in big-company life. Meetings, meetings, meetings are necessary, but involve twenty hours per week. Scrambling to squeeze out quarterly earnings requires an enormous amount of time, creativity, and energy. Relocations are on the decline, but they are still necessary every three or four years for up-and-comers in many companies. Some thrive on this life, others don't. If you don't, plan your eventual exit.

Here's an increasingly popular and smart way to work smarter, not harder: Stay with premier companies long enough (a decade?) to get leading-edge skills and career marketability; then leave. Go to a smaller organization where your skills can make a difference, yet you can work fifty hours per week. Big-company life was not for Ron, who was eventually going to end up in a death spiral of stress and burnout. As it turns out, Ron is richer, both financially and personally, working in a smaller company.

Some talented people work smarter by becoming entrepreneurs. Dozens have broken away from Intel and Microsoft to start their own companies. Being an entrepreneur is not an easier life, but can be more satisfying than clawing one's way up the corporate ladder. "I'm working as hard, but at least it's all productive work," one entrepreneur told me. He's working smarter, but still has to get a life. "After my IPO," he said. Uh-huh.

Since the 1980s a lot of B and C players have been nudged out of large companies, victims of productivity improvements, outsourcing, you name it. Instead of disappearing into the corporate hinterlands, many achieved remarkable success in smaller organizations. In initially lower-level (lower-paying) jobs, they were A players—ones with terrific disciplines learned at

Motorola, 3M, Citibank, or the like. Their title was usually bigger, their scope wider, but they were a bigger fish in a smaller pond. They stretched, succeeded, and eventually made more money than they would had they stayed at a bigger company. One said, "I have control over my life; I can work out at noon, attend my daughter's softball game, and have dinner with the family, and I'll do homework at 9:00 P.M. or Saturday." Another told me, "Brad, I knew I spent a lot of time in meetings (at Intel), but now I'm free! I have ten meetings per week, not twenty. All that coordinating crap is cut in half!"

Topgrading had better incorporate the *needs* of A players, not just their skills. Premier companies are slowly adapting, so that managers can work smarter, not harder, and enjoy reasonable balance in life. These favorable trends are just beginning to occur in most large companies, however. For those managers who just cannot achieve balance, moving to a simpler company might be best.

## 9. Topgrade in Business and Personal Life

This entire book is about topgrading in business, which can help you gain a competitive edge in your career. It can also help you get balance in your life.

---

**Instead of working seventy hours per week with your group of three A players, two B players, and two C players, topgrade and work fifty hours per week.**

---

Perhaps the single most powerful lever for achieving balance in life is getting more time, and topgraders do that. We've heard thousands of happy stories from managers who topgraded, and with a team of all A players, the job was a heck of a lot easier. The A team was smarter, more proactive, and more able to prevent problems, so the manager could get superior results working fewer hours. Is that manager you?

But what about topgrading in your personal life? Do you have trouble getting and keeping good help? Are the nannies you hire not good enough for your kids? Does your cleaning service rip you off? Does your dry cleaner trash compact your clothes? If so, it's time to topgrade.

I have noticed a high correlation between business and personal topgrading. Topgraders in business get all A players, so their career is successful and they enjoy going to work each day. They recruit rigorously, check references, and hire in the top 10 percent of talent available. They treat their A players with respect and caring and are repaid in loyalty and superb performance. To assemble dream teams in their personal lives, they use their resourcefulness and follow the topgrading principles in this book. They hire A players. So, their personal lives run smoothly. They aren't constantly frustrated with C player mechanics, accountants, and cleaning people.

## TOPGRADE YOUR KIDS

My daughter, Dr. Kate Mursau, is a family therapist and topgrading consultant, and she and I wrote a book: *CAN-DO KIDS: How to Raise Resourceful, Happy Children* (AMACOM, 2005). A different publisher suggested the title *Topgrade Your Kids,* and Kate went berserk. "What?! Set high goals for your kids and dump them if they don't perform?!" The publisher said, "Some parents might approve. Just kidding. *Topgrade Your Kids* could teach parents how to coach their kids to be resourceful." Nice try, but Kate nuked the idea.

Kate's doctoral dissertation showed that high achievers, all highly resourceful, have kids who are typically NOT resourceful. How interesting! All six thousand of the high achievers I've Topgrading interviewed are superresourceful, and they live to figure things out each day. But they tell me their kids lack the one skill they would most like them to have—resourcefulness. Society today (including parents) bestows on kids a PHD:

**P** for passivity ("You give me everything so I don't need to be resourceful.")

**H** for helplessness ("Since I've never figured much out for myself, I don't know how.")

**D** for dependency ("Because I'm passive and helpless, I continue to depend on parents, teachers, coaches, and so on, to give me advice, to figure things out for me.")

Our book has activities you can do with your kids, developing their re-sourcefulness, and stimulating their passion to take responsibility and fig-ure things out. The basic formula is deceptively simple: listen, bond, and coach your kid to set goals, evaluate options, implement a plan, and at the end of the activity give you a high five: "This has been fun. I like it when I figure things out and you are my helper!" Kids can get better at figuring things out, develop a passion for it, and learn to apply it in all areas of their life—relationships, school work, health, and so on. *CAN-DO KIDS* shows how resourcefulness parenting helps kids grow up to be happy, successful adults, because they are resourceful in all their Critical Life Dimensions—exactly what this chapter has focused on for you.

One activity is Build Something Together, like a playhouse. Instead of buying one at Wal-Mart or hiring Home Depot to build it, you ask your kid, "Do you want to build one together?" On Saturday you encourage your kid to make decisions, and that means you NOT choosing the site (though you can), NOT designing the playhouse (though you can), and NOT doing 95 percent of the building (though you can). Instead, you ask questions to coach your kid to be the real estate decision maker and con-tractor. "What are some different possible locations?" and "What's good and bad about this location?" stimulate your kid's resourcefulness.

It's hard for A player parents to zip it up, show patience, and STOP GIV-ING ADVICE! A little advice is OK, as is pounding a few more nails so the playhouse doesn't fall down. You can stop giving advice, however, I learned. Several years ago Kate and I were in Zambia, both invited to be interviewed on *Good Morning Zambia* (about Kate's high school club that worked to reduce poaching elephants), and I declined. Kate was nervous about a solo interview, so I helped her by asking, "What do you think their questions will be?" and "What are some possible responses?" She did so well they ran the TV interview again and again for two weeks in Zambia and Zimbabwe. I had to hire armed guards because we were told poachers didn't appreci-ate her fifteen minutes of fame criticizing their livelihood.

Geoff wanted to learn to fly a glider (a real plane with no engine). When we found ourselves in heavy snow over the Tetons, he did most of the fig-uring as to how to get us down safely. Flash forward—both Geoff and Kate love being resourceful and ol' Dad (and Mom, Mary) wouldn't dare offer an opinion or advice about whom to marry or how to build their own busi-ness . . . unless asked! It's initially tough to hold back, following resourcefulness parenting guidelines, but having energized kids who never got in trouble, who constantly delight in "I'll figure it out," is worth it.

*CAN-DO KIDS* is an antidote to these parenting challenges. Since your most important competency is resourcefulness, wouldn't it be nice—no, not just nice, but thrilling—to give your kids the gift of resourcefulness? You get to be a proud parent of self-reliant, responsible kids, confident that your kids are laying the foundation to eventually be resourceful adults who have their cake and eat it too.

## CHAPTER 7 CHECKLIST: CAN YOU HAVE YOUR CAKE AND EAT IT TOO?

**YES NO**

☐ ☐ I have completed my Life Balance Scorecard and have a plan to achieve all "Good Enoughs."

☐ ☐ I have a plan to fix all Very Poor or Poor competencies in my present job.

☐ ☐ (For those with no Poor or Very Poor competencies) My Individual Development Plan (IDP) seeks to improve the Only Fair competencies.

☐ ☐ (For those with all Good or better competencies) My IDP seeks to develop A player competencies I'll need in the next job.

☐ ☐ I'm in the personal development business for life.

☐ ☐ I'm highly resourceful in pursuing balance across all my Critical Life Dimensions.

☐ ☐ I have conducted a Personal Career Review, and my IDP incorporates my needs to stay on top of career trends.

☐ ☐ In job interviews, I put my best foot forward, but I reveal my negatives.

☐ ☐ I only enter jobs where I can be an A player.

☐ ☐ I live below my means, saving 25 percent pretax.

☐ ☐ I carefully consider if I am suited to big-company life, and plan my career accordingly.

☐ ☐   I topgrade in both my business and personal lives.

☐ ☐   (For those with three- to nineteen-year-olds) I use resourcefulness parenting techniques to raise can-do kids, kids who are resourceful in all their Critical Life Dimensions and thus have the
best chance to be happy and successful in life.

☐ ☐   All things considered, I am having my cake and I am eating it too.

The nine career-development principles comprise a strategy that is
unique; it flies in the face of the American "get ahead at all costs" mythology. By playing your cards right, you can win with happiness and success.

Job security no longer exists, but career security does, for A players. Follow the guidelines in this chapter, ignoring the bad advice infused in our
society, and you can be in the ninety-ninth percentile—that rare 1 percent
for whom "Life is good, the career is going great, and I wouldn't trade
places with anyone else!"

*Eight*

# FIXING WEAKNESSES IN EACH OF FIFTY COMPETENCIES: THE STRAIGHTEST PATH TO SUCCESS

*There is no growth without discomfort.*
Author Unknown

So you want to become an A player in the biggest league possible? After learning about career successes and failures from more than six thousand managers, I said in Chapter 7 that the best way to become an A player is to fix your weaknesses. This chapter presents practical advice for improving in each of fifty competencies.[38]

Managers are most promotable when their strengths are solid and they have no serious weaknesses. Nothing derails management careers faster than one or two fatal flaws. Therefore, the time you spend on professional development should be spent more on overcoming Achilles' heels, than on attending yet another seminar on the functional area you have mastered. It's not all or nothing; allocating some (10 percent) of your developmental time to maximizing strengths will help you maintain those as strengths.

This chapter will help you figure out your potentials—in what league you might be an A player, and what it will take to get there. It will also help calibrate you as a topgrader, so you more accurately peg A, B, and C players and better understand what people are capable of in their developmental efforts. Finally, it will give you developmental ideas in fifty managerial competencies, which can be useful in maximizing your growth and helping you develop your team members.

---

[38]The fifty competencies are skills, knowledge, and behaviors hundreds of companies have considered important for success in management.

This chapter is not assumed to be sufficient to inspire you to change, and makes no effort to coach you. It succinctly conveys opinions on what it takes to be an A player and which are the most important competencies.

## HOW A PLAYERS ARE PICKED

Over the years I have participated in hundreds of meetings in which candidates for promotion or for hire were discussed, dissected, and then chosen—or not chosen. I usually have conducted Topgrading Interviews and have coached the candidates, so I try to contribute opinions about individuals as well as process—how to validly and fairly compare talent. Consistent with the points made in Chapter 7 (key #5: "Work on Overcoming Your Weak Points More Than on Maximizing Your Strengths"), here's what happens:

---

**Candidates with the fewest serious flaws get the job. Candidates with the most impressive strengths get the job *only* if they do not have any major flaws. Companies outgrow people. Fast-growing companies can outgrow people fast.**

---

A lot of the coaching I do is with A players who are developing themselves like crazy, across dozens of dimensions, so they remain A players as their jobs get bigger and more complex.

Fortunately, day-to-day working develops not just a few competencies, but many. You got yourself organized with a department of ten, and you'll figure out how to do it for fifty. You'll learn. If you used tandem Topgrading Interviews to hire specialists, you'll use them to hire managers, adding the management questions. You used to interact with customer managers, and you'll figure out how to comport yourself with customer vice presidents. Your boss will drop hints about which fork to use, and you will sense when your humor was appropriate. Experience is not always the best teacher, but survivors survive. Every day is a training course in all fifty competencies at the next higher level. If you don't develop across all fifty competencies, your nondevelopment in any will stick out like a sore thumb. Your minor shortcomings might eventually be seen as major. If you fall far short on a competency—being Only Fair for one in which Very

Good is the minimum necessary—you will have a fatal flaw and that could be career stopping. Better fix it. If in Communications—Oral is a real strength, but Team Player is a fatal flaw, do you want to devote your developmental time to take public-speaking courses? If so, you had better plan to be a professional speaker after you're fired for not being a team player.

At the end of the fifty management competencies listed in Appendix G, there are 12 common career derailers. It has become clear that in hundreds of talent-assessment meetings over the years, these career derailers continue to overshadow a person's strengths. If someone is poor in even one of these, the result could be termination. The 12 common failings related to needed competencies, are in these areas:

1. Resourcefulness—"too passive," "doesn't create opportunities," "always trying to delegate upward"

2. Selecting A Players and Redeploying B/C Players—"mis-hires too many," "has a team of B and C players," "afraid to hire someone better than he is," "just won't topgrade"

3. Passion—"not highly motivated," "lacks drive," "goes through the motions"

4. Integrity—"lies," "can't be trusted to keep promises," "breaks confidences," "gossips," "pushes legal boundaries too far"

5. Ambition—"too ambitious," "always trying to get the promotion rather than serve the company"

6. Political Savvy—"a dirty politician," "backstabber"

7. Adaptability—"over her head," "can't adjust to our reorganization," "job is too complex for her"

8. Team Builder—"can't empower anyone," "control freak," "old-fashioned autocrat"

9. Team Player—"builds silos," "thinks his department is the only one," "won't coordinate across departments, causing major production waste," "not a team player"

10. Track Record—"missed her numbers again," "sandbagger," "more excuses than reasons"

11. Intelligence—"lacks the brainpower to adapt," "slow learner," "just doesn't get it"

12. Likability—"arrogant," "condescending," "egotistical," "doesn't treat people with respect," "makes a mockery of our people values," "know-it-all," "sarcastic," "demeaning," "acts superior"

Which competencies are career enhancers? All fifty, but some stand out. Resourcefulness has been mentioned in previous chapters as the most important competency. A players are all strong in their driving passion to figure things out. Resourcefulness is a megacompetency, because it incorporates many intellectual, personnel, motivational, and management competencies. Of course, the topgrading competencies are all-important—Selecting A Players, Redeploying B/C Players, and Coaching. Self-Awareness is essential, for with it A players figure out how to be successful. If your Self-Awareness tells you that a weak point isn't being topgraded, your Resourcefulness can help you develop Selecting A Players, Redeploying B/C Players, and Coaching.

The topgrading competencies ensure that your delivery system is good—the engine (Resourcefulness) is in the right vehicle (your dream team of A players). There are exceptions—that's why we have fifty, not five, management competencies. With Resourcefulness, Self-Awareness, Selecting A Players, Redeploying B/C Players, and Coaching, all the other forty-five competencies frequently (but not necessarily) can fall into place.

## A FIX-MY-WEAKNESS PLAN

Let's draw these interrelated points together in a simple action plan.

First, think of the next job you want (or a longer-term present job, if you prefer). Write the job description for it. Ask some A players in that job to help you. Next, go to Appendix G and revise the behaviorally anchored descriptions for thirty, forty, or all fifty competencies, so they fit whatever the job requires. On a six-point scale (Excellent, Very Good, Good, Only Fair, Poor, Very Poor), rate the minimum necessary to earn a promotion. This is important:

---

**A players need not be Excellent in all competencies, but they must meet the minimum standard for a particular job on all of them.**

---

If your goal is to become an accounting manager, you probably can get by nicely if your writing skills are Good and your First Impression is Only Fair, as long as you are Excellent in Analysis Skills and Very Good in Organization/Planning and Excellence Standards. You get the picture.

Next, rate yourself currently. Ask coworkers to rate you. Note the discrepancies between current ratings and the minimum necessary in the desired job. Where are you Only Fair and need to be Good? Where you are Poor and need to be, at a minimum, Only Fair? It's time for Self-Awareness. If you are Very Poor on four competencies and need to be Very Good, are you being unrealistic in your Ambition? Do you have too many fatal flaws? Never underestimate Resourcefulness. If your passion is to start your own company, rise to president, or sing at the Met, good luck to you and God bless. Perhaps your Resourcefulness can take you all the way.

Figure 8.1 is a sample Fix-My-Weakness Plan. A more comprehensive Individual Development Plan sample, like what managers have in topgrading companies, is presented in Appendix H and described in Chapter 10. Where your current rating falls short of the minimum rating necessary, create action steps, your plan to overcome the deficit.

## Figure 8.1
## Sample "Fix My Weakness" Plan

### Job: Accounting Manager

| Competency | Minimum Rating Needed | My Current Rating | Plan |
|---|---|---|---|
| Education | 4 | 3 | Complete BS/BA nights. |
| Experience | 5 | 3 | Get it on the job. Visit two companies this year with best practices I need to know. |
| Hiring A Players | 5 | 3 | Ask HR for Topgrading training. Volunteer to tandem Topgrading Interview accounting candidates. |

Team Building        4            2            Volunteer and within two years become
                                               officer of community organization. Read
                                               three books on team building. Perform 360-
                                               degree feedback survey to monitor progress.

Scale: 6 = Excellent, 5 = Very Good, 4 = Good, 3 = Only Fair,
2 = Poor, 1 = Very Poor

You can attend a five-day career assessment course that essentially performs this exercise. If you do a quick-and-dirty version in one hour, it probably will be 95 percent on target.

## THE BOTTOM LINE ON FIFTY COMPETENCIES

The rest of this chapter addresses all fifty competencies. A chapter could be written about each one—what it is, how important the competency is to becoming an A player, how amenable it is to development, and exactly how people fix a shortcoming in it. However, this overview provides some insight, for your own career development as well as your capacity to topgrade. I've chosen a self-assessment/advice format to capture as many truths as possible from my six thousand files, with their sixty thousand job case studies. To avoid platitudes, I opt for bluntness, and exaggerate to make the point. Blunt advice is not a good coaching technique, but it uses the sort of language savvy executives blurt out when they state the unvarnished truth to a subordinate. That bluntness is also the way A players think about their own developmental needs. The situations are designed to cross all levels of management, all industries.

### Intellectual Competencies

## 1. Intelligence

*Self-Assessment:* I'm not as smart as my peers.

*Advice:* Senior managers in complex, fast-changing industries must be smart as heck. Either aim for more of an implementer job, or change to more of a static, slow-moving industry.

*Self-Assessment:* I'm too smart and quick for people.

*Advice:* You might confuse people, interrupt, or win every argument because you are too intense, not too smart. Join companies in which there are equally smart people. Hire people who have better people sense than you and who can buffer your intensity.

## 2. Analysis Skills

*Self-Assessment:* My boss says my analyses are shallow.

*Advice:* Show your analyses to smart coworkers before showing them to your boss. Or, determine if you are smart enough for this job.

*Self-Assessment:* My analyses are good when I take my time, but my boss wants them done quickly.

*Advice: Make* the extra time you need—evenings, weekends, whenever.

*Self-Assessment:* I'm quick as hell, but sometimes I miss things.

*Advice:* You're hip-shooting. Slow down, or you probably won't get promoted. You can be off 10 percent, causing a tolerable $20K mistake at your present level. At a higher level, that mistake might cost $200K—which is enough reason to not promote you until you show more maturity and discipline.

## 3. Judgment/Decision Making

*Self-Assessment:* My decisions are good 75 percent of the time, but my subordinates feel I exclude them.

*Advice:* Your subordinates are probably frustrated; they don't buy into your decisions, and the A players feel stifled because they know they could help you on the 25 percent of your decisions that are bad. Allocate time for more participation. Do damage control. But always reserve the right to call the really big plays.

*Self-Assessment:* I just can't get my people to make decisions. They keep asking what I want to do. Why do I need them?

*Advice:* You don't. Maybe they are C players. If they were previously managed by an autocrat, coach them and give them a chance to become people whom you can empower. If they continue to delegate upward, remove them.

## 4. Conceptual Ability

*Self-Assessment:* I'm OK with concrete, tangible situations, but not vague concepts.

*Advice:* Senior-management jobs all have a strong conceptual component. Read a lot, and pick the brains of good conceptual thinkers.

*Self-Assessment:* To get ahead in line management, I need to take a staff marketing job for a year or two. It's a conceptual job and I'm scared.

*Advice:* Compensate. Beg or hire smart conceptual types to back you up and do some of your thinking for you.

## 5. Creativity

*Self-Assessment:* I'm criticized for not generating many ideas.

*Advice:* Lack of creativity is rarely a career derailer, but lack of resourcefulness is. Attack problems forty ways, not four; steal best practices and tailor them to your needs; conduct brainstorming sessions.

*Self-Assessment:* I feel it's my job as leader to think of the most creative ideas.

*Advice:* Think again. Your job is to build a team of A players with whom you can brainstorm and jointly produce creative ideas. If you try to do it all yourself, you're a C player.

## 6. Strategic Skills

*Self-Assessment:* I'm a VP and won't make SVP until I'm considered a strategic thinker. But I'm not strategic.

*Advice:* Topgrade, so your A players include strategists. Or, hire a consultant. You can't afford McKinsey for $500,000 per month? Then hire a recently retired strategist, or a sharp marketing strategist between jobs. And, read *Competitive Advantage* by Michael Porter.

*Self-Assessment:* Six months ago I was named division general manager. My people say they're confused. They don't know my vision for the division.

*Advice:* You might be confusing the heck out of them with conflicting directions as you sort things out, or with apparently contradictory goals, such as "increase profits but lower prices." Go off-site with your team and hammer out a credible vision, then a credible strategy, and finally a plan.

## 7. Pragmatism

*Self-Assessment:* A 360-degree survey showed me to be lacking in street smarts.

*Advice:* No one will promote you until you are at least Good in pragmatism. Spend time with the most savvy opinion leaders and bounce any ideas off of them. Be careful not to speak before thinking.

*Self-Assessment:* I'm an idea guy, and people say half my ideas are great, a quarter need work, and a quarter are lousy.

*Advice:* Separate brainstorming sessions, where no idea is bad, from decision-making sessions. Let your coworkers persuade you to scrap the nutty ideas after brainstorming, before decision making.

## 8. Risk Taking

*Self-Assessment:* They say I'm too conservative for this gun slinging, fast-growth high-tech company.

*Advice:* Maybe "they" should listen to your caution. If you are thorough but slow, then continue being thorough but speed up your analyses. If you are a chronic naysayer, change companies.

*Self-Assessment:* I'm a newly appointed VP who has achieved success taking chances, with an occasional big mistake. My new boss says I have to tone myself down.

*Advice:* Your boss could be right. Missing a $100,000 budget by 10 percent isn't as serious as missing a $20 million budget by 10 percent. Be more thorough and buttoned up and your hip-shooter image will soften.

*Self-Assessment:* The biggest risks I've taken have been in changing companies and not knowing what a rats' nest I'd entered.

*Advice:* You are hurting your marketability with your passiveness and lack of judgment. Be resourceful. Every company, every boss, every job can be checked out. Talk with people who left the company. Insist on seeing the financials before you accept an offer. Talk with your prospective coworkers about the culture. Know your first-year accountabilities and be sure you can achieve them.

## 9. Leading Edge

*Self-Assessment:* Best practices is a lot of baloney; it's TQM one day, then reengineering. Now outsourcing is in. Why learn all that crap?

*Advice:* To save your career, that's why. If you don't search the world for best practices to do your job, someone else will, and will probably get your job. Read, build your network, and use judgment in modifying leading-edge approaches that can help your business. Don't be an opponent of necessary change.

*Self-Assessment:* The corporate office checks out leading-edge approaches. Their jobs are to benchmark and alert us in the field to best practices. So, why should I do their jobs?

*Advice:* You peg yourself as a change implementer, not a change agent, if you wait for others to lead you. You sound like a "tell me how to do it" mid-manager, not a visionary future leader. Show some intellectual curiosity and thought leadership by searching for best practices yourself.

## 10. Education

*Self-Assessment:* For twenty years I've learned on the job. Most executives here have MBAs. Should I?

*Advice:* If you are working seventy hours per week, read a lot, know the financials cold, and have a reputation for leading-edge thinking, forget the MBA. You probably have the equivalent of two MBA degrees in your head. However, if you have the time for a weekend MBA and need more breadth and depth, get the degree—at the best MBA program you can attend. Otherwise, take selected courses and seminars.

*Self-Assessment:* What business periodicals do managers read?

*Advice:* Everyone reads the trade rags. Executives and future executives read *The Wall Street Journal* (including "Fact and Opinion," the editorial section), *BusinessWeek, Forbes,* and *Fortune.* At least scan each issue for pertinent articles. *Harvard Business Review* or *Sloan Management Review* should be circulated. *International Herald Tribune* and *The Economist* are favorites for international insight.

*Self-Assessment:* Why should I work all day and then take evening finance courses?

*Advice:* If you are getting feedback that you are weak in finance, you'd better do it. Finance is the language of business. If you aren't keeping up, aren't showing keen awareness of all the financials, then you're probably a B player, maybe a C. To be an A player candidate for any senior-management role, master the nontechnical aspects of finance. Ask your CFO or CEO what specific financial skills you should master. Courses in the evening are less of a pain than cozying up to a complex book on mergers and acquisitions at 9:00 P.M.

## 11. Experience

*Self-Assessment:* I've risen to VP Controller, but I've always wanted general management.

*Advice:* Be the most field-oriented controller you can. Learn operations, learn manufacturing, and help salespeople construct winning bids. Accept a lateral move into operations, sales, or marketing to broaden your base. Work in a company with a history of moving finance people into general management.

*Self-Assessment:* What types of experience are generic and increasingly important?

*Advice:* To maximize your marketability, it's useful to have participated in successful growth, severe belt tightening, major transformations, and international. Ask A players in the job you want what experiences they feel are crucial.

## 12. Track Record

*Self-Assessment:* I'm much more talented than my track record indicates. I've had bad bosses, and economic downturns have hurt.

*Advice:* Be careful! Your track record *is* your talent manifested. Research prospective bosses more thoroughly. Even in recessions, talent shines. Maybe your talent lies in a narrower or lower-level domain.

*Self-Assessment:* I have an excellent track record in a large company. What are the problems in moving to a small company?

*Advice:* Get a deep understanding of what resources will exist. Most people making such a change grossly underestimate the problems. They assume all sorts of talent exists to help them, in all departments, but it usually doesn't. Be specific—check out exactly how many people, with what talent, will be in your department and other departments; know your budgets. People talk too much in generalities, when understanding the hard-core specifics will help you picture whether you will have all the skills, resources, and will, to make such a change.

## Personal Competencies

### 13. Integrity

*Self-Assessment:* My boss says people don't trust me because of white lies. So what? Everyone lies, even U.S. presidents.

*Advice:* Lack of integrity is a career derailer in the business world. Just the perception that you tell white lies makes you a C player, at best. Read *The Seven Habits of Highly Effective People* by Steven Covey. Reference checks that disclose a perception that you aren't 100 percent trustworthy will severely hurt your career.

*Self-Assessment:* It's a lot easier to say I'll do it and then *not* do it, than admit I have no intention of doing it.

*Advice:* Your integrity will be questioned. If people can't trust you, you're dead.

*Self-Assessment:* Everyone breaks a confidence now and then.

*Advice:* Wrong! It's your responsibility to let people know your boundaries of confidentiality. Say, "If I know the answer to your question and was sworn to confidentiality, I won't respond." Say, "I'm sorry, but I can't promise confidentiality in advance, but if you choose to tell me something, I'll tell you if I can maintain the confidence." Learn to avoid certain topics. Loose lips sink careers.

### 14. Resourcefulness

*Self-Assessment:* Given direction, I'm an excellent implementer, but, to be honest, barriers thwart me.

*Advice:* You sound like a career midmanager and a B player at best. One competency separating A players at all levels is figuring out how to get over, around, under, or through obstacles. It's Resourcefulness, the single most important, the single best distinguisher among A, B, and C players.

*Self-Assessment:* I have all sorts of ideas for making improvements. I work weekends to put the plans together. But, my boss and, frankly, the whole company, are risk averse—chicken, slow, and bureaucratic. The competition is killing us and we languish in old ways of doing everything.

*Advice:* Join one of those aggressive competitors. Then write at least one "white paper" each year, developing an original idea into an action plan for the company. Submit your white paper through your boss to senior management.

## 15. Organization/Planning

*Self-Assessment:* I was OK in my last job, but since my promotion I can't get organized.

*Advice:* Every promotion brings new complexity. Get to know the capabilities of your new team, using Topgrading Interviews. Then organize your time focusing on three top priorities, delegating a lot to your A players. Remove the chronic B/Cs or you might never get on top of your job.

*Self-Assessment:* I have no administrative assistant, and I'm dying.
*Advice:* Get one *now*—an A player temp. You could get fired for not producing results, and no one will accept the excuse that you didn't have an admin.

*Self-Assessment:* I've taken time management courses and sort things into different priorities, but my people say I keep changing priorities.

*Advice:* Then communicate a lot more with them. Go from biweekly to weekly staff meetings. Go to daily conference calls. A players do not confuse their teams with changing priorities that cause a lot of wasted time.

## 16. Excellence

*Self-Assessment:* I've always been conscientious, but a 360-degree survey indicates people feel my standards are dropping.

*Advice:* Raise the bar. Competition is forcing higher standards in every industry; the Information Age means everyone can instantly know what products and services are best. When you stop performing at the highest level in the marketplace, your career is going to slip.

*Self-Assessment:* My standards are too high and I'm impatient and intolerant of C players.

*Advice:* Your standards for yourself sound too low. You keep C players and beat them up, when instead you should nudge them out. Perhaps you also pound on A players, demeaning them and motivating them to quit. You accept behavior in yourself that brings out the worst in others, not their best. Fix your leadership style so that people will embrace your high standards.

## 17. Independence

*Self-Assessment:* I've always been a rugged individualist, figuring all this team malarkey is for followers, not leaders.

*Advice:* Keep your individualism, and call the difficult plays yourself. But embrace teams because they aren't going away. The old hierarchy is gone forever, because it is beaten by a flat structure, with flexible teams.

*Self-Assessment:* My manager says I'm high maintenance, always bugging her with questions.

*Advice:* With flat organizations, the span of control for managers is broader, with more subordinates. It sounds as though you'd better act more on your own. The wave of the future is for Independence to be a more important competency.

## 18. Stress Management

*Self-Assessment:* I'm 50 and seem calm on the job, but I'm going nuts. Delayering gave me two jobs, so I'm working seventy hours per week with no time for exercise or family.

*Advice:* Maybe there is time: one-and-one-half hours for family, one-half hour for exercise, *every* day. Topgrade to be able to delegate more to A players and waste less time cleaning up after C players.

*Self-Assessment:* Exercise burns off stress, but my hectic work schedule doesn't permit a good one-hour workout three times a week.

*Advice:* I'll bet it can. I studied two hundred on-again, off-again exercisers who became regular exercisers. Their secret has worked for many others, including me. Their secret? *No pain, I gain.* Make a lifetime commitment to exercising and *never* experiencing pain. Exercise five times per week for half an hour, but start slowly. Take six months to get to an aerobic level, if that's what it takes to never feel the exercise is too hard. Have a cold? Then ease up. But work out. Chart your workouts; if you want twenty per month, and you fall behind, do double workouts (big deal, one hour on Saturday). Alternate aerobic and light-weight exercises.

*Self-Assessment:* A players seem driven yet calm. How do they do it?

*Advice:* Most are not calm, but some of those who are calm practice some form of meditation. They avoid burnout and keep everything in perspective with one or two fifteen-minute quiet periods each day—eyes closed, total calm, not sleep.

## 19. Self-Awareness

*Self-Assessment:* Every two years my company puts all managers through a 360-degree feedback exercise. Is this enough?

*Advice:* Because you're asking the question, I'll bet the answer is no. Senior managers all have blind spots, and 5 percent or more of the perceptions about these managers are typically untrue. Regular feedback from a trusted A player subordinate and a trusted A player peer can help you manage perceptions by figuring out which perceptions of you are positive and negative, and which are true or false. Isolate yourself only at risk to your career.

*Self-Assessment:* I've worked in the same company fifteen years and we're not good at giving feedback, so I wonder if . . .

*Advice:* Say no more. You are experiencing feedback deficit. You can't calibrate yourself in relation to the rest of the world. Build a network of A players outside the company from seminars or professional organizations, trade shows, and vendors. Find out what A players know and do by watching, talking, and probing.

## 20. Adaptability

*Self-Assessment:* Some change is OK, but I struggle with so much change.

*Advice:* Warning! Warning! Lack of Adaptability is a career derailer. A players are Excellent in Adaptability. They tolerate ambiguity, and make decisions on the fly. They not only tolerate changes in structure, processes, and locations, but seek them out in order to gain a competitive advantage.

*Self-Assessment:* I'm certain I am right, but people accuse me of being inflexible.

*Advice:* If ordinarily you are considered adaptable, then perhaps you *are* right, and the others are wrong. You owe the shareholders perseverance, not acquiescence. Show the others you fully understand their perspectives (use active listening a lot); get a solid, impartial, outside opinion; and stick to your guns.

## Interpersonal Competencies

## 21. First Impression

*Self-Assessment:* I'm slow to get promoted because of my image—dress and slang, I guess. People say I lack "presence," but I get the job done.

*Advice:* Without being a phony, always cultivate an image appropriate for the next-higher level—attire, bearing, hair style, language, and so on. Don't upstage your boss. Look and act the part, and you might get promoted a little sooner.

*Self-Assessment:* I'm in high tech, where substance, not image, counts. Every day is a casual day.

*Advice:* Great, but be careful. In management, your jeans may hurt you. In an IPO, Wall Street might think your casual attire is flaky. If your stock price suffers and the senior team looks sloppy to analysts, well—they might suspect that the business processes are sloppy too.

## 22. Likability

*Self-Assessment:* I'm not much of a people person.

*Advice:* Become a monk. Just kidding. Warmth and charm are wonderful, but rarely necessary. Sincerity, credibility, and willingness to listen are essential. You can become more likable without a personality transplant by holding "town meetings" or brown-bag lunches, and managing by wandering around (MBWA). With all of these, you must really listen, tell people the truth, and follow through on any promises. Read *Good to Great* (by Jim Collins), highlighting fourteen outstanding CEOs who were humble but not super-outgoing.

*Self-Assessment:* I'm confident, but people say I'm arrogant.

*Advice:* Arrogance is a career derailer. It motivates people to undercut you, to deliberately let you hang yourself. It destroys teamwork and insults everyone. You don't have to be Excellent in Likability, but below Good, you're in trouble.

## 23. Listening

*Self-Assessment:* I finish people's sentences and interrupt, but I know where they are going.

*Advice:* Either let people finish or else tell them what you think they are getting at. Let them confirm you were on target. Use active listening; that is, play back to people what you think their point of view is, and when they feel listened to, you will find them more willing to listen to your point of view. To be considered empathetic, you have to play back some unstated feelings (frustration, anger) along with the content. Active listening really works. Improving listening skills is one of the most pervasive needs of leaders. Read *People Skills* by Robert Bolton for good chapters on the sub-ject. Start each day with ten dimes in a pocket, and each time you use active listening very well, transfer one to another pocket. Managers who transfer ten dimes daily overcome perceptions that they are arrogant, stubborn, or lacking in emotional intelligence.

*Self-Assessment:* I listen, I understand, but then I usually do what I feel is best.

*Advice:* "Usually"? Calling the big plays can show your leadership, but be careful. Don't stifle your subordinates, or the As will leave.

## 24. Customer Focus

*Self-Assessment:* I do exactly what my boss calls for—generate profit and expand market share. Yet I was passed over because customer complaints are up.

*Advice:* Good for you for stealing profitable business from competitors. With more sales, naturally there are more customers to complain. You sound defensive, however. Someone thinks you are screwing customers or taking some other shortsighted approach. *Never, ever* be accused of being out of touch with customers. It's career suicide. Visit customers, take surveys, run focus groups. Every meeting should bring up the customer.

*Self-Assessment:* I know what customers are thinking without having to be out in the field with them.

*Advice:* That's doubtful, though possible. Surveys and other metrics (complaints) are usually insufficient. Senior managers are so busy, they try to justify being removed from the customer. A players must be Very Good, at a minimum, in this competency, and they make time for face-to-face customer interaction.

## 25. Team Player

*Self-Assessment:* In meetings with my peers and boss, I'm kind of quiet because everyone else is trying to grandstand.

*Advice:* Sounds like defensiveness on your part. You have an obligation to make your opinions known. You have a responsibility to make the team a team—to reach out to help others, to actively tear down organizational silos, to intervene in disputes to resolve differences. Read *The Wisdom of Teams* by Jon Katzenbach.

*Self-Assessment:* My boss says I'm not a team player because after a course of action is determined, I'm not always the most enthusiastic supporter.

*Advice:* You're *not* a team player. You should argue, disagree, fight for what you feel is best for the company, but only behind closed doors. If there is a major philosophical difference, A players will offer to resign. When a decision is made, you must support it 100 percent. Don't go to your people and say your boss has required X or Y. Get behind it. Make it work. Use your resourcefulness!

## 26. Assertiveness

*Self-Assessment:* I'm blunt, honest, direct, and forceful. However, I'm told I have too many rough edges for a promotion.

*Advice:* Keep your openness, but eliminate the most outrageous 5 percent of your behavior (publicly embarrassing people, temper outbursts, anything smacking of meanness). Doing that can improve your image not just 5 percent, but 50 percent.

*Self-Assessment:* I'm the opposite—not assertive enough. I never have been.

*Advice:* Look for a five-year improvement plan, at best. The hyper-assertive person tones himself down every day, in meetings with bosses and customers. He can easily increase his control of assertiveness. You must develop new muscles, and it takes a lot longer to show improvement. If you are Poor in this, management is probably not for you.

## 27. Communications—Oral

*Self-Assessment:* I'm an organized but dry speaker in formal presentations.

*Advice:* Join Toastmasters or get a public speaking coach, to gradually add charisma without phoniness. I've seen terrible speakers become great. Anyone can become good. Anyone. A wonderful woman with Down syndrome earns a living giving speeches after years of public speaking training.

*Self-Assessment:* I don't want some public speaking coach to try to change my personality. I'll appear phony and too packaged, like a politician.

*Advice:* Good speaking coaches will study your style and leverage your strengths—using *your* humor with better timing and emphasizing *your* gestures for better emphasis.

## 28. Communications—Written

*Self-Assessment:* I'm just not a polished writer.

*Advice:* This is one area where a formal course should help. Do reference checks to be sure the course gets rave reviews.

*Self-Assessment:* I can't stand proofing documents and I'm not permitted to have an administrative assistant. The typos are getting embarrassing.

*Advice:* A players don't let typos kill their chances for promotion. Figure it out. Put up with the pain and proof better, beg your boss for help, or pay someone outside of work to proof the most important documents.

## 29. Political Savvy

*Self-Assessment:* I'm not a gutter politician, but people say I'm naive.

*Advice:* You need to become politically aware—in tune with political forces that can help or hinder you and your group. Have lunch once a month with someone who will clue you in.

*Self-Assessment:* I'm sick of having to wire every decision with ten people before going into a big meeting.

*Advice:* Welcome to corporate life. Wire or die. Suck up a little or get left in the dust. Figure out how to lay the groundwork honestly and efficiently. Figure out how to assertively advocate your opinions on big matters *and* defer to top execs on unimportant matters. Or consider moving to a smaller company or a smaller job in your company.

*Self-Assessment:* I'm above politics.

*Advice:* Or, is your head in the sand? Develop at least one solid, trusting relationship in each area of the company that powerfully affects you—someone who will give you a "heads up" when you need it.

## 30. Negotiation

*Self-Assessment:* I'm a win/win negotiator, but I'm criticized because banks get the best of me.

*Advice:* You're not win/win. You lose. For win/win you probably need a lot better information on the other person's hand and less puppy-dog gushiness in showing your hand.

*Self-Assessment:* I'm just not quick on my feet in negotiations.

*Advice:* You don't have to be. A players are thoroughly prepared. Know everything about the other guy: his positions, needs, leverage, and vulnerabilities. Know thyself too. Preparation beats flash every time.

## 31. Persuasion

*Self-Assessment:* I'm not a dynamic, outgoing salesman. I've done well in manufacturing operations and asked for a key-account sales position to show I can be a general manager. I got the sales job, but I worry that I'll fail.

*Advice:* Stop worrying. The most effective salespeople are not superextroverts and many aren't really people-oriented. Instead of "bonding," they listen carefully to what customers want, they study customers to know their marketing strategy cold, and then they deliver. This world rewards salespeople who are competent and driven, not bubbly.

*Self-Assessment:* I'm not quick on my feet in sales situations.

*Advice:* See #30—preparation beats flash. Do your homework. Know your prospects' company strategies and marketing plans, their appraisals of other vendors, and their personality quirks. Listen. Then listen some more. Promise, but always deliver.

## Management Competencies

## 32. Selecting A Players

*Self-Assessment:* I have a mediocre hiring batting average.

*Advice:* Read this book and follow its advice. There is no more powerful lever for career success than topgrading. It's an A player's secret weapon. If you try to topgrade by removing Cs, but inadvertently replace them with more Cs, you will create a mess. Use tandem Topgrading Interviews to hire As.

## 33. Coaching

*Self-Assessment:* I'm a compulsive doer, too impatient for coaching.

*Advice:* You can still coach after hiring people using a Topgrading Interview. Chapters 9 and 10 will help.

*Self-Assessment:* I hire A players who don't need much coaching.

*Advice:* Good for you. But sometimes managers can get more talent for the buck with less experienced hires. Their potential is high, but they need coaching.

*Self-Assessment:* A 360-degree feedback survey showed that my people are frustrated; they rated me Only Fair as a coach.

*Advice:* Meet with each, discuss the survey, and work out a program with each one—a plan you and they can live with. Maybe a few group sessions would efficiently meet their needs. Monthly one-on-one meetings might help. Find out what are their legitimate needs to perform and to grow. Respond, or you will have a big strike against you.

## 34. Goal Setting

*Self-Assessment:* Subordinates say my goals for them change too much. I am just being flexible.

*Advice:* Are you a little flighty too? Your people should sense you're driving toward completion of your top priorities, and it's OK to flex around ways to achieve them. But if you change your mind because of new data, communicate with your people, ask their opinions, and get their buy-in.

*Self-Assessment:* I'm very participative and empowering; I think my subordinates will set higher goals than I could impose.

*Advice:* You sound a little passive and perhaps naive. Your goals must be congruent with overall corporate goals, so you can't delegate setting them. Your team has to be coordinated to achieve their combined goals, so you must be engaged. If bonuses are tied to individual performance, their incentive is to sandbag.

## 35. Empowerment

*Self-Assessment:* With each promotion I'm hesitant to empower people until I know whom I can trust to do the job.

*Advice:* Use the tandem Topgrading Interview for new hires, to learn whom you can empower, to coach As and Bs, and to quickly redeploy chronic Cs. The alternative is to work a hundred hours per week and frustrate your A players.

*Self-Assessment:* I've learned to empower my people, but it still scares me. Our organization culture punishes mistakes, and I'm afraid this empowerment could blow up.

*Advice:* Find a middle ground—emails from your people on their decisions before they act, or discussion of key decisions in your staff meetings.

## 36. Accountability

*Self-Assessment:* My new boss is moving from operating reviews every six months to every three months, because we are in a turnaround crisis. Quarterly reviews require preparation and I'd rather do the work, not prepare for so many meetings. Who's right?

*Advice:* Could be you're both wrong. Operating reviews every six months are for smoothly running teams of A players. Quarterly reviews are for mild turnarounds. Monthly mini ORs are for turnarounds.

*Self-Assessment:* I like my people to learn from mistakes.

*Advice:* Fine, but that doesn't mean you don't hold them accountable. If there is a promise to do X by a certain date, follow up. Build a team culture in which everyone holds everyone accountable.

## 37. Redeploying B/C Players

*Self-Assessment:* I inherited two B/C players, but at least they know how things operate around here. How long should I keep them?

*Advice:* Historical knowledge is overrated. Almost always topgraders say they should have moved quicker to remove B/C players, those who won't develop into As. Parachute As in and retain the B/Cs until the As feel the B/Cs are no longer needed. Then redeploy the B/Cs. Almost any team can be topgraded in six months.

## 38. Team Building

*Self-Assessment:* My people are scattered throughout the world. Monthly staff meetings seem too costly.

*Advice:* Try meeting in person twice per year, and twice monthly by teleconference or videoconference. At the end of each meeting, do a "process check" to see if you need to meet more or less often. Ask key team questions: "Do we need better teamwork, and, if so, what can we *all* do [not just you] to produce a more cohesive, effective team effort?"

*Self-Assessment:* OK, I've topgraded and half my team is new. But, we're disjointed.

*Advice:* Go off-site for team building.

## 39. Diversity

*Self-Assessment:* Frankly, we're a white male senior group, but we've done OK with diversity down in the organization. We've had no charges, so why sweat it?

*Advice:* If your strategy is to branch out beyond Duluth or Peoria, diversity isn't a nicety or a legal insurance policy, it's a necessity. Globalization requires diversity, so get with it.

*Self-Assessment:* I don't believe in quotas or tokens, but we need more minorities in management.

*Advice:* Then recruit like crazy. Require recruiters to produce A player candidates including blacks and women for *every* opening. Get the numbers not through lowering the bar but through creatively and aggressively recruiting.

## 40. Running Meetings

*Self-Assessment:* My people complain that my staff meetings aren't very productive. I've tried preparing better agendas and moving people along, but if I cut people off, I'm accused of being domineering.

*Advice:* Read two current books on meeting effectiveness—any two. They all say to empower the participants to take full responsibility. You speak as though it's all your responsibility, and it's not. *They* are copping out. Hold a "meeting on meetings"; address all of the factors listed in the books (clear goals, high commitment, widespread participation, mutual trust, timing, separate note taker, tight follow-up on actions, and so forth). If it doesn't improve, hire a facilitator.

*Self-Assessment:* How often do A players hold staff meetings?

*Advice:* Weekly. At a minimum, everyone can say what's going on. Better yet, participants interact for better coordination. Better yet, key decisions are made.

*Self-Assessment:* I don't know what an A player staff meeting looks like. Should it be friendly and professional?

*Advice:* Intense and chaotic is more typical. Everyone is active. The managers make sure that every meeting addresses all four key priorities for the year. Every issue gets out on the table and is addressed. Commitments are made. Follow-up is guaranteed, so everyone holds everyone accountable. These meetings are fast paced. No one attacks anyone personally, but no one avoids attacking an issue just to be nice.

## Additional Leadership Competencies

### 41. Vision

*Self-Assessment:* Should vision be the ideal or the practical?

*Advice:* Both. The balance must be credible. To be credible, the vision must be understandable and then understood by all. It must be alive—constantly reinforced and brought into decision making. When it is a mockery, hypocritical, or ridiculously unrealistic, scrap the vision and start over to create a better one.

## 42. Change Leadership

*Self-Assessment:* I drive change pretty hard and I'm told too many people are confused and scared.

*Advice:* You probably need to communicate 300 percent more. That means listening to people's concerns, responding, explaining, and involving people more in the change efforts. Some decisions must be participative to get buy-in. John Kotter's book *Leading Change* is good, but perhaps you need a workshop (National Training Laboratories, phone: 703-548-1500) or the help of a change consultant.

*Self-Assessment:* I'm a change agent; I love it when I can show that I welcome a new program that will beat the competition. More than just accepting it, I make it work.

*Advice:* You sound like a wonderful change implementer, taking others' initiatives and making them happen. A players are more apt to be true change masters, authoring changes and making them happen.

## 43. Inspiring "Followership"

*Self-Assessment:* I'm not a natural leader, and my people seem to go off in their own directions.

*Advice:* So-called natural leaders count for 1 percent of leaders, and all the other successful leaders are *made.* Get a credible strategy (#6) and vision (#41), topgrade your organization (#32, #33, #37), conduct good meetings (#40), and people will follow.

*Self-Assessment:* Peter Drucker writes that charisma is not as important as substance.

*Advice:* He's right, but even he agrees that charisma can help in times of great change—"selling" hundreds or thousands on accepting a new direction. A quiet, cold leader won't be very effective in the constant communications necessary to drive change; a dynamic, positive, charismatic leader has an advantage.

## 44. Conflict Management

*Self-Assessment:* Two of my subordinates can't resolve a major difference, and they have reluctantly brought the issue to me to resolve.

*Advice:* Bring them together NOW. Ask each individually to explain (a) her point of view, (b) the other's point of view, (c) what she will "give" for a solution, and (d) what she asks the other to give. Go through all four lists with a major goal of mutual understanding, and that's all—*not* necessarily a resolution. There is one ground rule: on any points of disagreement, X must state Y's point of view to Y's satisfaction, before stating her (X's) point of view. You are the referee. This is powerful: it ensures mutual understanding. Then resolution can finally be achieved.

*Self-Assessment:* I'm an A player, newly introduced into a C organization that fights everything I try to do. I get no air cover.

*Advice:* Shame on you for bad judgment in accepting an offer for a job in which you will probably fail. After getting a lot of scars, you'll either quit or get fired. In the meantime, talk to your boss about getting protection.

## Motivational Competencies

### 45. Energy

*Self-Assessment:* My energy level is declining. I eat right and take vitamin and mineral supplements, but I just can't find the time to exercise. My doc says to make the time.

*Advice:* Listen to your doc. See #18 (Stress Management).

*Self-Assessment:* I don't take much vacation. We're so delayered, everyone is doing at least two jobs.

*Advice:* Sounds as though your life is out of control. I've never known a manager who could not take full vacation, barring a crisis, if he or she had topgraded. No vacation might mean B/C players are killing you.

### 46. Passion

*Self-Assessment:* I feel enthusiastic, but don't show real passion.

*Advice:* If rah, rah is important, like in selling change, and if you are low key, express your enthusiasm other ways: videos that capture you at your best, celebrations of success in which others play effusive roles, well-written pieces for the house organ, and so on. Public relations coaches can sometimes tweak a presentation style, adding enthusiasm without attempting to remake a person's personality. Phony, plastic gimmicks backfire.

*Self-Assessment:* I'm not really passionate. I just do my job, and damned well. I'm serious and purposeful, and I'm an A player—except for enthusiasm.

*Advice:* Chances are you don't need to change. But progressing from Poor to Only Fair in Enthusiasm could spark the organization culture a bit. Without changing your personality, you can probably give a few more deserved pats on the back, say a few more positive things in staff meetings, and smile a bit more.

*Self-Assessment:* I'm the naysayer who keeps the nuts around here from going off in foolish directions.

*Advice:* You'd also better be a yeasayer. Any attorney or financial controller can say no, even a B/C player. A players have to add value to the yeses.

## 47. Ambition

*Self-Assessment:* I'm considered a high-potential manager. I'm only forty-five, but everyone sees me as a future CEO of a public company. Trouble is, I want my health and a real family life more than the CEO title.

*Advice:* Good for you. Follow your heart and you'll be happier than 90 percent of the ambitious strivers. Read Chapter 7 carefully. You can have your cake and eat it too. Either forget the CEO title in a large company, or, if you decide you want it but can only get a life in a smaller company, leave. You probably have twenty years of experience, so get 15 percent equity in a small company when you can be CEO *and* go to your kid's soccer game *and* eat dinners with the family *and* work out regularly. This could be more satisfying, more fun, more autonomous, and more lucrative.

*Self-Assessment:* People say I'm too ambitious, too eager to get ahead.

*Advice:* Don't trip over your ego. Let the powers above you know your desires, but your peers and subordinates should see only your deep commitment to your *current* job. If people see you as sacrificing future results to look good now, your integrity becomes suspect.

## 48. Compatibility of Needs

*Self-Assessment:* My leading candidate for VP of marketing really wants a GM job. She had one, but then her company relocated and she didn't go. She says she can be happy as VP of marketing, but maybe she's just saying that to get a job. I'm afraid that if she joins me as VP of marketing, she'll continue looking for a GM job.

*Advice:* Cut a deal. If she does an excellent job as VP of marketing, you'll help her get positioned again for general management in, say, three years. Special projects, a task force, a couple of seminars, and acting as GM for a vacationing GM can be part of the plan. Promise her only development, not a GM job. If your company cannot credibly develop her, don't hire her—she'll be trolling for that GM spot from the day she begins as VP marketing for you.

*Self-Assessment:* You can't find out what a job or company is really like until you get there.

*Advice:* Yes, you can. A players do it. They perform due diligence, thoroughly. Organize multiple visits. (See Chapter 3.)

## 49. Balance in Life

*Self-Assessment:* What balance?

*Advice:* Life is a process, not a forty-year career goal. Most senior managers who sacrificed balance for more than a year or so every five years gave up too much. They ultimately regret it. Balance of work, family, wellness, community, spiritual expression—that is the endgame. Balanced people are the most fulfilled. If your organization uses people up, QUIT.

## 50. Tenacity

*Self-Assessment:* A talented subordinate of mine gives up too easily, saying that frantic pursuit of work goals sacrifices his balance in life.

*Advice:* That's a cop-out. Of fifty competencies, Tenacity, the passion to succeed, is not last, but right up at the top, a component of Resourcefulness. Tenacious, resourceful people figure out how to serve customers and get quality time with the family. People generally low in tenacity should not be hired, except for a few mechanical, low-level jobs.

Did you see yourself and your subordinates in many of these situations? I suspect so.

Is such a focus on fixing weaknesses "negative thinking"? I hope you don't feel so. If you were an otherwise great surgeon, but your surgical knots were just a bit sloppy, unnecessarily stressing the adjoining skin, what would you do? You're Only Fair at knot tying, and you really want to be Very Good. Let your assistants suture for you? OK. Not bad—that's like a manager hiring people to compensate for his shortcomings. Or you could focus on knot tying and become Very Good at it. Is that negative thinking? A players don't think so. This is reality. Fixing weak points separates a lot of us from Bs and Cs. That's reality.

### CHAPTER 8 CHECKLIST: DO YOU HAVE WEAKNESSES TO FIX?

**YES NO**

☐ ☐ I recognize that my developmental time is better allocated to overcoming a potential fatal flaw than to maximizing an existing strength.

☐ ☐ I know what are the twelve most common career derailers.

☐ ☐ I am particularly interested in developing the most important competencies—Resourcefulness, Self-Awareness, Selecting A Players, and Redeploying B/C Players.

☐ ☐ I have a fix-my-weakness plan in progress.

With this groundwork laid on how As differ from others, how A players are picked, what competencies are most important, and how fatal flaws are fixed, let's move to how you can coach your people to maximize *their* strengths and, yes, fix *their* weaknesses.

# Nine

# COACHING 101:
# THE TOPGRADING-BASED MODEL

*Treat others as ends, never as means.*
> Immanuel Kant, 1724–1804

*I guess old dogs can learn new tricks.*
> Jack Welch

Coaching continues to be an important leadership competency. A players are selective, favoring jobs with a boss who can help them develop. Trouble is, research shows most managers to be mediocre coaches. Is your coaching reputation a draw for A talent? B/C players need good coaching to help them become As or realize they won't, so they become receptive to redeployment. Are you underdeveloping B/Cs who with coaching could become As? This chapter (essential theory and coaching tips) and Chapter 10 (case studies) will help you become a significantly more effective coach.

## A BRIEF HISTORY OF TOPGRADING COACHING

The history of topgrading is closely connected to coaching. Early in my career I polished the Topgrading Interview and, as a management psychologist, I coached people I assessed with Topgrading, shortly after they joined the company. I wanted feedback to help me assess hiring candidates better. A three-hour coaching session seemed to help new hires assimilate quicker, and beginning the Individual Development Plan process seemed to accelerate their overcoming weak points and maximizing their strengths. This was fun—A players were eager to get feedback and advice. And, it was easy, because A players are not only receptive, they are nondefensive and so resourceful that they figure out ways to improve on their own. I learned a lot about how to help sharp managers get even sharper because they gave me practical ideas that worked for them.

Then clients said, "Brad, you're pretty good at assessing candidates for selection, so how about assessing internal people?" The tried and true Topgrading Interview worked as well with internal managers, and the conclusions seemed credible to managers, because oral 360s were conducted to supplement Topgrading. Knowing I would be talking with their boss, peers, and subordinates, managers were very honest with themselves and with me, and the A players were predictably eager to learn how coworkers viewed them, and to get advice for how they could improve. Chronic B/C players found the process credible, a powerful supplement to their boss's feedback, because usually that was sparse and not so helpful. The combination of Topgrading-based coaching (which helped identify As to keep and B/Cs to replace) and Topgrading interviewing for hiring constituted topgrading. And for three decades I've passed on the topgrading principles, enabling managers like you to use the same process I used to become a better coach.

Flash forward. In the late 1980s I met Jack Welch of GE, who hired me to develop the process in which Topgrading-trained managers spend a week doing what I usually did individually—Topgrading Interviewing, 360s, coaching. Well, actually Jack didn't believe much in coaching. "Give the managers the report; an A player will figure out how to improve," he said. I told him that three hours of feedback would enable half the managers to improve a lot more and faster, and so he permitted it for the GE assessment and coaching process still used today. Then Jack asked me to personally assess and coach some GE executives, which helped him create the values/numbers model explained in Chapter 7. Many people thought Welch had gone soft, since "Neutron Jack" suddenly required managers to be good coaches, treat people with respect, and exhibit emotional intelligence. However, Welch's choice paid off; autocratic GE leaders were coached to be better, and one got so much better results that his business progressed from contributing $300 million to over $1 billion annually. Since GE embraced Topgrading-based assessment and coaching, thousands of managers have concluded, "I can learn and apply the same coaching techniques professionals use."

## DEFINITION OF COACHING

Coaching is a one-to-one-dialogue in which the coach helps a person understand his strengths and weak points and build commitment to improve performance. Coaching helps unlock someone's potentials. But which of the following is it?

- **Counseling**—to help someone improve self-awareness and change points of view

- **Mentoring**—sharing sage advice to help someone become more savvy in matters of organization culture, networking, and career planning

- **Teaching**—instructing someone in order to improve expertise

- **Confronting**—addressing nonperformance to help someone either achieve performance goals or accept the necessity of redeployment

You guessed—it's all of the above.

## THE COACHING CHALLENGE

Most managers are mediocre coaches. Surveys of more than five hundred thousand people conducted by Smart & Associates in the past thirty years show that 75 percent of employees rate their managers Only Fair or Poor as coaches. In my files of thousands of finalist candidates for senior management, only 25 percent qualify as having coaching as a standout strength. That leaves most of my management sample in need of improved coaching skills.

When people describe coaching deficiencies, they commonly describe their managers as:

- Inaccessible to me

- More results-oriented than people-oriented

- Too impatient to coach

- Hypercritical

- Stingy with praise

- Unconcerned with my career development

- Poor at listening

- Late and/or shallow in performance reviews

Looking at their mediocre ratings by subordinates in 360-degree surveys, managers have common excuses:

- *"I'm just too busy."* Downsizing and constant reorganizations require seventy hours of work per week. Delayering produces more subordinates, too many to coach.

- *"I don't know how to criticize without seeming hypercritical."* It's management by exception; in the crunch of time people have to learn that no news is good news. A players realize that if there is a problem, they'll hear about it fast.

- *"I just don't have those great coaching qualities: empathy and sensitivity."* Besides, the shareholder wants results from aggressive leadership. You don't rise in management by being Mother Teresa.

I've found that even the excuse makers find the promise of coaching alluring. Most senior managers I've interviewed have known at least one supercoach, and that coach led a charmed life. Coaching turbo-boosts talent, so the manager doesn't have to fight fires. With a trusting, supportive partnership forged with each subordinate, the coach is a nonstop inspiration to greatness. Each member of the team is coached to be better at problem solving, decision making, and team building. Are you short on time? Coaching helps—delegate more to people who have grown through good coaching. Are you hypercritical? No problem for a supercoach, who has so minimized his people's shortcomings; criticisms are positive tweaks, little nudges here or there. The noncoach is impaired, stifling his people through inattention, and sentencing himself to having a group of passive, dependent, nitpicked perpetual trainees with low morale.

A supercoach is a genius—initially coaching a lot, then empowering more but continuing coaching dialogue; she is able to play golf more because the job is done better. A supercoach is a talent magnet: "Susan doesn't use up talent, she grows it." A players flock to her to realize their full potential. Her well-coached flock flies on to bigger and better jobs, opening up slots for the lucky few who will reap the benefits of her coaching wisdom. She is a net provider of talent to other parts of the organization, which earns her accolades from the CEO. In times of fast, complex organizational change, her folks are the change agents, the fully developed leaders.

Some weak coaches burn out from trying to do it all themselves. Meanwhile, a supercoach has balance in life. Because she coaches regularly and effectively, she has time for herself—for thinking strategically, for special projects that give her visibility and promotability. Even a supercoach can't salvage most C players. Her coaching skills are so good, however, that she rarely has to fire someone, because chronic C players thank her for her sincere coaching and find another job. Hundreds of topgraders have told me that C players they fired ultimately thanked them.

Some managers experience a death spiral. There is "no time to coach," so they micromanage and nitpick, which fails to improve people, leaving less time for the "luxury" of coaching. As they micromanage, they drive away A players, have even less time to coach, and so on. As for those inspirational human qualities, forget it! No time. No time.

## THE MAGIC OF TOPGRADING-BASED COACHING

Put simply, when you topgrade, you automatically possess supercoach advantages. Really. Pull it off as this chapter and Chapter 10 teach, and you will find yourself improving as a coach with every member of your team; it's the equivalent of teaching you a good five-iron swing; master it, and the principles will transfer to other clubs. Use Topgrading-based coaching to help your new hire assimilate, begin to fit, and start a long-term development plan. Use these coaching skills to assess and develop all members of your team. When you have a topgraded team of A players who respect you and ask for your feedback and counsel (A players aren't shy about requesting feedback), you just naturally exude supercoach qualities. A players are more coachable than C players! Develop your subordinate managers to use Topgrading-based coaching as they topgrade, and pretty soon your entire team will be better coaches, maximizing the talents of A players on your dream team. I'm not just guessing that this happy scenario can take place.

As thousands of managers have topgraded, their 360 surveys have shown better and better coaching qualities.

## CHARACTERISTICS OF A SUPERCOACH

Coaching is important to, perhaps even the essence of, good leadership. What exactly are the characteristics of a good coach or supercoach?

1. **A partner.** "Hey, you've got a problem, let's work on it together." Interested, engaged, respectful, and respected.

2. **Promotes autonomy.** Helps the coachee to independently diagnose problems and consider solutions; makes informed choices regarding development.

3. **Positive.** Is supportive, builds confidence, is an enthusiastic motivator. Uses praise and recognition for progress and accomplishment. Never ridicules. Is passionate. Has a sense of humor.

4. **Trustworthy.** Is honest and open. Maintains confidences. Admits when wrong. Doesn't overpromise.

5. **Caring.** Is compassionate, empathetic, and sincere.

6. **Patient.** Understands how hard it is to change. Is tolerant and reasonable.

7. **Results-oriented.** Focuses only on important issues. Is proactive and infectiously committed to helping coachee perform. Follows through on promises.

8. **Perceptive.** Understands coachee's strengths, shortcomings, goals, and needs.

9. **Authoritative.** Is knowledgeable and wise. Is clear and specific in feedback. Has common sense. Generates valid measures of improvement. (Don't confuse *authoritative* with *authoritarian,* which means dictatorial.)

10. **Active listener.** Plays back content and underlying feelings. Summarizes, clarifies.

If such superb human qualities are necessary for coaching, it's no wonder most managers are found deficient. However, ordinary solid human qualities blended with topgrading best practices frequently result in leaders rated "very high" on coaching scales. This becomes clear during assimilation coaching, a disciplined process to help your new hire adjust and to begin a comprehensive developmental process.

## ASSIMILATION COACHING

During the first few weeks after starting to work, the new A player mostly is listening and getting to know people. The shortcomings you know exist in your new hire aren't apparent . . . yet. How does your new hire regard you? Chances are you stack up extremely well against the ten characteristics of a supercoach. The typical 25 percent success rate in hires makes an assimilation-coaching meeting awkward three-quarters of the time. Mishiring destroys a mutually trusting "partnership" and usually triggers mutual blaming. "You didn't tell me about all these problems." "Oh, yeah, you didn't tell me you had so little project management experience." So much for the honeymoon! But Topgrading Interviews produce good hires (meaning A players), and they are much easier to coach than B/C players.

Fortunately, you conducted the (tandem) Topgrading Interview and half a dozen revealing reference checks. Your new hire is almost certainly an A player and was not hesitant to ask you penetrating questions. You both concluded this is a good match. At the beginning of your Topgrading Interview you promised assimilation coaching, and this is it. The Topgrading Interview introduction promised coaching for short-term performance and long-term development. Several weeks after the new hire started, you are meeting to begin fulfilling these promises.

Of course, you're regarded by your new hire as a *partner* (supercoach characteristic #1). Extending the job offer was a vote of confidence by you and an indication of respect for you. You are the *authoritative* boss, in charge, which is supercoach characteristic #9. The Topgrading Interview provided extremely thorough insights into your new hire; assuming you performed a 360-degree survey within the past few days, your new hire is eager to learn "How am I doing?" You know the hiree's strengths and weaker points better than anyone, making you *perceptive* (#8). You accurately perceive the hiree's needs because you've already asked about them in dozens of ways. You have shown you understand. So, in this honeymoon period there is no doubt you are *caring* (#5) and *trustworthy* (#4). You both want that new hire to achieve high-performance goals; you both are *results-oriented* (#7) in this coaching. You've hired an A player, who doesn't want dependency on you, so you are regarded as *promoting autonomy* (#2). Expect a never-ending process of coaching As to successfully take on more responsibility, of actively monitoring and training them as needed, but empowering them as soon as they have proved worthy. If there have been missteps in the first few weeks, now is the perfect time to nip problems in the bud. If you have insights and a willingness to coach for long-term growth, hey, that's what A players want.

"Bonding" naturally occurs in Topgrading interviewing and hiring A players, so it's pretty hard for you not to be *patient* (#6) and a good *active listener* (#10), even if these generally are not your strengths. Without being a psychologist, you already have a good idea of the thinking style (intuitive, analytical, participative, experimental, emotional) of the hiree and vice versa, and you both have figured out how to adapt to the other's style. You know what the hiree expects in a manager—you've noted it in the Topgrading interview and many reference checks. You both know you can work together. Your new hire is all ears, open, responsive, and truly in a "teachable moment." You are apt to be *positive* (#3) and perceived to be positive by your new hire, because your new hire is probably doing just fine. Hey, it doesn't get any better than this.

Take advantage of this golden moment! First-time Topgrading interviewers have fun in assimilation coaching, a high-powered, positive coaching session. You feel empowered, so it is relatively easy to empower your new hire. There are fewer problems to fix with A players than with C players, so there is little inclination to push, cajole, or demand certain changes. With an initial coaching meeting a success, you become positively reinforced to polish your skills, to extend coaching to other subordinates.

---

**Hiring an A player using Topgrading interviewing and thorough reference checking automatically endows you with supercoach characteristics.**

---

## CAN LEOPARDS CHANGE THEIR SPOTS?

Coaching requires a complex interplay of assumptions regarding:

- Whether people in general can change

- Whether this individual can change

- How amenable specific competencies are to change

- What circumstances trigger unusual change

As an interviewer you should bet that people will change only when they already have demonstrated an ability to improve in a particular competency; that is, assume people can change when they already have changed. If someone is improving teamwork skills, believing further improvement will be possible is justified. Don't be naive and assume someone will finally get organized when every boss in the past ten years has criticized him for being disorganized. You can be sure that at every job change, he promised, "I'll improve, I'll improve. I really mean it this time!" Sure.

Let's investigate this subject in more depth. We all know that we have changed for the better. We mellow, become wiser, and acquire maturity and judgment. We all know individuals who dramatically changed—a hard charger who slowed down after a heart attack, for example. However, no hiring manager, no coach, can count on life-altering epiphanies.

A Topgrading-based coaching meeting, whether for assimilation or another purpose, is not a love-in. It's not always warm and fuzzy. Even A players have weak points—plenty of them. Coaching need not be acrimonious, but to be effective it must be hard hitting. Even A players can become defensive. My advice is not simplistic. But it can simplify the complexity of trying to figure out the likelihood of changing fifty different competencies. Let's take a look at those fifty.

The positioning of competencies in the three columns in Figure 9.1 is not carved in stone. Specific competencies are "relatively easy to change" or "harder but doable" for different individuals and in different circumstances. The "very difficult to change" list fits almost everyone in my experience. No matter how much we might want to change, there is simply no way an adult can acquire significantly more Intelligence, more IQ points.

We may learn to stretch our intelligence through hard work and listening to smart people, but it is rare for people to transform shallow Analysis Skills into deep ones, dullness into Creativity, lack of Conceptual Ability into a strength. There aren't many places to go for a character transplant to improve one's Integrity. Some sort of religious conversion might do it, but that is hard to incorporate in a developmental plan. So-called "natural" leadership components of Assertiveness and Inspiring Followership take years and years of serious work to improve from weaknesses to strengths.

## Figure 9.1
## The Ease of Changing Competencies

| *Relatively Easy to Change* | *Harder but Doable* | *Very Difficult to Change* |
|---|---|---|
| Risk Taking | Judgment | Intelligence |
| Leading Edge | Strategic Skills | Analysis Skills |
| Education | Pragmatism | Creativity |
| Experience | Track Record | Conceptual Ability |
| Organization/Planning | Resourcefulness | Integrity |
| Self-Awareness | Excellence Standards | Assertiveness |
| Communications—Oral | Independence | Inspiring Followership |
| Communications—Written | Stress Management | Energy |
| First Impression | Adaptability | Passion |
| Customer Focus | Likability | Ambition |
| Political Savvy | Listening | Tenacity |
| Selecting A Players | Team Player | |
| Redeploying B/C Players | Negotiation Skills | |
| Coaching/Training | Persuasiveness | |
| Goal Setting | Team Builder | |

| Empowerment | Change Leadership |
|---|---|
| Performance Management | Diversity |
| Running Meetings | Conflict Management |
| Compatibility of Needs | Credible Vision |
| | Balance in Life |

Tough SOBs, short on Likability, can be coached to be nicer; they are "nicer" every day with their boss and customers, so it's a matter of figuring out how to broaden the range of already existing skills. "Meek Mike" is always lacking in Assertiveness and if he suddenly tries to be forceful, he blows it. It takes him a long time to develop muscles he has never used. Better wellness and balance can jack up Energy a bit, but both require major commitments and real discipline. Enthusiasm can be faked a little better, but in general the motivational competencies—Energy, Passion, Ambition, and Tenacity—are ingrained and hardwired. They are very difficult but not impossible to change; people who had it but lost it when stifled can get it back under new A player leadership. Ditto for Resourcefulness, the megacompetency; it is very difficult for a manager to instill it where it has never been a strength, but wake-up calls can work if Resourcefulness has been dormant. All the other competencies are more fixable; that is, for most people, a conscientious effort can correct an Only Fair rating to Good. Is change from Very Poor to Good possible? Anything is possible, but the only Very Poor competencies I have frequently seen become Good are Education (take the courses), Experience (grow in a job), Communications—Oral and Written (take classes or get a tutor), Political Savvy (after getting burned), Selecting A Players (use Topgrading interviews), Redeploying C Players (you can just do it), and Compatibility of Needs (take the right job).

Chapter 8 provided advice for all fifty competencies, with the general perspective that a manager can do a lot to improve those in the Relatively Easy to Change category, but should change jobs if there is a major weakness in the Very Difficult to Change category. As a manager, devote your energies to helping people change in competencies that can be changed, and don't waste a lot of time trying to create a competency that has never existed.

## WHY PEOPLE CHANGE

The crocodile theory of change is simple, but explains a lot. We all live on tiny islands separated from danger. If a big, nasty crocodile comes ashore, we become highly motivated to change, to escape. But, jumping in the water with more crocs is also scary. Without a credible way to get to safety, why risk changing? If more crocs come ashore, we'll just go nuts. Welcome to the business world! The more responsibility you get, the more crocs come ashore, first nipping at your feet, then your ankles, then higher.

You discover a rowboat, a way to escape! But, it's leaky, so why risk it? Aha, now you find a speedboat, gassed and ready to go! That makes change easy.

---

### People change when the avoidance of pain seems worth the risk.

---

If one baby croc crawls ashore and I offer you a speedboat to escape, your decision is easy to make—you'll do it, you'll change. If fifteen full-grown crocs come ashore and I offer you only a leaky rowboat, you might risk leaving the island, because you have to. But no boat, no change. No crocs, no change. It's all a calculus—a balancing of developmental options (boats) in relation to anticipated pain (size and number of crocs) if you don't change. Anticipated career failure is ten big crocs, but if you don't see any escape boats, what can you do? The coach provides boats. If you don't know there are crocs on your island, you won't be motivated to change. The coach points out the crocs— a 360-degree survey showing arrogance combined with a "not promotable" rating because of it, for example.

---

### Rational belief is frequently insufficient to effect real change.

---

There are a few baby crocs on your island, and you know they will grow bigger and you know that your boat is beginning to leak and will only rot more, so you suppose you should change, one of these days. Or maybe you'll depart next year, when the crocs are bigger. Everyone tells you that you should listen better and get organized, but why should you? After all, you're getting top performance reviews. There are only baby crocs motivating you to get better organized. But when they are suddenly full grown, your emotions enter. Real fear. What a great motivator! If your boss tells you your 50 percent bonus will be zero if you don't get organized, that's like having ten hungry crocs licking their lips (do they have lips?).

I have coached dozens of managers who were fired because they didn't see the crocs coming. Paul was heir apparent at a major Chicago-based company, but his sense of humor was lethal. He constantly zeroed in on his people's most embarrassing vulnerabilities and ten times each day would utter a clever, but painful comment. I assessed twenty candidates for promotion to president two years before the planned retirement of his company's excellent president. The oral 360s I conducted led to this feedback: "Paul, ten of twelve peers will quit if you are named president." The CEO said, "Paul, fix that smart-ass mouth of yours! I won't promote you if there will be a mass exodus, and if I don't promote you, you're a blocker, and I'll fire you." Paul just couldn't control his hurtful sarcasm and was fired. He blamed the CEO, saying, "For twenty years you knew my personality and always suggested I cut the sarcasm, but you never held back a bonus, and you promoted me faster than my peers. You should have withheld both to get my attention." Paul was making excuses, but he also made a good point:

---

**Do not promote managers with a serious weakness until after they have fixed it.**

---

The nicest thing you can do for high-potential managers is tell the truth and hold them accountable for growth. That means becoming like a big croc and saying, "Improve, and only then will you get promoted."

You're getting along adequately living on an island, eating mostly bananas. The menu is a little boring, but the sea is wavy most of the time and your rowboat leaks. It's not worth the effort to fix the leaks . . . yet. You're not motivated . . . yet. But after a couple of months you are very tired of eating bananas. You look through your binoculars and see on a distant island, a McDonald's. Yum! Now you're motivated. You hadn't figured out how to fix the leaky boat, but now you're eager to be resourceful and figure it out. You try filling cracks with mud, melt some plastic bottles and pour the liquid into the cracks—whatever it takes.

Similarly, suppose you are thirty years old and would like to retire at fifty, and you could save 25 percent of your income, but that intuitively seems too little. So, why try? Motivation is lacking. Then someone teaches you the magic of compounding, and you see how saving and investing can lead to financial independence. Now you're motivated, so you begin saving and investing. Your hunger for independence wasn't sufficiently motivational until you understood the means (like fixing a leaky boat).

You get it. Coaches point out the fast-food restaurants (the vision of an exciting, better life), the crocs (pain in not changing), and the boats (developmental avenues). In thirty-four years of coaching I have found the most significant and enduring change to take place when the manager perceives a lot of fast food stores, a lot of crocs, and a lot of speedboats, or in ordinary terms:

---

**People change the most when they sense pain in not changing and benefits in changing, and fully embrace developmental activities to achieve their goals.**

---

## WHY PEOPLE DON'T CHANGE ON THEIR OWN

Why don't we, you and I, change on our own? Even when we realize we will be happier making a change, why don't we? Would coaching help us?

People don't change because:

- **It's impossible.** A subordinate may correctly conclude that he lacks the innate capacity to play for the Chicago Bulls or become a CPA. No coaching would help.

- **We have blind spots.** Sue simply doesn't know what it takes to succeed, what career paths would match her talents and interests. Charlie does not realize how offensive he can be barking out orders. Coaching can help.

- **We have normal defense mechanisms.** We all rationalize failures, blame others, project our own foibles into others, and deny that an "idiosyncrasy" could be a career derailer. Coaching can help here.

- **We fear changing.** Although we in organizations are supposed to welcome and even initiate change, many people truly fear radical change, avoid it, and resist it.

## PSYCHOLOGICAL STAGES IN CHANGE

Whether for coaching a new hire, addressing a newly observed problem, or facilitating change in any performance-management or career-development system, the steps are the same:

1. *Awareness.* "I seem to have a need to change."

2. *Rational acceptance.* "I definitely need to change."

3. *Emotional commitment.* "I not only own the problem, I own the responsibility to fix it."

4. *Individual Development Plan for development.* "I fully embrace this program, with specific activities."

5. *Reinforcement.* "I need internal and/or external reinforcement and feedback for maximum growth."

6. *Monitoring progress.* "I embrace measurement of my progress."

7. *Conclusion.* "I've fixed this problem; while recognizing that for some issues a lifelong effort is necessary, I have achieved the specific goal of eliminating a potential career derailer."

Let's consider the context, the implicit psychological contract in a constructive coaching session.

---

**Implied in all seven steps is who's in charge—
not the coach, but the person receiving the coaching.**

---

Even if you have to confront nonperformance in a C player, the most constructive outcome (even if it is a friendly termination) comes not from a trash compactor, beating a person with failure, but from a dialogue in which the person arrives at self-awareness and the conclusions necessary to change. A players always say, "Give me the unvarnished truth, don't beat around the bush." They want your insights and advice; then they will figure out how to change. Great! All seven steps might be addressed in five minutes. With C players it's slower, much slower, but the basic principle is the same: We all change fastest and deepest when we own the process.

If you buy the assumption that you as a coach are a change facilitator, not a change intimidator, a lot of supercoach qualities emerge. Instead of blaming, you problem solve. Instead of focusing on the person, you focus on the problem. You come across as "I'm OK, you're OK," and never, ever the condescending "I'm OK, you're NOT OK." Questions help the coachee diagnose and fix problems, rather than respond defensively. Instead of "Why weren't you generating more leads?" it's "How many leads did you generate in relation to the performance standard?" If you already know the answer, ask, "How do you feel about last month's performance?"

A wonderful technique for communicating those supercoach qualities is *active listening*—playing back what you hear and the feelings underlying it. Active listening is more than simply echoing back what you have heard. It involves paraphrasing the essence of the person's point of view. An active listener grasps and reflects back people's intent, reading between the lines. Body language is observed, and unstated feelings are accurately interpreted. It is much more helpful to reflect content and feelings by saying, "You're stumped by that problem," than to fake understanding ("I think I know what you're saying"), feign empathy ("I feel your pain"), or talk about yourself ("That reminds me of a time . . ."). Active listening is a powerful coaching tool when you want to avoid an argument, help a person become more dispassionate and objective, or guide the person to diagnose and solve a problem without giving your solution. Forget trying to use active listening when you are angry at the person, when trust is an issue in your relationship, or when you are too hassled or frustrated to calmly tune in to both the other person's feelings and your own.

Summarizing the three reasons why a goal was not met does not mean you agree with excuses, but simply that you care, you are listening, and you understand. Saying, "You missed quota three months in a row. One more month and you're fired," is clear, but a more motivational coaching approach might be "Joe, you've indicated three reasons for not making quota, you've shared how difficult and frustrating this is, and you just can't see how you will make quota in the future." This opens the door for the salesperson to take responsibility for either changing the results or considering job options. Putting the coachee in control means a chronic C player will be more apt to fix his behavior or, if not, more apt to depart on friendly terms (meaning no lawsuit).

Topgrading-based coaching builds in all seven of the psychological stages in change. Let's pause on each step for some coaching tips.

## 1. Awareness

Awareness is essential for change. How can we change if we aren't even aware of a reason to change? People who have never been given honest feedback can be oblivious to their weaker points. Coach a person toward awareness by:

- *Encouraging the person to solicit feedback.* If you have heard customer complaints, present your data and perhaps the salesperson will suggest a customer survey, which is bound to make the person aware that there are major problems.

- *Granting that 5 percent of negative perceptions of a person are typically not true.* Coworkers tend to assume the worst, even to an unfair degree, when they don't like or respect someone. Suppose you want to coach your subordinate to stop publicly berating others on your team. You've witnessed name calling and know your coachee is disrupting teamwork. You conduct an email 360 survey that solidly documents name calling, but written comments also criticize the person for breaking confidences, slacking off, and poor listening—all without clear examples. When you review the 360 results your coachee owns up to name calling and poor listening but vehemently denies breaking a confidence or slacking off. The best approach is to deal with the hard facts on name calling and listening and avoid dealing with confidences and slacking off, saying, "Those criticisms may not be true but just part of an increasingly negative image that makes people *think* you are guilty of more negatives than are true. That's all the more reason to fix the two big issues—name calling and poor listening."

- *Conveying that the higher the management position, the more true is the statement "Perception is reality."* Even if the person is not lazy, if that is the perception it is worth being aware of it. Then a program must manage the perception, even if the perception is inaccurate.

• *Doing a "data dump" on resilient, confident A players ("I don't think you are fitting in very well yet.") but inching into it more gradually with B/C players ("How do you feel you are fitting in?").* The more defensive the person, the more dialogue is necessary in order to know when there is receptivity to more negatives.

• *Being prepared with useful data that is specific (not general), is descriptive (not evaluative), is objective (not subjective), conveys "I" (accurately describe what you experience without blaming the person), and is well timed.* Unuseful data would be "You're running to catch a plane (poorly timed) but you've (blame) screwed up (evaluative) on that software project (general), and I think you are deliberately undermining a project you never wanted (subjective)." Here's a better approach: "Jan, thanks for carving out half an hour to discuss the software project (well timed); the flow chart (objective) shows three weeks of slippage (specific), and I (saying what you experience without blame) can't deliver on my goals without it."

• *Suggesting that any data can be checked for accuracy.* If there is disagreement, you will be happy to help the person test the data further. In fact, you are not on a witch hunt, and if the negative data are invalid, you want to know it. If someone says, "I'm not a poor team player. I'm very cooperative," conduct an anonymous email survey to see.

## 2. Rational Acceptance

A person can be aware that they have a shortcoming but not rationally accept its seriousness. For example, a 5'2" man can be aware that it is unusual for someone his height to play professional basketball, but not rationally accept the futility of trying out, year after year. Acceptance is rationally understanding connections and consequences. Coach the person by:

• *Connecting the Awareness of the person's stated short-term performance goals and long-term ambitions.* If a person is hesitant to take the CPA examination, ask, "How much more marketable will you be with the CPA?" When people grasp logical consequences, they are more apt to rationally (but not necessarily emotionally) agree that a developmental activity should be embraced.

- *"Visualizing"* what the person's life (job, career) would be with improvement. Be colorful and enthusiastic. Visualize what consequences there will be without change. The video generations respond to scenes vividly described, so paint word pictures with crocodiles, Big Macs, rowboats, and speedboats.

- *Explaining interaction effects among weaker points.* "The 360-degree feedback shows your team considers you aloof, uncommunicative, inaccessible, unconcerned with teamwork, and uncaring. When you fail to return phone calls promptly, all five negatives are exacerbated. On the other hand, as you fix each, the perception will eventually be that you are fixing others. If you return calls promptly, you show caring, demonstrate communicativeness, and so on."

This interaction effect is complex and merits more comment because using it in coaching can cause positive breakthroughs: "Now I get it—these interrelated weaker points feed off each other and produce a death spiral in which people expect the worst of me. I have to break up that death spiral!"

The executives I coach who have a serious weak point, a fatal flaw, all suffer from an interaction effect. They are shocked to realize how a lot of different, but related, weak points feed off of each other in a death spiral and create a much bigger composite weak point. That's when coaching is particularly effective, for it takes the manager from the awareness stage to rational acceptance, making the person all ears for the next stage, commitment.

Here's an example of how the interaction effect works: A busy manager can readily understand the criticisms, "You're inaccessible," "You're slow to return emails," and "you could communicate more to team members." However, oral 360s connect the weaker points: "Ron is a selfish SOB who frankly doesn't give a damn about anyone except himself; he destroys teamwork with incomplete or contradictory directions, never asks how my spouse with cancer is doing, and has ignored all of our requests for career planning. We're all stuck in our jobs, and the A players are looking for jobs elsewhere."

Ron might have been on the phone with the CEO and couldn't arrive at a particular staff meeting on time, but the team assumes he is tardy because he is inconsiderate, uncaring, and selfish. It's not so much each individual weak point that's the fatal flaw, it's the mutually reinforcing negative composite perception that magnifies each of the negative perceptions, even if they aren't true. Helping a subordinate recognize how the interaction effect works can lock in acceptance, because it provides a psychologically sophisticated rationale for why, in this case, the perceptions of coworkers seem negative. But a person can say, "I get it! I get it!" and still lack a deep emotional need to change.

## 3. Emotional Commitment

If awareness is understanding a fact ("I'm 5'2" tall.") and acceptance is rationally grasping consequences ("It will be extremely difficult to make the team."), commitment engages the person emotionally ("I know in my gut I should pursue a different occupation."). Coach the person by:

- *Explaining how the interaction effect can be reversed.* By making small improvements in each weak point, the death spiral becomes, eventually, a positive snowballing effect in which coworkers actually assume positive behaviors ("Ron is probably late because he's helping Jan prepare her PowerPoint presentation."). The emotional commitment becomes locked in as the person experiences more positive interactions.

- *Showing understanding of how difficult it is to change.* Build emotional commitment by acknowledging that some changes take years, that it's normal to take two steps forward and one backward. Sometimes having empathy with the person, acknowledging what a huge effort is necessary, helps make the emotional connection ("Someone understands and cares that I will be making such a big sacrifice to improve, so I'll give it a try.").

- *If interpersonal changes are needed, saying that a 5 percent change in behavior can improve ratings from Only Fair to Good.* For example, when hypercritical, condescending, volatile managers eliminate the most outrageous 5 percent of their behavior, coworkers genuinely feel the manager has improved a lot. Coworkers of the manager then become less defensive and are more willing to admit mistakes. Teamwork improves because there is less inclination to point fingers. A manager I have coached every three years for the past decade saved his job by eliminating the most outrageous, offensive 5 percent of his behavior. Instead of

A players fleeing from him, he attracted them. His business has improved from contributing $50 million in profits to more than $500 million yearly. This approach sometimes helps people by showing that their efforts can pay off, that changing is not such a daunting task.

• *Not trying to change anyone's character or basic personality.* People can accept being coached, helped, and facilitated, but resent being changed, manipulated, or "saved." Even people who have improved dramatically in their relationships when they have become a heck of a lot more considerate and human as a result of coaching, say, "OK, I changed my behavior, I've mellowed and improved my listening skills, but I'm basically the same person." People are more committed when they're in charge, not when you have forced them to become more committed. We all thrive best on free, informed choice.

• *Avoiding overload.* An eager beaver might initially be committed to a twenty-point personal development program, but lose commitment when things start to slip. Focus on the most important issues, particularly potentially fatal flaws.

The major challenge in helping someone move from rational acceptance to emotional commitment is showing how little wins can result in big successes.

## 4. Individual Development Plans (IDPs)

The Individual Development Plan (IDP) operationalizes awareness, rational acceptance, and emotional commitment. When a person is committed, creation of a workable plan is necessary. Strike while the iron is hot! IDPs should be composed with new hires (as part of assimilation coaching), during topgrading assessments (to determine who are the A/A potentials), and during coaching (to help people become As), and IDPs should be composed annually because everyone has developmental needs . . . forever. The IDP comprehensively states what the person will do, why (this is very important to lock in commitment), when, and how the results will be measured. Key principles are:

• *Encourage the person to write it.* It's not your program. I have found over the years that three-quarters of the people who compose their own plan after my coaching interview follow through on it quite conscientiously. Of those who do not compose their own plan, only one-third follow through. Appendix H is a sample Individual Development Plan; please read it now.

• *Stimulate multifaceted activities.* One-shot fixes rarely work. Suggest or be supportive of the person's planning to involve many avenues— learning a skill from one person, observing another, reading, taking a seminar.

• *Add your suggestions.* Although you want the person to design a solid program, you have more experience. It won't kill the person's initiative if you offer a couple of ideas. The important thing is for the person to want them in the program, not to feel manipulated into including your ideas.

• *Use an annual calendar.* For a fairly comprehensive plan covering three or four issues, an annual calendar works best. One intensive learning experience (say, a seminar) is OK, but continuing the learning process by visits with experts and readings spread out over a year can make it stick better.

• *Inspire with a positive vision.* Frequently paint a positive picture of what life will be like to your subordinate when the IDP is implemented— the greater effectiveness as a leader, more fun meetings, challenges, and perhaps promotion opportunities.

## 5. Reinforcement

Implementation of IDPs can falter, simply because, as with New Year's resolutions, people have good intentions but then get busy with other activities and . . . you know the rest. Fortunately, there are easy, powerful reinforcers you can use to keep people focused on their development:

• *Email 360-degree surveys.* Done properly, they can be enormously useful. Typically, 360s are so long that respondents blow through them, and useful written comments are few. We parachute into companies to topgrade, and oftentimes the performance appraisals fail to identify the chronic B/C players, making it costly in severance to remove them. So we look at 360 surveys, and those are usually flawed. Email 360s completed by B/C players value the wrong behaviors; As are rated low by Cs because Cs are lazy and don't want to be held accountable. With proper Topgrading assessments, the feedback is complicated when a C says, "I'm confused—my performance appraisal and 360 show I'm an A player."

As topgrading professionals, we include in our assessments the Topgrading Interview supplemented by oral 360s. We and higher-level A players choose the respondents, so a C player can't stack the deck. We redo the email 360, emphasizing inclusion of A players, to measure improvement in weak areas and verify strengths. The Mursau Group (Appendix J) has developed a wonderful email product that:

- *is short.* Following the Topgrading Interview, a ten- to fifteen-item survey is written by the professional, with perhaps ten strengths and five weak points.
- *values opinions of A players.* The topgrading professional and A player bosses salt the mines with A player respondents.
- *protects anonymity.* Only the computer knows who has responded.
- *provides full frequency distributions.* Most 360s provide a range of ratings, but it's much more useful to see all the ratings. It's nice for a manager to know he's widely considered trustworthy, but he also needs to know if two out of twelve respondents said he's "never" trustworthy.

In Chapter 10, the T. J. Johnson case study has an example of this email 360 survey, with charts showing how he improved.

- *Suggest keeping a log.* People rarely think of this on their own. Interpersonal (such as giving praise), emotional (such as blowing up), and organizational (such as time spent on top priorities) improvements are reinforced by a daily log. Recording successes and failures need take only five minutes a day. More successes over time fortify commitment, because the act of recording more successes and fewer failures is self-reinforcing ("Hey, I'm really improving.").

- *Include some easy fixes.* Although the program should primarily address the most important developmental needs, include some activities to tweak minor shortcomings in order to boost motivation. "Take a PC class" is a simple activity. Checking it off is a reinforcer of the entire developmental program.

• *Offer a reminder card.* I sometimes give people laminated credit-card–size reminder cards. Million-dollar-a-year executives have said, "I pull the card out with my credit cards, and it reminds me to stay on the program." Here's an example:

---

### Management Development Reminders

**Pat Jones**
**Hold weekly staff meetings.**
**Email boss monthly results.**
**Give praise ten times each day.**
**Read *The Wall Street Journal* daily.**
**Take one peer to lunch each week.**

---

• *Offer regular coaching.* You can be the most powerful reinforcer, meeting weekly (for serious people problems) or quarterly (for all other issues) to review progress, praise accomplishment, and tweak the program. Regular meetings for feedback from a customer, a peer, or a subordinate who will tell the truth in feedback sessions can also be useful. Remind your coachee to never punish honest feedback—to accept it appreciatively, or else the feedback sources will dry up.

## 6. MONITORING PROGRESS

• *Convey a bias for metrics.* You love data. Your A player coachees will too—say, measurements of production, customer complaints, quality, and other indications of good achievement. Email 360 surveys efficiently measure "soft" issues, like teamwork, trust, values, and emotional intelligence. Although A players thrive on metrics, C players have to be nudged toward objective measurement of reality. If measurements of hard results and soft issues are both spiraling downward, it could be time for a job change.

## 7. CONCLUSION

*Celebrate wins!* Don't let your A players move on to the next Individual Development Plan (they always seem to be doing that) without popping the champagne to celebrate big improvements. C players who have hung in there and fixed a fatal flaw deserve to have not only a sincere pat on the back, but assurances that the fixed issues will not be brought up as a negative again and again.

Many topgrading professionals have contributed to these best practices in coaching. This chapter has provided a distillation of psychological principles that really work as well as practical tips from the most successful professionals and hundreds of supercoaches. In Chapter 10, case studies will clarify how theory and practical application combine in coaching best practices.

### CHAPTER 9 CHECKLIST: ARE YOU BECOMING A SUPERCOACH?

**YES NO**

☐ ☐  I conduct (tandem) Topgrading Interviews, so I hire coachable A players at least 90 percent of the time.

☐ ☐  While introducing the Topgrading Interview, I promise coaching for assimilation, short-term performance, and long-term growth.

☐ ☐  I conduct oral 360-degree interviews in preparation for Topgrading-based assimilation coaching.

☐ ☐  I understand which competencies are relatively easy to change, which are harder but doable, and which are very difficult to change.

☐ ☐  I understand the crocodile and fast-food theories of why people change.

☐ ☐  I can list four reasons why people do not change.

☐ ☐  I can list the seven stages in change.

☐ ☐ I understand that the most dramatic and enduring change occurs when the coachee is in charge.

☐ ☐ Following coaching interviews, my coachees write their own Individual Development Plans (IDPs) and follow-up reports.

☐ ☐ I use short, tailored email 360s, with A player respondents, to measure improvement on my team members' IDPs.

The next chapter converts this theory into practice, beginning with a hypothetical case study for your first Topgrading-based assimilation coaching session.

# Ten

# CASE STUDIES:
# COACHING TO FIX WEAKNESSES

*It is not the strongest of the species that survives, nor the most
intelligent; it is the one that is most adaptable to change.*
                                                          Charles Darwin

Applying the theory of coaching is easier than you think and more effective. As promised in Chapter 9 and elsewhere in *Topgrading,* having conducted a Topgrading Interview gives you instant coaching advantages.
Having hired an A player, you automatically are 20 percent better as a
coach. This chapter will help you become even better. This chapter begins
with a simple case study outlining the model, the specific steps in conducting a Topgrading-based assimilation coaching session. Then a case study
shows how to use topgrading techniques to soften the blow when firing an
underperformer. The Tom Brock and T. J. Johnson case studies showing
how applying best practices in coaching can produce dramatic improvements in leadership style. The Johnson case study uses the simplest, most
powerful, most valid email 360 technique we've seen to monitor and measure coaching effectiveness and to motivate and guide people in their development.

## AN ASSIMILATION COACHING MODEL

I assume that you have passed Coaching 101 (Chapter 9). This chapter lays
out the structure and sequence of actual coaching sessions. It's like a videotape of what actually happens during successful coaching meetings.

In this fictitious case study, pretend you are the vice president store operations who hired Pat, a store manager, two weeks ago. Based on your tandem Topgrading Interview and thorough reference checking, you are sure
that she is the A player you need to turn around an underperforming store
with high theft, poor sales, lousy morale, C players, and red ink. You are not

surprised that she is ruffling some feathers. It's time for Topgrading-based assimilation coaching. The goals are to:

- Smooth the transition into her new job as store manager,

- Help Pat create an Individual Development Plan, to maximize her strengths and minimize her weaknesses in order for her to achieve the highest level of performance, and

- Include in her IDP activities to help her reach her long-term goal of vice president operations (your present job, for you want her to be your A player successor).

Why not begin a comprehensive, hard-hitting developmental-planning process now, during the honeymoon period? This is when problems can be nipped in the bud. Why wait for more serious problems to occur or for an annual performance appraisal? Pat is coming on strong, as you hoped and expected, but in bulldozing her way toward achieving business goals she is too pushy with some corporate people and irritating her staff enough that they are complaining to merchandisers visiting the store. You provided some air cover by warning Corporate that in changing red to black ink she would be demanding, even brusque. You briefly coached her on her first day on the job, noting that though she comes from a rough-and-tumble, high-performing retail chain, she's now entering the kinder and gentler organization culture of your company. You told her she was being hired to be a change agent, and you advised her to use you to help with the politics. She listened, but didn't really hear you. So, two weeks into her job you asked her if she was interested in assimilation coaching, and she said, "Of course, you promised it in the Topgrading Interview and I'm sure I can benefit from your coaching." A players are eager for coaching. You asked her if she would like 360-degree feedback from confidential interviews you could conduct with her department managers and corporate people to check their perceptions of how she's doing. She replied, "Yes, but I'm not here to win a popularity contest with C players I'm about to demote or with thieves I'll fire," and you assured her you were not looking for her to tolerate mediocrity.

You conducted oral 360-degree interviews with ten coworkers at all levels, including two C players she would probably replace. Why include them? Because their opinions are important in assimilation—she needs to get the most possible out of the Cs until they either become As or leave. Now you are preparing for an assimilation coaching interview with Pat. You have reviewed your tandem Topgrading Interview notes, the notes from structured shorter selection interviews, the Candidate Assessment Scorecard, your confidential reference notes, and, of course, the current 360-degree survey comments. Let's begin.

1. **Greet** Pat, offer her something to drink, and chitchat a minute to bond a little.

2. Restate the general **purposes**—assimilation and developmental planning for short-term performance and longer-term career success.

3. Restate your intent to have a **midyear career review** in five months (six months after she started), separate from the formal performance management system. The purpose of the midyear career review is to update her development plan and career goals in an atmosphere less charged with emotion than an annual performance review (when pay and bonus are discussed).

4. Begin with your **conclusions**—you believe that Pat can turn the store around, be an A player store manager, and eventually become a good candidate for vice president operations, but that it's important for her to file down her rough edges.

5. State your first **recommendation,** which is for her to take the information from today and write her own plan saying what she intends to do, why and when she'll do it, and how the results will be measured. Her IDP, written in her words, will be implemented more conscientiously than your recommendation in your words.

6. Review her **strengths.** Your list is apt to be long—maybe two dozen competencies. Include a couple of easy developmental items to address strengths to be maximized. For example, she is smart and wants to learn the total business, so she can attend the upcoming trade show and can represent her district in a best-practices conference in three months. Easy!

7. After there's a warm glow from discussion of her strengths, insert a **weak point** that might be an overused strength, such as her sense of

urgency that becomes pushiness at times. Discuss the shortcoming knowing she acknowledged it in the Topgrading Interview; she predicted references would comment on it. Tell her what some said (while honoring the confidentiality you promised). Advise Pat on how to best approach various Corporate people. Acknowledge some of them can be a little difficult at times but they are the executives who will someday advise the CEO to promote her to VP . . . or not. Let her come up with ideas to improve, such as initiating lunches with some Corporate people to build more mutual understanding and respect.

8. Discuss the **remaining weak points,** leveraging off her self-insights. "In the Topgrading Interview you said you thought previous bosses would say you can be too insistent on doing things your way. Even the strongest on your staff are feeling you don't value their ideas enough." Let her generate ideas for involving them more, such as asking them to participate in an in-store task force. This is the meat of this coaching interview. Ninety percent of her personal development time should be spent on fixing her weaknesses, only 10 percent on maximizing her strengths. As suggested in Chapter 9, it can be appropriate to make a few suggestions: "How about keeping a weekly log on how you're doing controlling pushiness?" or "How about making up a wallet-size card with three or four reminders?"

9. Suggest that a main reason for toning down her abruptness is very practical—**to get the most out of B/C players** until she replaces or develops them. C players probably commiserate about Pat's high expectations and their hope that she fails . . . and leaves. You suspect that they go through the motions instead of truly embracing necessary changes. They probably decline to share information with her that could help the store perform. Their passive aggressiveness is understandable—she has been impatient with them and openly intolerant. So, they probably undermine her rather than try extra hard to succeed.

   Draw out of Pat *her* conclusion: "I must treat even the Cs with more respect because everyone deserves respect, and if I show more appreciation of even small improvements, I'll get the best out of them until they improve or are replaced."

10. **Suggest that Pat use Topgrading-based assessment and coaching** with all her direct reports. These will lead to Individual Development Plans for all—to retain and develop As and A potentials, and to give the others a fair chance to become As . . . or else consider a demotion or leave.

11. **Conclude** the meeting. Pat should summarize all the key points—her conclusions, her strengths, her weak points. The two of you have discussed perhaps fifteen developmental activities, and she has already indicated which ones she embraces. Her plan is only in draft form, to be finalized in a week or two, by her. You should document your discussions too, to be sure Pat has heard you, and, just in case, for your legal protection. This brief summary will help her and you sense if it is a comprehensive and workable plan. Did she bite off more than she can chew?

12. Conduct a **midyear career review** in five months. A follow-up email 360 survey will provide both of you with a good indication of how she is perceived by her managers (minus B/C players she has probably replaced) and corporate staff. You and she created the survey of twelve items.

Pat will begin the review with a summary of the first six months as store manager—her accomplishments, her failures, her progress on achieving the turnaround. She will restate her career goals, summarize her strengths and weak points, and assess her progress on her developmental plan. Then you chime in, adding your thoughts, observations, insights, and advice. This is her meeting, but it is a partnership dialogue. This is not her performance review. You don't adjust her pay or inform her if she will get a bonus. It will be easy for you to discuss monitoring her progress, because her results are apt to be good. Praise and recognition are apt to flow from you, because she deserves it. And she is making you look good. As an A player, Pat will naturally move to the next step, which is a revised, updated IDP. She promises to give you the final plan, in writing, in a week.

One final step in that midyear career review is Pat's rating of you. Ask her for feedback and discuss what she feels are your strengths and weak points as a boss and coach and how you can best manage her. Maybe by now she would like less air cover, less of your running interference, so she can more easily build collaborative relationships with Corporate. To review, the four essential steps in coaching a new hire to succeed are:

---

### Assimilation Coaching Model

#### 1. Hire A player with
Tandem Topgrading Interview
Reference checks with all bosses in past ten years
Coworker competency interview (one hour each)
Conclusions stated in Candidate Assessment Scorecard

#### 2. Oral interviews or Email 360 survey
Two to four weeks after hire
Purpose: measure first impressions

#### 3. Coaching Interview
Two to six weeks after hire
State conclusions, strengths, weak points
Create IDP together

#### 4. Midyear Career Review
Discuss follow-up email 360 survey results
Include feedback to you too

---

This rather typical assimilation-coaching session progressed through the seven psychological stages in change (Chapter 9) of Awareness, Rational Acceptance, Emotional Commitment, Program for Development, and even some Reinforcement. Pat accepts the Monitoring, because she will write the plan to include it. And you and she will ensure a favorable conclusion.

You don't have to be a natural, warm, and fuzzy counselor to make Topgrading–based assimilation coaching potent. You are armed with compelling data. No doubt you are a very credible source of insight for Pat. Leadership involves coaching—bringing opportunities and problems to the surface, getting ownership, setting goals, planning, empowering, and implementing the plans. It is much more difficult if you don't have a coaching relationship for a year and then attempt to deal with a nasty, negative issue during the formal annual performance review.

If you require your managers to embrace this recommended coaching process, your team will be among the top 10 percent I know of in coaching effectiveness, which is typical of A players. Topgrading-based assimilation coaching bolsters topgrading by turbo-boosting A players from the start. If you mistakenly thought you were hiring an A player, but that person turns out to be a C player, at least there will be early recognition of a fatal flaw, so the person can be redeployed sooner, not later.

## COACHING A MIS-HIRE TO LEAVE

Phil, Division Controller, had impeccable credentials and a winning personality. He was tough-minded but warm, friendly, and self-effacing. Unfortunately, the division president had conducted a superficial screening process, consisting of round-robin, shallow interviews and nothing close to a Topgrading Interview, let alone a tandem Topgrading Interview. The division president conducted no reference-check interviews (the search firm did those, but no significant weak points were revealed). I was brought in to assess whether Phil (a real person, name changed) could make it and, either way, coach him. I conducted my own Topgrading Interview plus oral 360-degree interviews with his seven peers and six subordinates. If this case study seems reminiscent of the Chapter 4 dialogue with the C player, it's because many of the same approaches and principles apply. The different developmental issues will be illuminating for you, reinforcing techniques for successfully coping with underperformers.

To make this case study more relevant to your needs as a hiring manager, picture yourself as the newly appointed division president inheriting Phil, a recently hired controller. You are both new, but Phil had been on board two months when you arrived. In order to get to know your staff, you conducted Topgrading interviews with all of them plus 360-degree interviews.[39] (You quickly learn that A players welcome your interviewing them.) These were tandem Topgrading Interviews—you asked an HR

---

[39] Specifically, you asked each of your subordinates about each other, and each of their subordinates, saying, "So I can get to know the whole team, please give me your frank, confidential opinions about each team member's strengths and areas for improvement."

manager to help out. Particularly where there might be legal issues in firing someone, you properly concluded that two heads would be better than one.

So, you are the hiring manager, replacing Brad Smart as assessor and coach. You tandem Topgrading Interviewed Phil during your first month as division president, conducted oral 360-degree interviews, and concluded that Phil was a chronic C player and over his head in this turnaround situation. The Topgrading Interview showed Phil to be OK maintaining a solid department, but previously at Acme Corporation he had failed twice—once in a complex corporate function and later in a division-controller job. Phil was open and honest with you and the HR manager in the Topgrading Interview; it's too bad those revealing Topgrading Interview questions weren't asked *before* he was hired! Phil had been nudged out of Acme Corporation, and in order to maintain his income he foolishly accepted an offer for a job he couldn't perform. Here is your assessment of Phil:

| Strengths | Weak Points |
|---|---|
| "Stretches" intelligence through effort | Technically deficient (weak in all aspects of basic accounting) |
| Listens to others' ideas | Shallow analytic approaches |
| Experienced, savvy business perspective | Not creative |
| Not apt to shoot from the hip | Slow to learn our business |
| Willing to try new ideas | Unable to get a handle on our software mess ("It's just too complex for me.") |
| BA in business and economics | |
| Ten years' experience, all with Acme | Monthly reports still inaccurate; blames staff but has no fix in place |
| Well grounded in Acme disciplines (planning) | Very limited experience improving talent; has not hired/ fired many people; relied on Acme in this regard |
| Down-to-earth | |
| Expressive | |

| | |
|---|---|
| Widely liked | Asks two people to do the same task without telling each the other is involved |
| Exhibits a positive "can-do" attitude | |
| Extremely hard worker (fifteen hours per day) | Frazzled; overreacts ("Phil's temper could get him in trouble.") |
| Results-oriented | Has not yet won the respect of his team; not empowering anyone (even his strongest subordinates) |
| Responsible | |
| Honest and open | |
| Trying to improve systems and accuracy of monthly reports | At times overwhelms subordinates with requests for detail |
| Accessible | |
| Willing to remove chronic C players | |

If you had an A player replacement, you'd probably cut your losses and offer Phil a severance. But you don't. Your plan is to immediately begin recruiting an A player replacement, but give Phil a chance to succeed, a fair chance, with your serving as a partner, a positive coach. If he surprises you and succeeds, great. If not, either he will quit or you will nudge him out. In any event, the organization culture (nervous in this turnaround as it is) will be enhanced if Phil is widely perceived to be treated fairly, with integrity and compassion. Morale will be harmed if Phil is a C player and remains in the job, or if he is widely perceived to be mistreated.

So, you set up the assimilation coaching session, similar to what was done with Pat; you have your tandem Topgrading interview notes and 360-degree comments, but no reference check notes. (Phil was already on board when you started as division president.) The HR manager who was a tandem interviewer is out of town for a month, so you decide to handle the coaching solo. You greet Phil, chat a moment, and restate the purposes, which are assimilation and developmental planning, both to improve present performance and to help Phil achieve his long-term goal of becoming a chief financial officer (CFO) of a small company. Please assume that several hours of interaction preceded this scenario, and that you ("Manager") used a lot more dialogue to build and retain professional rapport. The following script is abbreviated for ease of reading, so it reads as much more blunt and harsh than what actually took place. Now for the coaching dialogue, starting from when you present your Conclusions:

*Manager:* Phil, we're both new and struggling, and we both are eager to succeed. Thank you again for being so honest with me in the Topgrading Interview the other day. Based on that, if you were my next door neighbor considering a job offer here, I'd have advised you to turn it down. You were happy and successful in three different jobs at Acme, but you struggled with your last two jobs as complex as this one, and I'm doubtful this is a good match here.

*Phil:* I just can't afford to fail in this job. Are you letting me go?

*Manager:* Let's give it the good ol' college try, if that's what you want. Our purpose for meeting this morning really is coaching. Let's work toward developing a plan to help you succeed. If we're both satisfied with the plan, let's forge ahead. Within a couple of months we'll know if the plan is working.

*Phil:* That's fair. I need help. I can't figure out which software package to purchase, and I don't have time to study it because my team keeps pumping out incorrect monthly reports. I'm firefighting. How can I run the business without reliable metrics?

*Manager:* You can't, but let's not start with analyzing the problems. From the Topgrading Interview and 360-degree interviews with your peers and direct reports, I've concluded you have a lot of strengths, Phil. Today we're going to also discuss how you can maximize your long-term career success, so getting a consensus on your strengths is really important.

*Phil:* Great!

This hard-hitting beginning is exactly what I did with Phil in real life. Bonding in the Topgrading Interview ensured that Phil would not be too defensive. You spend the next forty-five minutes going through your list of Phil's twenty strengths. It's a dialogue; Phil is taking notes. This session is not for you to bludgeon him with his nonperformance and weak points. It's coaching, a partnership. You ask Phil for additional strengths, and he lists "family man." This is a useful addition, for the career coaching might lead to a conclusion that Phil should pursue a smaller, less complex job, one that affords him more time for family.

*Manager:*  That is an impressive list of strengths, Phil! In the right job you can be an A player. Now, you know what's next.

*Phil:*  Here comes the most valuable stuff, the negatives.

*Manager:*  You know your weak points pretty well. Most of your peers are extremely smart, and you recognize that you have to work harder to learn and analyze things. Good for you for being so conscientious, but in this very complex job you're in, you seem to be working eighty hours per week!

*Phil:*  It's hard on me to come home after the kids are in bed. But, I've got to get on top of things.

*Manager:*  You're not a technical accountant, and you don't really want to be one.

*Phil:*  Right, I want to be a manager, not a technician.

*Manager:*  That's OK if you have A players who are doing a great job.

*Phil:*  And I don't. I've got a couple of As, but mostly B and C players.

*Manager:*  A players can offset your lack of experience in the industry and lack of accounting expertise. They can also offer creative ideas.

*Phil:*  Right. I'm trying to get all their ideas, to learn as much as I can and check to see who's screwing up.

*Manager:*  It'll come as no surprise, Phil, that the 360-degree interviews show you're driving them a little batty. They know you're still new and learning, but . . .

*Phil:*  I know, I'm micromanaging.

*Manager:*  Even the A players.

*Phil:*  I guess so.

*Manager:*  Careful, you don't want to drive them away.

*Phil:*  But I don't want to show favoritism.

*Manager:*  Phil, the frustration level is really pretty high. Just like what you told me occurred in the division controller job at Acme, you're overwhelming your people with requests for detail. People started transferring out of your area at Acme because of your micromanaging.

| | |
|---|---|
| *Phil:* | OK, item #1 on my plan will be to empower people more, particularly the A players. Damn! I swore I'd trust people more. I'll ease up, and at least stop micromanaging the A players. |
| *Manager:* | There was another thing you swore you'd stop doing after you were removed from the division controller job at Acme. Remember? |
| *Phil:* | Yeah, stop asking two people to do the same thing. I ask X, but if X drops the ball, I'll ask Y and not tell X. |
| *Manager:* | Right. |
| *Phil:* | OK, item #2 on my plan will be to discuss the situation with X and if I decide to give the task to Y, I'll tell X. It's an excuse, but I figure I can save time if I just give it to Y. X will find out soon enough, anyway. But I'll talk with X and try to find other ways to save time. I really am drowning in the problems; that's why I need help. |
| *Manager:* | Come to me, Phil, with your key decisions. For now, anyway. Maybe you can seem more decisive to your people if I help you sort things out. I have the experience you lack here. I'll be sort of a quality check, a sounding board. |
| *Phil:* | That's item #3. |
| *Manager:* | Good, let's talk about talent next. Acme promoted from within and we're in a turnaround without much promotable talent. External hiring is now necessary, and this is new territory for you. |
| *Phil:* | It sure is. I can use some help. Maybe I've been hard on the C players, but at least they know where they stand. I don't have replacements internally or externally. |
| *Manager:* | Let's ask your peers for names of people to replace your C players. Work with Susan in HR, who can partner with you. I want to interview finalists with you in a tandem Topgrading process. |
| *Phil:* | Sounds good. |
| *Manager:* | I have a lot more experience interviewing. I have a 90 percent success rate so probably the single best things I can do for you are help you pack your team with A players and teach you Topgrading interviewing. |
| *Phil:* | Got it. Can Susan recommend an interviewing course? |

*Manager:*  Good idea. Yes. That's another good item for your plan.

*Phil:*      Is that it?

*Manager:*  Not quite. In all your jobs you have been a great team player with peers.

*Phil:*      I know what you're gonna say. I get frazzled when these guys get on me about the inaccurate reports. But C players are pumping out garbage. I exploded a couple of times, but I apologized.

*Manager:*  They like you and sort of forgive you. I see an interaction effect here, Phil. You're over your head, so you work harder trying to do the jobs of your staff. Even the C players know more than you in some technical areas. But in order to get results, you inundate them with requests for detail. You work harder trying to learn, you get impatient and frustrated, and you lose your cool. People lose a little respect for you. Instead of helping you with solutions, they give you data, data, data. You work even harder, get more frustrated, and request more data. It's a death spiral, and lashing out at people will eventually turn them against you. Your winning personality won't win if you blow up at people.

*Phil:*      You're right. I hardly know these guys and I'm acting like a jerk.

*Manager:*  Your personality is a strength. How can you win them over other than fixing the problems in the department? You did it at Acme.

*Phil:*      Yes. When I was doing the best job, I was in the service business, asking my internal clients how we could better serve them. I've just been swamped here.

*Manager:*  And in two jobs at Acme, you weren't so successful at it.

*Phil:*      I'd better schedule meetings with each internal client to say I really want to help them, to show I'm trying, and to ask them to be patient with me as I learn. And to listen to them.

*Manager:*  Listen! Aha! That's a strength of yours!

*Phil:*      So . . . additional items are to stay calm, offer service to peers, and listen more.

*Manager:*  Sounds like a comprehensive plan for the next two months that includes maximizing some underutilized strengths and minimizing some weaknesses. Let's see a written copy of your plan in a couple days.

Phil orally summarizes his Individual Development Plan and promises to write it out—what he intends to do, why and when, and how the results will be monitored. (You write a memo summarizing these discussions, providing the legal documentation HR and legal counsel expect of you.) Phil is committed. You still don't think there will be a conclusion that saves Phil, but at least you can start topgrading his department now. Before you conclude the meeting, you want to be sure Phil has more realistic career goals than that of becoming CFO of your large company.

*Manager:* One more thing. Let's talk about your career goals.

*Phil:* I have only one—succeed in this job. I'm not looking so good for CFO, am I?

*Manager:* Let's look at two scenarios: one if you remain in your job, one if you don't. If six months from now you are happy and successful, and you are working sixty rather than eighty hours, what would you think?

*Phil:* That becoming CFO is a possibility.

*Manager:* CFO of what? How complex a job?

*Phil:* Hmm. I see what you're getting at. I'd be silly to go after another complex job, like CFO. First things first. What if I haven't improved to the A player level? What do you think? Should I go back to a staff-planning job?

*Manager:* At Acme you were a terrific planner, not a creative strategic planner, but a great tactical planner. You rolled up the numbers A players generated. If a division controller was late, you would appeal nicely, and they'd cooperate. You weren't a cop. That certainly is an option, even something to consider here, at Corporate.

*Phil:* What else? You've got broader experience than me.

*Manager:* I can envision your succeeding as CFO of a small company, one in good shape, not too complex, in an industry you know. Maybe a supplier to a company like Acme would be an alternative where you could be an A player. You'd still have to take a lot of accounting courses to get up to speed, however. In the meantime, you're performing as a C player now and it's most important to see if you can move up to the B and A levels in the next few months.

One more summary by Phil concludes the coaching session. He reviews the lists of his strengths and weak points, sincerely commits to each developmental item, and even summarizes the career options that make sense. He knows that his job is on the line. He has to get the financial numbers right, install a good software package, build a team, and earn the respect of coworkers. With weekly checkpoints written into Phil's plan, Phil's lack of progress will result in more heart-to-heart talks. (No doubt HR will insist on retaining records of them to show the company has been fair and legal, if Phil is fired and sues.) It becomes obvious he is not going to succeed in this job. You offer to cover for him if he wants to take a day here or there to check out other jobs, jobs where he can be an A player.

Let's review the structure of the coaching session with Phil, following your Topgrading Interview and confidential 360-degree discussions with Phil's peers subordinates:

1. Stated purposes (coaching for short-term results and longer-term career moves).

2. Conclusions. ("I'm doubtful there is a good match here.")

3. Strengths (so Phil feels appreciated and understood).

4. Weak points (positive, through frank dialogue).

5. Individual Development Plan summarized by Phil:
   a. Empower staff more.
   b. Stop asking two people to do the same task.
   c. Use my boss for key decisions.
   d. Do tandem Topgrading Interviews with boss.
   e. Stay calm.
   f. Offer service to peers.
   g. Listen a lot more and better.

6. Career discussion. (Seeking a complex CFO job was discouraged, but two options where Phil could be an A player were explored.)

7. Summary of career options by Phil.

You didn't have to be a supercoach, just a conscientious manager armed with tandem Topgrading data on Phil's background and 360-degree data on present perceptions of him. A solid, credible, fair IDP was created and implemented by Phil, but his job performance continued to be poor. In real life Phil was asked to resign six months after he was hired. He was given a six-month severance. There were no hard feelings (and no lawsuits) because he was coached positively by both me and his boss. In fact, he called to thank me for coaching him to recognize that he should find a CFO job in a smaller, less complex company.

## TOM BROCK CASE STUDY: COACHING TO IMPROVE LEADERSHIP STYLE

The Tom Brock case study does not repeat much of what was covered in the Pat and Phil cases. Instead I'll show how leopards can change their spots, thus expanding your range as a coach.

After twenty years with General Electric, Tom Brock was the #2 executive at a troubled division. With a reputation as a smart, hard-driving leader who quickly turns operations around, Brock was the obvious choice to replace the retiring general manager. The division was profitable, but in jeopardy because:

- No credible strategic plan existed. ("Everything including R&D is sacrificed for short-term results.")

- Morale at all levels was poor; people felt like they were treated like machines, unloved, and unvalued.

- Finger pointing, bickering, and politics were rampant.

- Customers threatened to take their business elsewhere.

- A top-down culture existed with little or no empowerment.

Brock was a controversial candidate for president. There was concern that Tom was not a good listener (in general), not a good team player (with Corporate), and not a team builder (with subordinates, because he insisted on doing things his way). Some rated Tom a C player candidate for GM. CEO Jack Welch said, "Get Brad Smart's opinion." I performed the Top-grading Interview plus oral 360-degree interviews. On a plant tour, I asked a group of workers several questions, the responses to which were, "Senior management can't be trusted," "Tom Brock is unknown," "Jobs are boring," and "The only job security comes from that guy over there—the union steward."

My report—all twenty-two pages—on Tom Brock went to Jack Welch. Here are excerpts from my Executive Summary:

## Executive Summary

- Mr. Brock is an excellent candidate for immediate promotion to general manager. He is an extremely bright, broadly based technologist/ executive, with extraordinary drive, creativity, vision, and resourcefulness.

- His strengths far outweigh his shortcomings. Although it ordinarily would seem that a person with such interpersonal shortcomings as his could not succeed, he will.

- Mr. Brock should be encouraged to continue his development and told directly that promotion to vice president (a title change, but at GE it means a lot to move from GM to VP) will be contingent upon his demonstrating considerably more maturity and interpersonal flexibility.

| *Strengths* | *Weak Points* |
|---|---|
| Superior intelligence | Confuses people with quick thinking |
| A quick study | |
| Accurately "calibrates" people's technical expertise | Does not "wire" change with communications nearly enough |
| Unquenchable thirst for knowledge | At times appears arrogant, combative, tactless |
| Adept at figuring out the business equation | Breaks down C players rather than nudge them out |
| Excellent analytic and logical abilities | Interrupts people; at times poor listener; dominates discussions |
| Strong conceptual skills | Refers excessively to past successes |

| Strengths | Weak Points |
|---|---|
| Decisive | Politically insensitive |
| Strategic visionary | Stingy with praise; hypercritical (hurting peoples' esteem and teamwork) |
| Intellectually flexible | |
| Revolutionary change agent | |
| Respected by senior team | |
| Sets high goals | |
| Successful turnaround leader | |
| Maturing | |
| Becoming less intimidating | |
| Very confident | |
| Focuses on key priorities | |
| Listens to A players | |
| Powerful, dynamic leader | |
| Eager to be coached | |
| Cares about people (though doesn't always show it) | |
| A "doer" (do it now) | |
| Topgrader | |
| Principled | |
| Can make favorable first impression | |
| Open, direct person | |
| Leads with long-term perspective | |
| BSE from Georgia Tech | |

*Strengths*

21 years' experience with GE

Exceptional technical expertise; strong in manufacturing, finance; learning marketing

Achieves "scheduled invention"

High integrity; trustworthy

Extremely independent

Can be charming, smooth, and likable (socially, for example)

Effectively manages across functions

Highly energetic; passionate about success

Customer-oriented

Welch called to discuss Tom Brock. I predicted that Tom would succeed, but I would need a year to help Tom file down his rough edges. The team was solid with A players who needed leadership. Tom was respected, and no one in his career had quit because of his arrogance or impatience. "OK," Welch said, "Brock gets the GM job."

Six months later I met with Welch on several topics. Welch said, "By the way, Brad, I think you lost your marbles on Brock—he's as arrogant as ever with customers, employees, and his team." I said somewhat defensively, "One year, Jack. Remember, I said Tom would need one year to show significant change, and he has six more months to go." Exactly one year since the Topgrading Interview–based coaching began, Welch was so impressed with Tom's progress, he praised him in a public meeting, saying, "Tom Brock is a great model of the GE leader of the future."

At that one-year mark, an internal General Electric assessment of Brock's progress was made:

## One Year Into Coaching

People are saying of Tom:

- "authentic," "real"
- "open," "we trust Tom"
- "understands my problems"
- "most excitement I've had in years"
- "safe to express ideas; Tom listens"
- "love the adventure"
- "values teamwork"
- "never been happier, wanted to transfer but no longer want to"

Visible signs of teamwork include:

- people reaching out to help each other/other teams
- hunger for results, measurements, targets
- having fun
- walls are coming down
- real creativity, magic in the air
- new leaders and "old dogs with new tricks" are emerging; people are following

As for business results:

- Business results are beginning to show, and better than ever (27 percent earnings growth over previous year).
- Partnerships with other GE businesses are at record heights.

> **Describing what's happening is exciting. Tom Brock's time has come. He's risen to the challenge. A new culture has evolved; leadership is being born, encouraged, and cultivated.**

Eighteen months after Brock began Topgrading Interview–based coaching, Brock's boss wrote to Jack Welch, in high praise of Brock, "I have rarely, in my many plant and office visits, experienced such tremendous enthusiasm for employee involvement or teamwork. The dedicated leadership of Tom and his head of operations was clearly visible throughout our visit. . . . They are to be commended for their realistic viewpoint as well as their huge accomplishments."

## Coaching Tom Brock

A key to Brock's leadership transformation was an unusually comprehensive, detailed, hard-hitting Individual Development Plan. Wade through this with me, and you will get valuable insights into how you can coach a leopard to change it spots.

Following the Topgrading Interview and 360-degree data gathering, I met with Tom for four hours in person. He received my twenty-two-page report and five-page suggested development plan, and we touched base by phone almost monthly for a year. For fast-paced managers who think they lack the patience to coach, take note: Most Topgrading–based coaching may require periodic one-hour follow-up sessions, but the basic psychological steps (Awareness, Acceptance, Commitment, and so forth) can be accomplished in three to four hours (with Monitoring, Reinforcement, and Conclusion occurring later). The Brock coaching model can work for you, whether you are coaching a new hire, conducting a career assessment and development program for all your managers, or singling out a person for special coaching.

In Tom's case, initially he had general Awareness of shortcomings as perceived by his bosses, but he had no Commitment to change until we met. In the four-hour coaching interview we began with a restatement of goals:

- At a minimum, I would help Tom better understand how he is perceived by me, coworkers at all levels, and key customers.

- Together we would compose a draft of a development plan aimed at helping Tom maximize his results and leadership effectiveness over the next two years.

Next I shared with Tom my overall Conclusions. He took a lot of notes, but I promised to send him my written report anyway. The bulk of our time was devoted to reviewing the bullet points for his strengths and weak points—strengths first. I gave Tom my opinion, but then quoted coworkers and customers (anonymously). Some strengths ("socially very likable") were underutilized and resulted in specific action steps for his developmental plan (more informal interactions). Some strengths ("very quick thinker") were overused ("confuses people"), resulting in action plans to correct them. Instead of my recommending developmental activities that seemed appropriate, I presented data and conclusions so Tom would propose action steps to improve. I supported them or suggested alternatives.

Throughout, I used basic coaching techniques:

- **Be honest.** If I didn't think Tom could succeed at something, I'd say so. No phony praise. I care about Tom. I wouldn't insult him with insincerity.

- **I'm OK, you're OK.** Tom and I are colleagues. In a coaching interview there is no pulling rank. We're problem solving together, partners in Tom's development. No arguing. No criticism. My role is to be positive, even when discussing negative issues. I'm on his team, cheering him on, his biggest supporter.

- **No overload.** Most people eventually say, "OK, that's enough for now—I'll implement this plan and see if I need to do more." It's better for Tom to commit to a short plan and do it than to a long plan that is not completed.

- **Involve others.** Build a network of support for the plan. Tom met quarterly with his boss but twice weekly with his Human Resources professional, who would give Tom feedback on his progress, reinforce positive steps, bolster him when he was frustrated, and modify the plan as necessary. Phone calls to me at any time were encouraged.

- **Expect slow progress and some backsliding.** It's normal to progress two steps, then slip back one. Long-term progress is the goal. Indeed, a dramatic change in personality would scare people and make them wonder, "When is that phony warmth going to disappear?"

- **Look for a couple of quick fixes.** In Tom's case, eliminating just a few behavioral negatives (poor listening, interrupting) dramatically improved his overall image.

- **The best plan is authored by the counselee.** Tom's IDP (Figure 10.1) is similar to the one I sent him following our half-day coaching session. However, through his writing what he intended to do, why, by when, and how results would be monitored, his commitment was locked in. His autonomy was fortified. Sharing that plan with his boss made it "management by objectives (MBO) for development."

- **Acknowledge carrots and sticks.** This is part of being honest. Some coaches believe only positive communications can be helpful. I feel that positively acknowledging negative consequences is essential for success. Remember the crocodiles and fast-food theories of motivation (Chapter 9). For Tom, success would earn him at least another promotion (which he received in two years). Failure to show improvement from his plan would result in his plateauing or even being forced out of GE. That's reality. Don't dwell on the negatives, but don't think a lot of saccharine and smiley faces will suffice.

- **Have fun.** Coaching is serious, but improvement can sometimes be bolstered with whimsy. Tom was so quick to criticize coworkers, we addressed it several ways—including his framing and hanging a cartoon (a dead ringer for Tom Brock) I commissioned showing Tom "counting to ten." The joke—that his career development plan consisted of many aspects of the same item—"count to ten"—is on him. Displaying it in his office, Tom was publicly promising not to jump on someone, criticize unfairly, or lose his temper. It worked. Tom keeps his word.

- **Don't neglect topgrading.** Tom was lucky. GE had already packed his team with A players. Leadership at the top—Tom—was needed, not a new team. Don't expect your coachee to change if B/C players constantly drag the team down.

- **Use active listening.** I played back to Tom not only the content but the unstated feelings I sensed in him. I role modeled this crucial skill that he emulated and eventually mastered. Tom says his IDP succeeded, "because Brad grew me big ears."

- **Encourage keeping a log.** The log records successes and failures in the development plan. Tom made entries for five minutes at the end of each day. Recording those "best behaviors" and slips for eighteen months helped lock in his changes. Today, Tom is quite naturally a more sensitive, likable person.

# Figure 10.1
## Tom Brock's Individual Development Plan

### Part A: Do's and Don'ts

#### DO'S

- Articulate my vision for the business everywhere I go, every time I have an audience (hammer-repeat-repeat)
- Let go somewhat, depend on and "empower" A players
- Think before speaking and package comments better . . . be sensitive to new image (*the leader*)
- Play politics upward better . . .
- Show and express vulnerability, flaws, and shortcomings (shows realness—working to improve—it's contagious—*if he can, "so can I"*)
- Be consistent, predictable, encourage, and recognize "teamwork"
- Be loose, show flexibility, keen sense of humor, "pick up" people who *are* struggling with new culture or a business challenge
- "Stroke," reward, and recognize people constantly
- Communicate more effectively (town meetings, brown-bag meetings)
- Start a *new* "Brock Mythology" (let go of past image)
- Above all, listen . . . listen . . . and *listen* more

#### DON'TS

- Change what people admire and respect most of me for the division (technology, product, people, customer driven)
- "Gloat" in reversing people or challenging Corporate
- Kill messengers
- EVER . . . demean
- Talk so much . . . get on a "roll" and dominate the conversations, be an expert on everything

**Part B: Specific Action Items**

| Items or Ideas | Purpose | Timing | Notes |
|---|---|---|---|
| A. Brad Smart discussions | Utilize Brad's expertise, get suggestions, feedback and development ideas | Quarterly | Respect Brad's knowledge in the field and value his inputs |
| B. Solicit staff's organizational ideas | Get their ideas Obtain their "buy in" | 2/10 and 3/1 (done) | Most felt good about my new style |
| C. Social with spouses at Hunting Hills Country Club | Ice breaker and fellowship/team builder | 2/23 (done) | Very timely and well received Myth erased . . . some |
| D. Career discussion with each old/new staff members | Honest and real discussion on their role in new organization, potential and future roles in the business | 3/9 (done) | Buy into their new position. Some "pain," but minimal |
| E. Six-month "Walk the Plant" plan | Expose me, 1-on-1, to hourly associates in plant tours every six months | *First 3 months:* 10-15 mins. daily through 9 different office or plant areas *Second 3 months* every other day Ongoing once a week | I talked with everyone just to see how they're doing |
| F. Monthly "Breakfast with Tom" | Expose people to me, initially from areas where my "press" may be less positive or into less-known areas | Monthly | Could include a very short ice breaker questionnaire given out in advance and then discussed at breakfast |

| Items or Ideas | Purpose | Timing | Notes |
|---|---|---|---|
| G. *"Your Nickel"* 10-min. one-on-one's with me | Show that I *can* listen to others' input<br>Expose me to many other key people (in the business) | Monthly ongoing basis w/my staff; randomly w/others | *Samples:*<br>• "What do you like that we're now doing?"<br>• "How can we do better?"<br>• "What really irritates you on the job?"<br>• "How do you feel about our new direction?"<br>Use a one-sheet questionnaire |
| H. Second quarter 1990—feature video with me | Establish benchmark of my objectives/vision for the business<br>Show me "at my best"—animated, enthused, interested, wanting to motivate and lead others. Revisit . . . whys of recent organizational changes | Release mid-April | Talk about "shortcomings/misconceptions or of me"—and indicate my understanding of them and my intent and commitment to work on them<br>Shows realness |
| I. *"Climate Council"*—establish an ongoing council of 6 or 7 thought leaders—people who can read the pulse of the workforce and are candid | Meet every other month to discuss a continuing set of questions about the environment/climate.<br>Provide anonymous report to me: could include "what can I do to improve or enhance my effectiveness?"<br>Involve human resources (Roger Farley) as partner in my development | Either monthly or every other month | Must be anonymous<br>Must be chaired by someone highly respected by me so no concern about killing the messenger<br>Suggest report be written |

| Items or Ideas | Purpose | Timing | Notes |
|---|---|---|---|
| J. My *"In-Plant" Employee Press Conference:* have 3 or 4 different employees each time w/questions thought out in advance to ask; after 10 mins. or so of above, open to ?'s from the floor | Establish open forum for employees to ask me questions directly. Hold in auditorium at different times—open to any interested employees <br>• Some noon time <br>• Some 4:45 P.M. <br>• Some off-shift | Every other month | Capitalize on my open, enthusiastic, and contagious style |
| K. My *"Report to Employees"* | Report on ongoing basis on key business indicators/goals—progress and problems <br>Do through "Reporter" <br>Format could be like a report card (A–F) on ongoing key items . . . or like an open letter | Every other month | Take concept of "sharing everything" one step further in a structured manner that is ongoing and "state of the art" |
| L. Attend at least next couple General Electric social functions | Mingle with people <br>Exhibit intent to "be with people" in a real way <br>Would make strong positive initial impression of "caring" attitude of new leadership | Next year | To show my "real" or approachable side |
| M. Speaking coach | Polish my skills | | That I attend a seminar on "how *not* to alienate people" . . . "how to avoid pressing people's 'hot buttons'" |

Two years after I began coaching Tom, he was promoted from general manager to vice president. He reached the coveted officer level at GE. Tom really improved his leadership skills himself. The Topgrading-based coaching provided compelling data that Tom was at a crucial juncture where his career would plateau or move to the next level. He insisted on a "full-court press" development plan, and he was unusually disciplined and courageous in implementing it.

Having turned his company around and built it, and having matured into a truly fine leader, Tom opted to give something back. He resigned his position at General Electric and has been devoting his extraordinary energy and talents to various civic activities. He is one of the rare 10 percent of managers I have worked with who managed his career to fit into a life plan (Chapter 7) that would ensure him both short-term success and long-term fulfillment. Perhaps he will accept an offer to be CEO of a company. Perhaps not. He certainly has the talent. But he has managed his career to permit a lot of attractive options.

## T. J. JOHNSON CASE STUDY:
## A USEFUL EMAIL 360 APPROACH

Typically 360-degree surveys are too long, the wording is unclear, and B/C player respondents have the wrong values, so they give A players low ratings on items such as "maintaining high standards of performance." The Mursau Group (see Appendix J for contact information) has a simple process that works. The Topgrading interview and initial feedback/coaching session results in an IDP. Measuring improvement is necessary to motivate most people to implement their IDP and improve, so a short, tailored email 360 is perfect for tracking progress. This case study shows how it works.

T. J. Johnson was a vice president, general manager at Hill-Rom, a division of Hillenbrand Industries (a company case study in Chapter 5). Like dozens of other managers, he was assessed by me. I Topgrading interviewed him, conducted oral 360s, and held a feedback/coaching session that led to his working with his boss to finalize his IDP. T. J. had issues, some similar to Tom Brock's, but some quite different. T. J. conscientiously worked to improve. As part of his IDP, an email 360 was designed by me and was administered six months later to track his progress. Each item was

# Figure 10.2
## Follow-Up Survey at Ventana (And Means for Hill-Rom and Ventana)
### (Survey #2)

| | An effective decision maker | Sufficiently participative | Independently decisive, when necessary | Strategic | Results-oriented | An open, direct communicator | Sarcastic | Independent | Aloof | Focused on key priorities |
|---|---|---|---|---|---|---|---|---|---|---|
| | Item 1 | Item 2 | Item 3 | Item 4 | Item 5 | Item 6 | Item 7 | Item 8 | Item 9 | Item 10 |
| Never | 1 | - | - | - | - | - | - | 4 | - | 3 | - |
| | 2 | - | - | - | - | - | - | 3 | - | 1 | - |
| Sometimes | 3 | - | - | - | - | - | - | - | - | 3 | - |
| | 4 | - | - | - | - | - | - | 2 | 1 | 1 | - |
| | 5 | - | 1 | - | - | - | - | - | 1 | 1 | - |
| | 6 | - | - | - | - | - | - | 1 | - | - | - |
| Frequently | 7 | 1 | 2 | 2 | 2 | - | - | - | 5 | 1 | 1 |
| | 8 | 2 | - | 1 | 1 | - | 5 | - | - | - | 1 |
| | 9 | 2 | 3 | 2 | 1 | 4 | - | - | - | - | - |
| Always | 10 | 5 | 3 | 3 | 6 | 6 | 5 | - | 2 | - | 7 |
| | NA | - | - | 2 | - | - | - | - | 1 | - | - |
| Ventana | 2003 Mean | 9.1 | 8.4 | 8.8 | 9.1 | 9.6 | 9.0 | 2.4 | 7.1 | 3.0 | 9.4 |
| Hill-Rom | 2001 Mean | 8.2 | 7.2 | 8.2 | 8.3 | 9.4 | 7.8 | 2.6 | 6.7 | 4.6 | 9.0 |

| | Friendly | Defensive | A topgrader | Maintaining high performance standards | Losing my temper | An effective team builder | A change agent | Highly motivated to succeed | An effective leader, overall |
|---|---|---|---|---|---|---|---|---|---|
| | Item 11 | Item 12 | Item 13 | Item 14 | Item 15 | Item 16 | Item 17 | Item 18 | Item 19 |
| **Never** | - | 4 | - | - | 3 | - | - | - | - |
| | - | 2 | - | - | 1 | - | - | - | - |
| **Sometimes** | - | 1 | - | - | 2 | - | - | - | - |
| | - | 3 | 2 | - | 3 | - | - | - | - |
| | 1 | - | - | - | - | - | - | - | - |
| **Frequently** | - | - | - | - | 1 | 1 | - | - | - |
| | 4 | - | 1 | - | - | 5 | - | - | 1 |
| | 1 | - | 3 | - | - | 1 | 4 | 1 | - |
| **Always** | - | - | 2 | 5 | - | 1 | 2 | 2 | 5 |
| | 4 | - | 2 | 5 | - | 2 | 4 | 7 | 4 |
| NA | - | - | - | - | - | - | - | - | - |
| **Ventana** 2003 Mean | 8.1 | 2.3 | 7.7 | 9.5 | 2.9 | 7.8 | 9.0 | 9.6 | 9.2 |
| **Hill-Rom** 2001 Mean | 6.5 | 4.1 | 6.3 | 8.5 | 2.6 | 6.7 | 7.9 | 9.5 | 8.6 |

worded the way I heard people in oral 360s describe T. J., so the items would be clearer to respondents than typical "canned" survey items. Many valuable typed comments resulted from having a short survey (so respondents would not rush through it) and by having A player respondents (who are very conscientious and want to provide valuable feedback).

There were two surveys at Hill-Rom. In the initial 2001 survey, T. J. fell short on half a dozen items. He embraced his IDP, and a 2002 survey showed improvement. He was promoted to VP Global Marketing, but left for an exciting opportunity at Ventana Medical Systems. While at Ventana T. J. continued working to improve, and in 2003 retook his email 360 survey, documenting terrific improvement and achieving all of his developmental goals.

Figure 10.2 shows raw numbers for his 2003 survey. At the bottom of the chart you see his average ratings on his first (2001) and third (2003) surveys. The items were all worded "How frequently do you view me as . . . ?" and the scale is Always (10), Frequently (7), Sometimes (4), and Never (1). T. J.'s goals were a 7 or higher on the positively worded items, and 3 or lower on the negatively worded items.

As you can see, he improved in almost all areas. Nice going, T. J.! Figure 10.3 is a chart summarizing his progress on the six items of greatest interest to him.

T. J.'s note to me says what he experienced:

Brad,

First of all I believe my Topgrading assessment has had one of, if not the biggest, impact on my career and a positive carryover into my relationships away from work. As I told you, my *Topgrading* book is on my desk at all times. (By the way I would love to have you sign it for me.) I refer to it frequently and have adopted the Topgrading interviewing and selection process. I would like to think that I've become a topgrader. I also continue to assist others in becoming topgraders. I have passed along my experience to a half dozen people here at Ventana. They have all bought the book and have started their transformations.

It was interesting to me and might be to you that when I shared elements of your report with my boss and a peer, they basically said, "We don't see those weaker points in you!" That was music to my

**Figure 10.3**
**Developmental Items for T. J. Johnson Surveys #1 and #2**

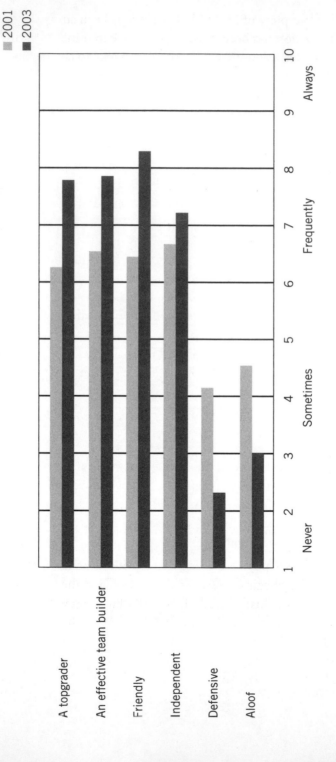

ears and a great piece of feedback. I've actually been surprised how easy my transition has been. I really don't have to think about my behavioral issues anymore. I really have been able to change my views and most importantly I am so much more aware of the dynamics going on around me and how I can either positively move things forward or damage the situation if I react in the wrong way. The hard part in the entire process was coming to terms with the initial feedback and accepting the perceptions that were there and impacting my effectiveness. Once I accepted the assessment, my improvement began immediately. It really is simple once you are willing to actively listen to what people are saying to you. I believe I'm an exceptional listener today.

I would also say that I'm a much calmer person in the heat of the business stresses. A few years ago it wasn't difficult to get my blood pressure up and for me to become emotional about a situation. I now sense this as it begins to happen and can channel the energy in a more positive fashion. The clue you gave me of the image of the chairman of the board watching me from a camera in the corner to see how I respond and to check if I have executive presence has had a great impact. I still think about that when I'm in a tough, stressful situation. I really do believe I've mastered the art of driving change and keeping the momentum moving in a fast-paced organization while not leaving a few bodies along the way. I truly try to keep a win/win attitude about all issues, even if I think I'm dealing with C players. As you know, I used to be pretty brutal with C players. I'm still very aware of who I'm dealing with, I still tend to grade them, but instead of being dismissive or even caustic, I go to work on changing them. Fortunately, Ventana is topgrading and there aren't many C players.

I sometimes see people in leadership positions behaving the way I used to. I quickly begin to diffuse the situation and then later work to coach the individual without them really knowing what I'm doing. I use my experience and the transformation that I've undergone to help others. I guess the moral to that story is once you have topgraded yourself, the process of helping others becomes easier and almost automatic.

On the personal front, my experience has changed me in many ways. I'm more approachable. I apply my learning with my wife, kids, and all interactions in general. With my oldest now being a teenager, I'm sure I'll have new frontiers to navigate and my topgrading experience will be instrumental. It was funny that when my wife read your report for the first time, she asked how much it cost to have it done. I told her it was expensive but worth it, and she laughed that she could have written it for free. Her feedback actually helped me accept the assessment all the more.

Brad, in summary, it has been a life changer for me and a process that I value a great deal. It's not over. I'm still working to improve my leadership skills. I have always had a relentless attitude of improvement. I now believe I channel that passion in a much more effective way because of my topgrading experience. I was skeptical at the beginning but I'm a devoted believer in and practitioner of topgrading today.

T. J.

## FINAL COMMENT

By now you know I am not recommending a soft, mushy coaching style. The business world is too fast-paced, too demanding for quiet, gentle little hints, except for a rare subordinate requiring your most flexible and sensitive care. No, this world requires hard-hitting constructive criticism. You want the straight scoop, no beating around the bush, if your boss is dissatisfied, right? But you want to be treated with respect, and you respond best when you are presented positively with an opportunity to improve, right? Your subordinates want and deserve the same thing.

This chapter has presented case studies in coaching to fix others' weaknesses, but has simultaneously given you insight into how to fix your own. (Will some of Tom Brock's or T. J. Johnson's developmental activities work for you?) Overcoming fatal flaws is not just satisfying, but thrilling. Being a hard-hitting but positive coach to help others grow is not merely a skill, but the essence of good leadership.

*Part Three*

# MASTERING THE TOPGRADING INTERVIEW GUIDE AND LEGALITIES IN USING IT

# Eleven

# YOUR MOST POWERFUL TOOL: THE TOPGRADING INTERVIEW GUIDE

*It takes a wise man to discover a wise man.*
                    Diogenes Laertius, c. 200–50

After reading Chapters 1 through 10, I hope you believe a 90 percent or better success rate in hiring is possible, and the assessment tool to help you achieve it is the Topgrading Interview Guide (Appendix A). If you haven't already done so, please take ten minutes now to carefully read Appendix A, the full Topgrading Interview Guide.

Topgrading is a crucial component of topgrading. To review: if you remove B/C players and suffer from a common 75 percent mis-hire rate using weak interviewing methods, you will fail at topgrading. You will appear to be a hatchet man flailing away, since you fire B/C players and three-fourths of the time replace them with B/C players. With the cost of mis-hires $1.5 million for a $100,000 employee, you waste $4.5 million in three mis-hires to hire one A player.[40] Topgrading in combination with other topgrading techniques promises a 90 percent or better success rate. Picture hiring nine A players for every single B/C mis-hire! With A players replacing Cs, positive morale mushrooms among your most talented people, and teams perform better. But you know that.

Part Three teaches the mechanics of Topgrading—it's sort of an operator's manual. Chapter 11 immerses you in the Topgrading Interview Guide, explaining every question and offering basic interview techniques and tips. The advantages of tandem (two) interviewers are explained and the disadvantages of competency-based interviews are spelled out. (For more thorough coverage of interviewing techniques, as they pertain to Topgrading, read *The Smart Interviewer* [Wiley, 1989]). Chapter 12 is the operator's

---

[40]These statistics are explained in Chapter 2.

manual of warnings—the do's and don't's to be sure your Topgrading Interviews are legal. Topgrading is becoming global, so a section in Chapter 12 advises you how to topgrade legally outside of the United States. Translations of *Topgrading* are available in several languages and the Spanish version (*El Valor del Capital Humano*) is available (Paidor Empen, publisher).

After reading Chapter 11 you will be able to:

1. Conduct the most valid interview of your career.

2. Conduct both solo and tandem Topgrading Interviews.

3. Better appreciate the validity of Topgrading.

4. Glean insights from a person's résumé and the Career History Form, incorporating that information into a smooth flowing Topgrading Interview.

5. Understand when and how to use the newly introduced Self-Administered Topgrading Interview Guide.

6. Know when and how to sell the job.

7. Take notes effectively.

8. Effectively conduct short competency-based interviews that appropriately supplement (not replace) Topgrading Interviews.

9. Conduct revealing reference calls (for external candidates) and 360 interviews (for assessing internal people).

10. Know how to continue improving your Topgrading Interview skills.

## ADVANTAGES OF USING THE TOPGRADING INTERVIEW GUIDE

Marshall McLuhan proclaimed, "The medium is the message," and so it is with interviewing. Thoroughness is the message, the passageway to truth. The Topgrading Interview Guide works better than highly canned structured interviews that omit a lot of crucial questions. It produces much more valid results than so-called targeted, or competency-based interviews that ignore dozens of important competencies as well as the chronology, the crucial patterns of *how* the interviewee developed throughout his career.

Despite the size of the Topgrading Interview Guide, it is like a manual that, when understood, permits you to perform a complex task easily, smoothly, and with confidence. The only disadvantage of using the Topgrading Interview Guide is that it takes longer than other interviews, particularly with a tandem approach. With an improved hiring batting average, however, in the long run you save an enormous amount of time, not only in the entire selection process but in managing A players rather than B/C players. Managers who say, "I don't have three hours for a Topgrading Interview," should finish the sentence with "so I will waste hundreds of hours when I mis-hire three out of four people." Some logic! The Self-Administered Topgrading Interview Guide (Appendix B) introduced in this revised edition of *Topgrading* can shorten Topgrading Interviews, but be careful! The risks in using it are thoroughly spelled out in this chapter.

Interviewing isn't easy, but this chapter will make it a little easier. In any given moment you naturally want to listen carefully to the response to a question and, in doing so, you might wonder if further clarification is necessary. If so, you might want to compose an original question, so you need to figure out the wording to it. (Try to make it open-ended, and don't bias the response.) You perform a quick memory scan to see if the current response possibly contradicts a previous response. You are trying to tune in to your gut feelings in order to develop the intuitive sense that can only be valid if anchored in facts. All the while you are trying to maintain adequate eye contact and a high level of rapport while taking appropriate notes and, by the way, carefully observing the candidate's body language. Phew! Interviewing is difficult!

The Topgrading Interview Guide simplifies this highly complex intellectual exercise by providing a clear, logical sequence of questions. The time-tested wording is presented, and there is space to take notes. If there is a blank after a question, this is a visual signal for you to ask the question (unless there is a good reason not to). By mechanizing the interview just enough, but not too much, you can look and feel professional and devote your energies to analyzing the candidate.

The Work History questions follow a logical pattern: what the expectations were coming into the job, what occurred, and why the person left. Chronology is all-important. Any interview process that asks what a person did in only the most recent job, or what would be done under hypothetical situations, misses the boat big-time. By tracing how a person developed over an entire career history, predicting the future becomes a lot easier. It's not that asking five questions about some competency (coworker relationships or whatever) is irrelevant; indeed, the latter half of the Topgrading Interview Guide is devoted to dozens of such questions. My point is, by asking about bosses a person has had over time and by asking how those bosses would appraise the candidate, revealing patterns of relationships emerge and current competencies are assessed with much greater accuracy.

The competency-based questions at the end of the guide are used to fill in the holes. If a very thorough job of interviewing was done throughout the chronology, only a handful of additional questions is worth asking. Those competency questions are grouped so that they can be used by interviewers conducting short, one-hour interviews.

The guide permits tremendous flexibility. It has been used for interviewing candidates for CEO of multibillion-dollar companies and for clerks. It is designed for one-hour to five-hour interviews, depending on how many jobs the person has had. Even without using the Self-Administered Topgrading Interview Guide, a Topgrading Interview can be completed in one hour for a recent college graduate. Its sole use is not just for assessment of candidates for external candidates for hire and internal candidates for promotion. It can also be used to get to know your team when you move into a new job. Finally, if there is a performance problem, the Topgrading Interview can serve as a solid foundation for you to really understand the strengths and weak points of your subordinate, permitting the powerful coaching described in Chapters 9 and 10.

Each of the questions in the guide has been filtered for legal acceptability. Anyone can sue for any purpose, but this guide has been constructed to minimize that risk. Chapter 12 ("Avoiding Legal Problems") says, "Stick to the guide, take notes, and you should be in pretty good shape."

The Topgrading Interview Guide is copyrighted. It's available in hard copy, and electronic versions can be licensed. (Visit www.Topgrading.com for information.)

## HISTORY AND ADVANTAGES OF TANDEM TOPGRADING INTERVIEW

The concept of multiple interviewers is not new. In fact, back in the 1980s the panel interview was popular. The educational community embraced it as a best practice, substantiated by, frankly, a gross misrepresentation of science. Teachers were selected based on opinions of a panel of ten interviewers, all present when the candidates answered the same eight questions. One of the many scientific definitions of reliability is "a high level of agreement among independent observers." Sounds good—the panel interview should be highly reliable. But it's ridiculous if only eight questions are asked, because it isn't valid, and it doesn't screen out B/C players or screen in A players! To make the point: if ten interviewers all observed the candidate respond to the question "How many noses do you have?" and the response was "One," all ten would agree that the response was "One"—perfect reliability! But there's zero validity, because As, Bs, and Cs all have . . . let's count . . . yup, one nose. For this reason, the panel interview has declined in usage. Or, more precisely, a panel of three or four interviewers is very occasionally used for some additional insights after all the topgrading steps of Chapter 3 are completed.

I began using two interviewers in Topgrading workshops thirty years ago. Topgrading was so complicated and difficult that two heads were better than one. Somewhat feebly I'd say toward the end of the workshop, "It may be hard to find a tandem interviewer for Topgrading, but you'll get better results in hiring and promoting people if you can do it." And maybe 5 percent took the advice. Next I went from one-day to two-day Topgrading workshops. My informal research showed that although one-day workshop participants became sold on the value of Topgrading Interviews, having role-played a few parts of it, only one-third actually were using it a year later. It's that complicated. So I conducted two-day Topgrading workshops, which were long enough that tandems conducted a full Topgrading, analyzed the notes, and completed feedback and coaching sessions. That doubled the one-year results, with two-thirds conducting good Topgrading Interviews the year following the workshops. More did tandems, about 10 percent, but at least 60 percent of my trainees were conducting Topgrading Interviews.

Enter Jack Welch. I thought tandem Topgrading Interviews would be great for training GE managers but too time consuming in real life, yet CEO Welch embraced it. If it would increase objectivity, validity, and credibility, then he would mandate tandem Topgrading Interviews. It started with the internal assessment and coaching process I designed for GE, but as Welch advocated more external hiring, divisions asked me to help train their managers. There was never a question about solo or tandem . . . if

Welch believed tandem was best for internal assessment, he'd expect it for external hiring as well.

Then the word got out. As GE expanded to prominence as one of the most respected companies and Welch became one of the most admired CEOs, companies copied GE, and tandem Topgrading Interviews have been the model embraced by topgrading clients achieving a 90 percent hiring success rate. Companies that are partial topgraders cut corners—tandems are not used, and the Topgrading Interview is not always followed by in-depth reference checks or a "second-opinion" Topgrading Interview by a professional. Topgrading corner cutters don't measure hiring success, but I'm sure their hiring results are (a) better than when Topgrading Interview not used, and (b) not as good as if they embraced the full topgrading process.

How are tandem interviewers best matched? The frank answer is "By expediency and trial and error." Senior managers usually ask (tell) their HR manager to be the tandem, if that HR manager is an A player, experienced in Topgrading Interviews, and paid a bonus if 90 percent As are hired. Easy choice. Many managers prefer the tandem to be with someone who is a terrific complement to them. Joe is kind of cold, so he chooses a warm tandem. Pat is technically weak, so she chooses a tandem who is a techie. Every day Jon works closely with Susan, so he wants her to be his tandem.

Actually the tandem process is robust. All sorts of rationales can be used for pairing people but only one is adhered to consistently: tandems are higher in the organization than the Topgrading interviewer. After that, toss A players' names in a hat, pick one, and the chances are good they'll figure out how to make tandem Topgrading Interviews work. Tandems review the résumé and Career History Form or SATI Guide, and then talk about how they want to structure it. Generally the hiring manager introduces the process and the tandem partner takes over as the principal interviewer for the first half (with the hiring manager taking most of the notes but chiming in with a question or comment periodically). There is a break (for drinks or the washroom) at about the midpoint. Then the hiring manager becomes the primary interviewer for the more recent (and relevant) half of the chronology, with the tandem interviewer taking more voluminous notes and periodically injecting rapport-building comments or asking questions. Then both ask a few competency questions at the end of the Topgrading Interview Guide. About one-quarter of tandems plow ahead with no one as the primary interviewer. Both know the Topgrading Interview sequence of questions, both take notes, and it's a free-flowing two-on-one. It's less organized but more spontaneous.

After the interview both tandems review all notes and reach consensus on rating all competencies. (This post-Topgrading Interview process is elaborated on in this chapter.)

## DISADVANTAGES OF COMPETENCY INTERVIEWS

The business world has flocked to so-called competency-based interviews, and they are better than "tell me about yourself" chats, but are weak predictors of job performance when compared with Topgrading Interviews. As the CEO of a prominent global financial services firm said, "How can a one-hour competency interview reveal as much as a four-hour Topgrading Interview that scrutinizes 100 percent of successes and failures?"

It can't. A lot of those companies experiencing 50–80 percent mis-hires use competency interviewing. A senior manager of one of the larger recruiting firms told me, "I can coach a candidate to successfully bullshit his way through any competency interview." I replied, "You coach them to lie?" and he responded, "No, no, no . . . just selectively disclose the truth."

The competency interview model sounds good—analyze the job, write a list of competencies necessary for success in the job, and prepare a list of behaviorally anchored questions that require disclosure of not just successes, but failures too. It's a structured process, with standardized questions, note taking, and face validity (meaning the questions all sound reasonable to candidates). It's like a pilot's preflight checklist, with fifteen crucial items to check (Are the flaps working? Do we have fuel?). Trouble is, there are fifty items, not fifteen, in a complete preflight checklist for a small plane. The other thirty-five items are vitally important, just not as important as having fuel. The competency interview overlooks too much; hence, the results are three out of four flights (hires) crashing (mis-hires).

Worse yet, even C player candidates can guess at what the competency questions will be and craft answers that hype positives and minimize negatives. Since the interviewee, not the interviewer, chooses which accomplishments and mistakes to discuss, the interviewee controls the process. In a Topgrading Interview, all jobs are scrutinized, 100 percent accomplishments are discussed, 100 percent mistakes/failures are discussed, and the interviewee knows you will talk with 100 percent bosses in the past ten years. Topgrading Interviews produce knowledge of *patterns* of success and *patterns* of growth in competencies, and those *patterns* enable the interviewer to zero in, laserlike, in follow-up questions to pin down exactly what the person can and can't do. Competency interviews miss all this; hence, their high rate of mis-hires.

Years ago GE arranged a "shoot-out" between the competency interview and the Topgrading Interview. A competency interview was conducted and thirty HR managers took notes behind a one-way mirror. Each wrote a report. Then the Topgrading was performed and reports were written. Everyone agreed that the competency interview produced a superficial picture of the person, a tiny fraction of the insights provided by the Topgrading Interview. You will experience the same thing. We topgrading professionals hear it all the time from managers we've trained.

## PREPARING FOR THE TOPGRADING INTERVIEW

Let's assume that you will enter the Topgrading Interview having gone through the various preparatory steps you have read about in Chapter 3. A thorough job analysis has been done, and a job description has been written that includes first-year accountabilities. Extensive competencies have been spelled out, written in behavioral terms, and assigned a minimum acceptable rating. For most technical or staff positions, approximately fifteen competencies should suffice. Any interview for a management position, however, should deal with at least four dozen competencies. (See Appendix G.)

## CANDIDATE ASSESSMENT SCORECARD (CAS)

With your tandem interviewer, complete a Candidate Assessment Scorecard (Appendix E). Decide which are the most important competencies and agree on a minimum accepted rating. After the Topgrading Interview, write comments, and then discuss your ratings/comments to gain a consensus. As mentioned in Chapter 2, retain your CAS to review it six months after a person is hired to see where your assessments were accurate or inaccurate and to review your Topgrading Interview Guide notes to see how you might have improved your assessment.

Let's assume that you have partnered nicely with Human Resources and the recruiter (if one is used), so you are all singing out of the same hymnal. You both met with the other interviewers a week or two before the first visit by the candidate in order to divvy up who will do which of the one-hour competency-based interviews—Intellectual Competencies, for example. The first visit resulted in your decision to have a second day of interviews. Your Topgrading Interview is scheduled on that second day. Just prior to the Topgrading Interview you review the individual's résumé and Career History Form or Self-Administered Topgrading Interview Guide. Let's push the Pause button.

## CAREER HISTORY FORM

The Career History Form (Appendix C) looks and feels like an application form. Many companies have licensed it (along with the Topgrading Interview Guide and other topgrading forms), put their logo on it, and tailored it to their preferences (with my permission), and it is their application form. Like the other topgrading guides and forms, the Career History Form is available in hard copy and electronic formats. (See Appendix J for contact information.) A players are usually in such demand that they don't want to think of themselves as out looking for a job. You have to go after them. They will fax or email you a résumé if they have one, but some are quite hesitant to complete an application form. If your previous interactions have lured the person into a full-day visit, however, and the candidate is willing to return for a second full day of interviews including your Topgrading Interview, you can probably induce the individual to kindly complete the Career History Form. Say something like this: "Thanks very much for sending your résumé, but now would you please complete the enclosed Career History Form? It asks for about thirty things not included in a typical résumé, so your interviews will go a lot smoother, and we'll then have plenty of time for you to ask us questions."

This Career History Form is a marvelously revealing document. Résumés are constructed with the help of others and are typically sanitized versions of the person's career history. This Career History Form accounts for every year and month since the person began working full-time jobs. That makes hiding an extremely short-term job or two very difficult. Compensation is specifically requested, and it is broken down into "base," "bonus," and "other." The name and title of each boss is requested, along with a clear statement that reference checks of finalists will be done (with the individual's permission); this helps inspire honesty. Dozens of inches of space are devoted to asking what was liked most and least about jobs. Educational performance is requested. Considerable space is allotted to asking not only what a person's strengths are, but also weak points and areas for improvement. There's more, but you get the picture. Perhaps one of the more revealing aspects of the Career History Form is an opportunity for you to understand chronological patterns before even conducting the Topgrading Interview. Sit back and look at the picture portrayed: In the twenty years (or whatever) since the individual started working full time, what have been the patterns for growth in title, compensation, likes, and dislikes?

The Career History Form requests dates for all full-time jobs, including dates college was attended, making it possible to guess someone's age. Legality of questions is dealt with in Chapter 12. Suffice it to say here that a company that discriminates against people over forty would be foolish to request education dates in interviews or application forms. But companies that do not discriminate against people over forty want to account for a complete chronology, at least from the time a person started college or full-time employment. It makes a difference if a person took four years or ten to graduate from college. Topgrading interviewers can get more valid insights into the candidate knowing that a person progressed from analyst to senior analyst in two years versus six years.

I have never heard of a company losing a lawsuit because the Career History Form makes it possible to guess age. Anyone can sue, however. The federal government of Canada questioned it, and when told that pinning down the full chronology was essential to topgrading, they hired me to train their top human resources professionals in Topgrading-based interviewing, using the Career History Form.

Don't necessarily conclude that a candidate today is weak in a necessary competency because she was weak in it during college. What happened back then is almost irrelevant in and of itself. However, the candidate reveals current competencies when reflecting on those early experiences. Some companies (and I) find, for example, candidates' reflections on what they did during school years produce insights into current decision-making modes and current needs. For example, someone might say, "I had a lot of activities in high school and was so disorganized I frankly didn't accomplish much in any, but I've really learned how to multitask and focus on the right priorities." This book suggests a cautious approach, beginning the Topgrading Interview with college, but tracking dates only from the first full-time job. Bottom line: Don't discriminate on the basis of age, do track dates as rigorously as your CEO will allow, and do read and follow the advice offered in Chapter 12.

I like to keep the Career History Form and résumé at hand when conducting the Topgrading Interview. There are a lot of papers to shuffle, but after a half-dozen interviews you can get to be pretty smooth at it. Having the Career History Form and résumé data convenient equips you to speed up or slow down the interview, ask probing questions or general ones, and essentially zero in on what will add even more depth to your understanding. If for some reason the candidate cannot complete the Career History Form, a lot of additional interview time is usually necessary. So, don't browbeat a superdesirable candidate into completing every item on the form. However, make the request, and if that sought-after individual wants to blow off the Career History Form, that's possible by just leaving a lot of blanks. The vast majority of candidates, however, conscientiously complete the form.

Since you have reviewed the résumé and Career History Form, you might be conscientious and enter some of the basic data—name of college, first employer, and so forth—in the Topgrading Interview Guide. This can make the interview proceed a little more smoothly.

## HOW TO USE THE SELF-ADMINISTERED TOPGRADING (SATI) GUIDE

The Self-Administered Topgrading (SATI) Guide is a twelve-page form in which the candidate responds to most Topgrading interview questions. The SATI Guide is potentially high in value, but its use is high risk too. When used appropriately, it can cut the time of a Topgrading interview by about one-third. Used improperly, it can destroy Topgrading effectiveness. Please go to Appendix B to review this newly introduced tool before reading further about the potential benefits and risks.

I hit on the SATI idea twenty-five years ago at HEB, now one of the largest private companies in the United States and a case study in Chapter 5.

Assessment centers were used to assess store managers as candidates for district manager, and of all the components of the center (in-basket exercise, group problem solving, performance appraisal role-play, speech, written tests, and more), only the Topgrading Interview was a valid predictor. However, it took a full day to conduct a Topgrading Interview in tandem and write a report. I designed the first SATI; it cut the Topgrading Interview process almost by a third; candidates (store managers) were internal, so they had to complete the twelve-page form. They were all eager to get a promotion, so they wanted to do whatever was asked of them. Topgrading interviewers read the completed SATI Guide and then set it aside, using the Topgrading Interview Guide (Appendix A) at a faster pace, given their keener insights into the person.

The best recruitment approach is for A players to contact As they have worked with, and very often those folks are happy and successful, progressing well in premier companies, but they might consider leaving if you offer terrific opportunity. You wouldn't email one and say, "Pat, how's it going? Say, I need a head of IT so let's talk and, by the way, please complete the twelve-page electronic form I've attached." However, after several meetings, when the prospect is willing to go through a couple of days of screening visits, you can use the four-page Career History Form, so all interviewers will have more than a résumé, or you can ask the candidate to complete the SATI Guide. Even prospects just remotely interested in applying will complete the Career History Form and share their résumé, because they want interviewers to know their career history and accomplishments. But many at this stage will decline to spend two hours completing a twelve-page SATI Guide. A very eager candidate, however, will complete it. Topgrading interviewers all want one of the two forms completed; deciding which depends on candidate eagerness and interviewer preference. Many experienced Topgrading interviewers prefer to see the Career History Form over the SATI Guide, saying, "I prefer to develop the interview data spontaneously, not see the answers in advance and then merely confirm them." I have observed some Topgrading interviewers become robotic, lacking in spontaneity, when substituting the SATI Guide for the Career History Form. If the SATI Guide doesn't produce a smoother, more efficient, more revealing interview, it should not be used.

Either way, the message is "In order for our interviewers to have considerably more knowledge of your career history and interests than a résumé presents, and in order for you and us to save some time, would you please complete the attached form? Thank you."

In this edition of *Topgrading,* the SATI Guide will be used a lot, and I'd appreciate hearing about your experience (please email me through my Web site, SmartandAssoc.com). For now I'll summarize advice gleaned from SATI Guide use by a few companies:

1. Use the SATI Guide as a substitute for the Career History Form, to supplement the candidate's résumé, but only when external candidates are very interested in the job (and willing to complete a twelve-page form) or are internal candidates (and are required to complete it).

2. Use the SATI Guide as you would the Career History Form: read it, set it aside to conduct a spontaneous Topgrading Interview, but keep it at hand, for a brief reminder of what the candidate wrote. You might probe by saying, "OK, as I see from your SATI Guide, you cut inventories 20 percent and lost-time accidents 50 percent. Please tell us exactly how you did it," or "Your SATI Guide indicates missing a couple of deadlines. Please explain, being clear about what in retro spect you could have done in that job."

3. Incorporate the SATI Guide only when tandem Topgrading interviewers are very experienced and very good.

4. Use it with care. Consider the SATI Guide experimental, until you are sure you can adapt to it, enabling you to save time and conduct a revealing, smooth-flowing dialogue.

## HOW TO ALLOCATE TIME

First-time Topgrading interviewers sometimes find so much revealing in discovering early positions or education that they run out of interview time. As interesting and job-relevant as an experience fifteen years ago might be, it is not sensible to spend twenty minutes talking about it, leaving only five minutes for your discussion of the present job. Here are some rough guidelines:

| | 4-Hour Interview (Career History Form at Hand) | 2-Hour Interview (SATI Guide at Hand) | 45-Minute College Interview (Career History Form at Hand) |
|---|---|---|---|
| Opening chitchat | 10 minutes | 5 minutes | 4 minutes |
| Education | 20 minutes | 7 minutes | 4 minutes |
| Work history | 155 minutes | 70 minutes | 20 minutes |
| Plans and goals | 10 minutes | 8 minutes | 4 minutes |
| Self-appraisal | 15 minutes | 10 minutes | 4 minutes |
| Competency questions | 30 minutes | 20 minutes | 9 minutes |

Let's dissect each of these segments of a Topgrading Interview, with insight and tips on how to be an A player interviewer.

## OPENING CHITCHAT

You're an experienced businessperson, so you know how to break the ice, or do you? Thousands of interviewees have told me that they and even CEOs at my client companies don't always do the obvious in interviews. After a couple of minutes of chitchat about the weather or yesterday's football game, don't forget to extend the common courtesy of offering the candidate something to drink. In this interview, the interviewee does most of the talking, so a dry mouth is inevitable. Add a little bit of nervousness, and dryness is exacerbated. People don't smoke anymore in interviews, but if the interviewee would like a moment to collect some thoughts, taking a sip of something provides a welcome crutch.

Some interviewers make a big point of sitting side by side with the interviewee rather than behind a desk. Do whatever is natural for you. If you manage behind the desk, interview behind the desk. That physical barrier does not necessarily constitute a psychological barrier. Indeed, interviewees like a physical barrier. If they want to cross their legs, or scratch their knee, the desk provides a little privacy. Twenty-five books on interviewing say you will have to go to detention if you interview from behind a desk, but those authors never asked interviewees their preference.

Remember a point previously made: You never stop selling the candidate! A players are in demand, so every step of the selection process should be designed to sell the candidate. That includes the Topgrading Interview.

Prior to the Topgrading Interview you might have had a preliminary telephone interview, and in addition to gathering information about each other, you no doubt gave a little sales pitch on why the opportunity is terrific, what a wonderful manager you are, and so forth. Then you met the candidate for breakfast, the day of visit #1, where you did a little more "selling." All interviews in visits #1 and #2 contain some selling, not so much a sales pitch but indirect selling through your being professional, alert, open, friendly, and very interested in understanding the interviewee's needs.

During the actual Topgrading Interview, you do not want to go too far afield in touting the features and benefits of your industry, company, job, personality, and the like. The single best thing you can do to sell the interviewee is to get to know her competencies and career needs in-depth, and on the basis of that information later structure your sales pitch. Too often interviewers make the huge mistake of trying to sell the candidate on something she couldn't care less about. You are not apt to know what an individual's real "hot buttons" are until completion of the Topgrading Interview. Although your company's stock options have been extremely lucrative, don't talk too much about them until you know if the individual is money-motivated. Perhaps the person really wants flexibility, independence, and job challenge and is not so money-motivated. All your talk about stock appreciation might make you sound greedy and turn the individual off.

Selection is like a mating dance. You spark the person's interest, then get information, return to intriguing the individual with the opportunity, then get some more information. You give information to the candidate, then get some, and it's really a two-way street. It's important to prepare the individual for the Topgrading Interview, however, because during that four-hour (or however long) interview, you get to ask the questions. At the completion of the interview, you should allot plenty of time for the interviewee to ask you his own penetrating, in-depth questions.

Even if the person is prepared for the Topgrading Interview, after the chitchat say something like

> Pat [tandem interviewer] and I appreciate your time today to review your background, interests, and goals to see if there is a good fit here at Acme Corporation. If there is and we offer you a job and you accept it, this interview and subsequent reference checks will help me

figure out how to help you enjoy a smooth assimilation here. Also, by getting to know your strengths and areas for improvement, I'll be able to work with you better to help construct a developmental plan right away. This is a two-way street, of course, so after I have interviewed you, you get to ask me all the questions you want. We both need to perform our due diligence to see if working together makes sense. How does that sound?

"Terrific!" is the response of most interviewees. A players like the thoroughness and professionalism of the Topgrading Interview. Naturally, they will expect reciprocity when they get to probe you.

## USE A NOTEBOOK

We're just about to the point of your asking your first Topgrading question, so let's deal with note taking. Many books on interviewing suggest that taking notes will impair eye contact, destroying rapport. Nonsense! Ask interviewees, and they say they very much appreciate your taking notes. Recording accomplishments and interests of the candidate shows you are conscientious and thorough. Momentarily losing eye contact to record the details of an accomplishment will give the interviewee an appreciated break. Note taking, done with a little finesse, is definitely a rapport builder.

---

**"He listens well . . . who takes notes."**
**Dante**

---

I like to use a notebook—you know, a leather-bound (vinyl will do) portfolio you open up and there is an 8½" × 11" ruled pad on the right, and a flap on the left to hold the résumé, completed Career History Form or SATI Guide, and job description. This arrangement permits you to take notes unobtrusively. Plopping the guide down on a desk or a table makes it obtrusive; as soon as you write anything the slightest bit negative, the interviewee's eyes will be drawn to the paper. Simply put the notebook on your lap and make no attempt to hide note taking.

The Topgrading Interview Guide is easily placed on the open notebook. You write on the guide, and the notebook provides a firm backing. If any questions require more elaboration than the guide has room for, simply make the notes on the 8½" × 11" tablet. When you go out for a break, you close the notebook and hide the guide without making a big point of it.

As you use the guide, you ask the questions you want answered and skip the rest. For some sections, like the Work History Form questions, don't go to the next page until there is something jotted after every one of the questions. However, for much of the interview you may proceed to the next page after a glance tells you that the questions of interest on a page have been answered. You'll naturally spend more time on the more recent jobs, so there will be more notes following each question on those pages.

One of the main advantages of a tandem interview is that the principal interviewer is focusing on asking the right questions and maintaining rapport, while jotting a *few* notes, while the tandem interviewer is conscientiously taking *voluminous* notes.

## THE TORC TECHNIQUE

TORC is an acronym for *threat of reference check,* and it is by far the most powerful technique to get the negatives. Candidates come to interviews well prepared to state accomplishments, strengths, and their needs. Although A player candidates are more willing to disclose the negatives than are B or C players, it is really your responsibility as an interviewer to provide a climate for truth for all candidates. This is somewhat complicated psychologically. Even A player candidates might not readily share negatives because:

- Your opportunity is fantastic, they want the job, and they fear that disclosing their weak points will hurt their chances for getting a job offer.

- Like all human beings, they have their defenses, and various individuals have a tendency toward denial, rationalization, and projection.

- Every book on job hunting encourages readers to be less than totally honest.

- Outplacement firms and recruiters tend to prepare people, sometimes too well, to put their best foot forward (and conceal negatives).

- Unskilled interviewers inadvertently invite candidates to minimize negatives by asking too few questions about failures and mistakes, not observing revealing patterns, and losing control of the interview.

The TORC Technique overcomes all that. It works, because interviewees are told that extremely thorough reference checking of finalists will be done. They conclude that you, the interviewer, will know so much about all aspects of recent jobs that honest disclosure is the best way to get a job offer; at least they have an opportunity to tell their side of a problem story before your possibly hearing a more negative version from a former boss. The TORC Technique is appropriate, legitimate, legal, professional, and fair.

Put simply, the TORC Technique says, "I'll be talking with your bosses, so tell me what they will say." By beginning the TORC Technique early in discussing a person's career, the interviewee becomes accustomed to the questions. As you come into more recent history, your follow-up questions are more detailed and probing, achieving greater specificity and revealing more of what the person is really like today.

The TORC Technique works in a very gentle fashion. You ask the questions, candidates respond, and you move on to the next questions. Question 13 under Work History in the Topgrading Interview Guide (Appendix A) simply identifies the boss by name, title, and current location. "Current location" reminds the candidate that a reference might be done with this person. It's most appropriate for jobs in the past ten years. With that information—including, "May I have permission to contact him/her?"—TORC is underway.

Question 14 in the guide's Work History section is an appraisal of that boss: "What (is/was) it like working for (him/her) and what were (his/her) strengths and shortcomings as a superior, from your point of view?" In order to accurately interpret what references might say, it is helpful to have an appraisal of that reference source. Beyond that, however, by asking your candidate about half a dozen different bosses, the patterns in responses tell you a great deal about what that candidate needs in you, the prospective boss. A candidate I Topgrading interviewed appraised various bosses as follows:

Boss #1:     "A real moron, with no brains."

Boss #2:     "Real turkey—ten years behind, definitely trailing edge, not leading edge."

| Boss #3: | "A moron." |
| Boss #4: | "Lacks basic common sense. Shallow technically." |
| Boss #5: | "Terrific. He was a technical guru. Taught me a lot." |
| Boss #6: | "A nice guy, but technically a dud." |

It does not take a Ph.D. in psychology to define this individual's mind-set, not just ten years ago, not five years ago, but today. If you aren't a technical wizard, you are going to be considered a "turkey," "idiot," and so forth. This candidate can only respect a boss with very strong technical expertise. You might want to hire someone to compensate for your lack of technical expertise, but it probably should not be this particular candidate. Ask yourself, "Can I effectively manage this candidate, and, if so, what is the best approach?"

Question 15 in the guide's Work History section is the guts of the TORC Technique—"What is your best guess as to what (supervisor's name) honestly felt were/are your strengths, weak points, and overall performance?" Deviate from that wording at your peril. Believe me, the wording of that question has been massaged over decades, through mistake after mistake on my part. For example, if you ask, "How did your boss rate your performance?" the interviewee might respond "Outstanding" while thinking, "I failed to meet my objectives, but my boss rated everyone Outstanding so I'll just answer the interviewer's question."

If an avoider says, "You will have to call her to find out what she thought of my performance," you can respond, "I'll do that, but I'm really interested in your insights into an important relationship—with your boss. I don't expect you to read your boss's mind, but do try to guess what she felt were your strengths, weak points, and overall performance back then. By responding thoughtfully and honestly to this question, you show that you are interested in what bosses think, you not only are interested but you are perceptive and understand their perceptions of you, and you show me that you trust me and my judgment."

What about the current employer? There is always turnover, and it is up to you to determine who among bosses, peers, and subordinates might have left and would make good reference sources. And, a final offer in any event should be contingent upon no surprises in reference checks. If a candidate is nervous about that, you might say, "Sara, if an offer is made in writing and you formally accept it, I'll naturally want to talk with your current boss. Now, don't worry. No offer has ever to my knowledge been withdrawn because of the current-employer reference check. But in talking with a current boss, I frequently get additional insights into how I can help a person succeed."

## ADDITIONAL INTERVIEWING TIPS

I've written two books on the fine art of interviewing, the more recent of which is *The Smart Interviewer* (Wiley). Briefly, some key principles are:

1. Use the Interviewer Feedback Form (Appendix F) twice a year. I do, and always get feedback to help me improve my interviewing techniques. My son, Dr. Geoff Smart, says I have a goofy laugh when the interviewee uses humor to avoid a question. My daughter, Dr. Kate Mursau, says I scratch my head when formulating specific, original questions. They rate me low on Unobtrusive Note Taking and give me explanatory feedback, and I try to do better.

2. Remind yourself to keep rapport high. Topgrading is demanding, and a conscientious interviewer can be concentrating so hard that a serious frown is the usual facial expression. Tandem interviewing makes it a lot easier for the principal interviewer to be warm and in control, and to bond with the interviewee.

3. Maintain control, and if the interviewee grabs it away more than once, say, "Pat, there are a lot of questions to be answered in this Topgrading interview, so I'll ask you to please stick with me." Any A player will get the message.

## SAMPLE TOPGRADING INTERVIEW

Have you thoroughly read Appendix A? Good. Let's begin a Topgrading Interview. Ever the gracious host, you have your interviewee at ease, ready to disclose all. You have prepared thoroughly. Almost all clients have licensed the various forms in the appendices, and suppose you went online and printed out the Topgrading Interview Guide. The first questions have to do with education. In order to fully understand why this oak tree looks the way it does, with its strength, its damage from lightning, its unique configuration of limbs, you want to begin early, with the acorn taking root, and come forward chronologically. Some interviewers actually like to begin interviewing twenty-five-year veterans with a discussion of high school days. I do. High school days are important developmental years. (If you prefer, begin with college, where the Topgrading Interview Guide starts.)

For example, Team Player might be an important competency. Asking about career influences in high school, you might hear, "My basketball coach taught me an important lesson. I was a loner, a great shooter, but a lousy team player. He benched me for a couple of games when I hogged the ball. I learned the lesson, and we won more games that season when I became a good team player. It was a tough lesson to learn, but it's stuck with me ever since. Now I'm chosen to head so many task forces I have trouble doing my regular job!"

When answering questions about education years, it is common for interviewees to switch to the present tense, helping you generate hypotheses about the present strength of various competencies. In the preceding scenario, is this applicant too hesitant to say, "No, I can't take on any more task forces without sacrificing my key goals"? With the person's full educational and career history to be explored, you will have multiple opportunities to confirm or disconfirm your hypotheses. By the time you are discussing the current job, you should feel confident that you have this person pegged.

Again, we're not so interested in what happened during the school days as we are in career influences and, more important, how the interviewee reveals current strengths and weak points when reflecting on those sometimes traumatic developmental years. Some psychologists (including me) feel that two-thirds of all people's careers can be accounted for in terms of living up to, or living down, one's high school reputation. If you are interviewing someone fresh out of high school, with no college, then there is no choice—modify the college section to fit high school, and begin with those high school experiences.

The Topgrading Interview Guide begins with college, because inexperienced interviewers, although they see value in starting with high school, feel squeamish because most expect to discuss jobs and, unless they've read

*Topgrading,* they might wonder, "What the heck does high school have to do with my ability to do the job?" OK. Let's assume you are interviewing a manager and begin with college.

The opening question makes your investigation of the college years seem quite job-relevant. You ask, "Would you please expand on the Career History Form (or SATI Guide) information and give me a brief rundown on your college years—particularly events that might have affected later career decisions. I'd be interested in knowing about work experiences, what the school was like, what you were like back then, the curriculum, activities, how you did in school, high and low points, and so forth."

This smorgasbord question lays out what you want, and the interviewee reveals a lot by what is answered, the order of the answers, what is avoided, and the relative emphases. Overly structured interview approaches amount to question–answer, question–answer, question–answer. You might as well use the Self-Administered Topgrading Interview Guide and have *no* interview. For management, and *Topgrading* is a book for managers, the smorgasbord question is most appropriate. It makes the interview more a spontaneous, ongoing dialogue than question–answer, question–answer.

Just fill in the responses to the questions in the "College" section of the Topgrading Interview Guide as the interviewee talks. Naturally, the interviewee will forget some of the components of the smorgasbord question, so go back and ask them again, and jot in the responses. When the two pages are full, it's time to go on to "Work History."

If the candidate has completed the Career History Form or SATI Guide and has loaded the "College" section up with accomplishments, this walk down memory lane will be quite positive. If there are a lot of blanks in this section, then you should assume that college was not the most positive time for the individual. Don't harm rapport by spending a lot of time on a negative part of the person's life, but at a minimum, ask for high points and low points, successes and failures. This is the pattern throughout the entire Topgrading Interview Guide: get successes, then failures—high points, then low points. This provides the "meat" for valid assessment. If the individual attended college twenty years ago and was a goof-off, but has been very successful since and takes full responsibility for immaturity back then, you might conclude that the candidate today is quite a mature individual. That's the whole point. This is a guided escort through the candidate's complete career history, and as you learn what this unique individual liked and disliked, succeeded at and failed at, across dozens of different competencies and, no doubt, several jobs, with lots of different challenges and people to interact with, you learn the truth.

If the candidate attended graduate school, request information about it, but do it in chronological order. If an MBA was acquired fifteen years into the person's career, ask the MBA questions after completing questions about the first fifteen years of the person's work history.

## WORK HISTORY

Ask every question in the "Work History" section for every job. Even if you allocate only three minutes for a very early job, nonetheless ask every question and jot a short response. With the later jobs you will be probing more, asking for more clarification, challenging apparent inconsistencies, and getting examples.

This is the guts of the Topgrading Interview. It comprises about two hours of a three-hour interview. Work History Forms 1 through 6 are all the same. If the person has had ten jobs, or five jobs within two employers, you will need to either add Work History Forms or take more notes on your yellow pad. If a person entered a large company that had job rotation consisting of four jobs in two years, and those all occurred fifteen years ago, group all four together on Work History Form 1. If the person is now in the second year of that job rotation, you might as well hear a little bit about each six-month job, using a separate Work History Form for each. If the candidate has a fifteen-year work history, spend at least half of the work history time on the most recent five or six years.

The "Work History" section of the Topgrading Interview Guide begins with another smorgasbord question. The purpose is exactly as it was for "College." You learn more if an individual has to organize the entire career history and present it, emphasizing this, excluding that, and so on, than if you conduct an interview in rapid-fire question–answer, question–answer, question–answer style. The latter format would probably take twice as long too.

So, the opening question is "Now I would like you to tell me about your work history. There are a lot of things I would like to know about each position. Let me tell you what these things are now, so I won't have to interrupt you so often. We already have some of this information from your

Career History Form and previous discussions. Of course, I need to know the employer, location, dates of employment, your titles, and salary history. I would also be interested in knowing what your expectations were for each job, your responsibilities and accountabilities, what you found upon entering the job, what major challenges you faced, and how they were handled. What were your most significant accomplishments as well as mistakes, and what were the most enjoyable and least enjoyable aspects of each job? What was each supervisor like and what would you guess each really felt were your strengths and weak points? Finally, I would like to know the circumstances under which you left each position."

Question 3 regarding compensation is important, because compensation is the single most common standard measure by which we can gauge employee value. It is the most important component of "availability" in determining if a person is an A, B, or C player. Books on how to get a job tell people to conceal compensation information, but by the time you get to the Topgrading Interview, sufficient trust should exist that the individual will not play games. Suppose someone balks. Simply say, "Compensation is a standard gauge of value, and in your case perhaps you were underpaid or overpaid. I don't want to either underpay or overpay you, but if I hire you I would view it as an important obligation on my part to get your pay right. And, I would hope that by now you would trust me enough to not feel you have to conceal something as basic as pay."

Question 4 asks what the person expected going into the job. This is a wonderful question, because if you hire the candidate, knowing her expectations in going to work for you will be crucial. Knowing the pattern of how her expectations met with reality across many jobs will tell you a lot about the individual's values, due diligence, ability to assimilate into a new job, and overall performance.

Question 5 asks for not just responsibilities, but also accountabilities—the metrics that determine bonus, for example. Question 6 asks what was found upon entering the job: the talent inherited, performance of the unit, resources available, the problems, and the major challenges. The next questions have to do with what happened—successes and accomplishments, failures and mistakes, what was most enjoyable about the job and what was least enjoyable. Probe for exactly how successes were achieved.

After conducting half a dozen Topgrading Interviews, you will not need to refer much to where each of the Work History Form questions is spelled out, with full wording. The smorgasbord question is so logical that you will remember it after a few tries. If you need a refresher on specific wording on any of the questions, you can easily flip back to it. For example, in any of the Work History Forms you can see that item 11 has one key word: *talent*. If you forget the question, you can flip back to and read: "(For management jobs) What sort of talent did you inherit (how many As, Bs, Cs)? What changes did you make, how, and how many As, Bs, and Cs did you end up with? (For the most recent two jobs, get A, B, C ratings and strengths/weak points of each subordinate.)"

Notice the smooth chronological flow guiding the interview. You have heard why the candidate left the previous job and what the expectations were for the next job. You learned the responsibilities and accountabilities, what the person found upon arriving, and then what the person did— specifically, successes and accomplishments, failures and mistakes, and what was most and least enjoyable. It's hard to ask all those questions without learning quite a bit about what talent the person inherited and what changes in people occurred (item #11), but if you need more information, ask for it. Then you ask reasons for leaving. Before going on to the next job, however, it's time to ask the TORC (Threat of Reference Check) questions, numbers 13 through 15.

## AFTER THE WORK HISTORY: PLANS AND GOALS, SELF-APPRAISAL AND COMPETENCY QUESTIONS

Most of the interview involves education and work history. We are still in chronology, however, asking the person to leap from the present into the future. Under "Plans and Goals for the Future," question 1 asks about the next job. It's straightforward. Question 2 could be interpreted as an inappropriate question, asking the candidate to divulge other private job discussions. If the interviewee balks, you respond, "I don't need to know the specific employers you have met with, but it would be helpful if you could tell me how the job opportunity here stacks up against those other opportunities—you know, what you're looking for and what is less important to you."

Question 3 asks about the ideal position, and Question 4 asks the candidate to compare that ideal with the job you are filling. Keep in mind, you've probably had at least a preliminary telephone interview, maybe a second preliminary interview, and a breakfast with the individual, and the candidate has been interviewed by some of your coworkers. You talked with the other interviewers about your candidate and read their reports. There has also been a tour of the facility. You already have a pretty good idea of how your job appeals to the candidate before your Topgrading Interview. But, after completing the "Work History" chronology, hearing why a person left each job to pursue the next, you should have an excellent understanding of exactly what turns this person on, what the candidate is really interested in. The advantages and disadvantages of your career opportunity should make a heck of a lot of sense, with no surprises. By discussing this topic for a few minutes, however, you are bound to get a few additional insights into the candidate's hot buttons. From this you should have "missile lock" on the importance of money, independence on the job, new responsibilities, location, or whatever.

The Self-Appraisal follows. If you only had ten minutes to interview someone, you would jump to this page and ask the questions. First ask for the pluses, since you are a positive thinker. Question 1 asks for "strengths, assets, things you like about yourself, and things you do well." That's four ways of asking for strengths. Get the grocery list of ten or twelve strengths, and then go back and get elaboration, digging for specifics on ones that are unclear. Question 2 asks for shortcomings, weak points, or areas for improvement. Again, get the grocery list of five or six weak points, urging the person to produce at least that many. Then go back and get the specifics. If impatience is a shortcoming, challenge the person on it. Almost every book on how to pass interviews suggests that candidates say that impatience is a shortcoming, "because my standards are very high and I mostly am just impatient with myself." Fire back at the person, "Exactly how is impatience a shortcoming? It sounds as though it's a strength to me!"

Get specifics, get specifics. Figure 11.1 explains what I mean. The first target shows "I sometimes procrastinate," as an example of an unclear shortcoming or weak point. Everyone sometimes procrastinates, right? Level 2 is a bit more specific. Missing three deadlines last year is precise, and if you already know that the person had thirty deadlines to meet and was given an overall performance appraisal of "outstanding," you might leave it at that. If not, it's time to go for the bull's-eye. You will want to know:

## Figure 11.1
## Interviewer Specificity

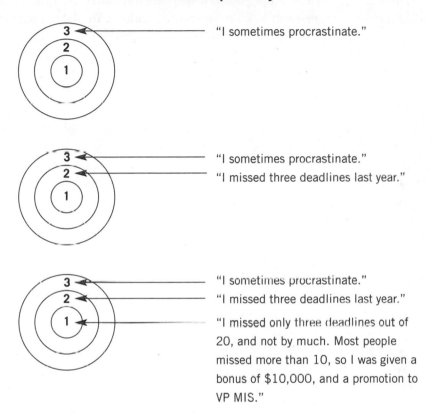

"I sometimes procrastinate."

"I sometimes procrastinate."
"I missed three deadlines last year."

"I sometimes procrastinate."
"I missed three deadlines last year."
"I missed only three deadlines out of 20, and not by much. Most people missed more than 10, so I was given a bonus of $10,000, and a promotion to VP MIS."

- Why did you miss three out of thirty?
- Was missing the deadlines your fault, or not?
- How late were you? What were the dollar consequences of missing the deadlines?
- What were the career consequences?

Level 1 hits the bull's-eye. The response convinces you that procrastination is not a major shortcoming. But suppose a level-1 response was "I missed all three out of three deadlines, and it was totally my fault; I got the reports in eight weeks late; consequently, we lost our best customer and I both lost my bonus and was told that I could lose my job." This probing to level 1 would reveal that procrastination is possibly a fatal flaw. The pattern of successes and failures revealed through a series of level-1 responses will surely permit you to rate the candidate accurately on many competencies.

Next are "Leadership/Management" questions. In each "Work History" section, you asked about talent. If you pass pretty quickly through this talent section of each Work History Form and haven't pinned down a lot of specifics on talent, asking all of the questions in the "Leadership/Management" section would be extremely important. Question 1 is a warm-up question—"How would you describe your leadership philosophy and style?" Since you probably already have some good insights into the answer, the response to this question will be mostly a "hype test." Question 2 gets a little closer to the mark, because it's like a 360-degree survey completed by subordinates. Question 3 is a pretty good test of a person's willingness to grow as a manager or leader. Question 4 is the most revealing and productive of all, however. It asks for a thorough account of the total flow of talent in and out of the last two jobs. You ask for a one-paragraph assessment of each subordinate, including his strengths and weak points. Were weak people coached and developed thoroughly, simply tolerated as C players, or coldly tossed overboard? What kind of recruitment efforts were there? These are the topgrading questions, so take your time. Get a good feel for what talent comprised the team, what changes were made, and what talent resulted. Is this manager inclined to topgrade, or not? In order to get some sense of patterns, the talent question is included in all of the Work History Forms, but I strongly encourage you to delve in-depth, getting the names, titles, and all the other information suggested for at least two recent jobs.

Candidates might sing a pretty tune when responding to Question 1 regarding their leadership philosophy and style. They absolutely have no idea how revealing the responses to Question 4 are, however. People can honestly think they are topgraders, but when you hear the long lists of terrible weaknesses in most of the subordinates and how this candidate carried C players, you get the true story. I have never seen an interviewing publication that suggested the interviewer pursue such detail about subordinates. Believe me, there is a mother lode of rich, revealing data in Question 4.

The Competency Questions are next. If you have done a thorough job throughout the chronological interview and Self-Appraisal, chances are you do not need to ask many more questions. Some interviewers prefer to have an "insurance policy," slicing and dicing the data different ways to be sure the conclusions are valid. I'm one of those interviewers. You should be able to accurately predict responses to the Competency Questions. Then you know you are on target.

There are asterisks before the questions I tend to ask of almost all candidates. One way to approach the Competency Questions is to say, "I have nineteen pages remaining of my favorite Competency Questions, and fortunately you have already answered most of them while discussing your career history. Why don't you relax a minute, and I'll read through these questions, asking only those where I feel I need a little bit more information."

For example, if a person's guess is that his boss ten years ago would say that he is "creative," you should not be satisfied with that. You'd pin him down to get specific examples of Creativity. And, when a candidate mentions a great idea, be sure to get the specifics—whose idea was it (the candidate's or someone else's), how good an idea was it? By the time you do this across three or four jobs, chances are you will have considerable information not just about Creativity, but also about Resourcefulness, Team Player, Energy, Conflict Management, and many other competencies. Naturally you will be particularly attuned to patterns for the most critical competencies.

These days, 360-degree surveys are so common, you might even ask to see the results. Or, if you have a question regarding any specific competency that comes up, you might say, "Have you gotten any 360-degree feedback on this skill?" Remember that there is a second use of the Competency Questions, and that is to provide sample interview guides for the other interviewers, those who conduct one-hour competency interviews. (See Chapter 3.)

You're done! Well, not really. Even if the Topgrading Interview has lasted three hours, if you have promised that you would respond to the candidate's questions at this time, do it. Some interviewers plan for a lunch break and suggest that the candidate use this more relaxed time for asking you probing questions.

## INTERPRETING ALL OF THE DATA

Having trained thousands of people in the Topgrading Interview technique, I have always tried to teach some of the most important principles for valid interpretation:

## 1. Observe Patterns.

Go to Las Vegas (or any other sports-betting venue), and you won't find anyone making money who considers performance in just the most recent athletic event—a basketball game, a horse race, you name it. Earthquakes are predicted with accuracy when not just the most recent history is concerned but the pattern of quakes across decades. It's pretty difficult to predict when a bridge will collapse unless you go back to the original drawings and note the various stress measurements across the years. A single cardiogram is not so revealing, in most cases, as the pattern of a series of cardiograms. Patterns reveal.

Let's review the data sources at your disposal just prior to your extending a formal offer of employment:

- Résumé analysis

- Candidate Assessment Scorecard

- Career History Form analysis or Self-Administered Topgrading Interview Guide analysis

- Preliminary telephone interview

- Five to seven one-hour competency interviews spread across two in-person visits

- Informal interactions during two visits

- Topgrading Interview, conducted by you and preferably a tandem interviewer

- Possibly another Topgrading Interview, conducted by a topgrading professional

- Preliminary record checks (by Human Resources)

- In-depth reference-check calls (or "coaching calls") conducted by you

- Your written report on the candidate

The data are similar for an internal candidate, with oral 360s replacing reference calls.

You are now equipped to provide valid assessments of your candidate across dozens (if necessary) of competencies. At this point, there is absolutely no excuse for unsubstantiated hunches. To validly interpret data, you don't need experience having conducted one hundred Topgrading interviews, but frankly you do need some life experiences and work experiences. Since this book is for managers, let's assume that you have considerable experience.

---

**"Use what words you will, you can never
say anything but what you are."
Ralph Waldo Emerson**

---

A fantastic psychiatrist or psychologist might be able to interpret a thirty-second video of a candidate and accurately rate the person on a few dozen competencies. You and I are not so gifted. That's OK—we have hundreds of thirty-second segments in a Topgrading Interview. The patterns of those statements given today, reflecting on an entire career history, give multiple vantage points from which to find out what makes a person tick, what the person's strengths and weak points are.

## 2. Assume That Strengths Can Become Shortcomings.

Under pressure, we all tend to overuse our strengths, and they can become shortcomings. During interviews, entertain this hypothesis frequently. For example:

- An ambitious person might sacrifice job performance in order to take additional classes and devote too much time to professional activities and expanding his professional network.

- A very conscientious, meticulous planner can become slow and indecisive.

- The friendly, affable customer-service representative might be easily dominated by assertive customers.

- Glib salespeople who are quick on their feet can manipulate bosses and be high-maintenance.

### 3. Assume Recent Past Behavior Is the Best Predictor of Near-Future Behavior.

Competencies have inertia. Success and failure patterns both persist. As you review an individual's chronological history, weigh the most recent behaviors most heavily. If the person was a goof-off in college but has been extremely conscientious and mature during the past five years, the previous adolescent immaturity can usually be disregarded. On the other hand, if a person was very mature and self-disciplined fifteen years ago, but has undergone a midlife crisis that has resulted in four job changes in three years, watch out.

### 4. Spot Red Flags and Look for Explanations.

Red flags are warning signals to the interviewer that something has gone wrong. Say, rapport suddenly declines or something changes in the interview to suggest that you have touched on a raw nerve. Either that, or it's time for a break. The signals are:

- Blushing

- Suddenly complex responses though previously they were more straightforward

- Loss of eye contact that had been quite good

- A significant change in pace (speeding up or slowing down)

- A significantly higher or lower voice

- Inappropriate use of humor

- Sudden changes in voice volume, pace (faster, slower), pitch (higher or lower), or pauses (more/longer or less/shorter)

- Twitching, stammering, drumming fingers though there had been none of that behavior

- Formality in style or vocabulary, when the individual had been informal

- Inconsistency between nonverbal behavior and words (e.g., saying, "I was very happy in that job," while frowning)

- Heavy perspiring though the person had been calm

It is the sudden change in the rhythm, style, or rapport of the interview that should tell you, "Pay attention. Something is going on here." Certainly make note of it in your Guide. Then go on a "fishing expedition," using follow-up questions to get additional information: "Could you tell me a little bit more about that?" or "Could you give me a specific example of what went on then?" If it is early in the interview, don't destroy rapport by probing too aggressively. You can always come back later in the interview, after you have more information that will help you figure it out.

## 5. Weigh Negatives More Heavily Than Positives.

I devoted a lot of Chapter 8 to the importance of fixing shortcomings in order that they not fall into that fatal-flaw, Achilles'-heel, career-derailer category. Naturally, as an interviewer, you should incorporate this perspective:

---

**Good-fit factors do not ensure success, but poor-fit factors can ensure failure.**

---

Clients frequently ask if I favor overall talent over experience. Should they hire a super sales manager from a different industry for their heavy machinery business (assuming the new hire could be less productive while learning a new industry, but presumably would outshine industry specialists within a couple of years), or hire an average sales manager in the industry (who will presumably be immediately productive, but never be a star)? My short answer is to be sure the sales team has enough experience, but hire the manager who's stronger on talent/potential than on specific industry experience. Sharp people can learn a new industry and a new product line very quickly.

## 6. Watch Out for Strong Feelings and Beliefs.

If you were at a party talking with someone who seemed to dwell on the topic of how volatile people are, after a while you would begin to develop a hunch about this person. Is he volatile? Is he hypercontrolled in order to deal with his extreme fear of volatility?

Naturally, strong beliefs can be an asset for any candidate. It's when the beliefs are accompanied by rigidity, intolerance, and extreme emotionality that you begin to wonder if there might be accompanying shortcomings. The person who vehemently and repeatedly says, "Insensitive people drive me nuts," might be insensitive. How tolerant is the individual who screams, "If there's one damn thing I can't stand, it's intolerance"? A Shakespeare quote is widely known because of the truth it reveals: "The lady doth protest too much, methinks."

## WRITE A REPORT

With all your data accumulated, take a few minutes to complete the Candidate Assessment Scorecard, and then write a report. It will force you (and your tandem) to crystallize your thoughts, to connect a lot of dots, and to question all of your conclusions. EEOC loves reports. And, by having a written record, you can review the report six months later to judge your own accuracy, and, by analyzing the data for any inaccuracies, you can learn how to become a more skillful Topgrading interviewer. Figure 11.2 is a sample report—not the fifteen-page report a professional topgrader provides, but enough of an executive summary in most companies.

I'd suggest for you what I do—take three passes through the data. One pass is just a refresher. Few of us took a shorthand course, so we simply scribble, scribble, scribble. Deciphering those scribbles immediately following an interview makes sense, because four days later they can look like hieroglyphics. After the first pass, go to the competencies (the last three pages of the Topgrading Interview Guide) and make a preliminary rating in pencil. Begin jotting comments in the space. Then take another pass through the data, to see if your preliminary ratings hold up. Next set the data aside for a few hours or overnight, and come back one more time to review your notes and be sure you are confident of your ratings. Fill out the Candidate Assessment Scorecard, with final ratings and comments. Then write a report (Figure 11.2). If you're not sure of some conclusions, remember that the Topgrading Interview for external candidates typically comes during the second day of interviews, so you can pick up the phone a day or two later and say, "Pat, I have a couple more questions . . ."

I hope you use a tandem Topgrading Interview. Most tandem interviewers use this approach following the interview:

1. Each tandem interviewer independently reviews her notes three times, rates the interviewee on all competencies (from the list of fifty in the back of the Topgrading Interview Guide), and makes brief summary comments in the space next to each competency.

2. The interviewers compare ratings and comments, spending less time on where there is agreement and a lot of time—enough to achieve agreement—where ratings differed.

3. Tandems next talk and gain agreement on overall conclusions: Is this person an A, A potential, or Non-A? What are the person's career goals and potentials? A joint report is written.

4. As in a solo Topgrading, call the candidate if you know you should have asked some more questions, conduct oral 360s (internal), or conduct reference calls (external), amassing all the data to feel 100

### Figure 11.2
### SAMPLE TOPGRADING INTERVIEW ASSESSMENT REPORT

#### GLOBAL COMPENSATION CONSULTANTS, INC.

NAME OF CANDIDATE:     Patrick Smith

POSITION APPLIED FOR:     Senior Compensation Consultant, Europe

INTERVIEWER:     Alan Jones, President, Europe

DATE:     August 15, 2005

TYPE OF INTERVIEW:     _____ Short Structured Interview

\_\_✓\_\_ Topgrading Interview

Chris Jones, VP HR, Europe
Tandem partner

percent certain you have the individual pegged. All the data should fit, so in your gut you are sure all the complexities, foibles, and inconsistencies (everyone has them) form a clear mosaic, with granularity that ensures you can predict the person's success.

## EXECUTIVE SUMMARY

Mr. Smith can relate credibly with Fortune 500 CFOs and VPs of HR and can become a recognized compensation specialist in Europe. He is a savvy businessman with a very professional image and plenty of substance as well. We like him and would be proud to have him as a professional associate, though we believe he lacks the fortitude and drive necessary to do the total job. Despite his "Exceeds" performance rating at General Motors, Mr. Smith acknowledges that senior GM executives would criticize him for not taking firm leadership stands on HR policy, and for taking far too long to remove C players in his HR organization.

Mr. Smith is being nudged out of GM by a new, dynamic division president who is determined to produce much better earnings. We'll call that division president for a confidential 360-degree discussion, but fear he considers Mr. Smith weak . . . perhaps in the top 10 percent of GM's Division HR VPs but not a sufficiently dynamic leader for a company undergoing a major transformation. We're concerned that Mr. Smith feels forty-five-hour workweeks are "too much." We need a senior compensation consultant to double our European executive compensation practice in the next three years. Furthermore, he is, as he put it, "not an aggressive salesman."

In short, we feel Mr. Smith lacks some of the "right stuff" to serve as senior compensation consultant. For the compensation he requires, we judge him (prior to my reference calls) a C player, lacking A player potentials in the foreseeable future.

| Strengths | Weak Points |
|---|---|
| Smart | Tired of 45-hour workweeks |
| Quick on his feet in conversation | Consistently criticized for placing himself above nitty-gritty details |
| Fluent; articulate | |

BA in economics from Dartmouth

MBA from Stanford

Strong general business perspective

12 years' work experience

Very strong analytic abilities

Quick and deep at "sorting"

Good writer; published two articles on compensation

Member of top 50 HR group (ASTD); knows best practices of premier companies

Prominent in HR community; was president of SHRM

Consistently earned top performance ratings at General Motors (though of questionable validity)

Excellent record in project planning and implementation

Reoriented IIR to be service-oriented at GM

Poised; at ease with senior executives

Sophisticated, yet down to earth

Strong team player

Positive, effective manager; sets clear direction, ensures accountability, attracts talent

More interested in strategic discussions than hands-on activity

Soft manager; does not confront negatives as he should

A relationship builder in NBD, but not a closer ("I'm not an aggressive salesman.")

Admits he is running from politics that exist in any company

### Draft Individual Development Plan

This can be the final section of your report. If your external candidate for hire is not an A/A potential, don't waste your time thinking of developmental suggestions. However, if your interviewee is internal, and if there is a good chance the external candidate will be hired, feedback will take place. Now, or after 360s/references are done, hammer out a draft of an Individual Development Plan, while all your interview data are fresh in mind. It will make preparing for the feedback/coaching interview in a few weeks a lot easier. Appendix H is a sample IDP.

## CONDUCTING REVEALING REFERENCE CHECKS

Many laws and company policies discourage managers from disclosing much of anything when people call for references on their previous employees. But the advice in this section works. Clients report that 85–90 percent of the references they want to talk with will not only talk, but give honest opinions of the candidate.

Chapter 12 points out that companies are penalized for giving out reference information only when they are determined to have disclosed false information or expressed malice. Most companies discourage managers, particularly low-level supervisors and managers, from giving out reference information; they prefer that Human Resources maintain tight control to be sure what is revealed is factual and devoid of malice. Carte blanche for managers to take reference calls could too easily lead a former employee to conclude a reference said something false or malicious. But companies cannot stonewall; they cannot refuse to give negative reference information without legal risks. If your company fired Joe for fighting, Human Resources had better reveal that to a prospective employer who asks. Otherwise, if Joe is hired and kills someone, your company might be found liable for not disclosing Joe's violence. Donald Weiss, author of several books on employment legalities, put it succinctly: "Asking for reference information is perfectly legal, giving out false or malicious information is illegal, and withholding certain negative reference information can be illegal."

Some companies are fairly loose in permitting upper managers to take reference calls. They say, "If you take a reference call, say you will give your *personal* opinion, not speak for the company; be truthful and nonmalicious, and be sure the reference source can be trusted to maintain confidentiality and not distort the truth." Almost all senior executives will take reference calls, no matter what their company policy, to discuss A players who worked for them. They believe (accurately) there is little risk in speaking highly of former employees.

Appendix D is a form specially devised to make your reference calling even easier. Read it carefully. Here is a summary of the major principles stated in the guide:

- You, the hiring manager, or your tandem interviewer conduct the in-depth reference calls. After conducting the Topgrading Interview, no one knows the interviewee better, and no one is better equipped to build rapport with the reference source. It's recommended that early in the selection process, Human Resources conduct preliminary checks with employers, credit agencies, and so forth (with written approval by the candidate). The Career History Form has such a request, but some attorneys want to have something more powerful (see Chapter 12). You as the hiring manager are apt to be the only one, however, with enough stature to call previous bosses (who are at your peer level) and earn credibility.

- Conduct in-depth reference checks after the Topgrading Interview. In the Topgrading Interview you asked the candidate to appraise the person you are calling, and this is enormously helpful in your later building trust and rapport with that individual. Ask the candidate to contact all bosses in the past ten years, plus two or three peers, subordinates, or customers, asking them to accept a call from you some evening or weekend soon. (It makes it easier for a person working for a company that has a policy against disclosing reference information to take the call away from the office.)

- If the candidate does not want the current boss contacted yet, make a written job offer contingent upon "no negative surprises" in the reference call that will take place after the offer is accepted. A player candidates don't often worry that their current boss would squash the job offer. In over thirty years I have never heard of even a single instance in which that "no surprises" clause was invoked and an offer revoked.

- Promise those contacted total confidentiality and honor that promise. Take notes, just in case someone's going to accuse you of making up a story.

- Create the tone that you are a trusted colleague, a fellow professional who knows the applicant very well, who just might hire that candidate, and who is apt to help the individual be successful with insights coming from this reference call.

If you really need to disclose to your boss what this reference source said, don't do it unless that person says it's OK. It's amazing, but if you say, "Is it all right if I share this confidential information only with my boss?" the person on the other end of the phone typically says, "I'll trust your judgment on that."

If your time is extremely limited and if the candidate is extremely eager to get the job, you can conduct five reference calls in a morning. Here's how: Establish half-hour time slots for the upcoming Saturday morning and ask the candidate to try to persuade people to take one. Many will, because they want to help former A player employees get ahead. Others will have to be contacted at a different time. Just follow these guidelines, and in-depth reference checking will go smoothly. One caution: Do not ask references for prohibited information on race, religion, and the like. You must operate within legal guidelines (see Chapter 12).

## CONTINUING TO DEVELOP INTERVIEWING SKILLS

If Topgrading interviewing is a silver bullet, capable of launching you to ever-higher career heights, what are the best ways to master the skill? Reading this book is a pretty good start. After that, I do have some suggestions:

- Practice, practice, practice. If you are not hiring these days, offer yourself as an interviewer for others. Do the shorter, one-hour interviews, but also volunteer to perform a tandem Topgrading Interview. Because the entire process is so time consuming, you are volunteering close to a full day by the time you meet beforehand and then understand the job and competencies to conduct a Topgrading Interview and write the report. Doing this twice per year is about all most managers can or need do.

- Get feedback. The Interviewer Feedback Form (Appendix F) was designed for this purpose. Someone need not sit in on an entire interview, but merely half an hour of one, to fill it out. Do this a couple of times per year, and you will continue to improve.

• Conduct your first Topgrading Interviews on candidates over whom you have psychological leverage. It takes only a few Topgrading interviews for most people to get the hang of it, but I wouldn't recommend trying it out on a likely A player who is far from being sold on joining you.

## BUT, ARE TOPGRADING INTERVIEWS VALID?

When I completed my Ph.D. in 1970, I had read every study on interviewing validity, and the results were pathetic—interviews did not predict job success. In preparation for my 1983 book, research continued to show interviews to be invalid; they still did not predict job success. And yet, I was sure I had created a magic bullet.[41] I was sure that the Topgrading Interview could achieve 90–95 percent good hires. Beginning around the early 1980s, research began confirming that interviews not only can be valid, but done properly can be the most valid predictor of job performance.

Research, for example, showed job analysis is essential. During World War II, armies (literally) of psychologists took job analysis to stratospheric heights. At low levels of organizations, job analysts, industrial engineers, and systems professionals joined with compensation specialists to promote efficiency and productivity. Years later job evaluation specialists such as Hay Associates, becoming quite proficient at assigning pay "points" to job "grades," found themselves competing with McKinsey MBAs looking to reengineer processes. But, somehow, job analysis rarely crept into the most senior management positions. It is still a casual undertaking in most companies. Nonetheless, all current research supports the importance of pinning down exactly what the job is (through job analysis).

"State of the art" today is commonly a process consisting of a job analysis, behaviorally anchored competencies, and then some sort of semistructured

---

[41]One book on interviewing influenced me early on: *The Evaluation Interview,* 4th ed., by R. A. Fear and R. J. Chiron (McGraw-Hill, 1990). It's still a classic, but seriously flawed. For example, whereas I might recommend a four-hour interview, Fear and Chiron say one and one-half hours is too long, producing "a lot of unnecessary and irrelevant information" (p. 71). Furthermore, by discouraging asking about performance appraisals for every job (p. 107), Fear misses the most powerful lever for understanding a person's failures, use of the TORC Technique.

interview format, so that questions focus on what is important to do the job. Topgrading offers even better approaches, but in most companies assessment continues to consist solely of invalid, unstructured interviews. Unstructured interviews include one or more of the following characteristics: lack a question format, short duration (less than an hour), casual questioning ("Tell me about yourself"), little planning (no job analysis, no job description, no written competencies), and no systematic analysis of data (the hire/no hire conclusion is made in minutes).

In 1988, in a review of 150 studies, Weisner and Cronshaw[42] found structured interviews over three times more valid than unstructured ones. Structured interviews are most valid when interviewers are trained, according to Pulakos et al.[43] Psychological testing is less valid than structured interviews, according to Van Clieaf.[44]

A study by McDaniel et al.,[45] analyzing 86,000 interviews by leading researchers in 1994, concluded, "Structured interviews were found to have higher interview validity than unstructured interviews." My graduate school colleague Frank Schmidt was an author of this study; he has done many meta-analytic studies of interviewing and tells me that the jury is definitely in: interviews must be structured if they are to predict job performance.

Perhaps you wing it in interviews because a tightly structured interview seems unbecoming, not as collegial as top-level interviews should be. Trouble is, the "wing-it" interviews can't address all of the competencies, so 250 of such interviews might be necessary for valid conclusions about a single interviewee!

---

[42]W. H. Wiesner and S. F. Cronshaw, "A Meta-Analytic Investigation of the Impact of Interview Format and Degree of Structure on the Validity of the Employment Interview," *Journal of Occupational Psychology* 61(4) (1988), pp. 270–290.

[43]E. D. Pulakos, N. Schmitt, D. Whitney, and M. Smith, "Individual Differences in Interviewer Ratings: The Impact of Standardization, Consensus Discussion, and Sampling Error on the Validity of a Structured Interview," *Personnel Psychology* 49(1) (1996), pp. 85–102.

[44]E. D. Pulakos, N. Schmitt, D. Whitney, and M. Smith. "Individual Differences in Interviewer Ratings: The Impact of Standardization, Consensus Discussion, and Sampling Error on the Validity of a Structured Interview," *Personnel Psychology* 49(1) (1996), pp. 85–102.

[45]E. D. Pulakos, N. Schmitt, D. Whitney, and M. Smith. "Individual Differences in Interviewer Ratings: The Impact of Standardization, Consensus Discussion, and Sampling Error on the Validity of a Structured Interview," *Personnel Psychology* 49(1) (1996), pp. 85–102.

[46]Pulakos, Schmitt, Whitney, and Smith, op cit.[47]M. A. Campion, J. A. Campion, and J. P. Hudson, "Structured Interviewing: A Note on Incremental Validity and Alternative Question Types," *Journal of Applied Psychology* 79(6) (1984), pp. 998–1002.

Let me cite two more studies. Pulakos et al.[46] found historical experience-based questions ("What were your accomplishments and failures in that job?") to be better predictors of job performance than hypothetical situational questions ("How would you restructure the finance department here?"). The Topgrading Interview approach does both. Campion, Campion, and Hudson[47] reported a respectable validity coefficient (.50), with a thirty-item interview of, half historical and half future questions. An interview consisting of thirty questions could take half an hour. Add half an hour to "sell" the candidate, and the interview would take an hour, which is the length of time scheduled for 90 percent of all management interviews. The one-hour time frames exist because interviewers don't know how to interview and because lawyers have frightened managers into avoiding so many questions. The Topgrading Interview approach, originated over thirty years ago and described meticulously in the two earlier versions of this book,[48] can easily ask two hundred questions. In this book I argue that there are more than four dozen competencies necessary (not just desirable) in any management job, so asking a lot more than thirty questions is necessary.

The tandem interview has yet to be researched to any degree. Having discussed the tandem approach, I believe that a solo Topgrading Interviewer who is very experienced is apt to be more valid than a tandem of moderately experienced interviewers. Pulakos et al. found multiple interviewers to reduce harmful effects of interviewer bias, but only if the interviewers did not share the same biases.

I hope this short stroll down Research Lane has convinced you that structured interviews are the only interviews that predict success for dozens of competencies. Topgrading interviewing is not a perfect science, and you will never be perfect at it. Nor will I. The tremendous saving grace of the Topgrading Interview approach is that it is resilient. You can miss the body language indicating a red flag, fail to delve into the specifics as deeply as you should have, bias responses to a question or two unintentionally, or

---

[47]M.A. Campion, J. A. Campion, and J. P. Hudson, "Structured Interviewing: A Note on Incremental Validity and Alternative Questions Types," *Journal of Applied Psychology* 79(6) (1984), pp. 998–1002.
[48]Bradford D. Smart, *Selection Interviewing: A Management Psychologist's Recommended Approach* (John Wiley & Sons, 1983), and Bradford D. Smart, *The Smart Interviewer: Tools and Techniques for Hiring the Best* (John Wiley & Sons, 1989).

even blunder into harming rapport. Because this is not a short interview, you have time to regain your insight and bond with the interviewee. Because so much stock is put on patterns, you can flat-out miss some important pieces in that jigsaw puzzle and still figure out if the candidate is an A player, B player, or C player. The resilience of the Topgrading Interview explains, in large part, why interviewers like it, A player candidates like it, and shareholders benefit from its use.

## CHAPTER 11 CHECKLIST: ARE YOU A TOPGRADING INTERVIEWER?

**YES NO**

☐ ☐ I use tandem Topgrading Interviews for assessing external and internal candidates for selection, getting to know my team in a new job, and coaching.

☐ ☐ I sell the candidate on completing the Career History Form or Self-Administered Topgrading Interview Guide at an appropriate time.

☐ ☐ I sell the candidate on the tandem Topgrading Interview by offering smooth assimilation and career coaching that rely on it.

☐ ☐ I ask all the Topgrading Interview Guide questions until the section on Competency Questions.

☐ ☐ I ask all the Competency Questions with asterisks and any remaining Competency Questions unanswered previously.

☐ ☐ I take some notes as the principal tandem interviewer, and copious notes when I'm not the principal interviewer.

☐ ☐ I ask all the Work History questions for every full-time job, but spend the most time on recent job history.

☐ ☐ I apportion my time so I am not caught short at the end of the interview.

☐ ☐ I get the specifics so as to be able to make judgments on all competencies for the job.

☐ ☐ After the tandem Topgrading Interview, I invite the candidate to ask me probing questions about the industry, company, job, and/or me.

☐ ☐ I review my Topgrading Interview notes a minimum of three times, rating the person on each competency.

☐ ☐ I ask someone to observe me and rate me on the Interviewer Feedback Form at least once per year.

☐ ☐ Because the Topgrading Interview addresses negatives, not just positives, I must make special efforts to bond with the candidates.

☐ ☐ I convey respect for the interview 100 percent of the time—no exceptions.

☐ ☐ I feel the TORC Technique is appropriate, legitimate, legal, fair, and powerful in getting the negatives.

☐ ☐ When interviewees avoid answering TORC questions, I always come back with a follow-up TORC question.

☐ ☐ After conducting the Topgrading Interview, the tandem interviewer or I personally conduct the in-depth reference calls.

☐ ☐ I realize that understanding patterns of behavior reveals the most valid insights into an interviewee.

☐ ☐ I understand that strengths, overused, can become shortcomings.

☐ ☐ I believe that recent past behavior is the best predictor of near-future behavior.

☐ ☐ When red flags shoot up, I go on a fishing expedition.

☐ ☐ I count on people improving a competency only when they have already demonstrated the ability to improve it.

☐ ☐ When a candidate has very strong feelings about something, I ask enough questions to figure out why.

☐ ☐ I complete a Candidate Assessment Scorecard before (Minimal Acceptable Ratings) and after (Rating by Hiring Manager) Topgrading.

☐ ☐ I write reports on all successful internal and all external people I interview.

# Twelve

# AVOIDING LEGAL PROBLEMS: A "BULLETPROOF" APPROACH TO SAFE HIRING, MANAGING, AND FIRING PRACTICES

"Bulletproof" is in quotes in the title of this chapter because bulletproofing, or certain protection, is only an ideal.[49]

In a perfect world, we probably would not need this chapter, but our world is far from perfect. Topgrading can embrace the spirit and letter of employment law or it can be abused. An effort to remove chronic B and C players can incur big risk if care is not taken to avoid a charge of discrimination—age discrimination, for example. Developing future A players can trigger litigation if disabled people protected by the Americans with Disabilities Act are overlooked. The EEOC will be knocking on your door if your infusion of new A players systematically excludes minorities. Employees and managers have discovered not only their civil rights, but also their contract and tort rights. Unless your company protects itself, it could face serious employment-related claims, including claims of wrongful discharge, breach of contract, discrimination, negligent hiring, or harassment.

---

[49]Many thanks to Seyfarth Shaw, LLP, a premier law firm in employment and labor law serving Fortune 500 companies, for updating this chapter. Seyfarth Shaw is based in Chicago (312-346-8000) and has more than six hundred attorneys in nine offices across the United States and one in Brussels. Eugene Jacobs, Ted Stamatakos, David Kadue, and Marty Golub of Seyfarth Shaw did a fine job of distilling U.S. and international law, providing understandable, solid insight and thoughtful recommendations. Seyfarth Shaw has relationships with employment law firms worldwide, and contributors to this chapter include Ius Laboris (Belgium), Lewis Silkin Solicitors (UK), Basham, Ringe y Correa, S.C. (Mexico), Cornelius, Bartenbach, Haesemann & Partners (Germany), Barthélémy & Associés (France), TransAsia Lawyers (China), and Matsuo & Kosugi (Japan).

Thanks are also due to Donald H. Weiss, PhD, and to Laser, Porkorny, Schwartz, Friedman, and Economos, of Chicago, for their contributions to this chapter in the first edition, which have been retained in this revision.

Three forms used in topgrading—the Topgrading Interview Guide (Appendix A), Self-Administered Topgrading Interview Guide (Appendix B), and Career History Form (Appendix C)—will help you meet legal requirements during the hiring process. The leading-edge practices in recruitment and selection we advocate—job analyses, behaviorally anchored competencies, structured interviews, note taking, and so forth—must be coupled with working hand in hand with your partner in Human Resources and your legal counsel to avoid legal problems. This chapter presents a general overview of legal considerations of topgrading. But state laws vary and your company might be vulnerable in ways that would prudently require more "don't's" and fewer "do's" than this chapter suggests. So check with your attorney before acting or failing to act.

This chapter includes sections on safe hiring and safe firing as well as a summary of risky versus less risky actions. Guidelines for legally topgrading in the United States are presented, followed by advice for topgrading internationally. The material in this chapter reflects many different pieces of legislation. You will gain particular insight into what you can and cannot do from points we raise regarding:

- Title VII of the Civil Rights Act of 1964

- The Civil Rights Act of 1991

- The Age Discrimination in Employment Act of 1967 (ADEA)

- The Americans with Disabilities Act of 1990 (ADA)

In these litigious times, it seems that almost every employee can sue for something. Why do they do it? Putting cynicism aside, a remarkable number of employment-related lawsuits (including actions for discrimination, defamation, etc.) are brought because employees perceive they have been treated unfairly. Employers often contribute to a sense of unfairness in at least five ways. First, managers make promises that can't be fulfilled, most often in the hiring process via overpromoting the positions and unrealistically raising the new hire's expectations. Second, managers artificially inflate performance evaluations because they can't stand confrontation. Grade inflation invariably flies in the face of the performance-based rationale for a demotion or termination and creates near-intractable hurdles in defending a lawsuit. It also can deeply affect workplace productivity and morale because mediocrity becomes the norm. Third, managers assume that policies are being followed and make disciplinary and termination decisions based on the false premise that similarly situated employees have been treated the same way. Fourth, managers fail to react promptly. Early intervention is the key to diffusing a host of potential employment claims, from workplace harassment allegations to reasonable accommodation requests by individuals with disabilities. Finally, managers do not listen well, apologize when appropriate, or follow the Golden Rule. The reality is that a very considerable percentage of employment lawsuits can be traced to these five mistakes.

In this chapter, you will see that, despite these mistakes and the inherent contradictions and complexities of U.S. employment laws, you can function reasonably easily and prevent lawsuits. Here's the secret: learn the law, treat people fairly, use common sense, and run your business—but check with HR and Counsel to avoid land mines.[50] That's all.

## SAFE HIRING AND FIRING PRACTICES
## FOCUS ON THE FUNDAMENTALS

Chapter 3 described practices designed to maximize the likelihood that you will hire the right people and improve or redeploy B/C players. But how can you actually hire the right people without sinking into the seemingly inescapable quagmire of employment litigation? Despite the complexities and contradictions of employment law, the answer is to focus on the fundamentals: (1) perform thorough job analyses; (2) write job descriptions with behavioral competencies; (3) use nondiscriminatory language in employment applications, topgrading forms and guides, job advertisements, and interviews; (4) use legally sound job offer letters; (5) avoid negligent hiring and retention claims; (6) use safe managing and firing practices; and (7) follow guidelines on how to topgrade outside the United States.

---

[50]One fifteen-minute telephone call with counsel now often saves you tens of thousands of dollars in attorneys' fees later. Likewise, leverage what you have—don't hesitate to call on your human resources and risk management professionals, managers with excellent judgment, and in-house counsel (if applicable).

## 1. Perform Thorough Job Analyses

Determine if the job is necessary. If you conclude it is, ask if it needs some tweaking, some reengineering before you hire someone. It is good business practice to streamline and simplify jobs to save time and money, but it is also important for legal reasons. To comply with the Americans with Disabilities Act (ADA), it is important to focus on the essential functions of each position and to document those essential functions as part of your ADA compliance. In identifying the essential functions of a job, it is important to distinguish between "fundamental" and "marginal" job duties.

Suppose you have an opening for an accounting manager. You might feel that an essential function of the accounting manager's job is to communicate frequently in order to successfully change processes in the department. You might conclude from your analysis that Managing by Wandering Around (MBWA) is essential, but maybe it's not. "Wandering" might imply "walking," when reasonable accommodations for a wheelchair-bound person could permit meetings in a central location or by telephone and email discussions, videotaped communications, or the like. Always remember, the key to ADA compliance is not whether a disabled individual could perform the job, but whether that individual could perform the "essential functions" of the job *when reasonably accommodated* (for example, could a person who cannot walk do the job if walkways were modified to accommodate wheelchairs?).

When hiring the accounting manager, ask people trained and experienced in doing the job you are filling to describe each function in detail. Ask the incumbent to write out all tasks, observe the person performing them, and ask others (internal clients, internal accountants, outside CPA firm) their opinions. Probe to determine what is not essential.

Consider, for example, how easy it was to reengineer a job, eliminating a nonessential function for a distribution center manager. Tradition required managers in a distribution function to load hundred-pound boxes for five minutes at the beginning of a shift. It ostensibly would show workers the manager is hands-on and not above manual labor. The job analysis showed the workers felt it was a silly tradition; they wanted their manager managing, planning better, and streamlining processes. Loading was eliminated, simultaneously permitting the distribution center manager job to be more productive and opening the position up to women and candidates with disabilities. Whether massive reengineering of hundreds of jobs is necessary, or simply tweaking one position is, the principles are the same: cut out the nonessentials, focus on what is absolutely necessary, reengineer for efficiency, and strive to include (not exclude) protected classes.[51]

## 2. Write Job Descriptions with Behavioral Competencies

Job descriptions can ensure that both the job applicant and everyone in-volved in the hiring process are on the same page, understanding what the job is. However, it is also important that a well-prepared job description re-tain flexibility by including not only a listing of the duties, responsibilities, and competencies entailed in the job, but also a catchall phrase: "and other duties as assigned by the employer."

Describe the job in terms of only the knowledge, skills, and abilities (KSAs) that are necessary for a trained or trainable person to perform the job. If the job analysis leads you to include peripheral activities that cannot be reengineered out, that's OK. But, you need to consider that possibility. It is also critical for ADA-compliance purposes that the job description state what you, the employer, consider to be the "essential functions" of the job.[52]

When possible, job descriptions should include objective, measurable performance accountabilities. For management jobs, this might mean specifying the achievements necessary to achieve the first-year bonus—production metrics, quality goals, productivity improvements, number of product launches, maintaining nonunion status, and so on. Specifying first-year accountabilities may offer some legal protection as well, by forc-ing a more detailed job analysis, a clearer job description, and a focus on most essential competencies.

---

[51]A "protected class" is a classification that has received protection from discrimination under federal and/or state law. Classifications and characteristics that have received federal protection include:
- People of race or color other than white
- People of any bona fide religious persuasion
- Members of either sex (yes, everyone is protected; there have been sex discrimination cases won by men, not just women)
- People over forty
- People with disabilities
- National origin classifications
- Veterans, current members, or applicants of the uniformed services or National Guard
- Pregnancy

[52]Although the employer's view is not determinative as to what is considered an essential function of the job, the employer's view is taken into account under the EEOC regulations.

Most courts and the EEOC agree with the Fourth Circuit Court of Appeals[53] that competencies based on soft or subjective criteria such as personal, interpersonal, and motivational competencies are acceptable where they are applied evenhandedly to all applicants for a position and when subjective competencies are job-related; that is, they meet the standard of business necessity.

Appendix G offers fifty management competencies, many of them "soft." Subjective competencies should be made as objective as possible. Avoid "feels comfortable talking with strangers" and instead say "builds credibility quickly with customers." You can measure, in surveys, whether customers feel the salesperson is a good listener, passionate about learning customer needs, knowledgeable, prepared, trustworthy, and conscientious in following up on promises. Customers would have more difficulty assessing how "comfortable" a salesperson actually felt, and who cares? So what if the salesperson is not very comfortable but customers buy because she is passionate about learning their needs and preferences and is credible?

"Good attitude" is too vague and is hard to defend legally. Specify the behaviors necessary, the behavioral competencies necessary to do the job. Use active verbs and observable results expected. Appendix G provides good examples of behavioral competencies.

Civil rights laws do not say that you must hire women, minorities, people over forty, disabled applicants, or war veterans. Nor do they say that you have to hire them in proportion to their numbers in the community. But, if you do not hire protected classes, you must exercise sound business judgment and base your decisions on how the candidates compared on necessary job-related qualifications or other valid business reasons. If practicing a particular religion—for example—Catholicism, is essential to being an officer in, say, a Catholic charity, then you may ask if the applicant is Catholic.

### 3. Use Nondiscriminatory Language in Employment Applications, Topgrading Forms and Guides, Job Advertisements, and Interviews

The primary federal anti–race-discrimination statute—Title VII—was signed into law in 1964. The federal age-discrimination statute—the Age Discrimination in Employment Act (ADEA)—became effective in 1967. Congress

---

[53]757 F.2d 1504, 37 F.E.P. Cases (BNA) 633 (4th Circuit Court).

passed anti–disability-discrimination legislation—the Americans with Disabilities Act—in 1990. The three primary pillars of antidiscrimination law thus are 40, 37, and 14 years old, respectively. Despite forty years of antidiscrimination legislation, some employers nonetheless continue to use employment applications, run advertisements, and conduct interviews that intentionally seek to exclude or, more often, unintentionally have the effect of excluding, members of protected classes. What follows is guidance on how to use application forms, prepare job advertisements, and conduct interviews in a way that should make you immune from claims that you discriminated against any applicant because of his or her race, color, gender, national origin, religion, age, disability, or military status.

*Application Forms.* Following this advice will help bulletproof the basic foundations of any hiring decision. With the job analyzed and described with behavioral competencies and with various communications broadcasting your recruitment, the next chronological step is scrutiny of completed application forms. Is your application form legal? The Career History Form (Appendix C) and Self-Administered Topgrading Interview Guide (Appendix B) are, in our opinion, legally defensible. They are designed to be completed by managers, who are not apt to feel that being asked to do so represents an offer of employment; for entry levels an application form including a disclaimer ("Completion of this form does not constitute an offer of employment.") is useful.

*The Career History Form and Self-Administered Topgrading Interview Guide.* These are not tailored for use in any particular state, but if your state allows you to express that "employment at will" is your policy, then an acknowledgment provision conspicuously stating, "I understand and agree that if hired, my employment is of no definite period and may be terminated at any time with or without cause or prior notice," provides important additional protection in connection with "at-will" employees. For additional protection, after the disclaimer we suggest you ask applicants to sign an acknowledgment stating, "I read and fully understand the terms set out in this application for employment and I certify that all statements contained in this application are true and complete to the best of my knowledge." Since disclaimer laws vary from state to state, check with your legal counsel. A section of this chapter spells out in more detail what should not be included on application or career history forms, but Appendix C is a pretty good sample.

*Interviews.* With résumés and application (career history) forms screened, interviews come next. The Topgrading Interview Guide is well structured, requires notes, and focuses on behaviors and results without asking forbidden questions. No interview guide ensures that the interviewer won't deviate and ask a forbidden question or make an unacceptable comment, because interviews are conversations. Chapter 3 discusses the different kinds of interviews and legal concerns pertaining to all interviews. The EEOC recommends interview guides, so stick with them. But when you make conversation and probe deeper, you should be very careful. This chapter presents quite detailed do's and don't's, but untrained interviewers violate them too often. Train your interviewers.

The EEOC accepts structured interviews, but suppose your company uses more than one structured interview—say, one for men and one for women? The Eighth Circuit Court ruled[54] that an airline discriminated against women for that reason, in that the interview process treated women differently from the way it treated men. If the airline decided not to hire a woman based on her answers to questions about child care and pregnancy, it would have blatantly violated Title VII of the Civil Rights Act of 1964. But more important, in this case, the Eighth Circuit Court ruled that it violated the law by asking one set of questions of men and a different set of questions of women. Needless to say, use one structured interview guide (like the Topgrading Interview Guide) for both men and women. (Some courts disagree with the Eighth Circuit Court. For example, the Seventh Circuit Court says, "Merely showing the questions were asked is not sufficient to prove intentional discrimination."[55])

You'd think that by now, after all the years since 1964 and with all that's written on the subject, interviewers wouldn't make the kinds of mistakes they often do. Some male and even some female interviewers ask female applicants:

- How many children do you have?

- Are you pregnant now?

- What arrangements do you have for childcare?

EEOC guidelines say it is not permissible to ask such questions of women if you don't ask them of men, and many state laws strictly forbid

---

[54]738 F.2d 255, 35 F.E.P. Cases (BNA) 102 (8th Circuit Court, 1984).
[55]950 F.2d 355 (7th Circuit Court, 1991).

them. Even if your state allows asking such questions, doing so could lead to evidence of sex discrimination under federal law. And, besides, if it is possible that a female applicant thinks they are illegal, why risk offending her? If you want to know if she can work the scheduled hours of 7:00 A.M. to 4:00 P.M., ask that and avoid intruding into the way she organizes her private life to meet her work responsibilities.

Each step of the hiring process carries with it possibilities for mistakes, with regard not only to EEOC issues but also to those related to employment contracts. In each step, avoid asking questions and making comments that can land you in trouble.

Whether for a telephone screening interview, a short structured interview, or the Topgrading Interview, the rules are the same. Questions you can't ever ask and comments you can't ever make during a selection interview are identified by EEOC laws, including the ADEA and ADA. All questions and comments must meet one simple criterion: they pertain to the essential functions of the job and qualifications that indicate a person's ability and willingness to perform those functions. Besides, why would you want to know anything else? If you wander from an interview guide, what exactly can you or shouldn't you ask?

*Age.* Avoid obvious age-related questions (which some people still ask), and beware of indirect questions that suggest age—for example, "Where were you when President Kennedy was killed?" Finally, watch out for smoking guns: "We need young blood here." A question of this kind can imply that you're looking for young people and that older people need not apply.

*Arrest Records.* Arrests without conviction can be irrelevant. Anyone "under suspicion" can be arrested for a crime he or she didn't commit. On the other hand, you do need to protect yourself if a person has been arrested and convicted of a crime that affects her ability to perform a specific job. You shouldn't hire a convicted embezzler as CFO.

In fact, if you don't pursue conviction records, hiring a convicted felon can leave you vulnerable to a repeat crime or can lead to lawsuits charging negligent hiring. However, be sure you have a good business reason for asking about convictions: "Have you ever been convicted of a crime related to this kind of work?" and "Have you ever been convicted of a violent crime?" are legitimate questions. That doesn't mean you can never hire an ex-convict, but if you do, it's wise to assign that person to work that reduces the potential for the individual to repeat the offenses or injure other people. It is important that you discuss such questions with your legal counsel because state laws regarding such questions vary; many states, in fact, require that questions about convictions be accompanied by a statement on the employment application that a conviction will not necessarily disqualify the applicant.

*Religious Affiliation or Group Membership.* Only if religious affiliation is a bona fide occupational qualification (BFOQ), should you question a person's religious practices, and you should question a person's group membership only if such group membership is job-related and not connected to a protected classification. What do you think would happen if, without a clear business reason, you asked any of the following: "Do you go to church on Sunday?" "Do you belong to the Knights of Columbus?" "Do you belong to the B'nai B'rith?" "Do you have a religious objection to working on Saturday?"

You may not think it, but questions such as "Do you belong to the NRA [National Rifle Association]?" and "Do you belong to the NAACP [National Association for Advancement of Colored People]?" are risky. They ask about affiliations that are totally irrelevant to the question "Are you capable of doing this job and are you willing to do it?"

*Health or Disabilities.* Under the ADA, during a screening interview or any time before offering a person a job (for example, on the application for a job), it's illegal to ask for his:

- Medical history

- Prescription-drug use

- Prior workers'-compensation or health-insurance claims

- Work absenteeism due to illness

- Past treatment for alcoholism, drug use, or mental illness

*Questions about Drug Use.* Except for positions that are safety-sensitive and governed by regulations from the Department of Transportation, Nuclear Regulatory Commission, or Department of Defense, drug testing is not mandatory. Likewise, it's best not to ask an applicant during a selection interview if she has ever experimented with or used any kinds of drugs (prescription or illegal). However, universal testing for illegal drugs for all new hires is acceptable as a condition of employment. Furthermore, it is permissible under the ADA to ask about an applicant's current illegal use of drugs.

Under the ADA, testing for illegal drugs is not considered a medical examination. Compliance with the Drug-Free Workplace Act of 1988 generally requires employers under certain government contracts or grants to forbid employees to manufacture, distribute, or use drugs illegally in the workplace; many employers outside the scope of the law voluntarily adopt the policies of this law. If public safety is at stake, as in the cases of school-bus drivers, train engineers, truck drivers, and other safety-sensitive jobs, then the Department of Transportation (DOT) mandates preemployment testing, periodic and random testing, as well as regularly scheduled testing of all such employees.

*Diversity.* To achieve more diversity in management, for market or legal reasons, be sure you select from a diverse pool of candidates. As obvious as that may sound, too often diversity goals are not achieved because recruiters did not look in the right pools.

When employers use a search firm to screen candidates for executive roles, they often ask to see only the top three applicants. That could be a mistake. What may appear to be the top three to someone outside your company may fall somewhere below your own estimates. Do the top three include members of protected groups you are seeking? Chapter 3 recommends that you initially screen résumés and Career History Forms with the recruiter to be sure you are both "singing out of the same hymnal." Further, weekly updates by the recruiter should involve discussing specific candidates. Talk about why they are included or excluded. Screen the papers and take recommendations from the search firm, but you decide which top three or more you want to see. This is one way you can achieve diversity with talent, not underqualified tokens.

*Multiple Interviews.* It makes good sense, from the management perspective, to have more than one person interview the candidates. A person reporting to you has to work with other people: peers, middle-level managers, and perhaps customers. How other people see the candidates can influence how well they work together with the person you hire. Chapter 3 recommends nine interviews, including two Topgrading Interviews, for management candidates. And don't even think of coding interview notes, your Topgrading Interview Guide, or any other forms for race or any other protected characteristics.

From a legal perspective, you reduce personal subjectivity or bias by adding properly trained interviewers to the process; this protects you from making decisions that could adversely affect members of a protected group. Having members of protected groups conduct interviews encourages fairness and removes the appearance of favoritism if you reject a member of a protected group applying for a position.

## The Education Date Dilemma

Is it permissible to identify information, such as age, that could be used for illegal discrimination? The answer is "probably." The biggest and most serious question is whether you should request education dates (such as year of graduation) in application forms or interviews. Make the request and you risk an age-discrimination suit, but fail to and you can leave yourself with such incomplete background information that you mis-hire more people. This is a complicated issue, but one worth studying because there are powerful forces in society working against your legitimate interests. The Topgrading Interview approach is in jeopardy because some groups want to prevent you from pinning down any dates—not just for education but for jobs too. If these forces prevail, you won't be able to effectively study applicants' work histories, rendering the Topgrading Interview impotent and causing your mis-hires to skyrocket from 10 to 75 percent. This would be an enormous impediment to your career success and it would put your company at risk.

Frankly, the whole issue could evaporate because brains and experience are eclipsing brawn. Companies are becoming more desperate for intellectual capital and are happy to hire older people whose jobs are less and less physical and more and more mental. But the issue is hardly dead. Picture this scenario:

*Complainant's*
*attorney:*     Your honor, the company discriminates against people over forty and we can prove it. They ask for college entrance and graduation dates, and since most people start college at age seventeen or eighteen, it takes about three

seconds to calculate age. Why would an employer want graduation dates, unless there was a conscious effort to discriminate against older, more experienced people?

Why, indeed. Here's why: You believe the Topgrading Interview is the most valid assessment tool on earth, and that studying the entire education and work histories reveals patterns crucial to understanding the candidate today. Knowing the dates of education are important for exactly the same reasons as for jobs. Precise dates (month and year) permit you to:

- Understand how rapidly and deeply competencies have been inculcated by knowing when each life segment occurred; for example, lacking energy and ambition during college and taking seven years to complete a degree are less serious if they occurred fifteen years ago than five years ago.

- Understand if the growth pattern for certain competencies is uninterrupted (and therefore is stronger now) or under pressure declines (and therefore is a riskier bet now). Education dates can establish both the base line in time and level from which revealing patterns emerge.

- Minimize gaps in chronology. Because education dates are easy to verify, candidates are less apt to hide them in an effort to conceal a failure (for example, flunking out or being fired from early jobs).

- Protect yourself and your company from a charge of negligent hiring.

Suppose you don't ask for date of graduation from high school and, unbeknownst to you, there is a gap between high school and the first full-time job John Jones lists on his résumé and his application form. Jones bummed around for three years, living off friends, gambling, and borrowing. He got into a lot of bar fights, broke a lot of noses, and was lucky no one pressed charges. Then he worked for ACME for three years, was never violent, and applies for a job with your company. His record is clean, you hire him, and six months later he breaks his supervisor's nose. The supervisor hires a lawyer, who figures Jones must have a violent past, digs up previous victims, and files a charge against your company for negligent hiring.

Had you requested education dates, you would have spotted that three-year gap. As a skillful Topgrading interviewer, you would have discovered the violence and probably not hired Jones. But your cautious company trained you to not request education dates, for fear of an age-discrimination suit.

The legal and HR communities are consistently against pinning down education dates, figuring the risks of negligent hiring are considerably less than the risks of age-discrimination suits. Their prudence does not eliminate the catch-22, but provides you the lesser of two legal risks. I have deferred to their prudence, suggesting that you use a carefully prepared Career History Form (Appendix C) that does not require any education dates but does require the applicant to provide information on all full-time jobs held; however, I encourage you to ask for education dates in interviews. In this manner, and with accompanying reference checks, you have been diligent in your efforts to cover gaps in the applicant's work records and education history while minimizing potential exposure to an age-discrimination claim that might result from using forms that might raise concerns to those who don't understand the appropriateness of having that information. Applicants participating in a Topgrading interview understand why education and work history dates are requested.

Sorry this is complicated (blame the lawyers!). In over thirty years I have not heard of even one legal challenge to whether education or work history dates can be requested in the United States. A client not in the United States was ordered by the equivalent of their EEOC to eliminate from their application form requests for high school and college graduation dates. They fought back. They explained that the Topgrading Interview would be hampered without pinning down those dates. "We need to know if there was a gap between high school and college, or if college took six years, because it gives us data to assess present competencies," they pleaded. They won. So, even if you are prudent (too cautious?) in not requesting education dates, please be willing to fight to know complete dates of all full-time jobs. That's the absolute minimum, in my opinion, to minimize mis-hires.

## Summary of What You Can Do, Can't Do, and Should Do to Avoid Discriminatory Language

You can become an employment lawyer, or walk arm in arm with an employment law specialist, but this is hardly practical . . . or necessary. You don't need total body armor, just a bulletproof vest. Just manage your business sensibly and honorably while remaining cognizant of legal constraints. We have walked you through the basics, and now, here are two tables of "do's" and "don't's"—first EEOC guidelines and then general advice on what and how to ask for information that will offer you a quick, handy reference to help you bulletproof your employment practices. The EEOC does not make law; it issues guidelines that have the force of law, however. If you do something EEOC regards as impermissible, you risk being investigated. If that investigation concludes there is disparate impact, for example, a lawsuit might follow. In addition, there are similar correlating state laws and agencies in many states. Finally, even without any federal or state investigation, violations could lead to or enhance a private employment-related claim from one of your employees or former employees.

## EEOC Guidelines

| Subject | Permissible | Impermissible or Suspect |
|---|---|---|
| Race, color, religion, national origin | Employers may lawfully collect such information for lawful affirmative action programs in accordance with Title VII, government record keeping, and reporting requirements, or studies to promote EEOC recruiting and testing. Employers must be able to prove these legitimate business purposes and keep this information separate from regular employee records. | All direct or indirect inquiries not serving legitimate business purposes may be evidence of bias. State laws may expressly prohibit this. |
| Height, weight | | If minorities or women are more often disqualified |

|  |  | than other people and if meeting height or weight limits isn't necessary for safe job performance |
| --- | --- | --- |
| Marital status, children, childcare | If information is needed for tax, insurance, or Social Security purposes, get it after employment. | Non–job-related and illegal if used to discriminate against women; may create exposure if only asked of (or have different policies for) women. |
| English language skill |  | If not necessary for job. |
| Education |  | If not directly job-related or no business necessity is proven and minorities are more often disqualified than nonminorities. |
| Friends or relatives working for employer |  | If preference for friends or relatives of current workers reduces opportunities for women or minorities. If nepotism policies barring hire of friends or relatives of current workers reduce opportunities for women, men, or minorities. State laws may expressly prohibit them. |
| Arrest records |  | If no subsequent convictions and no proof of business necessity. Mere request for, without consideration of, arrest record is illegal. |

| | | |
|---|---|---|
| Conviction records | Only if their number, nature, and recentness are considered in determining applicant's suitability. Inquiries should state that record isn't absolute bar and such factors as age and time of offense, seriousness and nature of violation, and rehabilitation will be (and must be) taken into account. | |
| Military service discharge | If information is used to determine if further background check is necessary. Inquiries should only be made if business necessity can be shown. If made, such inquiries should state that less than honorable discharge isn't absolute bar to employment and other factors will affect final hiring decision. | Honorable discharge requirement, because minorities are more often disqualified than nonminorities. Also, some state laws expressly prohibit this. EEOC says employers should not, as matter of policy, reject applicants with less than honorable discharges, and inquiry re military record should be avoided unless business necessity is shown. |
| Citizenship | Legal aliens, eligible to work, may only be discriminated against in interest of national security or under federal law or | If it has purpose or effect of discriminating on basis of national origin.<br><br>Note: Questions relating to citizenship must also |

| | | |
|---|---|---|
| | presidential order concerning the particular position or premises. | comply with requirements of the Immigration Reform and Control Act of 1986. |
| Economic status | | Inquiries re: poor credit rating are unlawful if no business necessity is shown. Other inquiries re financial status—bankruptcy, car or home ownership, garnishments—may likewise be illegal because of disparate impact on minorities. |
| Availability for holiday/weekend work | Only if employer can show that such availability is essential for the performance of the job, and that no alternatives with less exclusionary effect are available. | |
| Data required for legitimate business purposes | Information on marital status, number and age of children, etc. necessary for insurance, reporting requirements, and other business purposes should be obtained after the person is employed. "Tear-off sheets," preferably anonymous, which are separated from applications forms before the applications are processed, are also lawful. | |

## Additional General Advice

| Subject | Ask | Don't Ask |
|---|---|---|
| Physical condition, handicap, disability | "Can you perform the functions of the job with or without reasonable accommodation?"<br><br>Note: The ADA permits questions about an applicant's ability to perform marginal as well as essential job functions; however, an employer cannot refuse to hire an applicant based on his inability to perform marginal job functions.<br><br>Note: Except in cases where undue hardship can be proven, employers must make "reasonable accommodation" for the physical and mental limitations of an employee or applicant, including altering duties, altering work schedules, transferring the employee to a vacant position, altering the physical setting, and providing job aids. | "Do you have any physical disabilities or handicaps that would interfere with your ability to perform the job?"<br><br>"Do you need a reasonable accommodation to perform the job's functions?"<br><br>"Have you ever been treated for any of the following diseases?"<br><br>"How many days were you sick last year?"<br><br>"Have you ever had a drug or alcohol problem?"<br><br>"How much alcohol do you drink each week?"<br><br>"What prescription drugs are you currently taking?"<br><br>Questions regarding applicant's general medical condition, state of health, or illnesses.<br><br>Questions regarding receipt of or application for |

"Can you meet the attendance requirements of this job?"

"How many days did you take leave last year?"

"Do you illegally use drugs?"

Employer may tell applicants what is involved in the hiring process and then ask them if they need a reasonable acommodation for the process.

*Prior to making a job offer,* an employer may: Invite applicants to identify themselves as individuals with disabilities for purposes of the employer's affirmative action program (so long as they inform the applicant that information is requested on a voluntary basis, that it will only be used in accordance with the ADA, that it will be kept confidential and separate from the rest of

Workers' Compensation benefits.

Note: If no affirmative action plan is in place, an employer may not ask for voluntary disclosure of a disability.

If an applicant is screened out because of a disability, the employer must show that the exclusionary criterion is job-related and consistent with business necessity.

*Prior to making a job offer,* an employer may not: Ask questions about whether the individual is disabled, what kind of disability it is, or the severity of the disability. For example, it may not ask: Do you need an accommodation? Have you ever suffered any job-related injuries? Please list previous workers' compensation claims. How many days were you absent due to illness?

the application, that it is
being sought only for
affirmative action efforts,
and that refusal to
provide such information
will not result in adverse
treatment).
Ask applicants whether
they can perform
job-related functions in
a safe manner.
Ask applicants to
describe how they would
perform job tasks.
Obtain information
about the types of
accommodations needed
by an applicant whose
disability is obvious or
disclosed.

*After a conditional job
offer is made,* employers
may, provided such
information is treated
confidentially and kept
in separate files:
Ask disability-related
questions if these
questions are asked of all
employees who enter
into that job. Require a
medical exam if all
applicants for that job
category are required
to take such an exam.

| | | |
|---|---|---|
| Education | Inquiry into academic, vocational, or professional education and public and private schools attended and degrees received, but only where demonstrably related to the job.

Inquiry into language skills, such as reading, speaking, and writing foreign languages, but only where relevant to job applied for. | Any inquiry specifically about the nationality, racial, or religious affiliation of a school.

Inquiries concerning the dates of graduation or receipt of degrees may be legal but are risky (see discussion in this chapter).

Inquiry as to how a foreign language ability was acquired. |
| Citizenship | "Do you have the legal right to work for any employer in the United States?"

"Are you authorized to work in the United States?"

The Immigration Reform and Control Act of 1986 (IRCA) prohibits employers from knowingly hiring aliens not authorized to work in the United States. After being hired, an employee must provide the employer with proof (a driver's | "Of what country are you a citizen?"

"Are you (or your parents or spouse) naturalized or native-born citizens?"

"When did you (or your parents or spouse) acquire citizenship?"

Require that applicant produce naturalization papers.

It is unlawful under IRCA to discriminate on the basis of a person's citizenship status. This protection extends only to U.S. |

license and Social Security card) to establish identity and eligibility to work in the United States.

citizens and "intending citizens"—those granted permanent resident status, refugees, residents granted asylum, and those who have begun the application process for temporary resident status. However, the law provides that if a U.S. citizen and a non-citizen are equally qualified, an employer may give preference in hiring to the citizen.

**References**

Names of persons willing to provide professional and/or character references for the applicants.

"Who referred you for a position here?"

Require submission of a religious reference.

**Arrest, criminal record**

Inquiry into actual convictions that reasonably relate to fitness to perform a particular job. (A conviction is a court ruling in which the party is found guilty as charged. An arrest merely is the apprehension or detention of the person to answer a criminal charge.) But inquiries

"Have you ever been arrested?"

Any inquiry relating to an arrest.

Any inquiry into or request for a person's arrest, court, or conviction record if not substantially related to functions and responsibilities of the particular job in question.

about convictions should be accompanied by a statement that such convictions will not absolutely prohibit employment but will only be considered in relation to the job requirements.

Religion

Statement of regular days, hours, or shifts to be worked.

"Are you able to work weekends?"

An applicant may be advised by job announcements and advertisements concerning normal hours and days of work required by the job to avoid possible conflict with religious or other personal convictions. However, except in cases where undue hardship can be proven, employers and unions must make "reasonable accommodations" for religious practices of an employee or prospective employee. Reasonable

Questions regarding applicant's religion, religious affiliations, religious holidays observed.

Applicant may not be told, "This is a Catholic [or Protestant or Jewish] organization."

"Does your religion prevent you from working weekends and holidays?"

An applicant's religious denomination or affiliation, church, parish, pastor, or religious holidays observed.

Any inquiry to indicate or identify religious denomination or customs.

Applicants may not be told that any particular religious groups are required to work on their religious holidays.

accommodation may include voluntary substitutes, flexible scheduling, lateral transfer, change of job assignments, or the use of an alternative to payment of union dues.

The use of such preselection inquiries as "What days and hours are you available for work?" that determine an applicant's availability may be considered by the EEOC to be unlawful unless the employer can show that it did not have an exclusionary effect on the applicant or that it was otherwise justified by business necessity.

Generally, this ban on discrimination does not apply to religious institutions.

**Race or color, physical description**

Statement that photograph may be required after hire.

General distinguishing physical characteristics (such as scars) to be used for identification purposes.

Race may be requested (preferably not on the employment application) for affirmative action purposes but may not

Requiring applicant to submit a photograph at any time prior to hire, or requesting that the applicant, at his option, submit a photograph.

Race or color of applicant.

Inquiries regarding applicant's complexion or color of skin.

Question about an applicant's height or weight,

| | | |
|---|---|---|
| | be used as an employment criterion.<br><br>Height/weight may be requested if necessary after person is hired. | unless demonstrably necessary as requirements for the job. |
| Foreign language skills, ancestry, or national origin | Foreign languages applicant reads, speaks, or writes, if job-related. | "What is your mother (or native) tongue?"<br><br>Inquiry into how applicant acquired ability to read, write, or speak a foreign language.<br><br>Inquiries into applicant's lineage, ancestry, national origin, descent, birthplace, or native language.<br><br>National origin of the applicant's parents or spouse. |
| Organizations | Inquiry into any job-related organizations of which an applicant is a member provided that the applicant is warned not to name any organization if the name or character of the organization reveals the race, religion, color, age, disability, or ancestry of the membership. | "Are you a member of any union?"<br><br>The names of organizations to which the applicant belongs if such information would indicate through type or name the race, religion, color or ancestry of the membership. |

"List all job-related professional organizations to which you belong. What offices do you hold?"

| Prior military service | Questions about service in the U.S. armed forces or in a state militia or in a particular branch of the U.S. Army, Navy, etc. | "Did you receive other than an honorable discharge from the military?" (Note: questions about discharge are problematic in many jurisdictions.) |
| | Type of education and experience in service as it relates to a particular job. | |
| Personal finances | If car travel is required by the job, it is appropriate to ask whether the applicant has use of a reliable car. | Questions about wage garnishments, personal bankruptcy. |
| | | Questions about home or car ownership. |
| | | Future child-bearing plans. |
| Name | "State your name." "Have you ever worked for this company under another name?" | "State your maiden name." |
| | | "Have you ever used another name?" |
| | "Is any additional information relative to change of name, use of an assumed name, or nickname necessary to enable a check on your work records? If yes, explain." | Inquiries about the name that would indicate the applicant's lineage, ancestry, national origin, or descent. |
| | | Inquiry into the original name of an applicant whose |

name has been changed by court order or otherwise.

"Mr., Mrs., Miss, or Ms.?"

| Residence | The applicant's address. | "Do you own or rent your home?" |
| | | |
| | Inquiry into length of stay at current and previous addresses. | Specific inquiry into foreign residence. |
| | | |
| | "How long have you been a resident of this state?" | Specific inquiry into foreign address that would indicate national origin. |
| | | |
| | | Names and relationships of people with whom the applicant resides. |
| | | |
| Age | Statement that employment is subject to verification that applicant meets legal age requirements. | "State your age." (Questions regarding an applicant's age may be asked after hire.) |
| | | |
| | | "State your date of birth." |
| | Requiring proof of age in the form of a work permit or a certificate of age—if a minor. | "What are the ages of your children, if any?" |
| | | |
| | Requiring proof of age by birth certificate after being hired. | Requirements that applicant submit birth certificate or naturalization or baptismal record. |
| | | |
| | Inquiry as to whether or not the applicant | Questions concerning the dates of graduation may be |

meets the minimum age requirements as set by law; requirement that upon hire, proof of age be submitted in the form of a birth certificate or other form of proof of age.

If age is a legal requirement: "If hired, can you furnish proof of age?" or a statement that hire is subject to verification of age.

legal but risky. (See discussion in this chapter.)

The Age Discrimination in Employment Act of 1967 forbids discrimination against persons who are age forty or older. Avoid any advertising or age-based language that expresses limitations. The EEOC and the courts will determine if the advertisement has the effect of discouraging people age forty or older from applying, or if it limits or discriminates on the basis of age in any way.

**Marital status and family responsibility**

Whether an applicant can meet specified work schedules or has activities, commitments, or responsibilities that may hinder meeting attendance requirements.

Inquiries concerning duration of stay on job or anticipated absences that are made to both males and females alike.

"Do you have children?"

"Who will care for your children while you are working?"

"Are you married, single, divorced, or separated?"

"Do you plan to marry?"

"Do you wish to be addressed as Miss, Mrs., or Ms.?"

Name or other information about spouse. (After hire

|  |  | this is permissible to obtain a contact in case of an emergency.) |
|---|---|---|
| Names |  | "What are the names and ages of your children?" |
| Relatives | Statement of company policy regarding work assignment of employees who are related.<br><br>Names of an applicant's relatives already employed by the company. This inquiry, however, could increase the chances of a successful discrimination claim if it results in a preference to friends or relatives of employees, and minority groups are under-represented in the employer's workforce. Names and address of parents or guardian (if the applicant is a minor), but only after hire. | Name, address, or age of any adult relative of applicant not employed by the company. |
| Gender | Sex of the applicant may be requested (preferably not on the employment application) for affirmative action | Inquiry as to gender.<br><br>"Are you expecting?" or "Are you pregnant?" |

purposes under a lawful affirmative action program under Title VII, but may not be used as an employment selection criterion unless gender is a bona fide occupational qualification (BFOQ).

Inquiry or restriction of employment is permissible only where a BFOQ exists. (This BFOQ exception is interpreted very narrowly by the courts and the EEOC.) The burden of proof rests on the employer to prove that the BFOQ does exist and that all members of the affected class (e.g., females) are incapable of performing the job.

Inquiry into future childbearing plans. Any inquiry that would indicate gender of the applicant (for example, a statement that says, "Indicate Miss, Mrs. or Mr.")

Gender is not a BFOQ because a job involves physical labor (such as heavy lifting) beyond the capacity of some women, nor can employment be restricted just because the job is traditionally labeled "men's work" or "women's work."

The applicant's gender cannot be used as a factor for determining whether or not an applicant will be satisfied in a particular job.

Employers may not request information from female applicants that is not requested from males (such as marital or family status).

**Sexual harassment is prohibited by Title VII. Unwelcome sexual advances, requests for sexual favors, and other verbal or physical conduct**

| | | |
|---|---|---|
| | | of a sexual nature constitute sexual harassment when: submission to such conduct is made either implicitly or explicitly a term of employment; submission to or rejection of such conduct is used as the basis of employment decisions affecting that person; or such conduct substantially interferes with a person's work performance or creates an intimidating, hostile, or offensive work environment |
| Birth control | | Inquiry as to the capacity to reproduce, advocacy of any form of birth control or family planning. |
| Driver's license | "Do you possess a valid driver's license?" | Requirement that applicant produce a driver's license. |
| Person to notify in case of emergency | | Name and address of person to be notified in case of an emergency. (This inquiry should be asked only after a person has been hired.) |
| Place of birth | "Can you, after employment, submit a | Birthplace of an applicant. |

| | | |
|---|---|---|
| | birth certificate or other proof of U.S. citizenship?" | Birthplace of an applicant's parents, spouse, or other relatives. |
| | | Requirement that an applicant submit a birth certificate before employment. |
| | | Any other inquiry into national origin. |
| Experience | Applicant's work experience, including names and addresses of previous employers, dates of employment, reasons for leaving, and salary history. | |
| | Other countries visited. | |
| Miscellaneous | Notice to applicants that any misstatements or omissions of material facts in the application may be cause for dismissal. | |

## 4. Use Legally Sound Job Offer Letters

Offer letters are tricky because they serve different, often conflicting purposes. On one hand, the offer letter should be a feel-good communication that is somewhat informal and personalized and expresses enthusiasm about the prospect of embarking on an employment relationship. In this regard, the letter should convey the job being offered (including key duties and reporting relationships, if necessary), monetary terms and major benefit components, the location at which the work will be performed, and an expiration date for the offer. Despite the computer-enabled era of instant and informal communications, you should fight the temptation of extending an offer via a quick email or voice-mail message because those communications are often more notable—and legally risky—for what they don't say. Technology resources should be used to add a personal touch and supplement a good, old-fashioned, hard-copy offer letter.

On the other hand, offer letters present a unique opportunity to establish the legal framework for the employment relationship. Specifically, unless you contemplate entering into a written employment agreement with the candidate, every offer letter should contain language that establishes two key legal concepts. First, the letter should make clear that the employment relationship will be "at will"—meaning it can be terminated by either party at any time and for any reason, with or without advance notice. Second, the letter should make clear that the offer is not an employment contract, only the chief executive officer (or some other specified member of senior management) has the authority to enter into employment agreements on behalf of the company, and all such agreements must be in writing and signed by him or her. I wish there were a "nice" way to say these things, but there isn't, so just say them and move on.

The commencement of the employment relationship presents the optimal opportunity to enter into three related but distinct agreements, which I'll call "restrictive agreements" because they operate to restrict employees' latitude to do certain things. The three are a covenant not to compete, a trade secrets/nondisclosure agreement, and a confidentiality agreement. At their most fundamental, noncompete agreements serve to prevent the alienation of customers by requiring employees to agree to not solicit business from those customers for a limited period of time after the employment relationship ends. Trade secrets agreements prohibit employees and former employees from disclosing confidential and proprietary information outside of the organization. Some states have trade secrets statutes, but they often suffer from defining trade secrets in a narrow, unhelpful way. Finally, confidentiality agreements typically guard against the dissemination of confidential information that does not rise to the level of trade secrets but nevertheless is important to the employer. Confidentiality agreements thus often require departing employees to hold certain information in confidence and return proprietary information to the employer upon separation.

When drafted and implemented properly, noncompete, nondisclosure, and confidentiality agreements create a formidable legal security system for most companies' primary assets—customers and information (proprietary and otherwise). Yet they are not always desirable; not every employee needs to be bound by restrictive agreements, and requiring them across the board may well impair your ability to hire talented employees. Nor are they always enforceable. For example, courts typically are hostile to noncompete agreements, which accordingly need to be extremely finely tuned in their provisions. Despite these idiosyncratic characteristics, it is a mistake to let staffing exigencies trump the need to be thoughtful and prudent about restrictive agreements. Take the time to carefully assess your organization's needs regarding competition and confidentiality. Invest the money in skilled attorneys who can help in the assessment process and tailor the agreements to fit the organization's needs and the contours of the law. Do these things now, before it is too late—when you find yourself trying to explain why you'd like a long-term employee to enter into a noncompete agreement or when you've lost yet another big customer to your primary competitor and have no legal recourse against the former executive who lured them away.

## 5. Avoid Negligent Hiring and Retention Claims

As if navigating the hiring minefield isn't challenging enough, employers also risk exposure for negligent hiring, a legal theory now recognized by nearly every state. The legal theory originally arose out of the common law "fellow-servant" rule, which imposed a legal duty on employers to hire employees who would not endanger other employees. As now recognized, negligent hiring suits can be brought by employees as well as third parties, like customers or contractors. To win, the employee or third party must show that the employer was negligent because it hired a person with either known negative propensities or negative propensities that should have been discovered by a reasonable investigation, and then placed him in a position where it was foreseeable that he posed a threat of harm to others. For example, an employer can be found liable if it fails to examine information provided by an applicant or fails to conduct a background check to determine if the applicant has a conviction history.

Negligent retention claims are identical in nature except the alleged negligent act by the employer is its failure to take action—investigating, firing, reassigning, disciplining—after it became aware or should have become aware that an employee is "unfit."

So what is a prudent employer supposed to do, especially in light of the reality that most employers are so fearful of defamation and negligent referral claims that they won't provide anything but "neutral references," like verification of dates of employment? Adhere to all the basics in topgrading (Chapter 3) and advice given thus far in this chapter, and don't cut corners. Then use common sense. For example, it is obviously sensible to investigate the criminal history of an applicant who is seeking a job involving access to money or proprietary financial information.

We recommend that you conduct a background check on all new hires, from the entry-level administrative assistant to the chief executive officer. Background check service providers are everywhere (of course, some are better than others) and, in many instances, quite affordable. Significantly, conducting background checks has become so pervasive that failing to do so may well breach a general standard of care. In this world of transparent corporate governance, it is imperative to conduct comprehensive background checks of executive candidates. In this regard, if you are working with an executive search outfit to find a senior manager, don't get lulled into thinking that the search company is "taking care" of the background check; the fine print in search contracts often disclaims any responsibility for investigating the candidate's background. With executive candidates, go the extra mile. In fact, above and beyond the employment application, use the Career History Form (Appendix C) to elicit germane background information, and require the applicant to certify that the information she provides is complete, accurate, and truthful.

Despite the prevalence of background checks, many employers fail to comply with the federal law—the Fair Credit Reporting Act (FCRA)—that has long governed third-party access to credit, criminal, and other personal information. Work with your lawyers to ensure FCRA and state law compliance. A modest investment on the front end will preclude the risk of triggering legal land mines later on. What could be worse than unearthing disqualifying information via a background check only to learn that you can't use the information because the background check was unauthorized under the FCRA?

Finally, don't lose sight of your post-hire obligations and associated risks. Since it is often difficult to obtain thorough, accurate information during the hiring process, negligent hiring claims often morph into negligent retention claims when there is evidence that the employer obtained yet disregarded certain information after it hired the employee. This means that you should promptly investigate credible and troubling information regarding the employee's past work history that comes to your attention at any time during his employment; don't succumb to the temptation to disregard such information as essentially meaningless now that the employee has been hired and is making significant contributions to the organization. You should likewise look at the performance review process as an opportunity to assess foreseeable risks, like an imbalance in the employee's life that has manifested itself in a short temper and veiled threats to coworkers.

## 6. Use Safe Managing and Firing Practices

Employment law seems to be a contradiction. After all, nearly every state recognizes the cardinal principle of "at-will" employment, which means that employers can fire employees at any time and for any reason or no reason at all. Yet the wide-open rule of at-will employment is subject to a significant limitation. An employer cannot fire even an at-will employee for unlawful reasons. This means that an employer cannot terminate an employee solely because of her membership in a protected class as defined by antidiscrimination law, or violation of a union or employment contract, or in retaliation for exercising rights recognized as a matter of public policy (e.g., for filing a workers' compensation claim or engaging in protected whistleblowing). So, although at-will employment still has legal significance, it does not drive legal compliance and, indeed, in many respects serves as a starting point for devising a strategy that takes into account legal risks and seeks to minimize them.

Where does this leave employers? Safe managing and firing practices begin with safe hiring practices. When people have been hired the right and legal way, then if they turn out to be chronic B/C players (which *Topgrading* seeks to minimize), it is easier to fire them. Just as important, though, in managing and firing poor performers, employers' legal land mines can be avoided by designing and adhering to practices that are—above all—reasonable and fair.

## Promises That Bind

Most people get into trouble during the hiring interview more for what they say or offer (or don't say or don't offer) than for what they ask or don't ask. They commit four common errors that could later lead to charges of wrongful discharge:

- They promise more than they're personally authorized to promise (in compensation or job title, for example).

- They fail to cover the conditions of employment thoroughly in advance, especially with regard to employment at will (that is, that the company has the right to fire employees with or without notice, with or without cause).

- They don't give the new employee an employee's handbook (which should always contain the proper disclaimers that it does not create a contract, based on consultation with counsel because state laws vary).

- They lower their guard, getting too comfortable with the candidate, and say things that can be misconstrued as promises or, too often, as attitudes toward minorities, women, legal aliens, and the like.

Simple steps can prevent getting into such jams.

- Unless you're the CEO or president of the company, have in writing what the scope of your authority is when extending a job offer.

- If permitted in your state, make sure your company has an employment-at-will disclaimer that includes specific language that explains the limitations on employment (including that employment is for no specific duration). It should explain that either party can end the relationship at any time, with or without cause, with or without notice. It should then state that no one but the highest management authority in the group can alter the terms described in the organization's documents. Finally, ask all new employees to sign an acknowledgment that they have read and understood the disclaimer.

- Regardless of your personal attitudes or feelings toward other people, do not create any appearance of negative attitudes toward anyone. If you do harbor such feelings, don't assume that a person coming to work for you harbors them as well. Remember, anyone can be a witness against you if someone sues you for creating a hostile environment or for discrimination, even if she is not a target of your behavior.

## Real-Time Performance Monitoring and Progressive Discipline

There are three key principles that form the basis for the effective and legally defensible management and, ultimately, redeployment of B/C players. The first is borne in the recognition that effective management of weak employees begins well before the termination decision—performance issues should be addressed promptly as they arise and before they become serious, not once they have become serious. Why? Because prompt and constructive communication is the essence of fairness, lays the groundwork for future action, and helps render your decisions immune from legal attack.

What this means in the day-to-day context is that management-level employees should monitor the performance of their subordinates on an ongoing basis and, when problems develop, promptly raise them with the employee and suggest a strategy for improvement. Of course, adherence to this principle means fighting the urge to avoid conflict and put off performance assessment until the review cycle rolls around. But, holding off on communicating performance deficiencies until the problems become acute all too often substantially restricts your ability to take action that is legally defensible. This is so because courts refrain from throwing out discrimination cases and let juries decide them when there is genuine evidence that the employer's decision was "pretextual" (a phony reason or a lie). Remember: Jurors are free to infer discriminatory intent when the performance deficiency was not addressed—indeed, was tolerated—at length before that formed the basis for termination.

The second principle that should guide the process of managing and exiting B/C players lies in the usually unremarkable but often disregarded pages of applicable employment policies, typically contained in a handbook or manual.[56] Handbooks serve multiple functions, but their major attrib-

---

[56]It is essential that every employee handbook, and any personnel manual or guidelines, contain a clear, legally defensible disclaimer—a statement (usually at the beginning of the handbook) that disavows the creation of a contract, proclaims management's ability to supplement or change the handbook's terms, and reiterates employees' status as at-will employees. Insofar as legal requirements often vary state-by-state, you should work with your employment attorneys in preparing a solid disclaimer.

ute is that they announce the rules by which the employer intends to play. Virtually every handbook contains a progressive discipline policy. Even in the absence of a progressive discipline policy (but not in cases of extreme misconduct) employers should generally follow a course of progressive discipline because it comports with the bedrock value of fundamental fairness—it identifies the performance deficiency, gives the employee an opportunity to improve, and warns the employee of the consequences of poor performance. When followed, progressive discipline is honest, direct, and fair, and thus goes a long way to making separation decisions bulletproof.

Now a word or two about documentation and defamation. In litigation, proper documentation is the backbone of every defense. Conversely, improper—or, worse yet, nonexistent documentation—is the Achilles' heel of every defense. Nothing is more precious to a management-side attorney's eyes than documents that are dated, were created contemporaneously with the performance counseling and/or progressive discipline step, and summarize the substance of the communication with the employee. Better yet, communicate the counseling and progressive discipline in writing to the employee and place the documents in the employee's personnel file. To be sure, the twenty-first-century workplace moves very fast. But fast-paced work environments (typically laden with workplace technology) are a reason to document employee counseling and progressive discipline, not a reason to "get around to it later," disregard common sense, and create unnecessary risk.

## Documenting Nonperformance

Don't even think of creating documentation *after* making the decision to demote or fire someone. Entering into a file trivial things that happen after a charge of discrimination has been brought against you could be seen as retaliation and harassment and could expose you to a retaliatory-discharge claim.

Honest criticism of job performance may be painful to the recipient but is not itself unlawful. The Minnesota Supreme Court has ruled[57] that per-

---

[57]330 N.W. 2d 670 (Minn. Sup. Ct., 1983), superceded by statute, 392 N.W. 2d 670 (Minn. Ct. of App., 1986).

formance management systems that criticize an employee's performance do not constitute the infliction of emotional distress as long as the criticism meets four legal standards:

- The criticism is not extreme and outrageous.

- The criticism is not intentionally reckless.

- The criticism is not intended to cause emotional stress.

- The distress the criticized employee feels is not severe due to outrageous conduct by people in the company.

Document constructive discipline steps (consistent with steps listed in a well-prepared employee handbook) and lack of progress on developmental plans to achieve performance. Document not only the performance standards but the consequences of failing to achieve them. Ratings, critical incidents, and narratives all might simultaneously help the person understand what is expected and motivate and guide improvement while also protecting you legally. An extreme incident merits getting the employee's signature, admitting what occurred, and perhaps including a statement that without significant and immediate improvement, termination of employment will occur.

A solid performance management system is the best bulletproofing available when firing someone becomes necessary. It includes:

- Thorough job analysis, comprehensive job description, and behavioral competencies.

- Documented performance standards and accountabilities.

- Managers trained in performance evaluation, coaching, and interviewing.

- At least annual, and preferably ongoing, performance evaluation and coaching.

- An audit system to prevent bias.

- Documentation of performance problems in personnel files, job-related testing, rating systems, appraisal forms, signed memoranda, and so forth.

- Written policy statements regarding procedures for conducting performance appraisals and progressive discipline (verbal warning,
  written warning, ninety-day probation, termination, for example).

Watch out for what you put into employees' personnel files to document
nonperformance, and take care about what you say when you fire someone
for cause.

## Severance and Layoffs

Of course, if you want to fire someone, you can "buy" immunity in a severance arrangement. There are more and more out-of-court settlements that
avoid litigation fees and the possibility of higher jury awards. Indeed, companies with a strong culture of topgrading (1) experience fewer reductions in
force than companies run by B/C players, and (2) when they must lay off or
otherwise remove employees, they treat them with more humanity, sensitivity, and generosity. They provide outplacement counseling, initiatives to find
other jobs, early-retirement packages, and generous severances. The attitude
is "Why fight in court? We'll be fair and can part friends." Essentially the employee gives up the right to sue for some sort of payment. This is a very common approach at management levels. Use an attorney to construct a
severance agreement, because you must carefully follow the law with respect
to effectively releasing certain claims. For example, certain statutory periods
to review the release document and to revoke their signed release must be
provided in order to obtain a valid release of ADEA claims.

Severance agreements are so pervasive in the business world that we often fail to ask why they are used and, more significantly, fail to identify the
circumstances when they should not be used. There are several reasons
why employers often offer employees the opportunity to enter into severance agreements:

- **repose:** Severance agreements almost always include a waiver and
  release of all legal claims, which minimizes the risk of future litigation.

- **confidentiality:** The circumstances surrounding the separation remain secret, which usually is good for the employer and even better
  for the departing employee.

- **competition:** Severance agreements often contain the employee's agreement not to compete with the employer and/or raid its employees.

- **cooperation:** A cooperation provision will go a long way to ensuring the employee's assistance in future matters, including litigation, business planning, and consulting. This factor is especially significant if the company is engaged in litigation related to the employee or her area of responsibility. On the other hand, (1) employees who get good advice from their attorneys (which is not always the case) usually do not sue their former employers because litigation often results in a long stretch of unemployment inasmuch as prospective employers frequently are reluctant to hire employees who have sued their former employers; and (2) there is always the power of the subpoena: if a former employee does not have a severance agreement that requires him to cooperate, an employer can always use the legal process to compel him to appear and testify, even if that approach will make him unhappy.

- **precedent:** It has been done for employees in the past and thus is expected or is "good policy" to do so, especially with long-term employees.

- **fairness:** Employers want to fairly compensate employees who have been selected for separation as part of a workforce restructuring or reduction in force.

One final word about severance agreements. It is hard to imagine a set of circumstances under which an employer would offer severance pay and benefits yet not seek a waiver and release of all legal claims. But beware: the law of releases can be tricky, especially in situations where groups of employees are let go.

Be careful, during a layoff, not to let go a preponderance of members of protected groups. Too many executives remove themselves from the layoff decisions to the point that they don't know until it's too late that in attempting to downsize, their middle managers have laid off a disproportionate number of, for example, African Americans. This becomes painfully apparent if, after the downsizing, some rehiring takes place and the replacements are all, in this case, white. This type of approach may open up the employer to a charge of "disparate impact." Over the past ten years, a large manufacturer has had to settle several large age-discrimination suits for this reason. The moral: Be as careful in your firing processes as you are in your hiring processes.

## The "Comparable": How Have Similarly Situated Employees Been Treated?

Most discrimination claims are not won on what employment attorneys call "direct evidence" of discrimination (i.e., evidence that on its face demonstrates the intent to discriminate and does not require any inferences to reach that conclusion). Most plaintiffs win employment discrimination claims by using what lawyers call the "indirect method of proof," which usually requires evidence that the employer treated similarly situated employees who are not in the at-issue protected class more favorably. What does this mean? It means that the African American plaintiff in a race-discrimination action wins because he is able to show that a non–African American who performed substantially the same way under substantially similar circumstances was treated more favorably. Indeed, the essence of discrimination in the workplace is more favorable treatment of similarly situated employees who are not in the at-issue protected class.

## Email and Smoking Guns

It is beyond contention that computer-based technology has radically transformed the workplace for employers. However, the remarkable advances in productivity and efficiency have also created commensurate problems and legal risks, including the specter of financial liability via sabotage and the misappropriation of trade secrets, the creation of an "instant" hostile work environment, and the creation of indelible evidence (in the form of emails) of careless management communication. Indeed, in some respects employee misuse and abuse of workplace technology has decreased productivity and spawned liability. Although the magnitude of the problems and risks is almost impossible to quantify with accuracy, consider this:

- A May 2003 survey by the American Management Association of 1,100 U.S. employers showed that the average worker spends about 25 percent of the workday on email and 8 percent of workers spend more than four hours a day on email.

- In 2003, the *Chicago Tribune* and *Business 2.0* reported that monitoring by the U.S. Department of the Treasury of Internet use among IRS employees found that activities such as drafting personal email, participating in online chats, shopping, and monitoring personal finances and stocks accounted for 51 percent of employees' online time.

- Sextracker (an Internet-use monitoring company) reported in 2003 that 70 percent of Internet pornography is accessed between 9 A.M. and 5 P.M.

The reality is that technology resources in the workplace raise serious concerns about the accuracy, security, and control of information, including confidential and proprietary business information. This is especially true because electronic communications can be transmitted almost instantaneously, because they tend to be more immediate and informal than written communications, and because passwords and delete functions create an illusion of privacy, control, and confidentiality. Therein lies the single greatest risk of workplace technology: the permanent creation of damaging evidence. If you don't already, you must discipline yourself to carefully consider what you send via email before you hit the send key, and reflect on the reality that email often is forwarded inadvertently or intentionally and creates a permanent record (even if deleted) that may be subject to discovery in litigation. The cardinal rule of email related to employment matters is this: never, ever send anything via email that you would not send in a memorandum with general distribution, post on a bulletin board, place before a judge or jury, or share with the "wrong" person.

### The Termination Checklist

Here's a termination checklist that should be reviewed in advance of every termination decision:

- Is the rule or standard that has been violated published within the company?

- Did the employee ever receive a personal, written copy of the rule violated (e.g., a handbook)?

- Have you complied to the letter with any applicable progressive discipline policy? Unless termination is for gross misconduct that requires no prior warning, has the employee received oral and written warnings in compliance with applicable policy?

- If other employees have violated the rule, did they receive the same disciplinary action as the at-issue employee, are there supporting documents, and can the company identify witnesses, dates, times, places, and other pertinent factors regarding past violations?

- Was the incident that triggered the final warning or discharge carefully investigated before taking serious or final disciplinary action?

- Does company evidence include names of witnesses, dates, times, places, and other pertinent factors on all past violations, including the most recent one?

- Was the degree of discipline imposed on this employee reasonably related to the seriousness of the proven offense, the employee's past record, and her length of service?

- Review the decision from a jury's perspective. Ask the question that every jury in an employment-discrimination case asks itself: regardless of established policy and the law, does the decision seem fair? Put differently, does the punishment fit the crime?

- Take the time to weigh the cost of litigation (time, money, and potential effect on other employees) against the benefits derived from termination. Ask yourself if the decision will seem as right a year from now, when the company has paid $60,000 in attorneys' fees to defend a wrongful discharge case and the company's main witnesses will be tied up in court for a trial for two weeks.

## Communicating the Termination Decision

Very little in work life can be as difficult as terminating somebody's employment. Stress. Guilt. Fear. Anxiety. Yet, there are certain fundamental rules that, if followed, should minimize the trauma, respect the separated employee's dignity, and insulate the company—and you—from liability. Here are the top ten:

1. **Tell the individual in person.**

2. **Make sure that more than one person is present for the termination meeting.** Ensure that the company will have a witness in the event the substance of the meeting becomes an issue in litigation.

3. **Rehearse.**

4. **Take notes.**

5. **Don't fudge it.** If there are several reasons for termination and each represents an independent and sufficient basis for termination, then make that clear.

6. **Let the sun shine in.** Nothing offends a jury's sense of fairness more than an employee who has been accused of wrongdoing yet not given an opportunity to examine and seek to rebut the evidence against him.

7. **Avoid bomb throwing.** Every effort should be made to use the most appropriate and least inflammatory language feasible. Why create risk of liability for defamation by calling an employee a thief or incompetent when you can tell him that he breached trust or has performed inadequately? Empathize.

8. **Invite "your side of the story."** The conventional moral compass says that it is unfair to fire somebody without giving him the opportunity to tell his side of the story.

9. **Beware of high-risk situations.** Pay particular attention to "red-flag" situations. Red flags like these mean it is time to slow or stop the termination process and reexamine your approach: (i) the decision-maker is angry with the employee; (ii) the termination decision is precipitous and does not allow for a thoughtful review of the cir-

cumstances; (iii) the termination is being made by an inexperienced or new supervisor or manager; (iv) the employee has significant service with the company; (v) the employee is a member of a group protected by civil rights laws and is being replaced by an individual outside the protected group; and (vi) the employee has made a recent change in his life—say, a move or transfer—in reliance upon job security.

10. **Don't forget the simple stuff.** Nothing drives separated employees to attorneys faster than being jerked around in connection with notices (e.g., COBRA), benefits, and pay to which they are entitled. Make certain that the terminated employee timely receives all benefits for which she is eligible (e.g., vested vacation pay and sales commissions). Relatedly, long-term employees who may have to make pension or other benefits decisions deserve special consideration, including, for example, the opportunity to meet with your employee benefits personnel to discuss such matters.

## 7. Follow Guidelines on How to Topgrade Outside the United States

For decades I've heard, "You can't really topgrade in many countries because the laws make it almost impossible to fire people." For decades I've heard top CEOs at companies like GE, Royal Bank of Canada, Honeywell, and Barclays say, "Nonsense! Of course, you can topgrade!" You must know what you are doing, however. This final section of this chapter will inform you of major considerations and give practical advice for how to topgrade outside the United States. Laws vary considerably among nations and localities within nations, but representative guidelines are presented for the United Kingdom, France, Germany, Mexico, China, and Japan.

**a. Follow recommended U.S. topgrading practices for hiring and you will operate legally in most other countries, but be careful, because small violations can result in big problems.**

That's right, in most countries today, the laws concerning recruiting, interviewing, and selecting people are actually less stringent than in the

United States. Suggestions 2 through 7 in this chapter deal with firing, and in most countries the laws concerning firing are more stringent than in the United States.

With certain caveats, if you follow topgrading practices in the hiring process as you would in the United States, you will likely not run afoul of local legal requirements abroad. In preparing this chapter, we asked leading law firms specializing in employment law in France, Germany, the United Kingdom, Mexico, China, and Japan to review the Topgrading Interview Guide, the Career History Form, and the In-Depth Reference Check for compliance with their local legal requirements. Guess what! We pass legal muster. Not a single question in the Topgrading Interview Guide, the Career History Form, and the In-Depth Reference Check was found legally objectionable. Of course, we were not surprised with these conclusions inasmuch as all questions in the Topgrading interview process are job-related.

But be careful. Repeated throughout this section is the most practical advice: check to be sure you are operating in accordance with local, regional, and national laws. All countries in the world today have laws concerning hiring and firing, which include some differences from the laws in the United States, and if you operate outside of the United States, it is sensible to know them. Even if U.S. topgrading practices are 98 percent legal in another country, the 2 percent remaining can be problematic.

Some topgraders in the United States initially felt hampered by not being legally permitted to ask people's age, marital status, and so on, but we learned that such prohibited information was not job-relevant anyway. But topgraders in other countries are accustomed to relating such information to job relevance and say they need the information to understand "the whole person." OK, if it's legal and they want to ask it, fine. For example, in Germany it is very common (and legal) to ask selection candidates their age, marital status, and how many children they have. It's even legal to ask one's religion, but only after an employment contract has been signed. However, it's illegal to ask selection candidates about their political beliefs and *intent* to start a family. What? You can ask and learn that someone has eight children but not ask, "Are you intending to have more?" Yes, and that makes the point:

---

**There are so many differences and fine distinctions in hiring/firing laws that it is essential to know *all* legal requirements for the appropriate nation and governing entities within each nation.**

---

Perhaps the most serious legal issues raised concerning use of the Topgrading Interview Guide, the Career History Form, and the In-Depth Reference Check concern not the questions that they contain, but how the information sought by the questions is processed. In this regard, the United Kingdom, France, and Germany have all recently enacted legislation implementing European Union Directive 95/46/EC of 24 October 1995 on the protection of individuals with regard to the processing of personal data and on the free movement of such data. Japan has enacted comparable legislation (Personal Data Protection Law of May 23, 2003). Neither Mexico nor China has comparable legislation, but some of the concerns raised by such legislation also arise under the existing privacy laws in both countries.

Please note that "processing" is a broad concept that includes in the hiring context not only how personal data of a job applicant are collected from the applicant, used by the prospective employer, and stored by the latter, but also their collection from third parties (e.g., references supplied by the applicant) and transfer to third parties. In the latter regard, transfers of personal data outside of the country in which collected, even if within the same company, may very well be treated as a third-party transfer.

To give an example, in the United Kingdom, the Data Protection Act 1998 is a complex piece of legislation that, essentially, prevents an employer from processing personal data about individual data subjects (whether or not they are employees) unless certain criteria are fulfilled, including information being given to the data subject about how the data are to be used. It also gives a right to the individual data subject to access the data. While any data about the individual stored in electronic form can be accessed (subject to certain limited exceptions), data held in manual form can also be accessed if the data are stored in a "structured filing system" (a well-ordered file where it is easy to put one's finger on information of a certain kind about the data subject). The bottom-line implications for a prospective employer of an individual applicant therefore are as follows:

1. In order to "process" any information about an individual applicant, a prospective employer must advise the individual of the types of data they hold or anticipate holding and what they will do with them; and

2. The data that a prospective employer does hold about that individual can, in most cases, be accessed by that individual.

Therefore, a candid note made by an interviewer about an interviewee may well be read by that interviewee and, in a worst-case scenario, be used to found a lawsuit against the interviewer and/or the company.

Moreover, in the UK, this right of a person to access information includes seeing the contents of references given to the employer. (Reference sources are more candid when they are sure what they say is in confidence. The giver of the reference is to expressly state that the reference is her opinion and is given in confidence. This may allow the prospective employer to avoid disclosing the contents of the reference if a data protection access request is made as they are not obliged to disclose information pertaining to a third party without that third party's consent. This is not the case once legal proceedings are launched, however.) There are certain sorts of data about an individual that constitute sensitive personal data, and in order for the employer to "process" such data, express and informed written consent should be obtained. Sensitive personal data include:

- The racial and ethnic origin of the data subject;

- His political opinion;

- His religious beliefs or beliefs of a similar nature;

- Whether he is a member of trade union;

- His physical or mental health or condition;

- His sexual life;

- The commission or alleged commission by him of any offense; and

- Any proceedings for any offense committed or alleged to have been committed by him, the disposal of such proceedings, or the sentence of any court in such proceedings.

Therefore, where any of the above types of information is sought, it is advisable for a note to be given on the application form that sets out in reasonable detail the information being sought, the purposes for which it is sought, and how it will be used. Space should be provided for the prospective employee to sign to show consent to the data being used in these ways. A prospective employer should not process the data in any way that does not fall within the scope of the purposes that it sets out in the note. The scope for the information sought from references should also be made clear to the prospective employee. For evidentiary purposes, it is best to do this in writing also.

The key then in complying with data protection and privacy laws in the hiring context is to ensure that you obtain the applicant's *informed* consent. For the consent to be informed, the prospective employer should ensure that the applicant knows, among other things, how and from whom personal data will be collected, the uses to which the data will be put and by whom, how and for how long the data will be stored, and who will have access to the data. The consent should always be obtained in writing (even if this is not a strict legal requirement). And if you are asking the applicant to submit data online, be sure that the method used to record that consent meets local requirements (for example, a qualified digital signature in Germany).

The authorization given by the applicant on the Career History Form to investigate all statements made by the applicant is a good first step and in some countries may suffice, but in most instances it will have to be supplemented to ensure compliance with local legal requirements. Once again, we emphasize the need to obtain competent local legal advice.

Do not assume that if the form of consent works, for example, in the UK, it will also work in France, Germany and other member states of the European Union just because all are implementing the same European Directive. In most instances, it does not work that way: a European Directive sets forth guidelines and minimum requirements and must be implemented by national legislation; as a general rule, a directive will allow the member state some latitude in choosing the means of implementation and member states usually can and do supplement a directive with requirements of their own—all of which has occurred with respect to implementation of the Data Protection Directive.

The remainder of this chapter deals with firing, since many, if not most, other countries are much more stringent than the United States with respect to the termination of employment. Describing the laws governing termination of employment outside of the United States in generic terms is not an easy task and, indeed, even the attempt to do so may seem to contradict the most important rule that we can establish pertaining to such matters: seek competent local legal advice. A generic description, albeit imperfect, does provide us with a framework in which to understand conceptually how terminations are handled outside of the United States. The resulting understanding may very well not provide us with the answer to any particular problem that we may encounter, but it will help us to spot the problem. Thus we will make the effort.

### b. When firing, do not assume that U.S. law will apply to the employment relationship.

This rule may seem self-evident, especially with respect to local hiring at overseas locations, but a surprising number of companies simply assume that if the hiring decision is made in the United States or there is some other link to the United States in the hiring process, U.S. law will govern or may be chosen to govern the employment relationship. In many, if not most, countries outside of the United States, that assumption will turn out to be wrong. While the rules governing choice of law are frequently complex in employment matters, the law of the place of employment will most often apply, even if the employer and employee freely agree in writing otherwise. In many countries outside of the United States, employment matters are dealt with by specialized labor courts and such courts are, not surprisingly, very protective of their jurisdiction and, again not surprisingly, protective of employee rights.

Be wary of statements sometimes made by human resource professionals and legal advisers in some countries, such as Germany and Switzerland, to the effect that in their countries, employer and expatriate employee enjoy a "freedom to contract," and may agree to whatever requirements they wish, including choice of law. Such freedom is always subject to exceptions, the most important of which is the *public policy* exception: employer and employee have the freedom to write their contract except to the extent that it may conflict with public policy. In most countries, the laws pertaining to termination of employment are almost always deemed matters of public policy.

Do not let superficial cultural similarities lull you into believing that you have never left the United States. Many employers conclude that as long as you speak the same language, everything will be A-OK and that the most employer-friendly locations to operate in outside of the United States are those that share a common language and a common law heritage, such as the United Kingdom, Canada, Australia, and New Zealand. Unfortunately, it may talk like a duck, walk like a duck, and even dress like a duck (e.g., Canada), but it is not a duck—in many respects, for a U.S.-based employer, from an employment law perspective, the United Kingdom, Canada, Australia, and New Zealand may at times not even seem to be on the same planet as the United States and this is especially likely to occur in termination-of-employment matters.

### c. When firing, do not assume that your overseas employee is an employee at will.

In many, if not most, countries outside of the United States, the employment relationship is not defined by contract, but by statute (and, if not by statute, by a legal tradition that is quite different from ours), and, in such countries, the concept of employment at will is simply not recognized. Whether in London or Hong Kong, Paris or Tokyo, expect to enter into a written contract of employment that may augment, but not eliminate the rights granted to employees by statute. If there is no written contract, expect that statutes or jurisprudence will mandate in detail the provisions governing the employment relationship.

Expect that you will need a good reason for terminating an employment relationship and expect that terminating that relationship, even with a very good reason, will, with limited exceptions, require the giving of advance notice and the payment of severance or its equivalent. Also, expect to encounter situations that may seem—how shall we put it?—"counterintuitive" to the U.S. employer.

## Fair Reasons for Dismissal

In countries outside of the United States, what generally replaces the notion of employment at will are generous requirements for advance notice of dismissal and/or severance and the concept of unfair dismissal. The concept of unfair dismissal embodies two basic notions: (1) there must be a fair reason for dismissal, that is, there must be a reason that the law recognizes as valid; and (2) the employer must follow fair procedures in implementing the dismissal.[58] A third notion, that of constructive dismissal, further restricts an employer's ability to address, short of dismissal, an employee's failure to meet expected levels of performance.

What constitutes a fair or valid reason for dismissal varies from country to country. Frequently, the reasons are statutorily defined. The definition may be rather conceptual. For example, under the French Labor Code law, the dismissal of any employee with a permanent work contract must be supported by a "real and serious cause" based on *personal* reasons or *economic* reasons. The cause for dismissal must, moreover, be:

- objective—the grievance against the employee must be concretely verified;

- real—reasons submitted by an employer in support of the termination must be established as facts;

- precise—reasons submitted by an employer in support of the termination must correspond to the actual cause justifying the termination; and

- sufficiently serious to justify a termination.

An individual dismissal for personal reasons may be based on a variety of reasons including insubordination, professional incompetence, acts of disloyalty, failure to observe rules of security, or unfitness for work. An individual dismissal for economic grounds will only be justified if it is based on serious economic difficulties of the company (and the group to which it belongs) or the necessity to restructure the company in order to maintain its competitiveness.

Certain reasons are never recognized as legally valid. Thus, Article L.122–45 of the French Labor Code provides that an employee may not be dismissed on discriminatory grounds such as her sexual orientation, moral

---

[58]The term *unfair dismissal* is from the UK and is preferable to other terms, such as *wrongful discharge*, that are better used in a breach-of-contract situation.

opinions, family situation, appearance, ethnic origin, religious beliefs, trade union activities, political opinions, or state of health.

Or, as in Mexico, the statutorily defined reasons for dismissal may be quite precise. Thus, in Mexico, Article 47 of the Federal Labor Law enumerates fifteen specific kinds of conduct that are deemed cause for dismissal: (1) use of false documentation to secure employment; (2) dishonest or violent behavior on the job; (3) dishonest or violent behavior against coworkers that disrupts work discipline; (4) threatening, insulting, or abusing the employer or his family, unless provoked or acting in self-defense; (5) intentionally damaging the employer's property; (6) negligently causing serious damage to the employer's property; (7) carelessly threatening workplace safety; (8) immoral behavior in the workplace; (9) disclosure of trade secrets or confidential information; (10) more than three unjustified absences in a thirty-day period; (11) disobeying the employer without justification; (12) failure to follow safety procedures; (13) reporting to work under the influence of alcohol or nonprescription drugs; (14) a prison sentence; or (15) the commission of any other acts of similar severity. If the conduct said to justify the dismissal does not fall into one of these fifteen categories, the dismissal is invalid.

In Japan, the reasons for dismissal are defined in the first instance by the employer. Thus, an employer with more than ten employees must establish "Work Rules," which must include the grounds for dismissal and file these rules with the local Labor Standards Inspection Office. These can be quite elaborate and typically include such causes, among others, as misrepresentation of qualifications, unauthorized absences, violence or intimidation against other employees, insubordination, and failure to improve after having been sanctioned for previous violations. In Japan, as elsewhere, dismissal is considered a sanction of last resort, and only to be used in the most serious of situations.[59]

To be sure, the employer can expect to carry the burden of proof in establishing a fair reason for dismissal. This burden is not necessarily easy to meet (in some countries, justifying dismissal for misconduct, short of a felony committed in the workplace, is well nigh impossible). There are also certain grounds for dismissal that will never be deemed fair—for example, pregnancy, union membership, and transfer of undertaking (i.e., the sale of

---

[59]William L. Keller, editor-in-chief, *International Labor and Employment Laws*, Vol. I, pp. 32–9 et seq. (Washington, DC: Bureau of National Affairs, 1998).

a business). Moreover, establishing a fair reason for dismissal does not necessarily extinguish what rights an employee may have to notice and severance.

## Fair Procedures for Firing

What constitutes fair procedures for firing also varies widely. In some countries, it may simply consist of an employee's right of access to a court or specialized labor tribunal. In other countries, such as the UK, the test is rather subjective: in general, the procedures must be tailored to the circumstances, including the reason justifying dismissal. In still other countries, the procedures are objectively defined. In France, for example, the procedures to be followed in implementing a dismissal are quite formal and specific: among, other things, you must give the employee notice that you are *contemplating* dismissal and convene an initial meeting with the employee five days thereafter; the notice of termination must be sent no less than seven days after that. Failure to count correctly renders the dismissal ineffective.

In Mexico, an employee may appeal his discharge to a Conciliation and Arbitration Board, an administrative agency charged with resolving labor disputes, within two months of the dismissal.

In some countries, such as Germany and France, there is a requirement to consult with the Works Council or other body representing employees in addition to the requirement to consult with the affected employee.

The notion of constructive dismissal is fairly straightforward: the employer may not unilaterally (without the consent of the employee) vary the terms and conditions of employment. Promoting an employee to a higher position of responsibility with higher pay may very well prove to have been a mistake, but returning the employee to the original position without the employee's consent, even with the higher level of compensation, will likely be deemed a constructive termination, entitling the employee to invoke the legal remedies available for breach of the employment contract and/or unfair dismissal.

The notion of constructive dismissal is not recognized in Japan, which leads to another important element that must be taken into account when discussing the procedures to be followed in any dismissal, namely, local practices. In Japan, an employee is almost never dismissed; if circumstances warrant dismissal, the employee resigns.

The complexity of the legal rules governing the dismissal of employees may be even greater in a particular country (e.g., France or Germany) due to the presence of so-called collective agreements, which may provide employees with greater protections than those prescribed by laws and court decisions. These collective agreements may be company-specific or may be negotiated for an industrial sector or may even be of national application. And these collective agreements may apply to all employees, up to and including the most senior managers, as in France, or may exclude only the most senior managers, as in Germany.

## Consequences of Dismissal

In countries in which the concept of employment at will is not recognized, the consequences of dismissal can be costly for the employer, regardless of whether the dismissal is deemed "unfair" or a breach of the employment contract. The employee will frequently be entitled to advance notice (or payment in lieu thereof), severance, additional indemnities, or some combination of the foregoing. If the dismissal is challenged and found to be unfair or a breach of the employment contract, the employer may also be found liable for compensatory payments or damages, or both.

Under French law, an employee *properly* dismissed is entitled to minimum notice (or payment in lieu thereof) and severance. These provisions are generous and an employee with many years of service can be entitled to significant amounts. Additional compensation for unlawful dismissal and compensation equivalent to two or more years' salary and benefits is certainly possible. In appropriate circumstances, the employee may also be reinstated with back pay.

In Mexico, the employer has the burden of showing that the employee engaged in conduct described in Article 47 of the Federal Labor Law. If the employer fails to meet this burden, the employee can request either (1) reinstatement to her previous job or (2) a constitutional indemnification equivalent to three months' full salary, including premiums, bonuses, commissions, and all fringe benefits. The employee also has the right to receive back pay with no offset for interim earnings.

The employer is not obligated to reinstate an employee if the employee worked for the employer for less than one year, or if the employee must work in direct and constant contact with the employer and a normal work-related relationship is impossible, or if the employee rendered domestic services or worked on a temporary basis. If the employer does not reinstate the employee, the employer must pay the employee a lump-sum indemnification equal to three months' salary plus twenty days' salary for each year of seniority.

Employees dismissed with or without cause, as well as those who resign with fifteen or more years of seniority, are also entitled to a seniority premium equivalent to twelve days' salary for each year of service rendered. However, the seniority premium may not exceed twice the minimum salary in effect in the economic zone where the employer is located (plus prorated vacation, vacation premium, and year-end bonus as described below). In Mexico City, this currently amounts to approximately eight dollars per day.

Sometimes, the law's apparent simplicity can hide significant unfavorable consequences for an employer. For example, in Belgium, no cause is required for dismissal of an employee, but the latter is entitled by statute to "reasonable" advance notice. In order to determine what is reasonable, the courts have in practice adopted a formula that, not surprisingly, places heavy emphasis on the employee's seniority. Thus, a middle or senior manager will frequently be entitled to one or even two years' advance notice (or payment in lieu thereof). The notice requirement can only be avoided if the employee is dismissed for "serious cause," which involves a burden of proof that the employer can rarely meet. Not surprisingly, an employee dismissed for serious cause has a strong financial incentive to challenge the dismissal in court, and will almost always do so.

Please also keep in mind that in many countries, for middle and senior managers, the notice and/or severance to which they are entitled will be specified in the employment contract. These periods may be much longer than one would anticipate in the United States. For example, in Germany, six-month notice periods for middle managers and one-year notice periods for more senior managers, in each running from the end of the notice period following the period in which notice is given, are not unusual.

## A Specific Example: Individual Dismissals Under UK Law

In the United Kingdom, under the Employment Rights Act of 1996, in general, all employees with one or more years of continuous service, regardless of position, are protected against "unfair dismissal." The concept of unfair dismissal embodies two basic notions: (1) there must be a fair reason for dismissal, meaning there must be a reason that the law recognizes as valid; and (2) the employer must follow fair procedures (i.e., "act reasonably") in implementing the dismissal.

The following five reasons are recognized as fair reasons for dismissal:

- An employee's lack of capability for performing the work that she was employed to do;

- An employee's misconduct;

- An employee's redundancy;

- An employee could not continue to work in the position that he had held without contravening a duty or restriction under an enactment (e.g., loss of driver's license); and

- Some other substantial reason justifying dismissal of the employee from the position that the employee held.

On the other hand, some reasons for dismissal are always deemed "unfair," and if present, the analysis need go no further—the employer has lost its case. Such reasons include, among others, dismissals relating to

- pregnancy or for pregnancy-related reasons;

- union membership or nonmembership;

- a transfer of undertaking (for example, if a company sells its catering business, the new owner "inherits" all employee rights enjoyed before the sale);

- being a trustee of an occupational pension scheme;

- being an employee representative for collective redundancy/transfer of undertaking consultations, or being a workforce representative under the Working Time Regulations 1998;

- refusing to forgo rights under the Working Time Regulations of 1998 (which specify protected employees, such as union representatives);

- dismissal for whistle blowing; and

- dismissal for asserting rights to the national minimum wage.

More likely than not, an employer in the UK can find a fair reason to justify a dismissal. What constitutes fair procedures in implementing the dismissal is more problematic and, indeed, rather subjective, depending in large measure on the particular circumstances of a given case. Not surprisingly, it is here that most employers are likely to encounter problems.

Certain generalizations remain possible. Whatever the reason for dismissal, the employer must (1) allow employees to present their side of events and receive a fair hearing; (2) if there is conflict of evidence, give the benefit of the doubt to long-serving employees; and (3) once a decision is made, offer at least one internal appeal hearing. At the same time, however, the procedures must be tailored to the circumstances, including the reason justifying dismissal.

If the ground for dismissal is the employee's incompetence (i.e., the employee's lack of capability for performing the work that she was employed to do), the employer is not obliged to show that its belief in the employee's incompetence is correct, only that it had reasonable grounds for the belief and that it had taken reasonable steps to verify its conclusions. In addition, the employer must usually follow a progressive procedure with these basic steps:

- a careful, objective appraisal of the employee's performance (and failures of performance), including explanation to the employee of the deficiencies and the standards to be achieved;

- adequate warnings of the consequences of a failure to improve (oral or written as appropriate, according to the disciplinary procedure adopted and the stage reached);

- a reasonable opportunity to improve;

- reasonable support (e.g., further training) with a view to securing improvement.

Failing to follow any of these procedural steps is likely to render the dismissal unfair. If the employee still fails to meet the required standard, the employer should also consider alternative employment more suited to the employee's ability. There is no duty to create a new position, only to give reasonable consideration to whether there is scope for redeployment.

If an employer seeks to dismiss an employee for the latter's misconduct, the employer must genuinely believe in the guilt of the employee; have reasonable grounds to sustain that belief; and have carried out as much investigation as was reasonable at the stage at which it formed its belief. The employer need not have conclusive direct proof of misconduct. A genuine and reasonable belief, reasonably tested, is sufficient. Here are some guidelines for handling disciplinary misconduct dismissals:

- Investigate the alleged or suspected misconduct objectively;

- Constitute a disciplinary panel with different membership to the investigation panel;

- Ensure the employee is warned at all stages of the possible consequences;

- Allow the employee to be accompanied at the disciplinary hearing by a trade union representative (keep in mind that professionals and managers might belong to a union) or a fellow employee of his choice;

- Inform the employee before the hearing of the details of the complaint(s) made against the employee;

- At the hearing, allow the employee a chance to answer fully the allegations made; allow the employee or representative to ask questions, explain their case, and put forward mitigating factors that may have an effect on the sanction;

- Where appropriate, allow the employee to call witnesses and consider allowing cross-examination by the employee or her representative;

- Ensure consistency between employees with respect to sanctions imposed;

- When deciding a sanction, take into account work record, length of service, conduct during proceedings, and objective seriousness of the offense;

- Provide a right of appeal with a panel independent of the investigation and disciplinary panel, and specify the appeal procedure to be followed; and

- Take very careful notes of all investigations and disciplinary and appeal hearings.

Do all of the above and you can probably escape liability for an unfair misconduct dismissal, provided, of course, that you can also show that the misconduct complained of arises to a level justifying dismissal.

Redundancy situations arise where the business as a whole is closing down; the particular part of the business in which the employee worked is closing down; the business is closing down in a particular location; or the business needs fewer employees to carry out the work that the particular employee is employed to do. To dismiss fairly for redundancy an employer should:

- warn about possible redundancies;

- consult with the individuals likely to be affected;

- agree on objective nondiscriminatory criteria with union or employees' representatives (if appropriate) for selecting employees for dismissal;

- ensure that selection is fair and in accordance with the criteria; and

- inquire whether suitable alternative employment can be offered to selected employees.

Where twenty or more employees from the same location are made redundant within ninety days or less, special rules regarding collective dismissals apply. Consult your lawyer.

An employee fairly dismissed is entitled to receive minimum advance notice, based on seniority, and a redundancy payment, if dismissed on economic grounds, and whatever else her contract of employment may contractually provide. For the employer, the additional consequences of an unfair dismissal are usually monetary. The employee unfairly dismissed is entitled to a basic award and a compensatory award, both of which are subject to ceilings on recovery, which are in turn subject to economic adjustment. As of early 2004, the combined maximum exposure for the employer is approximately £62,500. An employer may also be ordered to reinstate or re-engage an employee, but in practice such orders are rare.

We now continue with practical advice on how to topgrade outside the United States.

### d. Calculate the costs of mis-hires, and of retaining underperformers, and of firing underperformers.

Since the costs in demoting or firing people are higher in many countries than in the United States, it's especially important to "run the numbers" abroad. In Chapter 2 we showed the average cost of mis-hiring someone whose compensation is $100,000 to be $1,500,000. And, because typically (without topgrading best practices) there are three mis-hires for every A player hired, it costs 3 × $1,500,000 or $4.5 million in mis-hires to finally hire an A player. With the higher costs of firing, that $4.5 million can double in some countries.

Run the numbers. Just as in the United States, we recommend using the Appendix I template to calculate the recurring, annual costs of retaining an underperformer. Weigh those costs against the costs of firing the person. For example, if you mis-hire a division CFO for Italy, what will the severance cost be? If the annual recurring costs are $2 million to retain the CFO, and it will cost $500,000 to fire him, the decision becomes obvious.

### e. Hire and promote only A players.

This advice may seem obvious, but global companies embracing topgrading best practices should master them with even greater urgency abroad than in the United States.

### f. Fire or demote B and C players.

When the costs of mis-hires are calculated, and when the costs of re-taining versus severing B and C players are nailed down, topgrading com-panies do *not* live with underperformers. However, a B player may have to be given a little longer to become an A, or be kept for a couple more years until retirement.

Time and time again it has become clear to global topgrading compa-nies that trying to prop up, for example, a C player global accounts man-ager does not make economic sense. That C player closes $10 million in new sales, whereas an A player would close $100 million. After calculating the higher profits on sales, the sales rep's commissions, the costs of disrup-tion, and the (high) cost of firing the C, it becomes a simple decision, and they let the person go. And, as noted previously, by quietly recruiting an A player replacement, performing the tandem Topgrading interviews and reference checks, it typically becomes glaringly obvious that this A will not only outperform the C by 1000 percent but will be a team builder, con-tribute creative ideas, be fun to work with, and cause fewer disappoint-ments. After topgrading, everyone says, "Although it cost us a lot to fire the C, we should have done it years ago!"

Some scenarios like this make topgrading compelling, but there are many less dramatic examples, gray areas. In the final analysis, most global topgrading companies lower the bar just a hair. Instead of 92 percent A/A potentials, the higher cost of firing results in living with a few more Bs, so the overall percentage is 90 percent A/A potentials. But, they still topgrade!

---

**Global companies topgrade, despite laws that make firing expensive. They enjoy a huge advantage over companies that resign themselves to living with underperformers.**

---

### g. "Sell" topgrading to fit the local culture.

Topgrading can fit every culture if it is sold properly. Four-hour tandem interviews are counterculture in the United States, until they are used and hiring success improves from 25 to 90 percent. Then they fit the cultures of both the company and the United States. There are more than two dozen

U.S. laws that make it very risky for a former employer to criticize a fired C player in a reference call, but 85 percent of the time former bosses open up, taking the risk. When topgraders realize the benefits of reference calls and realize that the reference source, usually the former boss, is incurring the legal risk, it becomes "culturally expected" to do references in every country.

In some national cultures there is a deference to authority that makes it counterculture to honestly criticize bosses in Topgrading Interviews. In some cultures performance management is soft and mushy (as it is in most U.S. companies), so asking interviewers in Topgrading Interviews to criticize subordinates results in bland appraisals. In some cultures eye contact is considered impolite, not an indication of deviousness. In some cultures a lukewarm "yes" may mean "no." Although most senior executives in global companies speak English, some don't. These considerations lead to recommendations that are not legalistic but culturally sensitive:

- Conduct tandem Topgrading Interviews in the native language, if the candidate is not fluent in English.

- Be aware of national cultural idiosyncrasies and adapt Topgrading and references accordingly.

- Educate and persuade candidates about the underlying philosophy of topgrading and the good reasons for having A players and conducting Topgrading Interviews.

Follow these principles and you'll find that A players in all cultures will embrace topgrading and that you can topgrade in all countries.

*Epilogue:*

# TOPGRADING IN THE FUTURE

*Here is Edward Bear, coming downstairs now, bump, bump, bump, on the back of his head, behind Christopher Robin. It is, as far as he knows, the only way of coming downstairs, but sometimes he feels there really is another way, if only he could stop bumping for a moment and think of it.*

A. A. Milne, Winnie-the-Pooh

It's hard to imagine an organization that cannot benefit from topgrading. From hot dog stands to the United Nations, A players get results, C players don't. What organization cannot benefit from a 90 percent success in hiring versus 25 percent?

The world zoomed through the Agricultural Age, Industrial Revolution, and Information Age. What's next? Futurist Jim Taylor suggests the Age of Chaos. If authors get a vote, I vote for:

## The Age of Talent

Peter Drucker, possibly the most respected management guru of the past fifty years, sees trends that can only mean elevated importance of talent. He said:[60]

- "The industries that are moving jobs out of the U.S. are the more backward industries. What outsourcing does is not [cut costs], but greatly improve the job quality of the people who still work here."

- "White collar workers are grotesquely unproductive."

- "The smart CEOs methodically build a great management team around them."

---

[60]"Peter Drucker Sets Us Straight," *Fortune,* January 12, 2004.

In other words, the future is all about talent, highly specialized blue collar talent, and ... uh ... "grotesquely unproductive" white collar talent. Those of us in management might take exception to Drucker's characterization of us, but maybe he's correct. Throughout this book we have referred to harsh realities: 25 percent As hired or promoted, leaving 75 percent of those hired/promoted B/C players, mis-hires, mistakes. And, recall the research in Chapter 2 showing those are costly mistakes—for $100,000 managers, $1.5 million mistakes, three of them to be precise, totaling $4.5 million, for every A player selected.

If your favorite professional sports team had 75 percent underperformers, meaning 75 percent mis-hired athletes, their performance would be ... how should you put it? ... "grotesquely unproductive." I'll bet Drucker would be quite complimentary of the "skilled labor" Super Bowl, World Series, and Olympic medalist athletes as well as their "white collar" coaches and managers. And I'd bet he'd be impressed with the management teams of topgraded companies, with 90 percent (plus) A players. But if only 7 percent of companies are topgraded, there is a galaxy of opportunity for talent improvement. Consider just a few future venues for topgrading:

## 1. COMMUNITY SERVICE

The increase in multimillionaires has resulted in a new form of philanthropy, results-oriented giving. Instead of throwing money at problems, as old foundations sometimes appear to do, the new megawealthy want to see results. They worked hard to earn the money, and increasingly I hear, "It's almost as hard giving it away." They don't want to write a check for $1 million to an organization run by C players. Smart not-for-profits like American Heart Association "get it" (see their topgrading case study in Chapter 5).

Community-service organizations can attract more money in the future by topgrading them and advertising, "We have a team of A players who will spend your donations for maximum results." Rich givers will increasingly require, perhaps even fund, topgrading in order that their money be donated wisely.

## 2. GOVERNMENT

U.S. presidents, governors, and mayors all promise dream teams, and too often C players are elected or appointed. Why not screen political candidates for financial support by submitting them to Topgrading Interviews?

In office, politicians perform political favors, but why not use Topgrading interviews to staff key positions with A players? Any politician could benefit from reading a ten-page Topgrading Interview report on every finalist, to choose the best and to know how to work most effectively with each.

I'm hesitant to date myself, but my first big client was Chicago's Mayor Daley. No, not the twenty-first-century Mayor Daley, but his dad. Back in the 1970s, I Topgrading interviewed and recommended individuals for management jobs up to, but NOT including, the commissioners. Daley never required me to attend a rubber chicken dinner fund-raiser. But for a few years, Daley accepted almost every recommendation I made for promotion. No doubt he had his favorites for various reasons, but topgrading helped him pick honest A players. He had an exceptional management team that made Chicago "the city that works" . . . work well. I never asked why he didn't topgrade the commissioners, a group for which "grotesquely unproductive" would be a generous description.[61]

This is just one small example. Why don't more political leaders topgrade? Clients three times handed President Bush (the son, not the dad) *Topgrading,* saying that for no pay I'd be happy to assess candidates for positions. He never called. I think topgrading might have helped, say, pick a stronger team to oversee the rebuilding of Iraq.

## 3. FINANCE

Half of all mergers and acquisitions fail, and the biggest reason is inadequate talent. Many financial wizards just can't get the people thing right. Some do—Dr. Geoff Smart's doctoral dissertation research[62] showed that the most successful venture capitalists (VCs) are very rigorous in assessing management in organizations in which they invest; they qualify as top-

---

[61]After Daley died I worked on some projects, then resigned the account, telling one aspirant to mayor, "I don't think your level of character and moral stature would qualify you."
[62]Geoffrey H. Smart, "Management Assessment Methods in Venture Capital: Towards a Theory of Human Capital Valuation," Ph.D. dissertation, Claremont Graduate University, 1998.

graders. The least successful VCs are cursory in their assessment of talent; they aren't even upgraders, for they consider only the deal, the financials, the products, and not the management talent. In eighty-six deals analyzed, the topgraders achieved a spectacular 80 percent return (IRR) versus a 30 percent return for the VCs who were cursory in assessing management talent. *Topgrading* offers the world of finance accurate insight into that unfathomable black box—people.

Topgrading companies do not acquire other companies without assessments of talent. Generally they have learned the hard way, making acquisitions that bombed, regretting that "the management team wasn't as good as promised." Hillenbrand Industries and MarineMax dispatch Topgrading interviewers into companies they consider acquiring, to determine if management talent is strong enough. In some acquisitions a very strong management team might be necessary, perhaps to maintain dominance in a market, perhaps because the acquiring company lacks the bench strength to topgrade the acquisition quickly. In other acquisitions a lot of A players in the acquired company are desirable, but not necessary. Sometimes an acquisition is cheaper because management is weak, and a strong bench of As in the acquiring company ensures rapid topgrading.

Topgrading companies are not so foolish as to trust the talent judgments of management in companies to be acquired. At an appropriate time (usually when a letter of intent has been signed) the acquiring company conducts Topgrading interviews to make valid, effective assessments of management talent.

## 4. GOVERNANCE

In my opinion, the single biggest flaw in our economic system is governance. Sarbanes-Oxley legislation and New York Attorney General Eliot Spitzer have aggressively addressed corporate scandals, threatening heavy fines and even jail time when dishonest C players cheat shareholders. Boards of directors have had too many C players, who didn't look after the best interests of the company and didn't topgrade the CEO job—their #1 responsibility. To hire a CEO, boards have historically trusted the search firm's interviews and report, with directors performing perfunctory interviews. With directors taking more (deserved) heat and incurring more legal risk, it would seem prudent to select a CEO by topgrading.

Shareholders are more inclined to shout to boards of directors, "Top-grade the CEO and top team or we'll force you out!" In the past it was rare for someone like Michael Price (of mutual fund Mutual Shares) to use the power of his funds' shares to break up companies, remove CEOs, and force the sale of CEO toys (planes, fancy offices, etc.). Dun and Bradstreet and Dial Corp. were busted up, with pieces sold off, due to Price's determination. Abby Joseph Cohen, a Goldman Sachs director, sees more and more shareholders pushing corporate executives toward reform. TIAA-CREF is a huge institutional investor, using its billions in shares to change corporate governance (although there are concerns about its influence to install pro-union directors). Pension funds and labor unions forced Sprint to have shareholder proposals reviewed by an independent committee. Vanguard approved 90 percent of the full slates of directors of companies in its mutual funds in 2002, but subsequently approved less than one-third. It's the shareholders, more than Congress, who will improve corporate governance, but as Vanguard said in a letter to CEOs at several hundred of its top holdings, "There is much more change needed." Recently we have been asked by boards to assess top executive teams, and clearly Sarbanes-Oxley legislation motivated their (finally) taking more responsibility for talent.

Geoff Smart's company (ghSMART & Company) has dozens of private-equity clients who don't have a governance problem. Geoff notes, "The shareholders dominate the boards, insist on executive teams being top-graded, and have financial interests perfectly aligned with management." It's less likely that Enron-, WorldCom-, or Tyco-type shenanigans will take place in private equity because those who bought the company have their net worth tied to its success, serve on boards, and are hands-on with management to monitor activities.

---

**Shareholders should demand topgraded boards and senior management. Boards should topgrade the CEO position and require the CEO to topgrade the company, beginning with senior management.**

---

## 5. LEGALLY MANDATED TOPGRADING

A billion-dollar legal industry thrives on invalid selection and promotion. "We didn't discriminate against him because of race. We just felt the white person was more qualified." "No, he wasn't." "Yes, he was." Variations on that scenario produce expensive, embarrassing lawsuits.

Selection systems have been mandated by courts because they promise validity with minimized illegal discrimination. A major metropolitan police department, for example, was required to select officers through assessment centers (case studies, interviews, tests, exercises that replicate the job). Having devised a dozen assessment centers, one five days and nights long, I have concluded that the most valuable component is the Topgrading Interview. It is the one assessment-center component that draws *all* the information together in a consistent package. Multiple assessors help make assessment centers nondiscriminatory; tandem interviews in centers can achieve the same.

With research finally showing structured interviews to be valid predictors of job performance, the Topgrading Interview is bound to be tested against its shorter, less comprehensive counterparts, as well as long and expensive assessment centers. I believe it will outshine them.

If I were a judge looking at discrimination that emerged "innocently" from sloppy, shallow selection procedures, I would require:

- Tandem Topgrading Interviews for hiring and promoting, and

- Thorough training in Topgrading interviewing for all interviewers.

With race norming and quotas illegal, yet the pressure for affirmative action continuing, valid approaches for hiring truly talented protected groups is the solution.

## 6. EDUCATION

The business of education is crying out for topgrading. Are 90 percent of the teachers in your school system A players? C player administrators hire C player teachers, and teachers' unions protect C players. European high schools surpass U.S. schools on standardized tests, yet our per-pupil cost is sky high (six times what French students are allocated, for example). The Chicago public schools were so bad, emergency legislation permitted the mayor to fire everyone—administrators, teachers, staff. That was an opportunity for topgrading. Must our educational system be flat on its face in order to topgrade?

Perhaps an argument in favor of school choice (e.g., vouchers and charter schools) is that topgrading is more apt to take place in these private institutions than in public schools. When administrators and teachers work in topgraded organizations, the quality of education can soar overnight.

## 7. CAREER PLANNING

High schools, trade schools, colleges, universities, and all types of organizations offer some sort of career planning, but it is usually weak. Counselors look at test profiles and say, "You're good in math, so how about a career in engineering?" Topgraded organizations use Topgrading Interviews to get "missile lock" on people's talent—accurate appraisals of managers on dozens of competencies. Topgraded companies rarely promote people over their head or leave a supertalent languishing and underutilized. Educational institutions could assess students' career talents a lot better if they would incorporate a Topgrading Interview.

The Internet already provides job information and plenty of ways to apply for jobs. Someone is going to offer, perhaps on the Internet, a library of extensive career information. An interactive software package will no doubt be created to help a newly graduated accountant learn all the relevant career paths. Salary data are already available, but how about videotaped interviews with CPAs, vice presidents of finance, and analysts? Then a Topgrading Interview by a career counselor can help that graduate determine if being an individual contributor or a leader makes more sense.

A client professional services company experienced extremely high turnover in its field consultant ranks. Many candidates applied for the job, thinking the high pay and freedom would be terrific. The eighteen-hour workdays were killers for many, however. A thirty-minute video was created that accurately portrayed the good and bad elements of the job. Candidates participated in Topgrading Interviews to better understand their talents. The combination of Topgrading Interviews and the descriptive video dramatically reduced turnover in the field consultant job and greatly increased job satisfaction and performance. This sort of practical education is technically feasible.

Just think, what if students and job candidates all had the benefit of both Topgrading Interview insights and descriptive videos of various jobs? What if interactive media were also available to answer all their questions about careers? Talent utilization and human fulfillment would both skyrocket, and the world would be a little better for it.

## 8. FUTURE RESEARCH ON TOPGRADING

Talent as an issue, or opportunity, is as old as the human race. Publications about it began with the advent of printing in China and later in Europe, when Gutenberg's printing presses began cranking out bibles. Business books and articles on how to maximize human capital abound. Yet research lags. Most economic research deals with numbers (pay, turnover) but not with individual human beings. The psychological literature is scientific, but too narrowly focused and too short on economic factors.

I fervently hope this book stimulates more research, a lot more research, and that some economists and behavioral scientists link up to study topgrading. I would hope for an explosion of field research—sloppy science but "real life" that eventually becomes solidly scientific and more beneficial to society. Many companies could contribute to the body of scientific literature, and hundreds of master's theses and Ph.D. dissertations could refine and connect individual corporate studies. A few topics might be:

- *Definition of A, B, and C players.* "Top 1 percent" is a more useful definition of A player than "top 10 percent" in some companies or industries. Would the addition of D player and F player categories be useful designations?

- *Cost of mis-hires.* Let's move beyond our studies and really nail down the costs across all jobs, all job levels, and all types of organizations.

- *Hiring success rates.* We performed small studies for this book, and topgrading clients are studying their own success. But we need to have more precise definitions of success and more objective measurements of it.

- *Screening approaches.* I obviously consider a tandem Topgrading Interview the most accurate selection interview for managers. It's high time to see scientific research prove it.

- *Topgrading-based coaching.* How many Bs with A potential become As? How do they do it? Topgrading-based coaching seems to be the most powerful developmental system. How about more research to show what system is most effective?

- *Impact of topgrading.* This book cites quite a few case studies. How about research on one thousand case studies, or ten thousand, to elucidate the benefits and risks of topgrading in various companies, industries, and countries? Research should slice and dice data to continuously refine patterns that will show best practices for small versus large companies, failing companies versus successful companies striving to become ever more successful, different industries, various nationalities, you name it!

- *Relationship of happiness to topgrading.* I think A players are happier than C players, but there are a lot of "it depends" conditions. This book presents my conclusions based on my sample of several thousand senior managers, but it's hardly definitive. Longitudinal studies of happiness as it relates to the career myths as well as advice presented in Part Two offer the prospect of increased happiness and well-being for those embarking on careers in management.

In the meantime, you can conduct your own research on talent maximization every day. You know topgrading is not easy. There are lessons to be learned, by you and me, about what topgrading approaches work best. Your personal "case study" is an art form, a work in progress. I sincerely hope this book helps you in your daily laboratory to become the best topgrader you can, for your company, your career, and your personal happiness.

APPENDIX A

# APPENDIX A

Applicant    _____

Interviewer   _____

Date   _____

# TOPGRADING
# INTERVIEW GUIDE

Bradford D. Smart, Ph.D.

**"There's something rare, something finer far,
something much more scarce than ability.**
*It's the ability to recognize ability."*

Elbert Hubbard

This Guide seeks to provide you with the most accurate, most valid insights when assessing internal talent and candidates for selection or promotion. Companies can achieve a record of 90 percent A players hired when a tandem interview (two interviewers) is conducted and the interviewers have been trained in the Topgrading Interview techniques.

Maximum benefits in using this Topgrading Interview Guide can be achieved through applying the principles stated in the book.

*Topgrading: How Leading Companies Win by Hiring, Coaching, and Keeping A Players*
(Dr. Bradford D. Smart, author; Portfolio Viking Penguin, publisher, 2005)

This Guide is intended to make the interviewer's job easier. It is a comprehensive, chronological guide, providing plenty of space to record responses. Thousands of hiring managers have felt that following this Guide has permitted them to gain the deepest insights ever into an interviewee. Experience has shown the following guidelines to be helpful when hiring:

1. Review the candidate's **Career History Form (or Self-Administered Topgrading Interview Guide)** and résumé.

2. Be sure that the **Job Description, Competencies, and first-year Accountabilities** are clear to you and the team the successful candidate will work with.

3. Review this Guide prior to the interview, in order to:

   • **Refresh your memory** regarding the sequence and wording of questions, for a smoother interview.

   • **Add or delete questions** based upon what previous information (résumé, Career History Form, Self-Administered Topgrading Interview Guide, preliminary interviews, reference checks) have disclosed about the individual.

   • Scratch on this Guide your **estimated time** to spend on each section.

4. Use a **tandem** (two-interviewer) approach.

   A tandem interview is more valid than a solo interview, unless the Topgrading interviewer is highly experienced. Two heads are truly better than one when asking the Topgrading Interview questions, analyzing the interview responses, arriving at conclusions, and providing useful feedback and coaching.

5. After a couple of minutes building rapport, give the interviewee an idea of the expected time frame (three hours?) and then *sell* the person on being open and honest. For an external candidate for selection, you might state *purposes* such as to:

- *"Review your **background, interests, and goals** to see if there is a good match with the position and opportunities here."*

- *"Determine some ways to assure **your smooth assimilation** into your new position, should you join us."*

- *"Get some ideas regarding what you and we can do to maximize your **long-range fulfillment and contributions.**"*

- *"Tell you more about the **career opportunities** we have to offer and answer any questions you have."*

- *"Understand your **career history,** which will be thoroughly verified in reference checks we'll ask you to arrange with a minimum of all bosses you've had in the past ten years."*

6. Following the Topgrading Interview:

- **Review** the completed Guide three times.

- Conduct in-depth **reference checks** and accumulate opinions from coworkers who conducted interviews with the person.

- **Write comments** about each Competency on the last three pages of this Guide, on a Job Description, or on Candidate Assessment Scorecard.

- **Make final ratings** on the Competencies.

7. **Write a brief report**—an Executive Summary, followed by a list of Strengths and Weak Points and Developmental Recommendations.

## COLLEGE

So that I can get a good feel for your background, first your education and then work experience, let's *briefly* go back to your college days and come forward chronologically, up to the present. Then we'll talk about your plans and goals for the future.

Note to Interviewers: Start with college or first full-time job, whichever came first.

1. I see from the Career History Form (or Self-Administered Topgrading Interview Guide) that you **attended** _____ (college). Would you please expand on the information provided and give me a **brief rundown on** your college years, particularly events that might have affected later career decisions. We'd be interested in knowing about **work experiences,** what the school was like, what you were like back then, the curriculum, activities, how you did in school, high and low points, and so forth. (Ask the following questions to obtain complete information not included in responses to the general "smorgasbord" question.)

2. Give us a feel for what kind of **school** it was (if necessary, specify large/small, rural/urban, cliquish, etc.), and generally, what your college years were like. _____

   _____

   _____

   _____

3. What was your **major?** (change majors?) _____

   _____

4. What school **activities** did you take part in? (Note activities listed on Career History Form, and get elaboration.) _____

   _____

   _____

5. What sort of **grades** did you receive, what was your class standing, and what were your study habits like? (Confirm data on Career History Form.)

    GPA: _____/_____(scale)

    Study Habits _____

6. What **people** or events during college might have had an influence on your career? _____

    _____

    _____

    _____

7. Were there any class **offices, awards, honors,** or **special achievements** during your college years? (Note Career History Form or SATI Guide responses, and get elaboration.) _____

    _____

    _____

    _____

    _____

8. What were **high points** during your college years? (Look for leadership, resourcefulness, and particularly what competencies the interviewee exhibits *now* while discussing those years.) _____

    _____

    _____

    _____

9. What were **low points,** or **least enjoyable occurrences,** during your college years? (Again, what happened back then is only important in relation to what is revealed about the interviewee *now*.) _____

    _____

_____

_____

_____

10. Give us a feel for any **jobs** you held during college—the types of jobs, whether they were during the school year or summer, hours worked, and any high or low points associated with them. (Don't spend much time on these jobs, but look for indications of extraordinary resourcefulness, motivation, etc.; if the person did not work during the summer, ask how the summer months were spent.) _____

_____

_____

_____

_____

11. (TRANSITION QUESTION) What were your **career thoughts** toward the end of college? _____

_____

_____

_____

_____

## GRADUATE SCHOOL

Note: If graduate school occurred later in the interviewees' life, complete this section later. Stay in chronological order.

1. _____ 2. _____

   School                                      Degree

3. **Why did you attend this school** and pursue this degree?_____

_____

_____

_____

4. High Points _____

_____

_____

_____

5. Low Points _____

_____

_____

_____

6. Work Experiences:

   a. _____

_____

   b. _____

_____

   c. _____

7. Career Thoughts/Opportunities _____

_____

_____

_____

_____

# WORK HISTORY

Now we would like you to tell us about your work history. There are a lot of things we would like to know about each position. Let me tell you what these things are now, so I won't have to interrupt you so often. We already have some of this information from your Career History Form (or Self-Administered Topgrading Interview Guide) and previous discussions. Of course we need to know the **employer, location, dates** of employment, your **titles,** and **salary** history. We would also be interested in knowing what your **expectations** were for each job, your **responsibilities/accountabilities,** what you **found** upon entering the job, what major **challenges** you faced, and how they were handled. What were your most significant **accomplishments** as well as **mistakes,** and what were the **most enjoyable** and **least enjoyable** aspects of each job? What was each **supervisor** like and what would you **guess** each really felt were your strengths and weak points? Finally, we would like to know the circumstances under which you **left** each position.

Note: If the person recently worked for a single employer and had, say, three jobs of two years each with that employer, consider each one of those a separate position and complete a Work History Form on it. The following is suggested wording for information requested on the Work History Form:

1. What was the name of the **employer, location,** and **dates** of employment? (Get a "feel" for the organization by asking about revenues, products/services, number of employees, etc.)

2. What was your job **title?**

3. What were the starting and final levels of **compensation?**

4. What were your **expectations** for the job?

5. What were your **responsibilities** and **accountabilities?**

6. What did you **find** when you arrived? What shape was the job in—talent, performance, resources, problems? What major **challenges** did you face?

7. What results were achieved in terms of **successes** and **accomplishments?** How were they achieved? (As time permits, get specifics, such as individual vs. shared accomplishments, barriers overcome, "bottom line" results, and impact on career—bonus, promotability, performance review.)

8. We all make **mistakes**—what would you say were mistakes or failures experienced in this job? If you could wind the clock back, what would you do differently? (As time permits, get specifics.)

9. All jobs seem to have their pluses and minuses; what were the **most enjoyable** or rewarding aspects of this job?

10. What were the **least enjoyable** aspects of the job?

11. (For management jobs) What sort of **talent** did you inherit (how many As, Bs, Cs)? What changes did you make, how, and how many As, Bs, and Cs did you end up with? (For most recent two jobs, get A, B, C ratings and strengths/weak points of each subordinate.)

12. What **circumstances** contributed to your leaving? (Always probe for initially unstated reasons.)

13. What was your **supervisor's name** and title? **Where** is that person now? May we **contact** him/her? (Ask permission to contact supervisors in the past ten years, in order to understand the candidate's developmental patterns.)

14. What is/was it like working for him/her and what were his/her **strengths** and **shortcomings** as a supervisor, from your point of view?

15. What is your **best guess** as to what (supervisor's name) honestly felt were/are your **strengths, weak points,** and **overall performance?**

NOTE: An easy transition to the next job can occur by simply determining employer/title/dates, and then asking **WHAT** DID YOU DO, **HOW** DID YOU LIKE IT, AND **HOW** DID YOU DO?

# WORK HISTORY FORM 1

1. _____
   Employer          Starting date (mo./yr.)        Final (mo./yr.)

   _____
   Location                                    Type of business

   Description _____

2. Title _____

3. Salary (Starting) _____

   Salary (Final) _____

4. Expectations _____

   _____

5. Responsibilities/Accountabilities _____

   _____

6. "Found" (Major Challenges) _____

   _____

7. Successes/Accomplishments (How achieved?) ___

8. Failures/Mistakes (Why?) (Do differently?) ___

9. Most Enjoyable _____

10. Least Enjoyable _____

11. Talent (topgrading) _____

12. Reasons for Leaving _____

# SUPERVISOR

13. _____
   Supervisor's Name                          Title

_____
Where  Now                    Permission to Contact?

14. Appraisal of Supervisor
   His/Her Strengths _____

   His/Her Shortcomings _____

15. Best guess as to what he/she really felt at that time were **your** strengths, weak points, and overall performance rating:

| STRENGTHS | WEAK POINTS |
|---|---|
|  |  |
|  |  |

Overall Performance Rating _____

# WORK HISTORY FORM 2

1. _____
   Employer          Starting date (mo./yr.)    Final (mo./yr.)

   _____
   Location                                Type of business

   Description _____

2. Title _____

3. Salary (Starting) _____

   Salary (Final) _____

4. Expectations _____

   _____

5. Responsibilities/Accountabilities _____

   _____

6. "Found" (Major Challenges) _____

   _____

7. Successes/Accomplishments (How achieved?) _____

8. Failures/Mistakes (Why?) (Do differently?) _____

9. Most Enjoyable _____

10. Least Enjoyable _____

11. Talent (topgrading) _____

12. Reasons for Leaving _____

# SUPERVISOR

13. _____

Supervisor's Name                    Title

_____

Where Now                    Permission to Contact?

14. Appraisal of Supervisor
His/Her Strengths _____

His/Her Shortcomings _____

15. Best guess as to what he/she really felt at that time were **your** strengths, weak points, and overall performance rating:

| STRENGTHS | WEAK POINTS |
|---|---|
|  |  |
|  |  |
|  |  |

Overall Performance Rating _____

# WORK HISTORY FORM 3

1. _____
   Employer　　　　Starting date (mo./yr.)　　　Final (mo./yr.)

   _____
   Location　　　　　　　　　　　　　Type of business

   Description _____

2. Title _____

3. Salary (Starting) _____

   Salary (Final) _____

4. Expectations _____

   _____

5. Responsibilities/Accountabilities _____

   _____

6. "Found" (Major Challenges) _____

   _____

7. Successes/Accomplishments (How achieved?) _____

8. Failures/Mistakes (Why?) (Do differently?) _____

9. Most Enjoyable _____

10. Least Enjoyable _____

11. Talent (topgrading) _____

12. Reasons for Leaving _____

# SUPERVISOR

13. _____

Supervisor's Name                    Title

_____

Where Now                    Permission to Contact?

14. Appraisal of Supervisor
His/Her Strengths _____

His/Her Shortcomings _____

15. Best guess as to what he/she really felt at that time were **your** strengths, weak points, and overall performance rating:

| STRENGTHS | WEAK POINTS |
|---|---|
|  |  |
|  |  |
|  |  |

Overall Performance Rating _____

# WORK HISTORY FORM 4

1. _____
   Employer         Starting date (mo./yr.)    Final (mo./yr.)

   _____
   Location                               Type of business

   Description _____

2. Title _____

3. Salary (Starting) _____

   Salary (Final) _____

4. Expectations _____

   _____

5. Responsibilities/Accountabilities _____

   _____

6. "Found" (Major Challenges) _____

   _____

7. Successes/Accomplishments (How achieved?) _____

8. Failures/Mistakes (Why?) (Do differently?) _____

9. Most Enjoyable _____

10. Least Enjoyable _____

11. Talent (topgrading) _____

12. Reasons for Leaving _____

# SUPERVISOR

13. _____

Supervisor's Name                    Title

_____

Where  Now                    Permission to Contact?

14. Appraisal of Supervisor
    His/Her Strengths _____

    His/Her Shortcomings _____

15. Best guess as to what he/she really felt at that time were **your** strengths, weak points, and overall performance rating:

| STRENGTHS | WEAK POINTS |
|---|---|
|  |  |
|  |  |
|  |  |

Overall Performance Rating _____

# WORK HISTORY FORM 5

1. _____
   Employer              Starting date (mo./yr.)        Final (mo./yr.)

   _____
   Location                                      Type of business

   Description _____

2. Title _____

3. Salary (Starting) _____

   Salary (Final) _____

4. Expectations _____

   _____

5. Responsibilities/Accountabilities _____

   _____

6. "Found" (Major Challenges) _____

   _____

7. Successes/Accomplishments (How achieved?) _____

8. Failures/Mistakes (Why?) (Do differently?) _____

9. Most Enjoyable _____

10. Least Enjoyable _____

11. Talent (topgrading) _____

12. Reasons for Leaving _____

# SUPERVISOR

13. _____

   Supervisor's Name                    Title

   _____

   Where Now                    Permission to Contact?

14. Appraisal of Supervisor
   His/Her Strengths _____

   His/Her Shortcomings _____

15. Best guess as to what he/she really felt at that time were **your** strengths, weak points, and overall performance rating:

| **STRENGTHS** | **WEAK POINTS** |
|---|---|
|  |  |
|  |  |
|  |  |

   Overall Performance Rating _____

# WORK HISTORY FORM 6

1. _____
   Employer        Starting date (mo./yr.)      Final (mo./yr.)

   _____
   Location                              Type of business

   Description _____

2. Title _____

3. Salary (Starting) _____

   Salary (Final) _____

4. Expectations _____

   _____

5. Responsibilities/Accountabilities _____

   _____

6. "Found" (Major Challenges) _____

   _____

7. Successes/Accomplishments (How achieved?) _____

8. Failures/Mistakes (Why?) (Do differently?) _____

9. Most Enjoyable _____

10. Least Enjoyable _____

11. Talent (topgrading) _____

12. Reasons for Leaving _____

# SUPERVISOR

13. _____

    Supervisor's Name                 Title

_____

    Where Now                Permission to Contact?

14. Appraisal of Supervisor
    His/Her Strengths _____

    His/Her Shortcomings _____

15. Best guess as to what he/she really felt at that time were **your** strengths, weak points, and overall performance rating:

| STRENGTHS | WEAK POINTS |
|---|---|
| | |
| | |
| | |

    Overall Performance Rating _____

# PLANS AND GOALS FOR THE FUTURE

1. Let's discuss what you are looking for in your **next job.** (Note "Career Needs" section of Career History Form.)

   _____

   _____

   _____

   _____

2. What are **other job possibilities,** and how do you feel about each one?

   _____

   _____

   _____

   _____

3. Describe your **ideal position** and what makes it ideal.

   _____

   _____

   _____

   _____

4. How does this opportunity square with your ideal position? What do you view as opportunities and **advantages** as well as risks and **disadvantages** in joining us?

   Advantages _____

   _____

   _____

   _____

   _____

Disadvantages _____

_____

_____

_____

_____

# SELF-APPRAISAL

1. We would like you to give us a thorough **self-appraisal,** beginning with what you consider your **strengths, assets,** things you **like about yourself,** and things you **do well.**

> (Ask follow-up questions, and urge the person to continue. For example, you might say such things as "good," "keep going," and "oh," nod, and ask questions such as "What other strengths come to mind?" and "What are some other things you do well?"
>
> Obtain a list of strengths and then go back and ask the person to elaborate on what was meant by each strength listed— "conscientious," "hardworking," or whatever.

2. OK, let's look at the other side of the ledger for a moment. What would you say are your **shortcomings, weaker points,** or **areas for improvement?**

> Be generous in your use of the pregnant pause here. Urge the person to list more shortcomings by saying such things as "What else comes to mind?" and "Keep going, you are doing fine," or just smile, nod your head, and wait. When the person has run out of shortcomings, you might ask questions such as "What three things could you do that would most improve your overall effectiveness in the future?"
>
> Obtain as long a list of negatives as you can with minimal interruptions on your part, and then go back and request clarification. (If you interrupt the individual for clarification on one,

there might be so much time spent on that one negative that the individual will be very hesitant to acknowledge another one.)

## SELF-APPRAISAL

| STRENGTHS | WEAK POINTS |
| --- | --- |
|  |  |

## LEADERSHIP/MANAGEMENT

1. How would you describe your **leadership philosophy** and **style?**

_____

_____

_____

2. What would you suppose your **subordinates** feel are your strengths and shortcomings, from their points of view? What have 360-degree feedback surveys shown?

| STRENGTHS | WEAK POINTS |
| --- | --- |
|  |  |

3. In what ways might you want to **modify** your approach to dealing with subordinates? _____

_____

_____

# TOPGRADING

4. Question 11 in each Work History Form addresses topgrading. Ask question 11 for every management position, but ask the more complete topgrading questions in this section for the most recent **two** management jobs.

When you began your present (or most recent) position:

How many subordinates do (did) you have total, direct and indirect? _____

How many direct subordinates do (did) you have? _____

Of the direct reports you inherited, how many were in each of the following categories? (Explain definitions of A, B, C.)

A player (or A potential) _____

B player (without A potential) _____

C player (without A potential)_____

Describe the most valuable direct reports you inherited:

| NAME | TITLE | A, B, C | STRENGTHS | WEAK POINTS |
|------|-------|---------|-----------|-------------|
| 1. | | | | |
| 2. | | | | |
| 3. | | | | |

Describe the least valuable direct reports you inherited.

| NAME | TITLE | A, B, C | STRENGTHS | WEAK POINTS |
|------|-------|---------|-----------|-------------|
| 1. | | | | |
| 2. | | | | |
| 3. | | | | |

Ask about all management actions with direct reports, accounting for how the "inherited team" became the "at-the-end" team. Ask how many people were recruited and **selected,** what **approaches** were used, how the people were **trained** and developed, and how each **worked out** in the job. For those who did not work out well, ask what **happened** with them (transferred to a job where successful, fired, or simply tolerated?). Determine the hiring **"batting average"** (how many good hires/promotions versus mis-hires/mis-promotions). Also look for indications of **diversity,** positive versus negative **feedback** given, **empowerment,** fostering **teamwork,** and how people were/are held **accountable.** Most of all, look for success in packing the team with **A players** and redeploying chronic B/C players.

_____

_____

_____

_____

_____

# SPECIFIC COMPETENCIES

The following questions are optional in the Topgrading Interview. Those with an asterisk (*) are asked of all candidates, unless they have been answered in the chronological portion of the Topgrading Interview. Get specific examples, not general responses.

A general item format, applicable to all the Focused Questions, is "Please describe _____ and what specific examples can you cite?" Or, "If a 360-degree survey included an item on _____, how were you rated?"

These questions can also be used by interviewers performing one-hour competency-based interviews.

## INTELLECTUAL COMPETENCIES

### 1. INTELLIGENCE

a. Please describe your **learning ability.** _____

_____

_____

b. Describe a **complex situation** in which you had to learn a lot, quickly. How did you go about learning, and how successful were the outcomes? _____

_____

_____

_____

### 2. ANALYSIS SKILLS

a. Please describe your **problem analysis** skills. _____

_____

_____

_____

b. Do people generally regard you as one who diligently pursues every **detail** or do you tend to be more **broad brush?** Why? _____

_____

c. What will references indicate are your style and overall effectiveness in **"sorting"** the wheat from the chaff? _____

_____

_____

d. What **analytic approaches** and tools do you use? _____

_____

_____

e. Please give me an example of **digging** more **deeply** for facts than what was asked of you. _____

_____

_____

## 3. JUDGMENT/DECISION MAKING

* a. Please describe your **decision-making** approach when you are faced with difficult situations, in comparison with others, at about your level in the organization. Are you decisive and quick, but sometimes too quick, or are you more thorough but sometimes too slow? Are you intuitive or do you go purely with the facts? Do you involve many or few people in decisions? _____

_____

_____

b. What are a couple of the **most difficult** or **challenging** decisions you have made recently? _____

_____

c. What are a couple of the **best** and **worst** decisions you have made in the past year? _____

_____

_____

d. What **maxims** do you live by? _____

_____

### 4. CONCEPTUAL ABILITY

Are you more comfortable dealing with concrete, tangible, short-term issues, or more abstract, **conceptual**, long-term issues? Please explain. _____

_____

### 5. CREATIVITY

\* a. How **creative** are you? What are the best examples of your creativity in processes, systems, methods, products, structure, or services?

_____

_____

_____

b. Do you consider yourself a better **visionary** or implementer, and why? _____

_____

_____

### 6. STRATEGIC SKILLS

\* a. In the past year, what specifically have you done in order to remain **knowledgeable** about the competitive environment, market and trade dynamics, products/services and technology trends, innovations, and patterns of consumer behavior? _____

_____

_____

_____

b. Please describe your experience in **strategic planning,** including successful and unsuccessful approaches. (Determine the individual's contribution in team strategic efforts.) _____

_____

_____

c. Where do you predict that your (**industry/competitors/function**) is going in the next three years? What is the "**conventional wisdom,**" and what are your own thoughts? _____

_____

_____

## 7. PRAGMATISM

Do you consider yourself a more **visionary** or more **pragmatic** thinker, and why? _____

_____

_____

## 8. RISK TAKING

\* What are the **biggest risks** you have taken in recent years? Include ones that have worked out well and not so well. _____

_____

_____

## 9. LEADING EDGE

\* a. How have you copied, created, or applied **best practices?** _____

_____

_____

b. Describe projects in which your **best practice solutions** did and did not fully address customer/client needs. _____

_____

_____

_____

_____

c. How will references rate and describe your **technical expertise?**
Are you truly leading edge, or do you fall a bit short in some areas?

_____

_____

d. How **computer literate** are you? _____

_____

e. Please describe your professional **network.** _____

_____

_____

10. **EDUCATION**

a. What **seminars** or formal **education** have you participated in
(and when)? _____

_____

_____

b. Describe your **reading habits** (books and articles on global factors, general business, functional specialty, industry). _____

_____

_____

11. **EXPERIENCE**

a. Compose a series of **open-ended questions**—"How would you
rate yourself in _____, and what specifics can you
cite?" For Finance, learn expertise in Treasury, Controller, Risk
Management, etc., areas. For Human Resources, learn expertise
in Selection, Training, Compensation, etc.

- Question: _____? _____
  _____

- Question: _____? _____
  _____

- Question: _____? _____
  _____

- Question: _____? _____
  _____

- Question: _____? _____
  _____

- Question: _____? _____
  _____

b. What are the most important **lessons** you have learned in your career? (Get specifics with respect to when, where, what, etc.) ____
_____

_____

## 12.  TRACK RECORD

Looking back in your career, what were your **most and least successful** jobs? _____
_____

_____

# PERSONAL COMPETENCIES

## 13. INTEGRITY

* a. Describe a situation or two in which the pressures to **compromise your integrity** were the strongest you have ever felt. _____

_____

_____

b. What are a couple of the most **courageous actions** or unpopular stands you have ever taken? _____

_____

_____

c. When have you confronted **unethical behavior** or chosen to not say anything, in order to not rock the boat? _____

_____

_____

d. Under what circumstances have you found it justifiable to **break a confidence?** _____

_____

_____

## 14. RESOURCEFULNESS

* a. What actions would you take in the **first weeks,** should you join our organization? _____

_____

_____

* b. What sorts of **obstacles** have you faced in your present/most recent job, and what did you do? _____

_____

_____

c. What are examples of circumstances in which you were expected to do a certain thing and, on your own, went **beyond the call of duty?** _____

_____

_____

d. Who have been your major **career influences,** and why? _____

_____

_____

e. Are you better at **initiating** a lot of things or hammering out results for fewer things? (Get specifics.) _____

_____

_____

15. **ORGANIZATION/PLANNING**

* a. How well **organized** are you? What do you do to be organized and what, if anything, do you feel you ought to do to be better organized? _____

_____

_____

b. When was the last time **you missed a significant deadline?** _____

_____

c. Describe a **complex challenge** you have had coordinating a project.

_____

_____

_____

d. Are you better at **juggling** a number of priorities or projects simultaneously, or attacking few projects, one at a time? _____

_____

e. Everyone **procrastinates** at times. What are the kinds of things that you procrastinate on? _____

_____

_____

f. How would you describe your **work habits?** _____

_____

g. If I were to talk with **administrative assistants** you have had during the past several years, how would they describe your strengths and weak points with respect to personal organization, communications, attention to detail, and planning? _____

_____

h. Describe a situation that did **not go as well** as planned. What would you have done differently? _____

_____

_____

## 16. EXCELLENCE

Have you significantly **"raised the bar"** for yourself or others? Explain how you did it—your approach, the problems encountered, the outcomes. _____

_____

_____

## 17. INDEPENDENCE

a. Do you believe in asking for **forgiveness** rather than permission, or are you inclined to be sure your bosses are in full agreement before you act? _____

_____

_____

_____

b. How much **supervision** do you want or need? _____

_____

### 18. STRESS MANAGEMENT

* a. What sort of **mood swings** do you experience—how high are the highs, how low are the lows, and why? _____

_____

_____

* b. What do you do to **alleviate stress?** (Look for exercise, quiet periods, etc.) _____

_____

c. How do you handle yourself under **stress** and pressure? _____

_____

_____

d. Describe yourself in terms of **emotional control;** what sorts of things irritate you the most or get you down? _____

_____

_____

_____

e. How many times have you **"lost your cool"** in the past couple of months? (Get specifics.) _____

_____

_____

f. Describe a situation in which you were the **most angry** you have been in years. _____

_____

_____

## 19. SELF-AWARENESS

* a. Have you gotten any sort of systematic or regular **feedback** (360-degree or otherwise) from direct reports, clients, peers, supervisors, etc., and if so, what did you learn? _____

    _____

    _____

    _____

    b. How much **feedback** do you like to get from people you report to, and in what form (written, face to face)? _____

    _____

    _____

    c. What are the **biggest mistakes** you've made in the past (ten) years, and what have you learned from them? _____

    _____

    _____

    d. What are your principal **developmental needs** and what are your plans to deal with them?

    _____

    _____

    _____

    e. What have been the most difficult **criticisms** for you to accept?

    _____

    _____

## 20. ADAPTABILITY

* a. How have you **changed** during recent years? _____

    _____

b. What sorts of **organization changes** have you found easiest and most difficult to accept? _____

_____

_____

c. When have you been so firm people considered you **stubborn** or inflexible? _____

_____

_____

21. **FIRST IMPRESSION**
(Judge directly in interview.)
What sort of **first impression** do you think you make at different levels in an organization? _____

_____

_____

_____

_____

## INTERPERSONAL COMPETENCIES

22. **LIKABILITY**
 * a. When were you so **frustrated** you did not treat someone with respect? _____

_____

_____

b. How would you describe your **sense of humor**? _____

_____

_____

c. Tell me about a situation in which you were expected to work with a person you **disliked.** _____

_____

_____

### 23. LISTENING
Are you familiar with the term **active listening?** How would you define it? What would coworkers say regarding how often and how effectively you use active listening? _____

_____

_____

### 24. CUSTOMER FOCUS
a. If you were to arrange confidential **reference calls with some of your major clients/customers,** what is your best guess as to what they would generally agree are your strengths and areas for improvement? _____

_____

_____

b. Relate an example of your **partnering** with a client/customer— helping the client/customer to achieve its goals and financial results.

_____

_____

_____

c. Give examples of your **going beyond** what was normally expected to enhance your company's reputation or image. _____

_____

_____

d. Describe your methods of **diagnosing client/customer needs.**

_____

_____

_____

e. What is your "track record" in both acquiring and **retaining clients/customers?** _____

_____

_____

f. Tell me about the most **frustrated or disappointed client/customer** you have had in recent years. _____

_____

_____

_____

## 25. TEAM PLAYER

a. What will reference checks disclose to be the common perception among peers regarding how much of a **team player** you are (working cooperatively, building others' confidence and self-esteem)?

_____

_____

_____

b. Describe the most **difficult person** with whom you have had to work. _____

_____

_____

_____

c. When have you **stood up** to a boss? _____

_____

_____

d. Tell me about a situation in which you felt **others were wrong** and you were right. _____

_____

_____

_____

## 26. ASSERTIVENESS

a. How would you describe your level of **assertiveness?** _____

_____

_____

b. When there is a **difference of opinion,** do you tend to confront people directly or indirectly, or tend to let the situation resolve itself? (Get specifics.) _____

_____

_____

c. Please give a couple of recent specific examples in which you were **highly assertive:** one in which the outcome was favorable, and one where it wasn't. _____

_____

_____

_____

_____

## 27. COMMUNICATIONS—ORAL

* a. How would you rate yourself in **public speaking?** If we had a videotape of your most recent presentation, what would we see? _____

_____

b. Describe the last time you put your **foot in your mouth**. _____

_____

_____

_____

c. How do you **communicate** with your organization? _____

_____

_____

## 28. COMMUNICATIONS—WRITTEN

How would you describe your **writing style** in comparison with others' styles? _____

_____

_____

_____

## 29. POLITICAL SAVVY

\* a. Describe a couple of the most difficult, challenging, or frustrating company **political situations** you have faced._____

_____

b. How aware are you of company **political forces** that may affect your performance? Please give a couple of examples of the most difficult political situations in which you have been involved, internally and with clients.

_____

_____

## 30. NEGOTIATION

Describe situations in which your **negotiation skills** proved effective and ineffective. _____

_____

_____

_____

### 31. PERSUASION

a. Describe a situation in which you were **most effective selling** an idea or yourself. _____

_____

_____

b. Describe situations in which your **persuasion skills** proved ineffective. _____

_____

_____

## MANAGEMENT COMPETENCIES

### 32. SELECTING A PLAYERS

\* a. What have your most **recent two teams** looked like (how many A, B, and C players) and what changes were made? _____

_____

_____

_____

b. Explain your **selection process** in terms of job analysis, job description, behavioral competencies, amount of structure to interviews, if there is an in-depth chronological interview, and how reference checks are done. _____

_____

_____

### 33. COACHING

How would subordinates you have had in recent years describe your approaches to **training and developing** them? (Look for coaching, challenging assignments.) _____

_____

_____

_____

### 34. GOAL SETTING

a. How do you go about **establishing goals** for performance (bottom up, top down, or what)? Are they easy or "stretch" goals?

_____

_____

_____

b. How are your **expectations** communicated? _____

_____

_____

_____

### 35. EMPOWERMENT

How **"hands-on"** a manager are you? (Get specifics.) _____

_____

_____

_____

## 36. ACCOUNTABILITY

* a. Tell me about the **performance management** system you now use.

_____

_____

_____

b. How effective have been your methods for **following up** on delegated assignments? _____

_____

_____

_____

c. Tell me about **accountability**. What happens when people fail to perform? _____

_____

_____

_____

d. What do you say or do when someone reporting to you has made a significant (serious, costly) **mistake**? _____

_____

_____

_____

e. Cite examples of your giving **negative feedback** to someone. _____

_____

_____

_____

_____

### 37.  REDEPLOYING B/C PLAYERS

 * How many nonperformers have you **removed** in recent years? What
   approaches were used? (Look for regular, honest feedback, sincere
   training and development efforts, B/C players more apt to ask for a
   different job or quit than to be fired, and redeployment in months,
   not years.) _____

   _____

   _____

   _____

### 38.  TEAM BUILDING

 a. How have you tried to **build** teamwork? _____

   _____

   _____

 b. Which of your teams has been the **biggest disappointment** in
    terms of cohesiveness or effectiveness? _____

   _____

   _____

   _____

   _____

### 39.  DIVERSITY

 * a. When have you actively confronted indications of **discrimina-
     tion** or prejudicial behavior? _____

   _____

   _____

   _____

b. How have you added to **diversity** (ethnic, cultural, racial, gender) in a workplace? _____

_____

_____

c. Have there been any successful **employment charges** against you (EEOC, sexual harassment, etc.)? _____

_____

_____

### 40. RUNNING MEETINGS

\* a. How **productive** are meetings you run? How could they become more productive? _____

_____

_____

b. How would you describe your role in **meetings**—ones that you have called and those in which you have been a participant? _____

_____

## LEADERSHIP (Additional Competencies)

### 41. VISION

What is (was) your **vision** for your present (most recent) job? How was the vision developed? _____

_____

_____

## 42. CHANGE LEADERSHIP

a. In what specific ways have you **changed an organization** the most (in terms of direction, results, policies)? _____

_____

_____

_____

b. What has been your approach to **communications** in changes? (Look for communicating like mad!) _____

_____

_____

_____

## 43. INSPIRING "FOLLOWERSHIP"

a. Are you a **"natural leader"**? If so, cite indications. _____

_____

_____

_____

_____

b. Give examples of when people might have readily **followed** your lead and when they did not. _____

_____

_____

_____

## 44. CONFLICT MANAGEMENT

    a. Describe a situation in which you actively **tore down walls** or barriers to teamwork. _____

_____

_____

_____

    b. Describe situations in which you prevented or **resolved conflicts.**

_____

_____

_____

_____

    c. If two subordinates **are fighting,** what do you do? (Look for bringing them together to resolve it.) _____

_____

_____

_____

_____

# MOTIVATIONAL COMPETENCIES

## 45. ENERGY

    * a. How many **hours per week** have you worked, on the average, during the past year? _____

_____

_____

_____

b. What **motivates** you? _____

_____

## 46. PASSION

a. How would you rate yourself (and why) in **enthusiasm** and charisma? _____

_____

_____

_____

b. Describe the **pace** at which you work—fast, slow, or moderate—and the circumstances under which it varies. _____

_____

_____

## 47. AMBITION (SEE "PLANS AND GOALS FOR THE FUTURE")

Who have been recent **career influences,** and why? _____

_____

_____

## 48. COMPATIBILITY OF NEEDS

Is there anything we and I can do to **help you** if there is a job change (relocation, housing, etc.)? _____

_____

_____

## 49. BALANCE IN LIFE

How satisfied are you with your **balance in life**—the balance among work, wellness, community involvement, professional associations, hobbies, etc.? _____

_____

## 50. TENACITY

a. What are examples of the biggest **challenges** you have faced and overcome? _____

_____

_____

b. What will references say is your general level of **urgency?** _____

_____

_____

# OTHER COMPETENCIES

## 51.

a. Question: _____? _____

_____

b. Question: _____? _____

_____

c. Question: _____? _____

_____

d. Question: _____? _____

_____

e. Question: _____? _____

_____

f. Question: _____? _____

_____

g. Question: _____? _____

_____

# SUMMARY

RATING SCALE: 6 = Excellent, 5 = Very Good, 4 = Good,
3 = Only Fair, 2 = Poor, 1 = Very Poor

| Competencies | Minimum Acceptable Rating | Your Rating | Comments |
|---|---|---|---|
| **INTELLECTUAL** | | | |
| 1. Intelligence | | | |
| 2. Analysis Skills | | | |
| 3. Judgment/Decision Making | | | |
| 4. Conceptual Ability | | | |
| 5. Creativity | | | |
| 6. Strategic Skills | | | |
| 7. Pragmatism | | | |
| 8. Risk Taking | | | |
| 9. Leading Edge | | | |
| 10. Education | | | |
| 11. Experience | | | |
| 12. "Track Record" | | | |
| **PERSONAL** | | | |
| 13. Integrity | | | |
| 14. Resourcefulness* | | | |
| 15. Organization/Planning | | | |
| 16. Excellence | | | |
| 17. Independence | | | |

| Competencies | Minimum Acceptable Rating | Your Rating | Comments |
|---|---|---|---|
| 18. Stress Management | | | |
| 19. Self-Awareness | | | |
| 20. Adaptability | | | |
| 21. First Impression | | | |
| **INTERPERSONAL** | | | |
| 22. Likability | | | |
| 23. Listening | | | |
| 24. Customer Focus | | | |
| 25. Team Player | | | |
| 26. Assertiveness | | | |
| 27. Communications—Oral | | | |
| 28. Communications—Written | | | |
| 29. Political Savvy | | | |
| 30. Negotiation | | | |
| 31. Persuasion | | | |
| **MANAGEMENT** | | | |
| 32. Selecting A Players** | | | |
| 33. Coaching** | | | |
| 34. Goal Setting | | | |
| 35. Empowerment | | | |
| 36. Accountability | | | |
| 37. Redeploying B/C Players** | | | |

| Competencies | Minimum Acceptable Rating | Your Rating | Comments |
|---|---|---|---|
| 38. Team Building | | | |
| 39. Diversity | | | |
| 40. Running Meetings | | | |
| **LEADERSHIP (Additional Competencies)** | | | |
| 41. Vision | | | |
| 42. Change Leadership | | | |
| 43. Inspiring "Followership" | | | |
| 44. Conflict Management | | | |
| **MOTIVATIONAL** | | | |
| 45. Energy | | | |
| 46. Passion | | | |
| 47. Ambition | | | |
| 48. Compatibility of Needs | | | |
| 49. Balance in Life | | | |
| 50. Tenacity | | | |
| **OTHER** | | | |
| | | | |
| | | | |
| | | | |
| | | | |

*Resourcefulness is the most important competency. It involves passionately finding ways to get over, around, under, or through barriers. It is a combination of many Intellectual, Personal, Motivational, Management, and Leadership competencies.

**Topgrading competencies are Selecting A Players, Coaching, and Redeploying B/C Players.

**SMART & ASSOCIATES, INC.**
37202 North Black Velvet Lane
Wadsworth, IL 60083
Phone: 847-244-5544 Fax: 847-263-1585
SmartandAssoc@aol.com    www.Topgrading.com
Revised 2004

# APPENDIX B

## SELF-ADMINISTERED TOPGRADING INTERVIEW GUIDE

This information will not be the only basis for hiring decisions. You are not required to furnish any information which is prohibited by federal, state, or local law.

| Last name | First | Middle | Social Security number |
|---|---|---|---|
| Home address | City | State | Area code + telephone no. |
| Business address | City | State | Area code + telephone no. |
| Email address | | | Date |

**I. BUSINESS EXPERIENCE** Please start with your present or most recent position, and complete a different section (A, B, C, etc.) for each job title. For example, if you have had two promotions at your present employer, ACME Corp., you have had three jobs, so complete sections A, B, and C for ACME, and D will correspond to a previous employer.

**A.** Firm _____ Address _____

City_____ State____ Zip _____ Phone ( )_____

Kind of business _____ Employed from____ to ____
(Show months as well as years.)

Staff: Number of direct reports: _____ Total staff: _____

Title: _____

Name & title of immediate supervisor:

Name: _____ Title: _____

What do you most enjoy about your job? _____

_____

What do you least enjoy? _____

_____

Describe the situation when you took the position. What shape was the job in with respect to talent, resources, systems, etc.? Specifically, what major challenges did you face? _____

_____

_____

_____

What are your key responsibilities and accountabilities? _____

_____

_____

_____

_____

List your major accomplishments. Please quantify the information (e.g., "20% increase in sales"). _____

_____

_____

_____

_____

_____

What mistakes have you made in the position? What would you do differently if you could start over in the job? _____

_____

_____

_____

What do you believe your current boss sees as your major strengths?

_____

_____

_____

What do you believe your current boss sees as your weaknesses and areas for improvement? _____

_____

_____

_____

What has been your most recent overall performance rating in this job? (Please explain the scale: 5 = "exceeds expectations," 4 = "meets expectations," or whatever.) If you have not had a performance evaluation in this job, what is your best _guess_ as to how you would be rated by your boss?

_____

_____

_____

_____

**B.** Firm _____ Address _____

    City_____ State_____ Zip _____ Phone ( )_____

    Kind of business _____ Employed from_____ to _____
                                       (Show months as well as years.)

    Staff: Number of direct reports: _____ Total staff: _____

Title: _____

Name & title of immediate supervisor:

Name: _____ Title: _____

What do you most enjoy about your job? _____

_____

What do you least enjoy? _____

_____

Describe the situation when you took the position. What shape was the job in with respect to talent, resources, systems, etc.? Specifically, what major challenges did you face? _____

_____

_____

_____

What were your key responsibilities and accountabilities? _____

_____

_____

_____

_____

List your major accomplishments. Please quantify the information.

_____

_____

_____

_____

What mistakes did you make in the position? What would you do differently if you could start over in the job? _____

_____

_____

_____

What do you believe your boss saw as your major strengths? _____

_____

_____

_____

What do you believe your boss saw as your weaknesses and areas for improvement? _____

_____

_____

_____

What was your last overall performance in rating this job? (Please explain
the scale: 5 = "exceeds expectations," 4 = "meets expectations," or whatever.) If you did not have a performance evaluation in this job, what is your
best *guess* as to how you would have been rated by your boss? _____

_____

_____

_____

**C.** Firm _____ Address _____

City_____State\_\_\_\_ Zip \_\_\_\_\_ Phone ( )_____

Kind of business _____Employed from\_\_\_\_ to \_\_\_\_
(Show months as well as years.)

Staff: Number of direct reports: _____ Total staff: _____

Title: _____

Name & title of immediate supervisor: _____

Name: _____ Title: _____

What do you most enjoy about your job? _____

_____

What do you least enjoy? _____

_____

Describe the situation when you took the position. What shape was the job in with respect to talent, resources, systems, etc.? Specifically, what major challenges did you face? _____

_____

_____

_____

What were your key responsibilities and accountabilities? _____

_____

_____

_____

_____

List your major accomplishments. Please quantify the information.

_____

_____

_____

What mistakes did you make in the position? What would you do differently if you could start over in the job? _____

_____

_____

What do you believe your boss saw as your major strengths? _____

_____

_____

_____

_____

What do you believe your boss saw as your weaknesses and areas for improvement? _____

_____

_____

_____

_____

What was your last overall performance rating in this job? (Please explain
the scale: 5 = "exceeds expectations," 4 = "meets expectations" or whatever.) If you did not have a performance evaluation in this job, what is your
best _guess_ as to how you would have been rated by your boss? _____

_____

_____

_____

**D.** Firm _____ Address _____

    City _____ State _____ Zip _____ Phone ( ) _____

    Kind of business _____ Employed from _____ to _____
                                      (Show months as well as years.)
    Staff: Number of direct reports: _____ Total staff: _____

Title: _____

Name & title of immediate supervisor: _____

Name: _____ Title: _____

What do you most enjoy about your job? _____

_____

What do you least enjoy? _____

_____

Describe the situation when you took the position. What shape was the job in with respect to talent, resources, systems, etc.? Specifically, what major challenges did you face? _____

_____

_____

_____

_____

What were your key responsibilities and accountabilities? _____

_____

_____

_____

_____

List your major accomplishments. Please quantify the information.

_____

_____

_____

_____

What mistakes did you make in the position? What would you do differently if you could start over in the job? _____

_____

_____

_____

_____

What do you believe your boss saw as your major strengths? _____

_____

_____

_____

_____

What do you believe your boss saw as your weaknesses and areas for improvement? _____

_____

_____

_____

_____

What was your last overall performance rating in this job? (Please explain the scale: 5 = "exceeds expectations," 4 = "meets expectations," or whatever.) If you did not have a performance evaluation in this job, what is your best _guess_ as to how you would have been rated by your boss? _____

_____

_____

_____

_____

Note: If you had additional positions within the past ten years, please attach a separate paper and follow the format for positions A–D.

## POSITIONS HELD PRIOR TO MOST RECENT DECADE

| a. Company<br>b. City, state | a. Your title<br>b. Name of<br>supervisor | Date (mo./yr.)<br>a. Began<br>b. Left | a. Type of work<br>b. Reason for<br>leaving |
|---|---|---|---|

**E.**
  a. _____ _____ _____ _____

  b. _____ _____ _____ _____

**F.**
  a. _____ _____ _____ _____

  b. _____ _____ _____ _____

**G.**
  a. _____ _____ _____ _____

  b. _____ _____ _____ _____

Indicate any of the above employers you do *not* wish to be contacted.

_____

## II. MILITARY EXPERIENCE

If in service, indicate branch _____

Date entered (mo./yr.) _____ Date discharged (mo./yr.) _____

Nature of duties _____

Highest rank or grade _____

Terminal rank or grade _____

## III. EDUCATION

High School               1    2    3    4

College/Graduate School    1    2    3    4    5    6    7    8

(Circle highest grade completed.)

**A.** High School

Name of High School _____

Location _____

Approximate number in graduating class ____ Rank from the top ____

Final grade point average _____ (A = _____ )

Extracurricular activities _____

Offices, honors/awards _____

Part-time and summer work _____

**B.** College/Graduate School

Grade point average _____ Total credit hours _____ Extracurricular activities, honors, and awards _____

| Name and Location | From | To | Degree | Major | Grade point average | Total credit hours | Extracurricular activities, honors and awards |
|---|---|---|---|---|---|---|---|
|  |  |  |  |  |  |  |  |
|  |  |  |  |  |  |  |  |

What undergraduate course did you like most? Why? _____

_____

What undergraduate courses did you like least? Why? _____

_____

How was your education financed? _____

_____

Part-time and summer work _____

_____

Other courses, seminars, or studies _____

_____

_____

## IV. ACTIVITIES

Membership in professional or job-relevant organizations. (You may exclude groups that indicate race, color, religion, national origin, disability, or other protected status.) _____

_____

_____

Publications, patents, inventions, professional licenses, or additional special honors or awards. _____

_____

_____

| STRENGTHS | WEAK POINTS |
| --- | --- |
|  |  |

## V. SELF-APPRAISAL

Please provide a thorough **self-appraisal,** beginning with what you consider your **strengths, assets,** things you **like about yourself,** and things you **do well.** What are your **shortcomings, weak points,** and **areas for improvement?**

## VI. LEADERSHIP/MANAGEMENT

1. How would you describe your leadership philosophy and style? _____

_____

_____

_____

_____

2. What would you suppose your **subordinates** feel are your strengths and shortcomings, from their points of views? _____

_____

_____

_____

_____

| STRENGTHS | WEAK POINTS |
| --- | --- |
| | |

3. In what ways might you want to **modify** your approach to dealing with subordinates? _____

_____

_____

_____

_____

## VII. TOPGRADING

When you began your present (or most recent) position:

How many subordinates do (did) you have total, direct and indirect?

_____

How many direct subordinates do (did) you have? _____

Of the direct reports you inherited, how many in each of the following categories did you have?

A player (or A potential) _____

B player (without A potential) _____

C player (without A potential) _____

Now (or at the end of your most recent position) how many direct reports are (were):

A player (or A potential) _____

B player (without A potential) _____

C player (without A potential) _____

In the past five years, how many direct reports have you hired or promoted who turned out to be:

A player (or A potential) _____

B player (without A potential) _____

C player (without A potential) _____

## VIII. CAREER NEEDS

Willing to relocate?     Yes _____ No _____ If no, explain. _____

_____

Amount of overnight travel acceptable? _____

What are your career objectives? _____

## IX. OTHER

Do you have the legal right to work for any employer in the United States?
Yes _____ No _____

Have you ever been convicted of a crime (other than a minor traffic violation)?    Yes _____ No _____ If so, explain. _____

_____

I certify that the answers given in this Self-Administered Topgrading Interview Guide are true, accurate, and complete to the best of my knowledge. I authorize investigation into all statements I have made on this form as may be necessary for reaching an employment decision.

In the event I am employed, I understand that any false or misleading information I knowingly provided in my Self-Administered Topgrading Interview Guide or interview(s) may result in discharge and/or legal action. I understand also that if employed, I am required to abide by all rules and regulations of the employer and any special agreements reached between the employer and me.

_____
Signature

_____
Date:

SMART & ASSOCIATES, INC.
37202 North Black Velvet Lane
Wadsworth, IL 60083
Phone: 847-244-5544 Fax: 847-263-1585
SmartandAssoc@aol.com www.Topgrading.com
1999 © Smart & Associates, Inc.

# APPENDIX C

## CAREER HISTORY FORM

This information will not be the only basis for hiring decisions. You are not required to furnish any information that is prohibited by federal, state, or local law.

*For Online Completion: This form is in table format. Move from cell to cell with the "tab" key.*

| Last name | First | Middle | Social Security number |
|---|---|---|---|
| Home address | City | State | Area code + telephone no. |
| Business address | City | State | Area code + telephone no. |
| Email address | | | Date |

Position applied for _____ Earnings expected $_____

**I. BUSINESS EXPERIENCE:** (PLEASE START WITH YOUR PRESENT OR MOST RECENT POSITION.)

**A.** Firm _____ Address _____

City_____ State____ Zip _____ Phone ( )_____

Kind of business _____ Employed from _____ to _____
(Show months as well as years.)

Base $ _____

Bonus $ _____

Other $ _____

Title _____ Initial compensation $ _____

Final total compensation $ _____

Supervisory responsibility _____

Name & title of immediate supervisor _____

What (do)(did) you like most about your job? _____

_____

_____

_____

What (do)(did) you least enjoy? _____

_____

_____

_____

Reasons for leaving or desiring to change _____

_____

_____

_____

**B.** Firm _____ Address _____

City _____ State _____ Zip _____ Phone (   ) _____.

Kind of business _____ Employed from _____ to _____
(Show months as well as years.)

Base $ _____

Bonus $ _____

Other $ _____

Title _____ Initial compensation $ _____

Final total compensation $ _____

Supervisory responsibility _____

Name & title of immediate supervisor _____

What did you like most about your job? _____

_____

_____

_____

What did you least enjoy? _____

_____

_____

_____

Reasons for leaving _____

_____

_____

_____

**C.** Firm _____ Address _____

City_____ State_____ Zip _____ Phone ( )_____

Kind of business _____ Employed from_____ to _____
(Show months as well as years.)

Base $ _____

Bonus $ _____

Other $ _____

Title _____ Initial compensation $ _____

Final total compensation $ _____

Supervisory responsibility _____

Name & title of immediate supervisor _____

What did you like most about your job? _____

_____

_____

_____

What did you least enjoy? _____

_____

_____

_____

Reasons for leaving _____

_____

_____

_____

## OTHER POSITIONS HELD:

| a. Company<br>b. City, state | a. Your title<br>b. Name of<br>supervisor | Date (mo./yr.)<br>a. Began<br>b. Left | Compensation<br>a. Initial<br>b. Final | a. Type of work<br>b. Reason for<br>leaving |
|---|---|---|---|---|
| **D.** | | | | |
| a. _____ | _____ | _____ | _____ | _____ |
| b. _____ | _____ | _____ | _____ | _____ |
| **E.** | | | | |
| a. _____ | _____ | _____ | _____ | _____ |
| b. _____ | _____ | _____ | _____ | _____ |

**F.**

   a. _____ _____ _____ _____

   b. _____ _____ _____ _____

**G.**

   a. _____ _____ _____ _____

   b. _____ _____ _____ _____

What employers do you not wish to be contacted?

_____

## II. MILITARY EXPERIENCE

If in service, indicate branch. _____

Date (mo./yr.) entered _____ Date (mo./yr.) discharged _____

Nature of duties _____

Highest rank or grade _____

Terminal rank or grade _____

## III. EDUCATION

High School                 1    2    3    4

College/Graduate School    1    2    3    4    5    6    7    8

                       (Circle highest grade completed.)

**A.** High School

   Name of High School _____

   Location _____

   Approximate number in graduating class _____ Rank from the top \_\_\_\_

   Final grade point average _____ (A = _____ )

   Extracurricular activities _____

   Offices, honors/awards _____

   Part-time and summer work _____

**B.** College/Graduate School

| Name and Location | Dates From | To | Degree | Major | Grade point average | Total credit hours | Extracurricular activities, honors and awards |
|---|---|---|---|---|---|---|---|
| | | | | | | | |
| | | | | | | | |
| | | | | | | | |

What undergraduate courses did you like most? Why? _____

_____

_____

What undergraduate courses did you like least? Why? _____

_____

_____

How was your education financed? _____

_____

_____

_____

Part-time and summer work _____

_____

_____

Other courses, seminars, or studies _____

_____

_____

_____

## IV. ACTIVITIES

Membership in professional or job-relevant organizations. (You may exclude groups that indicate race, color, religion, national origin, disability, or other protected status.) _____

_____

_____

_____

Publications, patents, inventions, professional licenses, or additional special honors or awards _____

_____

_____

_____

What qualifications, abilities, and strong points will help you succeed in this job? _____

_____

_____

_____

What are your weaker points and areas for improvement? _____

_____

_____

_____

_____

## V. CAREER NEEDS

Willing to relocate?     Yes _____ No _____ If no, explain. _____

_____

Amount of overnight travel acceptable? _____

_____

_____

What are your career objectives? _____

_____

_____

_____

## VI. OTHER

Do you have the legal right to work for any employer in the United States?
Yes _____ No _____

Have you ever been convicted of a crime (other than a minor traffic violation)?     Yes _____ No _____ If so, explain _____

_____

I certify that answers given in this Career History Form are true, accurate,
and complete to the best of my knowledge. I authorize investigation into
all statements I have made on this form as may be necessary for reaching
an employment decision.

In the event I am employed, I understand that any false or misleading information I knowingly provided in my Career History Form or inter-
view(s) may result in discharge and/or legal action. I understand also that
if employed, I am required to abide by all rules and regulations of the employer and any special agreements reached between the employer and me.

_____
Signature

_____
Date

**SMART & ASSOCIATES, INC.**
37202 North Black Velvet Lane
Wadsworth, IL 60083
Phone: 847-244-5544 Fax: 847-263-1585
SmartandAssoc@aol.com www.Topgrading.com
1999 © Smart & Associates, Inc.

# APPENDIX D

# IN-DEPTH REFERENCE CHECK GUIDE

Applicant _____

Interviewer(s) _____

Date _____


Reference Check Conducted By _____

Name of Applicant (A) _____

    Home Phone _____

    Office Phone _____

Individual Contacted _____

Title _____

Company Name _____

## GENERAL PRINCIPLES

- In-depth reference checks should be conducted by the **hiring manager or another Topgrading interviewer.**
- Checks should be performed **after** the Topgrading Interview.

- Contact **all supervisors** in the past ten years, minimum.

- Obtain **written permission** from (A) to conduct reference checks.

- During the Topgrading Interview ask the applicant the name, title, and location of each supervisor. Then ask (A), "Would you please contact (reference) **at home,** and ask if it would be OK to receive a telephone call at home sometime soon?"

- Contact the person **at home,** preferably on the weekend.

- Promise those contacted total **confidentiality,** and honor that promise.

- Create the tone in which you are a **trusted colleague** . . . a fellow professional who knows (A) very well, who just might hire (A), and who is apt to better manage (A) if (reference) will be kind enough to share some insights.

- Contact the **current** supervisor. If this is not acceptable to (A) until a written offer is formally accepted, make it clear that a job offer will be **contingent upon "no surprises"** in reference checks that **will be** performed at a mutually agreed upon time. In the meantime, perhaps you could contact someone who has left A's present employer.

- **Take notes,** and keep them six months.

## INTRODUCTORY COMMENTS

"Hello, (name of person contacted), thank you very much for accepting my call. As (A) indicated, we are considering hiring her and I would **very much** appreciate your comments on her strengths, areas for improvement, and how I might best manage her. Anything you tell me will be held in the strictest confidence." (Assuming concurrence . . .) "Great, thank you very much. (A) and I have spent _____ hours together. I have thoroughly reviewed her career history and plans for the future and I was particularly interested in her experiences when she reported to you. If you don't mind, why don't we start with a very general question . . ."

**COMPREHENSIVE APPRAISAL**

| "What would you consider (A)'s strengths, assets, things you like and respect about (A)? | "What are her shortcomings, weak points, and areas for improvement?" |
| --- | --- |
| | |

**NOTES**

- It is OK to interrupt strengths to get clarification, but do not do so for shortcomings. Get the longest list of shortcomings possible and then go back for clarification. If you interrupt the negatives and get elaboration, the tone might seem too negative, thus closing off discussion of further negatives.

- If you are getting a "whitewash," inquire about negatives directly. For example, "Pat said that she missed the software project due date by three months and guesses that that hurt her overall performance rating. Could you elaborate?"

## RESPONSIBILITIES/ACCOUNTABILITIES

"Would you please clarify what (A)'s responsibilities and accountabilities were in that position?" _____

_____

_____

_____

## OVERALL PERFORMANCE RATING

"On a scale of excellent, good, fair, or poor, how would you rate (A)'s overall performance?" _____

_____

_____

"Why?" _____

_____

_____

## CONFIRMATION OF DATES/COMPENSATION

"Just to clean up a couple of details:

What were (A)'s starting _____ and final _____ employment dates?

What were (A)'s initial _____ and final _____ compensation levels?"

## DESCRIPTION OF POSITION APPLIED FOR

"Let me tell you more about the job (A) is applying for." (Describe the job.)

## GOOD/BAD FIT

"Now, how do you think (A) might fit in that job?" (Probe for specifics.)

| Good-Fit Indicators | Bad-Fit Indicators |
| --- | --- |
| | |

## COMPREHENSIVE RATINGS

"Now that I've described the job that (A) is applying for and you've told me quite a bit about (A)'s strengths and shortcomings, would you please rate (A) on nine categories? An excellent, good, fair, and poor scale would be fine."

| | Rating | Comments* |
| --- | --- | --- |
| 1. **Thinking Skills:** intelligence, judgment, decision making, creativity, strategic skills, pragmatism, risk taking, leading-edge perspective | | |
| 2. **Communication:** one-on-one, in meetings, speeches, and written communications | | |
| 3. **Experience:** education, "track record" | | |
| 4. **Resourcefulness:** passion to surmount obstacles, perseverance, independence, excellence standards, adaptability | | |

| | Rating | Comments* |
|---|---|---|
| 5. **Stress Management:** integrity, self-awareness, willingness to admit mistakes | | |
| 6. **Work Habits:** time management, organization/ planning | | |
| 7. **People Skills:** first impression made, listening, the ability to win the liking and respect of people, assertiveness, political savvy, willingness to take direction, negotiation and persuasion skills | | |
| 8. **Motivation:** drive, ambition, customer focus, enthusiasm, tenacity, balance in life | | |
| 9. **Managerial Abilities:** leadership, ability to hire the best people, ability to train and coach people, willingness to remove those who are hopelessly incompetent, goal setting, change management, empowerment, promoting diversity, monitoring performance, and building team efforts | | |

*Note: Probe for specifics. Don't accept vague generalities ["(A) sometimes procrastinates."] but ask for concrete examples, dates, consequences, etc.

## ADVICE FOR ME AS HIRING MANAGER

"What would be your best advice to me for how I could best manage (A)?"

_____

_____

_____

_____

## FINAL COMMENTS

"Have you any final comments or suggestions about (A)?"

_____

_____

_____

_____

## THANKS!

"I would like to thank you very much for your insightful and useful comments and suggestions. Before we close, please let me know which of your comments I can share with others and which should be just between the two of us."

_____

_____

_____

_____

SMART & ASSOCIATES, INC.
37202 North Black Velvet Lane
Wadsworth, IL 60083
Phone: 847-244-5544 Fax: 847-263-1585
SmartandAssoc@aol.com www.Topgrading.com
Revised 2004

# APPENDIX E

# CANDIDATE ASSESSMENT SCORECARD

Position:_____ Date: _____

Hiring Manager: _____

First-Year Bonus _____

Accountabilities       1) _____

                                 2) _____

                                 3) _____

6 = Excellent, 5 = Very Good, 4 = Good,
3 = Only Fair, 2 = Poor, 1 = Very Poor

| Competencies | Minimum Acceptable Rating | Rating by Hiring Manager | Comments |
|---|---|---|---|
| **INTELLECTUAL** | | | |
| 1. Intelligence | | | |
| 2. Analysis Skills | | | |
| 3. Judgment/Decision Making | | | |
| 4. Conceptual Ability | | | |
| 5. Creativity | | | |
| 6. Strategic Skills | | | |

| Competencies | Minimum Acceptable Rating | Rating by Hiring Manager | Comments |
|---|---|---|---|
| 7. Pragmatism | | | |
| 8. Risk Taking | | | |
| 9. Leading Edge | | | |
| 10. Education | | | |
| 11. Experience | | | |
| 12. Track Record | | | |
| **PERSONAL** | | | |
| 13. Integrity | | | |
| 14. Resourcefulness | | | |
| 15. Organization Planning | | | |
| 16. Excellence | | | |
| 17. Independence | | | |
| 18. Stress Management | | | |
| 19. Self-Awareness | | | |
| 20. Adaptability | | | |
| 21. First Impression | | | |
| **Interpersonal** | | | |
| 22. Likability | | | |
| 23. Listening | | | |
| 24. Customer Focus | | | |
| 25. Team Player | | | |
| 26. Assertiveness | | | |

| Competencies | Minimum Acceptable Rating | Rating by Hiring Manager | Comments |
|---|---|---|---|
| 27. Communications—Oral | | | |
| 28. Communications—Written | | | |
| 29. Political Savvy | | | |
| 30. Negotiation | | | |
| 31. Persuasion | | | |
| **MANAGEMENT** | | | |
| 32. Selecting A Players | | | |
| 33. Coaching | | | |
| 34. Goal Setting | | | |
| 35. Empowerment | | | |
| 36. Performance Management | | | |
| 37. Redeploying B/C Players | | | |
| 38. Team Building | | | |
| 39. Diversity | | | |
| 40. Running Meetings | | | |
| **LEADERSHIP (Additional Competencies)** | | | |
| 41. Vision | | | |
| 42. Change Leadership | | | |
| 43. Inspiring Followership | | | |
| 44. Conflict Management | | | |
| **Motivations** | | | |
| 45. Energy | | | |

| Competencies | Minimum Acceptable Rating | Rating by Hiring Manager | Comments |
|---|---|---|---|
| 46. Passion | | | |
| 47. Ambition | | | |
| 48. Compatibility of Needs | | | |
| 49. Balance in Life | | | |
| 50. Tenacity | | | |
| **OTHER** | | | |
| | | | |
| | | | |
| | | | |
| | | | |

# APPENDIX F

# INTERVIEWER FEEDBACK FORM

Interviewer _____ Interviewee _____

Observer _____ Date _____

Number of Minutes Observed _____

Rating Scale: 6 = Excellent, 5 = Very Good, 4 = Good, 3 = Only Fair, 2 = Needs a Lot of Improvement, 1 = Good Grief, N/A = Not observed or would not have been appropriate or useful in interview.

## INITIAL RAPPORT BUILDING RATING

1. **Greeting** (warm, friendly, smile, handshake)

   Comments: _____

2. Offered something to **drink**

   Comments: _____

3. **Idle chitchat** (couple of minutes—enough to get interviewee talking comfortably)

   Comments: _____

4. Stated **purposes** and expected **timing**

   Comments: _____

5. **Mechanics** (appropriate seating, all forms handy, notebook used, private location)

Comments: _____

## THROUGHOUT THE INTERVIEW RATING

1. **All appropriate questions** in Interview Guide asked without harmfully altering the wording.
   Open-ended (not yes/no) questions favored

   Comments: _____

2. Interviewer **connecting** with interviewee on human level

   Comments: _____

3. **Eye contact** (minimum of 20 percent, but no staring)

   Comments: _____

4. **Friendliness**, warmth

   Comments: _____

5. **Enthusiasm**

   Comments: _____

6. **Control** maintained

   Comments: _____

7. **Humor**

   Comments: _____

8. Appears **sincere**

   Comments: _____

9. Thorough **note taking** on content and context

   Comments: _____

10. **Unobtrusive note taking**

    Comments: _____

11. **Follow-up questions** asked, with appropriate wording and style, and specific meanings determined for vague responses

    Comments: _____

12. **Absence of (unintended) biasing** of question responses

    Comments: _____

## RATING

13. **Interviewee talks:** 90% (6), 80% (5), 70% (4), 60% (3), 50% (2), less than 50% (1)

    Comments: _____

14. Appropriate **vocabulary** level

    Comments: _____

15. Voice **clarity**

    Comments: _____

16. Vocal **range** (not monotone)

    Comments: _____

17. **Expressiveness** (interested, friendly, half-smile; not blank, not excessive frowning)

    Comments: _____

18. Interview **pace** (neither too fast nor too slow)

    Comments: _____

19. Use of **applicant's name** (every 5–10 minutes)

    Comments: _____

20. **Show of approval** of openness or when interviewee is obviously proud of an unambiguous accomplishment

    Comments: _____

21. **Protection of interviewee's ego** (use of "weasel words" rather than unintended bluntness)

    Comments: _____

22. **Control of shock,** dismay, surprise, anger

    Comments: _____

23. **Breaks** (every 45 minutes)

    Comments: _____

24. Consistently shows **respect** for interviewee

    Comments: _____

## INTERVIEW PROBES RATING

*Note:* Not all probes are necessary.

1. Thorough **summary** (at least one every 10–15 minutes)

   Comments: _____

2. Pregnant **pause**

   Comments: _____

3. **Affirmation** of understanding ("I see," "uh huh," a nod, etc.)

   Comments: _____

4. **Echo** (repeating all or part of a response)

   Comments: _____

5. **Active listening** (reflecting interviewee's content and unstated feelings)

   Comments: _____

6. **Direct questions** (usually used when softer approaches have failed)

Comments: _____

7. **TORC** methods

Comments: _____

## SUMMARY

Overall level of rapport achieved:

_____ 6 Excellent

_____ 5 Very Good

_____ 4 Good

_____ 3 Only Fair

_____ 2 Needs a Lot of Improvement

_____ 1 Good Grief

# APPENDIX G

# SAMPLE COMPETENCIES— MANAGEMENT

The Management Competencies are generic, derived from job analyses and job descriptions from several companies. A Minimum Acceptable Rating will vary according to specific circumstances. For example, Strategic Skills (#6) might require a Minimum Acceptable Rating of 6 for president of a turnaround company, but only a 2 for store manager of a fast-food chain. When the Minimum Acceptable Rating is 1 or 2, the competency can simply be omitted.

Scale: 6 = Excellent, 5 = Very Good, 4 = Good, 3 = Only Fair,
2 = Poor, 1 = Very Poor

|  | Minimum Acceptable Rating | Your Rating |
|---|---|---|
| **INTELLECTUAL COMPETENCIES** | | |
| *Intelligence:* Demonstrates ability to acquire understanding and absorb new information rapidly. A "quick study." This competency reflects neither motivation to learn nor willingness to accept change; rather, it reflects the intellectual capacity that, when combined with motivation, results in learning. 6 = genius, 4 = average for college graduates. | ☐ | ☐ |
| *Analysis Skills:* Identifies significant problems and opportunities. Analyzes problems in depth. Relates and compares data from different sources. Sorts the wheat from the chaff, determining root causes and subtle relationships | ☐ | ☐ |

among data from various sources. Exhibits a probing mind.
Achieves penetrating insights.

*Judgment/Decision Making:* Demonstrates consistent logic,
rationality, and objectivity in decision making. Achieves
balance between quick decisiveness and slower, more
thorough approaches, i.e. is neither indecisive nor a hip-shooter.
Shows common sense. Anticipates consequences of decisions.

☐ ☐

*Conceptual Ability:* Deals effectively not just with concrete,
tangible issues, but with abstract, conceptual matters.

☐ ☐

*Creativity:* Generates new (creative) approaches to problems
or original modifications (innovations) to established
approaches. Shows imagination.

☐ ☐

*Strategic Skills:* Determines opportunities and threats
through comprehensive analysis of current and future trends.
Accurately assesses own organization's competitive strengths
and vulnerabilities. Makes tactical and strategic adjustments,
incorporating new data. Comprehends the "big picture."
Reads latest books and articles on strategy.

☐ ☐

*Pragmatism:* Generates sensible, realistic, practical solutions
to problems.

☐ ☐

*Risk Taking:* Shows evidence of having taken calculated risks,
with generally favorable outcomes. Does not "bet the farm."

☐ ☐

*Leading Edge:* Constantly benchmarks best practices and
expects subordinates to do the same. Strives to be as leading
edge as appropriate in light of costs.

☐ ☐

*Education:* Meets educational requirements, formal and
informal. Exhibits continuous learning through reading,
seminars, networks, professional organizations. 6 = MBA from
top-ten school or equivalent knowledge, 4 = undergraduate
degree from respected, above-average school or equivalent
knowledge.

☐ ☐

*Experience:* (Written specifically for job).

☐ ☐

*Track Record:* Has successful career history. Meets commitments. Repeated failures with "good excuses" probably not acceptable. Recent track record weighed heavily. □ □

## PERSONAL COMPETENCIES

*Integrity:* "Iron clad." Does not ethically cut corners. Remains consistent in terms of what one says and does and in terms of behavior toward others. Earns trust of coworkers. Maintains confidences. Puts organization's interests above self. Does what is right, not what is politically expedient. "Fights fair." Intellectually honest; does not "play games" with facts to win a point. □ □

*Resourcefulness:* Seeks out and seizes opportunities, goes beyond the "call of duty," passionately finds ways to surmount barriers. Action-oriented "doer," achieving results despite lack of resources. Restimulates languishing projects. Shows bias for action ("do it *now*"). □ □

*Organization/Planning:* Plans, organizes, schedules, and budgets in an efficient, productive manner. Focuses on key priorities. Effectively juggles multiple projects. Anticipates reasonable contingencies. Pays appropriate attention to detail. Manages personal time well. □ □

*Excellence:* Sets high, "stretch" standards of performance for self and all coworkers. Demonstrates low tolerance for mediocrity. Requires high-quality results. Exhibits conscientiousness and high sense of responsibility. □ □

*Independence:* While committed to team efforts, exhibits a willingness to take an independent stand. At times will "call the big plays." Is not swayed excessively by the last person talked with. □ □

*Stress Management:* Maintains stable performance and poise under heavy pressure from Corporate ("must make your numbers"), time (too little), unions (threat of strike), customers (dissatisfied). □ □

*Self-Awareness/Feedback:* Recognizes not just one's own
strengths but also weaker points and areas for improvement.
Demonstrates the courage not to be defensive, rationalize
mistakes, nor blame others for one's own failures. Learns from
mistakes. Builds feedback mechanisms to minimize "blind spots."
Institutes 360-degree feedback for self and subordinates.

*Adaptability:* Flexes to new pressures from competition, loss
of talent, new priorities. Converts high self-objectivity into self-
correction and personal improvement. Not rigid intellectually,
emotionally, interpersonally. Adjusts quickly to changing
priorities. Copes effectively with complexity.

## INTERPERSONAL COMPETENCIES

*First Impression:* Professional in demeanor. Creates favorable
first impressions through appropriate body language, eye
contact, posture, voice qualities, bearing, attire.

*Likability:* Puts people at ease. Warm, sensitive, and
compassionate. Builds and maintains trusting relationships
with all constituencies (associates, customers, community,
professional organizations). Does not "turn people off." Not
arrogant. Exhibits friendliness, sense of humor, genuineness,
caring. Even when frustrated, treats people with respect.

*Listening:* "Tunes in" accurately to the opinions, feelings, needs
of people. Understands impact of one's behavior on others.
Empathetic. Patient. Lets others speak; listens actively, "playing
back" a person's point of view.

*Customer Focus:* Regularly monitors customer satisfaction.
Meets internal and external customer needs in ways that
provide satisfaction and excellent results for the customer.
Establishes "partner" relationships with customers. Regarded as
visible and accessible by customers.

*Team Player:* Reaches out to peers to tear down walls.
Overcomes "we–they" relationships. Approachable. Earns a

reputation for leading peers toward support of what is best for total company. Cooperates with supervisors (but is not a "yes person") and establishes collaborative relationships with peers (without being a "pushover").

*Assertiveness:* Takes forceful stands on issues, without being excessively abrasive. 6 = optimally assertive, 1 = either insufficiently or exccessively assertive.

*Communications—Oral:* Communicates effectively one to one, in small groups, and in public speaking contexts. Demonstrates fluency, "quickness on one's feet," clarity of organization of thought processes, and command of the language. Easily articulates vision and standards. Keeps people informed.

*Communications—Written:* Writes clear, precise, well-organized emails, memos, letters, and proposals while using appropriate vocabulary, grammar, and word usage, and creating the appropriate "flavor."

*Political Savvy:* Shows awareness of political factors and "hidden agendas," and behaves shrewdly without being a self-seeking "backstabber." Recognizes where to go to get things done and builds informal network to "wire" information sources and influence.

*Negotiation:* Achieves favorable outcomes in win/win negotiations. Demonstrates effectiveness in salvaging tense negotiations (with customers, union, etc.).

*Persuasion:* Exhibits persuasiveness in change efforts, selling a "vision." Charisma is desirable, though soft sell and quiet credibility are acceptable alternatives.

## MANAGEMENT COMPETENCIES

*Selecting A Players:* Topgrades through effectively recruiting and selecting at least 90 percent "A players" (not more than 10 percent mis-hires).

*Coaching:* Actively and successfully trains people for current assignments. Coaches and develops them for promotion into positions in which they succeed. Provides challenging assignments. A people builder.          ☐     ☐

*Goal Setting:* Sets clear, fair "stretch" goals for self and others, encouraging individual initiative (preference for bottom up as opposed to top down).          ☐     ☐

*Empowerment:* Pushes decision making down to lowest (optimal) level; provides authority and resources. Is "hands on" when appropriate.          ☐     ☐

*Performance Management:* Fosters high levels of accountability through fair, hard-hitting performance management system. Measures performance thoroughly. Reinforces integrity in the system by personally monitoring performance of subordinates (without "oversupervising") and rating/ranking people honestly (no "gifts," no taking the easy way out). Ties in reward system (pay, promotion, removal). Free with deserved praise and recognition. Constructive in criticism. Provides frequent feedback.          ☐     ☐

*Redeploying B/C Players:* Redeploys chronic B/C players through transfer, demotion, termination, or quietly helping person understand it is best to leave.          ☐     ☐

*Team Builder:* Achieves cohesive, effective (positive, mutually supportive) team spirit with subordinates. Team "climate" characterized by open, honest relationships in which differences are constructively resolved rather than ignored, suppressed, or denied. Treats subordinates fairly. Shares credit.          ☐     ☐

*Diversity:* Achieves diverse workforce at all levels, for global effectiveness and legal compliance. Decries tokenism; topgrades with diversity. Actively breaks down barriers to diversity; visibly fights discrimination.          ☐     ☐

*Running Meetings:* Demonstrates ability to organize and run effective meetings.          ☐     ☐

## ADDITIONAL LEADERSHIP COMPETENCIES

*Vision:* Provides clear, credible vision for the future (what the company will be like internally and in the marketplace) when strategy successfully implemented.

☐ ☐

*Change Leadership:* Actively intervenes to create and energize positive change. Can cite specific examples of moving organizations through major change. Leads by example.

☐ ☐

*Inspiring Followership:* Through whatever combination of competencies, inspires people to follow the lead. Minimizes intimidation and threat. Takes charge. Motivates by pushing appropriate "hot buttons" for individuals.

☐ ☐

*Conflict Management:* Exhibits understanding of natural sources of conflict and acts to prevent or soften them. When conflicts emerge, effectively works them through to optimum outcome. Does not suppress, ignore, deny conflict.

☐ ☐

## MOTIVATIONAL COMPETENCIES

*Energy:* Exhibits energy, strong desire to achieve, appropriately high dedication level. Although hours per se are less important than results, 60 hours or more per week are probably necessary for results expected.

☐ ☐

*Passion:* Exhibits dynamism, enthusiasm, charisma, excitement, positive "can do" attitude.

☐ ☐

*Ambition:* Desires to grow in responsibility and authority.

☐ ☐

*Compatibility of Interests:* Demonstrates needs (for money, recognition, affiliation, achievement, prestige, promotion, power, location, amount and type of travel, or whatever) consistent with the opportunities available in the foreseeable future.

☐ ☐

*Balance in Life:* Achieves sufficient balance among work, wellness, relationships, community involvement, professional associations, friendships, hobbies, and interests. *Sufficient* may

☐ ☐

be defined variously, reflecting necessity of meeting current work challenges, the possibility of burnout, or the consequences of sacrificing so much currently that later in life there are severe regrets.

*Tenacity:* Demonstrates consistent reward of passionately striving to achieve results. Conveys strong need to win. Reputation for not giving up. ☐ ☐

## CAREER DERAILERS

- *Resourcefulness*—"too passive," "doesn't create opportunities," "always trying to delegate upward"

- *Selecting A Players* and *Redeploying B/C Players*—"mis-hires too many," "has team of B and C players," "afraid to hire someone better than he is," "just won't upgrade"

- *Passion*—"not highly motivated," "lacks drive," "goes through the motions"

- *Integrity*—"lies," "can't be trusted to keep promises," "breaks confidences," "gossips," "pushes legal boundaries too far"

- *Ambition*—"too ambitious," "always trying to get the promotion rather than serve the company"

- *Political Savvy*—"a dirty politician," "backstabber"

- *Adaptability*—"over her head," "can't adjust to our reorganizaton," "job is too complex for her"

- *Team Builder*—"can't empower anyone," "control freak," "old-fashioned autocrat"

- *Team Player*—"builds silos," "thinks his department is the only one," "won't coordinate across departments, causing major production waste"

- *Track Record*—"missed her numbers again," "sandbagger," "more excuses than reasons"

- *Intelligence*—"lacks the brainpower to adapt," "slow learner," "just doesn't get it"

- *Likability*—"arrogant," "condescending," "egotistical," "doesn't treat people with respect," "makes a mockery of our people values," "know-it-all," "sarcastic," "demeaning," "acts superior"

# APPENDIX H

# SAMPLE
# INDIVIDUAL DEVELOPMENT PLAN

To:        Immediate supervisor and Human Resources Manager

From:     Pat Smith

Re:        My Individual Development Plan

Having met with the tandem Topgrading interviewers, I have a clearer understanding of how my strengths and weaker points will affect my career progress, and know how I am perceived by my coworkers. I got some developmental recommendations from the interviewers, and have met with you two (boss and HR) for your thoughts—how you view me, and what you think of the various developmental activities we discussed. I have taken all of this and composed my own plan, which will be considered "final," pending your approval.

1. *Hire three A players this year.*

   Why: Our company's future and my career success depend on topgrading.

   How/when: Install *Topgrading* blueprint for recruitment for all three open positions reporting to me. I will:

- Work with a search executive (prescreened by HR), who will do the work himself and treat me as a client.

- Ensure well-organized visits to the company. I'll see to it that interviewers know the job and competencies, are prepared, are on time, and write brief reports.

- Personally conduct a tandem Topgrading Interview.

- Personally conduct final reference calls.

    Measurement: Six months after each of the three managers is hired, the executive committee will meet to decide whether I hired an A player (success) or a B or C player (failure).

2. *Improve my public speaking skills from a 5 to a 7 (on a ten-point scale).*

    Why: Public speaking is one of my strengths, but I'd like to improve it more. I'm frequently standing before groups trying to sell change. I've asked for feedback and understand that I am considered credible and organized, but a little dull and drab.

    How/when: Meet with a tutor (ask HR for recommendations) quarterly for 2.5 hours, throughout the next year.

    Measurement: Online survey of twenty-five people observing a presentation on mine each quarter in the next year.

3. *Improve as a team player.*

    Why: I admit it, I get impatient and tend to run over people. I dominate meetings, and people consider me a lousy listener.

    How/when:

- Read one book per month, such as *People Skills* (Robert Bolton), *The Wisdom of Teams* (Jon Katzenbach), *Leading Change* (John Kotter), *Why Smart People Do Dumb Things* (Mortimer Feinberg), or *Zapp! The Lightning of Empowerment* (William Byham).

- Ask one peer to give me regular feedback on my team play and listening skills. Take that person to lunch once per month to discuss it in-depth.

- Attend Center for Creative Leadership within the next year for a one-week program on the interpersonal aspects of leadership.

    Measurement: Feedback from my peer at lunch, observations by you, communicated in quarterly meetings I'll initiate. Online 360-degree every six months. CCL has a 360-degree survey to measure me as well.

4. *Clarify accountabilities with subordinates.*

Why: Although I occasionally am a bulldozer, some of my people have indicated that they aren't quite sure what I expect. I seem to change direction and not necessarily tell them, and it wastes a lot of their time.

How/when: Meet with each subordinate one hour in the next two weeks to clarify job description, performance standards, and accountabilities for the year. Clarify at my weekly staff meetings.

Measurement: Each subordinate must say he/she is totally satisfied with the clarity of accountabilities in staff meetings and online surveys.

5. *Improve direction in my team.*

Why: This is related to #4. My people are going in different directions as new information convinces me we should. But I'll tell X to do something, forget, then tell Y, and not let X know. We need to flex and change directions, but I need to get a lot better at coordinating, at staying in touch with each person, so that we don't waste time, energy, and effectiveness. We get so busy I too often cancel staff meetings, and my people are screaming for me to hold them regularly.

How/when: Conduct a staff meeting every week, on Monday from 9:00 to 10:00 A.M. This means *every* week.

Measurement: I'll submit a report to you at the end of the year, and if I have canceled more than 10 percent of the meetings, I will have failed. Furthermore, on a monthly basis I will be measuring the effectiveness of the meetings, asking everyone to say if the agenda is OK, if there is adequate participation, if the highest-priority issues are being discussed, if we are acheiving the necessary coordination, if my expectations for individuals are clear because of it, if people are being held accountable for follow-through, if trust is high, if one hour is enough, and overall how they feel about the effectiveness of the staff meeting.

6. *Control my temper.*

Why: I lose my cool a couple of times per week. It looks unprofessional, undermines teamwork, and causes people to cower rather than aggressively do the job. It might even drive away some A players if I am not careful.

How/when: I'll take a deep breath and count to ten whenever I am about to blow up. Then I'll go get something to drink or take a short walk, to calm down. Every Friday afternoon I'll spend ten minutes filling out a 3 × 5 card on how I did that week on temper control. On one side I'll record when I did a good job of controlling my temper, and the other side I'll record when I lost it.

Measurement: In my quarterly meetings with you I'll bring my card file, and both of us can give me a pat on my back if I'm progressing. Other measurements will be your observations as well as those of the peer I have recruited to give me feedback on my teamwork and listening skills.

7. *Conduct an email 360 survey regularly.*

Why: It's an efficient way to get honest measurement of my improvement.

When: Every six months until my goals are achieved.

Measurement: Goal is 7 (or higher) on most positively worded terms, though 8 for "topgrading" and "trustworthy." Goal is 3 or lower on negatively worded items.

# APPENDIX I

## COST OF MIS-HIRES FORM

Job Title of Person Mis-hired or Mispromoted: _____

**Dates person was in position:** _____ to _____
(If person was successful in previous job, but failed in a new job, just calculate costs for the years the person was in the new job.)

**Reason for leaving:**
Quit _____ Fired (or forced to resign) _____ Transferred _____
Demoted _____ Retired _____ Died _____ Other _____

This person is considered a mis-hire or mispromotion because:

_____

_____

_____

Note: Adjust the following costs for inflation (using your best guess for today's dollar values):

1. <u>**Total costs in hiring the person**</u>        **$**_____
   - Recruitment/search fees (Any guarantee? If so, was money recovered?)
   - Outside testing, interviewing, record checking, physical exam
   - HR department time (for all candidates)
   - HR department administrative costs (all candidates)

- Travel costs (for all candidates, spouses, other executives traveling to meet candidate)

- Time/expenses of non-HR people (all candidates)

- Relocation (moving household goods, purchasing house for candidate)

2. <u>Compensation</u> (sum for all years person was in job):          $_____
   - Base ($ _____ × number of years)

   - Bonuses ("signing," performance, etc.) for all years

   - Stock options (realized for all years)

   - Benefits (life/health insurance, 401(k), etc.) for all years

   - Clubs for all years

   - Car (including gas, insurance, etc.) for all years

   - Other forms of compensation

3. <u>Maintaining person in job</u> (sum for all years person was in job):          $_____
   - Administrative assistant for all years

   - Office "rental" (including electricity, etc.) for all years

   - Furniture, computer, equipment for all years

   - Travel (air, food, lodging, etc.) for all years

   - Training

   - Other "maintaining" costs

4. <u>Total severance:</u>          $_____
   - Severance fee (salary, benefits, use of office)

   - Outplacement counseling fee

   - Costs in negotiating separation

- Costs in lawsuits caused by the person (EEOC, harassment, EPA, OSHA, etc.)

- Administrative costs in separation

- Wasted time of people in separation

- "Bad press" (loss of corporate goodwill, reputation)

**5. Mistakes/failures, missed and wasted business**
   **opportunities:**                                        $_____
For example, drove a key customer away, mis-hired three people at total cost of $300,000, impaired customer loyalty, failed to enter new hot market, wasted $10M on software that had to be scrapped, embezzled $1M, launched three "dog" products.

Explain: _____

_____


**6. Disuption** (costs of inefficiency in the organization,
   lower morale, lower productivity, impaired
   teamwork):                                               $_____

**7. Other:**                                               $_____
Specify: _____

**8. Sum of all Costs** (#1–#7):                            $_____

**9. Estimated value of contributions of the mis-hire:**   $_____
Even if a $50,000-per-year store manager drove away customers and stole $1M, perhaps he contributed something—for example, hired five excellent employees or came up with a merchandising idea worth $500K per year to the bottom line.

Explain: _____

_____

**10. <u>Net cost of Mis-hire</u>** (#8–#9):

        Sum of all costs (#8)                    $_____
        – Value of Contribution (#9)
        = Net cost of mis-hire

Quality Check: Does the ratio of total costs to estimated value of contributions seem correct? If not, please go back and make adjustments.

# APPENDIX J

# TOPGRADERS—CONTACT INFORMATION FOR CONSULTING AND LICENSING FORMS

Consulting services include advising on topgrading projects, interviewing selection candidates, assessing and coaching internal talent, and one-hour to two-day presentations and seminars. A complete multimedia training option, with Topgrading interview demonstrations, is now available. See www. topgrading.com.

Contact information for topgrading companies is:

Dr. Bradford Smart
Smart & Associates, Inc.
37202 North Black Velvet Lane
Wadsworth, IL 60083
phone 847-244-5544, fax 847-263-1585
SmartandAssoc@aol.com, www.topgrading.com

Margaret Brask
Smart & Associates, Inc.
phone 847-265-7415, fax 847-265-7416
MBrask@aol.com

Dr. Geoffrey Smart
ghSMART & Company, Inc.
203 North LaSalle Street, Suite 2100
Chicago, IL 60601
phone 312-674-0945, fax 312-674-0955
ghsmart@ghsmart.com, www.ghsmart.com

Christopher Mursau
Dr. Kathryn Smart Mursau
The Mursau Group, Inc.
1041 Popes Creek Circle
Grayslake, IL 60030
phone 847-543-4840, fax 847-543-4817
chrismursau@ameritech.net, www.themursaugroup.com

# INDEX